For Diana—

Best wishes

Jonathan Montaldo
Sophia Center
December 2009

THE INTIMATE MERTON

BOOKS BY THOMAS MERTON

The Seven Storey Mountain
The Sign of Jonas
New Seeds of Contemplation
Conjectures of a Guilty Bystander
Zen and the Birds of Appetite
The Collected Poems of Thomas Merton
The Literary Essays of Thomas Merton
Mystics and Zen Masters
The Hidden Ground of Love (Letters I)
The Road to Joy (Letters II)
The School of Charity (Letters III)
The Courage for Truth (Letters IV)
Witness to Freedom (Letters V)
Love and Living
The Monastic Journey
The Asian Journal
Run to the Mountain (Journals I)
Entering the Silence (Journals II)
A Search for Solitude (Journals III)
Turning Toward the World (Journals IV)
Dancing in the Water of Life (Journals V)
Learning to Love (Journals VI)
The Other Side of the Mountain (Journals VII)

THE INTIMATE MERTON

His Life from His Journals

EDITED BY

PATRICK HART

AND

JONATHAN MONTALDO

HarperSanFrancisco

A Division of HarperCollins*Publishers*

HarperCollins books may be purchased for educational, business, or sales promotional use. For information please write: Special Markets Department, HarperCollins Publishers, 10 East 53rd Street, New York, NY 10022.

HarperCollins Web Site: http://www.harpercollins.com
HarperCollins®, ☕®, and HarperSanFrancisco™
are trademarks of HarperCollins Publishers Inc.

FIRST EDITION
Designed by Joseph Rutt

Library of Congress Cataloging-in-Publication Data
Merton, Thomas
The Intimate Merton : his life from his journals /
edited by Patrick Hart and Jonathan Montaldo. — 1st ed.
p. cm.
Includes index.
ISBN 0–06–251620–5 (cloth)
ISBN 0–06–251629–9 (pbk.)
1. Merton, Thomas, 1915–1968 Diaries. 2. Trappists—United States Diaries.
3. Trappists—United States Biography. I. Hart, Patrick. II. Montaldo, Jonathan. III. Title.
BX4705.M542A3 1999
271′.12502–dc21   99–33239
[B]
99 00 01 02 03 ❖/RRDH 10 9 8 7 6 5 4 3 2 1

The Intimate Merton is dedicated to
Naomi Burton Stone, Robert Giroux,
James Laughlin, Anne McCormick,
and Tommie O'Callaghan

CONTENTS

Either you look at the universe as a very poor creation out of which no one can make anything, or you look at your own life and your own part in the universe as infinitely rich, full of inexhaustible interest, opening out into the infinite further possibilities for study and contemplation and interest and praise. Beyond all and in all is God.

Perhaps the Book of Life, in the end, is the book one has lived. If one has lived nothing, one is not in the Book of Life.

I have always wanted to write about everything. That does not mean to write a book that *covers* everything—which would be impossible, but a book in which everything can go. A book with a little of everything that creates itself out of nothing. That has its own life. A faithful book. I no longer look at it as a "book."

July 17, 1956

A Path Through
Thomas Merton's
Journals

He kept a journal as early as 1931 when he was only sixteen. From boyhood he apprenticed himself to the notion that his life would be inexhaustibly rich if he wrote about it. Writing would make him a main celebrant at Life's infinite creation.

Writing became Thomas Merton's second nature: his mode of breathing from the diaphragm to take everything in. Writing was his way to taste and see. A smell became perfume when he had captured it on a page. "To write," he noted in his journal, "is to think and to live—even to pray" (September 27, 1958). By writing, "life lived itself" through him (April 14, 1966). He found himself a place to be within a written word. He wrote his heart out as if his heart's next beat depended upon his writing about it.

Blessed with an inclusive imagination, he wanted to write a "book" into which everything in his life was able to go. Life's very self would live through him as he explored a path through the world's ten thousand things by writing down their names. Life would remember itself through him as he compiled almanacs of the changes in his heart's inner weather. By creating within his journals a "book of everything," Merton was writing his paragraph into Life's autobiography.

Writing a journal was Merton's way of doing a poet's "heart work," a scholar's "inner work," a monk's "work of the cell." Writing a journal was the birth canal through which the myriad inner responses of his spirit to the world became enfleshed and took on a life of their own. Once born to the page, his words formed sentences with their own truth in them.

He wrote journals as a spiritual discipline: he kept "vigil" through making a journal until a pattern of experience would unfold into momentary epiphanies—"sparks of truth, small, recurring flashes of a reality that is beyond doubt, momentarily appearing"—which led him further in "the direction shown him and to which he was called" (March 3, 1966).

Writing was the religion that bound Merton over to his God. He would give birth to God in himself by writing about his need for God to be born in him.

Merton became a monk by writing about becoming a monk. He allowed the form of his particular monastic vocation to reveal itself to him in sequences of experience paradoxical to his readers but holding for him a dark clarity. He wrote about silence to become silent. He wrote about his being lost so that God would find him quickly. He hid himself from the world by fully disclosing himself to it.

To write of God's mercy was to be gathered by God's mercy. As Merton's words became more grateful, whatever was vile in him became precious, whatever was poor in him became infinite, his human frailty became powerful. God's "mercy within mercy" to him throughout his life is the code that breaks the mysteries at the heart of Merton's journal writing: "Suspended entirely from God's mercy, I am content for anything to happen" (November 29, 1952).

When Merton was born on January 31, 1915, in Prades, France, only the small-cloistered joy of his parents greeted his first sound. When he disappeared from view, accidentally electrocuted in Bangkok, Thailand, on December 10, 1968, his death was noted by millions and merited a front-page obituary in the *New York Times*. In fifty-three years he had written himself in large letters and with indelible ink onto his century's Book of Life.

Merton's memoirs made him famous. *The Seven Storey Mountain*, the narrative of his journey from self-intoxicated youth to sober novice at the Trappist monastery of Our Lady of Gethsemani in Kentucky, has remained in print since 1948. In the twenty years that followed this classic best-seller, Merton would write poetry, a play, popular books on the spiritual life, as well as essays engaging his wide, passionate interests: contemplative traditions East and West, world literature, politics and culture, social justice and peace. His magazine articles alone fill fifteen large volumes. He also revived an early novel he had written in 1941, *The Journal of My Escape from the Nazis*, which would be published after his death as *My Argument with the Gestapo* (1969). His collected correspondence to people high and low nears ten thousand items. Seventy "reading notebooks" exist to prove he read as carefully as he wrote. In the last year of his life he even edited a literary magazine, *Monks Pond*.

Through it all, below it all, he practiced his art of "confession and wit-ness" (April 14, 1966) by writing journals, portions of which he edited in his lifetime: *The Secular Journal, The Sign of Jonas, Conjectures of a Guilty Bystander,* and *Woods, Shore and Desert.* Editors would publish three of his journals posthu-mously: *A Vow of Conversation, Thomas Merton in Alaska,* and the *Asian Journal.*

Scholars call Thomas Merton a "spiritual master," and publishers imprint the jackets of his books with claims that he is among the twentieth century's most significant spiritual theologians. He was indeed a gifted writer and teacher. His free-ranging evocation of what it feels like to lead an examined, inner life marked by intense prayer rightly attracts the theologian and the lay reader alike.

But being the monk that he was, he could never confine his competing parts of himself and his contradictions into leak-proof compartments. Merton's left hand always knew what his right hand was doing. His genius for honesty thus made dark and hard his long, graced road to Joy. His journals reveal to him and to his reader that his life was no metaphor for mastery but rather an icon for spiritual mastery's salvific opposite: poverty of spirit. He allowed his journals to convince himself and his reader that he was "nobody's answer" (June 17, 1966). Not even his own.

The Seven Storey Mountain can mislead its reader into imagining Merton's spir-itual biography ever after as a gradual ascending path toward Truth. But much of his journeying was spent on the side roads and on an indirect path. The heights he sought were seldom in full view and then only in flashes. His lament at often losing his way and the tone of sadness and compunction at his evasions on his pilgrimage toward God are among the great monastic themes of his private journals.

When Merton was received as a novice into monastic community at Gethsemani, his first abbot, Dom Frederic Dunne, ritually asked him before all assembled, "What is it you seek?" The novice gave the ritual answer: "The mercy of God and of the Order." Merton lived out that answer every day of his monastic life for twenty-seven years. He wagered everything on God's mercy to him at Gethsemani.

Merton was no virtual monk. A reader should take literally his quest to find himself gathered by God's mercy, a mercy he knew he could never bequeath to himself. He actually sought to live for "God Alone" and actually desired to find himself hidden in the "secret of God's face." As he enjoyed international acclaim and literary success, the tears in Merton's journals would be pathological were it not for his desire to obey God's "voice" and go "clear out of the midst of all that is transitory and inconclusive [and return] to the Immense, the Primordial, the Unknown, to Him who loves, to the Silent, to the Holy, to the Merciful, to Him Who is All" (March 22, 1961).

To this great vocation of being human by flinging himself passionately toward God, Merton counted his golden reputation as so much dross. He trusted only his real, conflicted self and its inadequacies.

In his desire to master everything by writing about it, Merton learned that God was mastering him. With his sins always before him, he still hoped in the promise of God's mercy. Even on the bleakest nights, when his mouth turned mute and his heart turned into stone, his ears were always awake in the dark to Love's voice, which bid him welcome.

A reader best understands Merton's autobiographical art by reading his journal entries in their complete context. For serious study of and quotation from Merton's journals, it is necessary to read the journals Merton edited along with the seven volumes of the complete, extant journals published by Harper San Francisco under the titles *Run to the Mountain* (ed. Patrick Hart); *Entering the Silence* (ed. Jonathan Montaldo); *The Search for Solitude* (ed. Lawrence S. Cunningham); *Turning Toward the World* (ed. Victor A. Kramer); *Dancing in the Water of Life* (ed. Robert E. Daggy); *Learning to Love* (ed. Christine M. Bochen); and *The Other Side of the Mountain* (ed. Patrick Hart).

Since *The Intimate Merton* presents these seven volumes of journals in one volume, it is best regarded as a work of translation, compiled through selectivity and extensive cutting. *The Intimate Merton* is a re-visioning, and the reader should be aware that *The Intimate Merton* is not how Merton integrally presented himself and his experience in his journals.

We have divided *The Intimate Merton* into seven chapters that correspond to each volume published by Harper San Francisco. The chapter titles are taken from the subtitles of each respective volume. Thus, the journal entries selected from *Run to the Mountain* appear in chapter 1, "The Story of a Vocation."

The basis for our selecting a given journal entry over another was to produce a powerfully written, chronological presentation of his journals' major themes. Merton's hopes for more than a writer's identity by becoming a monk; his search for a monk's identity by writing; his appropriation of Holy

Wisdom as a metaphor for God; his failed search for the "perfect place"; and his strong sensitivities to the simple and the natural are just a few of the major themes unfolded in *The Intimate Merton.* We also consciously included every dream that appears in the seven volumes of the journal along with a generous portion of his prayers.

This presentation also displays other minor but important themes in Merton's biography. To give but one extended example, the role that "rooms" play in his journals. *The Intimate Merton* opens in Merton's rooms at 35 Perry Street in Manhattan, where he lived after his conversion to Catholicism. He remembers his room at the house of his maternal grandparents in Douglaston, New York. He moves through hotel rooms in Miami and Cuba. In the summer of 1940, after the Franciscans tell him he cannot become a friar, he leaves Perry Street and joins friends at "the cottage" in Olean, New York. He later decides to enter the Trappists in his room at St. Bonaventure College in Olean, where he had been teaching English for a year and a half.

Rooms become even more important to him after he enters the rigorous communal life at the Abbey of Gethsemani on December 10, 1941. His monastic history could even be divided into periods by citing important rooms: the infirmary room on St. Joseph's feast day, March 19, 1948; the vault for the abbey's rare books, where he was allowed to write and pray alone; the room of St. Anne's, a toolshed he christened his first "hermitage"; his Mount Olivet hermitage on Gethsemani's grounds; the hospital room in Louisville where he met a student nurse; and the bungalow in Bangkok where he died.

Merton figuratively resides in one last room: the Merton Room at Bellarmine College, where he insured his work against decay by donating manuscripts, photographs, calligraphy, what is now a collection of forty thousand items. He called himself Peter Pan for helping construct this posthumous existence for himself. He chided himself that the Merton Room would forever represent the classic Mertonian double bind: the writer in him wanted to extend his fame through time, while the monk in him wanted to disappear into the only afterlife that mattered.

Our editing the journals for *The Intimate Merton* required much more than selecting certain journal entries over others. If the nugget of a Merton insight or of his recording a moment of beauty is confined to a first and third paragraph in a seven-paragraph journal entry, only the first and third paragraphs appear, without elision marks to warn the reader that something is missing.

As this text was to have no footnotes, when a guide for the reader was needed, we enclosed it within the text. Thus, when his friend "Lax" first appears, he appears as "Bob Lax." We deleted anything that we judged weakened Merton's style or might disturb a reader who does not expect, in so limited a presentation, to encounter a good writer writing badly. We deleted, for example, his too-frequent use of *And* to begin his sentences. As for Merton's erratic punctuation, when his meaning was clear, we left it. When it muddled his thought, we unmuddled it. In sum, the mandate of making one volume of journals present the thematic thrust of seven required surgery enough, but as we were asked to confine the text to a certain length, we deeply edited Merton's text to present him as favorably and faithfully as we could.

The metaphor that mitigates the fault of our editorial procedures is that we cleared a path through the wood. If all seven volumes of journals are the wood, *The Intimate Merton* is only a path through them and not the wood itself. The metaphor of path clearing also connotes that we have cleared one path and not the only path that could have been taken through these thousands of paragraphs.

We make no claim that what we have rendered here is the "essence of" or the "best of" Merton's journal writing. Having read *The Intimate Merton,* readers can return to all seven volumes of Merton's journals by another way and clear their own paths through his "book of everything."

No one needs a tour guide, a spiritual director, or a mound of footnotes to enjoy reading Thomas Merton. His literary gift is to inspire readers to identify with him.

His writing operates for readers as both a window and a mirror. In Merton's journals readers catch a glimpse of their own "infinite possibilities" for "contemplation and praise." As he struggles with his life's contradictions, readers are self-examined in the mirror of his autobiographical art. By hearing Merton's literary voice, readers are seduced into listening to that still, quiet voice within themselves, one that longs to become incarnate in some outward gesture uniquely their own.

Merton's journals encourage his readers to write themselves as large as he did into the Book of Life by acknowledging their own hearts just as they truly are. Merton knew his personal dilemmas were universal. He knew his readers, too, longed to live their lives like a "book into which everything could go" for God and everyone to read, were it not that their hearts were shy and feared exhibition of their infinite possibilities. He knew that we all hide the mystery of our heart's complexities not only from the world, but from ourselves.

By writing journals Merton learned that at Life's banquet he ate the same food as everyone else. He learned that, like everyone else, he needed to take his place at the table and receive the sacrament of his life's particular moments. His journals were his way to time-share with his reader this universally precarious human existence through which everyone falters forward in alternating patterns of celebration and tears.

Merton's journals document, deeply below everything, his search for God's face reflected in *all* his experiences. He records how he listened for the Voice of Love, which called him out of self-exile from Love back to Love's garden. Merton wrote journals not just to find himself in words but to lose himself in words that exhausted themselves into surrender to Love's voice that called him out, beyond all words, to Love's own self.

His journals bear witness to his education as a human being. He gradually abandoned hope for a suddenly perfect life in some perfect place always elsewhere than where he actually was. He surrendered himself instead to the slow heart work of seeking God one day and one night at a time in the place where his eyes opened and shut every morning and evening. He got up and fell down, he got up and fell down, he got up over and over again.

Merton's journals in all their depth and scope are his gift to his readers of one human life's extended metaphor of hope that no human being is "Life's poor creation." We are loved by Love for precisely being the fallible, fragile creatures that we are.

Thomas Merton stumbled home, but he has made it home. No longer an orphan or an exile, no longer a solitary or a prodigal, in the company of all the saints he now listens with full clarity to the Beloved's voice. His journey has come to its end. His ever-searching spirit rests in God's peace.

P. H. and J. M.

PART I

The Story of
a Vocation

1939–1941

Lady, when on that night I left the Island that was your England,
your love went with me, although I could not know it and
could not make myself aware of it.
It was your love, your intercession for me, before God,
that was preparing the seas before my ship,
laying open the way for me to another country.

I was not sure where I was going,
I could not see what I would do when I got to New York.
But you saw further and clearer than I.
You opened the seas before my ship,
whose track led me across the waters
to a place I had never dreamed of,
which you were even then preparing for me
to be my rescue and my shelter and my home.

And when I thought there was no God and no love and no mercy,
you were leading me all the while into the midst of His love and
   His mercy,
and taking me, without my knowing it,
to the house that would hide me in the secret of His Face.

The Seven Storey Mountain

Have you had sight of Me, Jonas, My child?
Mercy within mercy within mercy. . . .

The Sign of Jonas

October 1, 1939. 35 Perry Street. New York City

Today has the smells of a feast. A girl sitting opposite me in the restaurant at breakfast: some perfume on that reminded me of several things. First, the perfume and the softness and complexion of her skin reminded me of a whole class of girls I had been in love with from fourteen on. The kind that are rather thin than plump, rather blonde than dark, who seem at the same time soft and sad, their sadness, a kind of mystery, a melancholy which makes them appear intelligent and good.

Then the perfume too reminded me of all sorts of Sundays and feasts and the rich smells going with them at Douglaston. The smell of powder and perfume in my Grandmother's room. The smell of the same room, with all the heat on in the morning, with my Grandfather having breakfast in bed: the room smelling of perfume, powder, cold cream, radiator heat, fried eggs, toast, strong coffee. All at once.

Other feast smells: Brilliantine I bought in Bermuda this year. Good, fat, lavender smell. Means sun and the white coral houses and the dark cedars. That nostalgia is now complicated by the fact that there's no going to Bermuda now, because of the war.

Feast smells at Douglaston: cigar smoke, meaning Uncle Charles and the funny sheets (he bought the *Tribune:* Pop took the *Times*). Candy. Smell of dinners, of course. Smell of Christmas tree, noise of steam chirping in the radiator, at the same time.

Noises:

Outside now it is raining.

Noises of a cocktail shaker at Douglaston, first with a martini being stirred in it, then with something being shaken in it. Generally, sun outside, or late slanting sun through the French windows.

Noise of a toy electric train going around its tracks. Noise of winding up a clockwork locomotive—slower turn of the key, thickening catch of the spring.

Noise of the cook chopping or pounding things in the kitchen.

Noise of tires singing past the house on the road outside, in winter or in autumn when the road is light and bare and hard.

Noise of a fire, cracking and snapping in the grate, just lit. The sheaves of sparks that rush up the chimney from time to time.

3

Noise of the dog jumping up inside the door and scratching on it as you come up the steps.

Noise of Pop walking upstairs, beating with his hand on the banister halfway between the beats of his feet on the hollow-sounding wooden steps.

Noises of someone (never me!) shoveling coal into the furnace downstairs, the shovel chunkily bites in under the coal, which smothers its sound: the coal rushing off the shovel into the fire, leaving the shovel ringing slightly, full of a load.

Noise of someone opening up the legs of a card table—a drag and a sudden catch.

Noise of starting the radio: click of the knob, the light comes on, then half a second later, a sudden swell of hum that dies again a little, while the radio settles down to think up a real sound. After that nothing very interesting comes out of the radio, as a rule.

Noise of the cellar door banging shut: never one bang, but a bang and a quarter because of the bounce. Noise of footsteps on the cement steps leading down to the cellar. Noise of dragging ash cans up the cellar steps, step by step, the heavy, muffled bumping, muffled by the weight of the fine pinkish gray ash. All this took place under the window of the room I slept in: that room was Pop's den. It had an office desk and a swivel chair. Noise made by the swivel chair when you turned on it completely. First no noise at all, then a kind of slight, singing protest. (Noise of the drawers opening and shutting.) The protest of the chair comes not from making it turn, but it is uttered by a tough spring as you lean back in the chair and tilt it quite a bit.

Noise of raking leaves, of mowing the grass, of digging with a spade, of raking ground or hoeing. Sweeping the sidewalk and the brick front steps.

Noise of the sprinkler, as it turns scattering whirling threads of water around the air over the front lawn. Twenty or thirty feet away the leaves of the privet hedge move where you would not have suspected water was falling.

Thank God then for all good smells and good sights and good sounds, but what is the good of being attached to them and sitting and turning over their memory and dwelling on the recollections they bring to you, cherishing a sadness for these things which are gone away? Pop and Bonnemaman are dead, and it will never again be the same as being sixteen and eighteen and living at Douglaston on vacations. What a vanity it would be anyway to moan over the happiness of those times because, at eighteen and twenty and twenty-one, while I was active and rushing about after all sorts of things, who can say those were very good or happy years for me when I was full of anger and impatience and ingratitude toward my family to an extent it is horrible to think about now? Then I was proud and selfish and denied God and was full of gluttony and lust. I was so filled with all these things that even now the unhappiness of them does not leave me at all but keeps forcing itself back upon me in thoughts and dreams and movements of anger and desire. I am still full of that same pride and wretchedness which is very strong and very hard to get rid of because of the strength of self-will which weakens love and prayer and resists God.

But all these things were much stronger because I did not resist them at all. Because of them I was very confused and unhappy. So it would be a lie to look back on those as happy days. It is vanity to desire anything that is past because you cannot bring it back again. If pleasure is vanity now, then pleasure in the past is twice as much vanity. The pleasure of making love now is poor enough by itself (that is, without enough love to want to marry the girl, which is not much!), but the pleasure of a first love when you were sixteen: you will never be sixteen again, and you will never be in love again for the first time, and anyway it was fairly silly and certainly not at all satisfactory. As to its injustice—seeing she was married—I think that doesn't matter, because of my own innocence, anyway. I did not conceive it was possible to do more than declare that I loved her and give her one kiss. The misery afterward was, of course, a luxury. It was all very well and nice, but to want such a stupid kind of thing to happen again would be crazy. Stupid: not the being in love part but all the dramatics and excesses and luxuries of sentiment that surrounded it when the object of my love was on her way to the other side of the earth.

Yet there are many good things to look back on because, before I had my first year at Cambridge, anyway, although I was always full of crazy pride, yet I did love God and prayed to him and was not completely full of sins. So there were good days at Oakham—and at Strasbourg and at Rome and earlier in France and in London on holidays from school. But I think that, even as a child, I was too full of anger and selfishness for me to want to recapture my own childhood at all now! In fact, to want to recapture anything you have had or owned or experienced is a bigger vanity and unhappiness than to want to possess some present good that is before you. And of course, Saint John of the Cross says the memory must be completely darkened as well as the intellect and the will.

It is not really true that I am sentimental about things I remember. That is not it, but I do find them easy and interesting to write about. They come readily and run fast off the pen. For me they have a kind of life and interest. I have been bothered, however, for a long time, wondering just what place they have—what place anything has I write down here.

October 14, 1939. Saturday

In returning the novel, Farrar and Rinehart announced they were not enthusiastic enough about it to publish it. Trying to find out more, I repeatedly got on the telephone and talked to a woman whose job it is to say "We never discuss refused manuscripts." Then, quite by chance, she suddenly relented, half hoping I would not turn out to be a maniac after all. She let me talk to a man who had not read the novel but whom, at any rate, I had seen. From the notes of the one who *had* read it, he told me the story was impossible to follow and shoddily written. That it often got dull and boring. That this man had not bothered to finish it. That the names of the characters were ugly and disconcerting, that the characters themselves were unreal.

Looking at the thing again, I find all that is true.

He said it was obvious enough I wanted to write a novel, and that it showed promise. I believed that in the first place.

He asked: what was I trying to do, create some utterly new kind of novel structure? The name of James Joyce slipped into one of his sentences, intimating that sort of thing was all right, perhaps, in Joyce. I hastened to deny that I was striving after originality, that is, originality for its own sake and apart from the novel.

Coming home, I rearranged all the chapters in a different order, and now I haven't any idea what to do with the thing. That was Thursday.

October 15, 1939. Sunday

Marcel Proust and memory: to Proust experience seems to be valuable only after it has been transformed by memory. That is, he is not interested in the present. I suppose that, while he was writing, his other possible present experiences did not appeal to him: sick in bed. The "present time of things present" was unbearable. What kept attracting him was the "present time of things past." Actually, what was important to him was writing—that is, writing was the one "present" he could put up with.

What is this terrific importance that memory seems to have for me?

Perhaps I am interested in it because it was so easy to write such a lot of autobiography this summer: but that may be putting the cart before the horse.

Is it a new interest? Or have I always been preoccupied over memory ever since I was a little boy?

October 16, 1939. Monday

When I first knew I must be a priest, I went to Father Ford, who put the idea in my head that I had never had: of being a secular priest. It was not long after that, that I went to ask Dan Walsh about it, and he told me to go into an order, suggesting that, from what he knew of me personally, I should go to the Franciscans.

He knows me better than Ford. I had his course in Saint Thomas last year. After classes we would talk and I would tell him about ideas that I was enthusiastic about, and in our conversations I am sure he found out enough about my intellectual and spiritual temper to give advice to me on such a subject. He introduced me to Jacques Maritain. After Maritain's lecture last spring to the Catholic Book Club, Walsh and I were both very stimulated and went off talking about miracles and saints. When I first mentioned my vocation he said immediately he had always expected I would want to go into the religious life.

November 8, 1939. Thursday

In the last three days I have written another 60 or 70 pages of new stuff for the novel, which I reread and found dull. Jinny Burton came around a couple of times, and this morning I stopped by the Franciscan monastery on Thirty-first Street. Tonight, taking a bath, I was led to reflect that this fall, since I am going into a monastery, is quite different from other autumns. Reading my diary for 1931, which I ought to destroy, I am surprised at my childish paganism. Announcing what I wanted: to be drunk.

November 20, 1939. Monday

I think everybody in the world wants people to read his autobiography or his letters or his diaries or his state papers or even his account books.

Everywhere I look people are full of their autobiographies or their own collected notes or something of the sort.

Bob Lax spent the summer writing an autobiography after he had spent the spring writing a journal. The best novel of the age—*Ulysses*—is autobiography.

Today there was a picture of Roosevelt dedicating a library or something he has had built at Hyde Park to house his state papers. In 1941 the library will be thrown open to scholars. The world thinks this means Roosevelt won't run for a third term, but all I care about is that here is another guy who realizes that the medium the whole age seeks expression through most readily is autobiography, and he is jumping right in with the others.

December 8, 1939. Feast of the Immaculate Conception

I wish nobody had ever told me it was a good thing to attempt to know myself. I used to write it down in my diaries in Greek—γνωθι σεαυτον. (Never knew anything about the accents.) I carted my diaries from Oakham to Rome to New York to Cambridge and knew—not myself or anything else—nothing. No-*thing*.

I read Jung and tried to figure out what psychological type I was and figured I was an "extraverted sensation type," whatever that is. I was certainly afraid of being an introvert because introversion is a sin for materialists and, what is more, it is used conversationally almost as if it were synonymous with "perversion."

(What a ridiculous thing it is to take oneself so seriously!)

December 11, 1939. Monday

Got back today from being in Washington the weekend with Ed Rice. Maybe I always was bad at picking hotels. Got a very bad one in Washington: the Harrington: not quite so modern or so comfortable as the Olean House. In fact, the Olean House had it all over this great firetrap. Bad rickety joint, people rattling on our doorknob all morning, dark black room on a court from which you couldn't see the sky. Crummy.

I wonder when I ever of my own good choice picked a good hotel? I let the Cook's Travel man sell me the Hamilton Hotel in Bermuda (what a ridiculous ramshackle depressing joint!). I stayed at the Alexandria Hotel near Hyde Park corner overnight once. I guess it wasn't so awful for the price, but then that was a hotel Pop had discovered and not I.

In Rome—a pretty vile place: although on the Via Veneto, it was small and black and stuffy and cramped and full of old ladies.

Did all right in Germany but not in Brussels. Oh no! not in Brussels.

Every hotel I have ever picked has been full of a kind of spiritual squalor, sometimes accompanied by actual physical squalor, too. All these hotels frighten me.

December 20, 1939. Wednesday

One reason why I can't write short stories to other people's formulas: I can't invent a character fast enough. I have to write twenty or thirty pages before I have any idea what kind of character I am writing about. Then I go on and on and on, pages and pages and pages, and maybe never get to the point when the character means anything to anybody else.

Another thing is that I have tremendous preoccupations of my own, personal preoccupations with whatever is going on inside my own heart, and I simply can't write about anything else. Anything I create is only a symbol for some completely interior preoccupation of my own. But symbols I have difficulty in handling! I start to write a short story, creating something new, I get distressed in the first paragraph and disgusted in the next. I try to create some new, objective, separate person outside myself, and it doesn't work. I make some stupid wooden guy.

Give me a chance to write about the things I remember, things that are in one way or another piled up inside me, and it is absolutely different. There are a whole lot of rich and fabulous and bright things in that store: whether things I remember or things that just make themselves there: deep and secret and well ordered and clear and rich and sweet thoughts and ideas are there, but they are all about things that are so close to me that I love them as myself. Some actual people—not enough of my neighbors, however. This makes one thing very apparent, doesn't it? Such things as I love as I love myself I can write about easier than about things that don't exist and therefore can't be loved. I guess I could write a much better short story about angels I love than about some purely fanciful person who cannot be conceived as having any of the characteristics of anyone I ever loved. I can start to write if they are symbols of something I love, but as symbols they are hard to handle.

Since there is a curiously close relationship between love and fear, I also write very readily but without pleasure about the things I fear, but then I am rarely happy about what I have written. I only know I am writing well when I am writing about the things I love: ideas, places, certain people: all very definite, individual, identifiable objects of love, all of them, because it is impossible to love what doesn't exist.

January 13, 1940. Saturday

If there is no important change in our lives, as we go on, there is no point in keeping journals. Journals take for granted that every day in our life there is something new and important.

I have been going through the *Spiritual Exercises* of Saint Ignatius. Not giving them four hours a day but at any rate two and a half.

The first day, didn't know where I was getting; didn't seem to see what I was supposed to *get out* of the meditations quite clearly. Just read what the book said and put the book down and repeated the words back.

Second and third days: temptation to think the thing was doing me harm. That is to be expected.

It is true the *Exercises* are quite tiring. The completeness of the meditations on mortal sin is impressive and also efficacious. The meditations on death are nothing new to me!

Not until I did the meditation on venial sin did the full impact of the greatness and horror of mortal sin really strike me, in spite of all that had gone before this meditation. Now I most fervently pray that I may altogether amend my life, utterly and completely, forsaking all things.

There is an absolute urgency for unrelenting combat with the passions and the weaknesses of our flesh. As far as I have been concerned, all the psychoanalytical arguments have only served me as the excuses that my laziness and cowardice required to avoid the struggle and so continue in misery. The only happiness I have known in the last six years has had some connection with my conversion and has been tied up with the increase in my belief and desire to serve God.

There is an utter necessity for giving up all things, taking up the cross and following Christ. Everything else is imprisonment and death. Before, I knew this intellectually: now I *know* it. I assent to it with my whole soul and heart, not only with my understanding.

January 25, 1940. Thursday

Most days begin the same way: I come home from Mass and breakfast and then begin a long and agonizing hunt for some small object without which apparently I cannot do any work—if it isn't reading glasses, it's a pencil or a pen or some paper.

Just now I filled my pen: I had been using little scraps of paper to clean it after filling it—now I couldn't find any. Yesterday, lost a red pencil.

Remember the times at Douglaston you would look up and down all over the house for a shoe, a hat, a sock, a book, a brush? In the matter of books, especially, it meant war. My Uncle and my Grandmother always suspected my Grandfather of picking up books and throwing them out or giving them to taxicab drivers—a lot of times they were right.

Today, however, today doesn't begin this way. I just had lunch, and there is no necessity to write in a journal. I could read or draw or think up a new way to make the novel end or study something. Anything.

When my handwriting gets smaller—not neater, just smaller—it seems that I have been reading something that requires a lot of concentration or that I have been trying to follow something that requires discipline.

The times at Cambridge when I got zealous for the reformation of my ways and started to work hard (for instance, Easter vacation, 1934) my handwriting got smaller. Just before Christmas, 1933, when I was in a pretty bad way, I made a deliberate effort to make my handwriting neat and precise. It didn't help very much.

January 26, 1940. Friday

I miss my novel. Macmillan has had it for over two weeks—no, three weeks. I telephoned Mr. Purdy this week, and he said the first reader had given a favorable report on it and so it had gone on to someone else. So now, instead of being suspicious of my novel and growling at it and kicking it around, I am happy about it. I would like to be kind to my novel and make up for the way I have scolded it. Maybe it is not so bad after all. I wish it was here so I could pat its shaggy head.

However, probably tomorrow—no, Monday is a better guess—I'll get a polite note from Macmillan's Mr. Purdy and I'll go over there and drag back my big heavy novel, not speaking to it; then I'll get it home and whip it and throw it in a corner and be mad at it. After about a week I'll make five corrections with this pen and retype the title page and haul the whole thing off to—whom? Harcourt Brace? I wish Macmillan would take it. I'd like the book to be published by a place that's as big and solid and shiny as a subtreasury or at least as a Federal Reserve Bank.

April 1940. Miami Beach

The Leroy Hotel is an okay place. It has a particular smell which I find hard to identify, but it is a smell that seems to be appropriate to a seaside hotel and indeed reminds me of some hotel I have stayed in sometime and somewhere. I can't remember which one.

Venetian blinds, stone floors, coconut palms making a green shade in the room: the smell is a sort of musty smell of the inside of a wooden and stucco building cooler inside than out. It is a smell that has something of the beach about it too, a wet and salty bathing-suit smell, a smell of dry palm leaves, suntan oil, rum, cigarettes. It has something of the mustiness which that immense and shabby place in Bermuda, the Hotel Hamilton, had: the salt air had got into the wood and the walls of that place. It smells also like the Savoy Hotel in Bournemouth, which stood at the top of a cliff overlooking a white beach on the English Channel. It had fancy iron balconies, and even when the dining room was full you could feel the blight of winter coming back upon it and knew very well how it would look all empty with all the chairs stacked.

I was in love there with a girl called Diane. The blight came upon our love that November, at which time they stacked up our chairs. I burned her letters in the fireplace of the Prefect's common room at Oakham: I tossed them in a packet into the flames with a grand gesture. Only once did I wish I had them back to read.

The smell of this Miami room, my ground-floor room that looks out on the patio, is further complicated by the presence of leather. My good new leather Gladstone bag, my saddle leather bag, bright, all leather, *limpio*, clean, unbanged, unstrapped, sweats aromatically in this heat and gives off a good smell of leather. The fellow who sold it to me didn't have the wit to say that this was the kind of a bag that would look better as time went on. However, the salesclerk in Rogers Peet (downtown New York) said just that of my new camel hair sports jacket.

Even the false leather suitcase I have had for a year, and bought for only five dollars as opposed to twenty, gives off its own kind of false leather happiness.

The cool shadows in the room remind me of a girl's house in Great Neck where I used to spend some time. She had a big cool living room with awnings on the screened windows, and some breeze circulated through it while we gently sweated in our tennis clothes and sat on the couch and sipped Coca-Cola and giggled at each other.

The smell and the light all belong to summer. I suppose I am above all impressed with them because of the suddenness of my transition into them from New York, which just now has got a pretty raw April.

Here it is as hot as August. Coming here overnight and stepping off the train into an August afternoon and riding in a car along blue bays where there is a lot of lush greenery is like the time I first got off the

English boat in August and drove out on Long Island, astonished at the heat and the haze and the profusion of weeds growing four and five feet high along the roads.

Driving out along these streets with shining new hotels and apartments everywhere (they put up forty-seven new hotels this year) was something like the time last spring I stepped out of the Long Island station into the garish brightness and gaiety and movement and the snoring tones of broadcast music blowing about in the air of the World's Fair, the musical horns of the buses, the foghorn noise of the huge locomotive by the Railroad Building.

But what is it that the smell in this hotel reminds me of? It is a typical summer resort smell, and maybe it epitomizes all the summer vacations I ever had in my life.

April 1940. Havana, Cuba

Havana is a thoroughly successful city, a good city, a real city. There is a profusion of everything in it, immediately accessible and, to some extent, accessible to everybody.

The gaiety of the bars and cafes is not locked in behind doors and vestibules: they are all open wide to the street, and the music and laughter overflow out into the street, and the passersby participate in it and the cafes also participate in the noise and laughter and gaiety of the street.

That is another characteristic of the Mediterranean type of city: the complete and vital interpenetration of every department of its public and common life. These are cities the real life of which is in the marketplace, the *agora*, the bazaar, the arcades.

Sellers of lottery tickets, of postcards, or late extra papers (there is a new edition of some paper almost every minute) go in and out of the crowd, in and out of the bars. Musicians appear under the arcade and sing and play and go away again.

If you are eating in the dining room of the plaza, you share in the life of the whole city. Out through the arcade you can see, up against the sky, a winged muse standing tiptoe on top of one of the cupolas of the National Theater. Below that, the trees of the central park: and everybody seems to be circulating all about you, although they do not literally go in and out of the tables where the diners sit, eating dishes savory of saffron or black beans.

Food is profuse and cheap: as for the rest, if you don't have the money, you don't have to pay for it: it is everybody's, it overflows all over the streets: your gaiety is not private, it belongs to everybody else, because everybody else has given it to you in the first place. The more you look at the city and move in it, the more you love it, and the more love you take from it, the more you give back to it, and, if you want to, you become utterly part of it, of its whole interpenetration of joys and benefits, and this, after all, is the very pattern of eternal life, it is a symbol of salvation. This sinful city of Havana is so constructed that you may read in it, if you know how to live in it, an analogy of the kingdom of heaven.

April 29, 1940. Camaguey, Cuba

The complete interpenetration of every department of public life in Cuba, the overflowing of the activities of the streets into the cafes and the sharing of the gaiety of the restaurants by the people in the arcades outside, also applies to churches. The doors being open while Mass is going on, you unfortunately get all the noise and activity of the street outside going on, too: the clanging of the trolley car bells, the horns of the buses, and the loud cries of the newsboys and sellers of lottery tickets. Outside the church of Saint Francis the Sunday I was there, a seller of lottery tickets was going up and down and shouting out his number with the loudest and strongest voice in the whole of Cuba, and Cuba is a country of loud voices. It was a fine-sounding number, four thousand four hundred and four:

> *Cuatro mil cuatro cientos CUA-TRO,*
> *Cuatro mil cuatro cientos CUA-TRO*

and so he went on, adding some half-intelligible yell now and then that had something to do with Saint Francis: probably that Saint Francis liked the number, too. *Cuatro mil cuatro cientos CUA-TRO!*

As I came in the front door of San Francisco, a crowd of children, from the school I suppose, filed in through one of the side doors two by two and began taking their places in the front of the church until gradually the first five or six rows were filled. Mass had already begun, and the priest was reading the epistle. Then a brother in a brown robe came out, and you could see how he was going to lead the children in singing a hymn. High up behind the altar Saint Francis raised his arms up to God, showing the stigmata in his hands. The children began to sing. Their voices were very clear, they sang loud, their song soared straight up into the roof with a strong and direct flight and filled the whole church with its clarity. Then, when the song was done and the warning bell for consecration chimed in with the last notes of the hymn and the church filled with the vast rumor of people going down on their knees everywhere in it, then the priest seemed to be standing in the exact center of the universe. The bell rang again, three times.

Before any head was raised again, the clear cry of the brother in the brown robe cut through the silence with the words "*Yo Creo . . .*" "I believe," which immediately all the children took up after him with such loud and strong and clear voices and such unanimity and such meaning and fervor that something went off inside me like a thunderclap, and, without seeing anything or apprehending anything extraordinary through any of my senses (my eyes were open on only precisely what was there in the church), I knew with the most absolute and unquestionable certainty that before me, between me and the altar, somewhere in the center of the church, up in the air (or any other place because in no place), but directly before my eyes, or directly present to some apprehension or other of mine which was above that of the senses, was at the same time God in all His essence, all His power, God in the flesh and God in Himself and God surrounded by the radiant faces of the thousands, the millions, the uncountable numbers of saints contemplating His Glory and praising His Holy Name. The unshakable certainty, the clear and immediate knowledge that heaven was right in front of me, struck me like a thunderbolt and went through me like a flash of lightening and seemed to lift me clean up off the earth.

May 21, 1940. New York City

I have been cleaning stuff out of the room I had on Perry Street. I lived in it all winter, sitting at the desk, spending more time in it than in any other room I ever lived in, for the same period of time.

What was I doing?

Going through the *Spiritual Exercises* of Saint Ignatius.

Correcting papers written by my English class in Columbia Night School: "My Favorite Movie Star." "Is It Possible to Be Happy Without Money?"

Lying on the bed with five or six stitches in my jaw where a wisdom tooth had been torn and hammered from the bone: the sweet smell of Gilberts antiseptic filled the whole place for weeks afterward. As a consolation, I feebly turned over and over the pages of travel folders about Mexico, Cuba, Brazil. (I knew all along I would only be able to afford Cuba.)

Most of the time I wrote and wrote: a Journal, longhand, in a ledger. A novel that has perplexed three publishers without any result. And also I read. Pascal, *The Little Flowers* and the *Rule* of Saint Francis, Lorca, Rilke, the *Imitation of Christ*, Saint John of the Cross, and also William Saroyan, when I was too tired to read the hard stuff.

June 16, 1940. The Cottage. Olean, New York

The French have been driven south to the Loire, all my friends have gone to the lake, and I am sitting by myself in the middle of the driveway outside the cottage, looking at the woods.

Just because nobody I ever knew wanted a war, I imagined the Germans didn't either, and all the time they wanted nothing else. No, not all of them. But you hear of the tremendous enthusiasm of some of the German troops in this fight: they like it, and that is why they are winning. Nobody else likes war.

Here it is very quiet and sunny. In front of me there is a bush covered with pale white blossoms that do not smell of anything much. Somewhere under some thorns and weeds a cricket sings dryly. Everything is quiet and sunny and good, but I am tempted to make no sentimental comparisons between this and the valley of the Loire.

It is possible to imagine a man coming silently out of these woods into the open grass space before me and aiming a gun and shooting me dead in this chair and going away.

Even though there is sunlight, the woods might well fill, all at once, with the clack and roar of tanks. The airplane that went by an hour ago might have been filled with bombs, but it just wasn't. There is nothing too fantastic to believe anymore because everything is fantastic. There is no fighting here now, but there could very well be plenty tomorrow.

The valley is full of storage tanks, and oil is for feeding bombers, and once they are fed, they have to bomb something, and they generally pick on oil tanks.

Wherever you have oil tanks or factories or railroads or any of the comforts of home and manifestations of progress in this century you are sure to get bombers, sooner or later.

Therefore, if I don't pretend, like other people, to understand the war, I do know this much: that the knowledge of what is going on only makes it seem desperately important to be voluntarily poor, to get rid of all possessions this instant. I am scared, sometimes, to own anything, even a name, let alone a coin or shares in oil, the munitions, the airplane factories. I am scared to take a proprietary interest in anything for fear that my love of what I own may be killing somebody somewhere.

June 28, 1940. St. Bonaventure College. Olean, New York

What (besides making lists of the vices of our age) are some of the greatest vices of our age? To begin with, people began to get self-conscious about the fact that their misconducted lives were going to pieces, so instead of ceasing to do the things that made them ashamed and unhappy, they made it a new rule that they must never be ashamed of the things they did. There was to be only one capital sin: to be ashamed. That was how they thought they could solve the problem of sin, by abolishing the term.

We are developing a new superstition: that people who think too much about a certain disease will give it to themselves by suggestion: we get ulcers from worrying about them. If we don't worry about them, says the converse of this argument, we won't get any diseases.

We have another superstition like this one. If we all agree that war is unpleasant and that we don't want it, then we won't have to fight. We think that just because we don't want to fight, nobody will ever come and take away our ice cream sodas, incidentally killing us. This is bound to happen if, in the same breath, we accuse them of being black dogs for coveting our ice cream sodas.

Then, of course, we have the vice of thinking that because something is successful, it is therefore valuable. The worth of a thing is in its profit to us.

Also we love facts for their own sake, in contradiction to the superstition just mentioned. The radio is full of question bees and information programs, and everybody reads the *Reader's Digest*, which pretends to give as many facts as possible in a little space. At the same time, the very hardest thing in the world to get is any real news about the war. We know the bare fact that France has been beaten. But what is going on there? It might as well be some country on the moon.

October 27, 1940. Feast of Christ the King

Today I saw a movie of London under bombing and heard the recorded sound of the air raid alarm and of the all-clear signal. For the first time in my life, I think, I momentarily wanted to be in the war.

There is a sort of fascination about it, too: something beyond patriotism or anything like that—and lower than that, too—a kind of animal curiosity to hang around the scene of danger and of killing, the scene of the most important and terrible killing that is being done in the world today.

The thing that shocked me as much as anything was the picture of Peter Robinson's store in Oxford Circus with a hole blasted out of the three top floors. In Peter Robinson's I bought a gray suit when I was sixteen, or fifteen, and wore it to Strasbourg and to Italy the first time I went there. I remember the suit very well. It was a gray herringbone tweed. Just up the street from Peter Robinson's, upper Regent Street, was the place where I used to take the Green Line bus to go to Ripley Court. Diagonally across Oxford Circus was Henry Long's Bar where I called up the Bennetts to say good-bye. Farther down from Peter Robinson's, eastward across Oxford Street, was the cinema where I first saw all the René Clair pictures, as well as that strange Freudian movie I went with Tom Bennett to see there, and many other things. All this was struck when Peter Robinson's was struck. Bombs are beginning to fall into my life. That wasn't true with Warsaw. I had never seen nor imagined Warsaw. This was a terrible thing to see.

But more terrible was seeing the line of people going down into the air raid shelter at dusk. Then seeing the empty streets and then an air raid warden walking slowly with his hands behind him in the sudden flash of a bomb: and then hearing the sound of that air raid alarm. This, for the first time, made me want to fight.

For the first time I imagined that maybe I belonged there, not here. I have responsibilities in England, I left my childhood behind there. Now that they are bombing it, perhaps I should go back to my childhood: except of course they don't, for the moment, need men.

Actually, all the propaganda needed to make me want to fight was uttered by the Germans. If they had never bombed any part of England, I would never have given a damn for the whole war, no matter what. Perhaps a bombing of Paris for two or three weeks might have done it. I don't know. The bombing of Rotterdam rather repelled and scared me. But the bombing of London, where I once lived, where there are so many people that were my friends in school and people that I loved, is certainly different.

I think this was one of the best photographed, best cut, best spoken documentary films I ever saw. No, some of the lines were pretty terrible: but the tone of the man's voice was good. The title was lousy: *London Can Take It.*

It showed a big gash blown in Somerset House, something that might have been a new wing of the Middlesex Hospital, burst wide open. Some of those Bermondsey Houses for laboring men were shown blown up. There were many places I didn't recognize—probably in the city. But what was impressive was the amount of life going on in the city; buses, people going to work, hurrying around the piles of stone and brick in the daytime—then going underground at night.

The town hall in Allegheny the other day, standing with its cupola among the bare branches against a gray sky and with its red bricks, might have been something in a Surrey village, a Victorian post office or something. In any case I was reminded of Surrey and felt strange. And I have been dreaming I was in London, often, at night.

November 12, 1940

I gave my class some Chaucer to put into modern English, and this will probably severely tax their brains and do violence to their tempers. Father Cornelius is mad at the *New Yorker* for being anti-Catholic, and I am mad at it for being anti-funny and extremely dull. Bob Gibney has got a cold. Lax is afraid to drive Gibney's car. The football coach has been bitten by Father Hugo's black spaniel. The football team has lost another game. Somebody told me that when a pig attacks a human being he (the pig) gores out the entrails and eats them and that is all the meat a pig will ever touch. I saw what I thought was a photograph of the three Ritz brothers dressed as women, but on closer inspection it turned out to be the three Andrew Sisters. Somebody said that they couldn't hold the College's Junior Prom in Bradford because nobody could drive back that distance afterward without cracking up against a tree somewhere in those 20 miles. They tried it once and that was what happened. This is a violent world in which I am not doing nearly enough work, although I appear to be busy all the time.

December 4, 1940

The poem I got back from the *New Yorker* today at least looked as if it had been handled.

Last night I tore a handful of pages out of last year's journal. It is nice to have a journal written at great length one year. The next year you fall upon it as idle as a king and read a page and tear the page out and throw it away; you have read the day's news.

Why would I write anything if not to be read? This journal is written for publication. It is about time I realized that and wrote it with some art. All that screaming last year to convince myself a journal was worth writing, but not to be read.

If a journal is written for publication, then you can tear pages out of it, emend it, correct it, write with art. If it is a personal document, every emendation amounts to a crisis of conscience and a confession, not an artistic correction. If writing is a matter of conscience and not of art, there results an unpardonable confusion—an equivocation worthy of a Wordsworth.

February 2, 1941

If I were not so mad with my own vanity and selfishness and petty cares for the ease of my flesh and my pride, I would see clearly how perhaps nothing I have ever done of any good was mine or through me but given by God through the love and gifts and prayers of people who have given me their whole life in fruit for me to pick and take or spoil according to my indifferent and cursed selfishness. That fruit has only nourished me in grace in spite of myself, so to speak, and accidentally given me a little health.

Look how the whole life of my grandfather, all his work of years, was poured out for my brother John Paul and myself, buying me what hundreds of things, Italy, France, England, Cuba, Bermuda, food and clothing and care and hundreds of curious books and besides that all the things I hate to think of. But Pop worked from a boy in an Ohio town for sixty years in order that I should run down Bridge Street, Cambridge, in the middle of the night, terrified because I had just thrown something, a bottle, a shoe, a brick, I don't know, through a shop window. He worked his whole life so Bill Finneran and I should lean on some poisonous little bar on 52nd St. in a half-empty place picking a fight with some long, callow, drunken kid whom some swept-up lousy old dames in the place seemed to prefer to us.

Look how he spent his whole life in working so that I could sit at the foot of the flagpole outside Columbia, in 1935, with a great pleasure and surprise in me about a girl I thought I was in love with.

What else did he buy for me with his blood? For not only Christ gave his life for me, but all who ever loved me have sacrificed some of their life's blood for me. How easily I take that gift, as if I were a god, to be sacrificed to—as if the sacrifice could really be mine, and not God's.

My grandfather bought me the day I came into the bar of the *American Merchant*, going up the Channel, around 3:30 in the morning, after I had fallen on my berth with all my clothes on and passed out. So I find this dame talking to the ship's doctor. That was a fine humiliation, me with vomit on my black pants. That was what I gave him back for loving me even with his life, and my grandmother too.

If father had not died ten years ago, how much would I have hurt him in that time? How could I spoil and waste so much love and so much care and so many gifts?

At Aunt Maude's funeral: I realized it was dramatic and was only secretly vain of it and congratulated myself that I was down from Cambridge and nobody knew the secret of where I had been the night before. Not that it was anything terrible, but I made it so in my imagination that I should come among the sober relatives at a funeral and could still taste this dame's perfumed mouth in my own mouth. So when good Aunt Maude, a saint, was buried, I had, I suppose, some decent regret she was dead because I did love her but was just as full of my own private seventeen-year-old drama that I applauded for a magnificent adventure, I am sure! That was what her love for me brought her at her funeral! For she had made it possible by her patient care for me to get to Oakham, and then to Cambridge.

All these things are easy to say, and the Lord suffered in everyone who ever loved me for Love's sake and was turned upon by my vicious ingratitude and pride, for I hated even to be loved in any such way.

How can anyone tell how much he owes to the goodness of those who love him? If we knew what people in their love for us do to save us from damnation by the simple fact of their friendship for us, we would learn some humility. But we take for granted we should have friends and are not at all surprised they should come seeking our company and liking us; we imagine we are naturally likable, and people flock to us to give us our real due, as if we were angels and attracted them by our great goodness to love us. It is only love that gives us life, and without God's love we would cease to be, and perhaps without our friends' good, natural love and charity, which argues for us always in God's sight without their always knowing it, He would long ago have given us up to our punishment and turned His face away and let us hurtle over the edge of the abyss, where the love of friends still holds us in their spoken or unspoken prayers.

I don't know what I have written that I could really call mine or what I have prayed or done that was good that came from my own will. Whose prayer made me first pray again to God to give me grace to pray? I could have fought for years by myself to reduce my life to some order (for that was what I was always trying to do—even to ridiculous extremes and the most eccentric disciplines, all pseudoscientific and pretty much hypochondriacal too; keeping records of what I drank, trying to cut out smoking by reducing the number of cigarettes each day, noting down the numbers in a book—weighing myself every few days, etc.!), and yet I would have slowly eaten myself out, I think. But someone must have mentioned me in some prayer; perhaps the soul of some person I hardly remember—perhaps some stranger in a subway or some child. Or maybe the fact that someone as good as Lilly Reilly happened to think I was a good guy served as a prayer. Or the fact that Nanny may have said my name in her prayers moved the Lord God to send me a little grace to pray again or first to begin reading books that led me there again—and how much of it was brought on by the war? Or maybe Bramachari in some word to the Lord in his strange language moved the Lord to let me pray again! These things are inscrutable, and I begin to know them better than I can write them. How many have become Christians through the prayers of Jews and Hindus who themselves find Christianity terribly hard?

February 11, 1941

Now I think of the days I sat in the May sun, cramped and curled on the loose rotting boards of the little balcony outside the Perry Street front room, and held a bottle of Coke in my hand and looked at the warm sun on the buildings—like Decoration Day, 1939. That was before there was a war, and the World's Fair was just beginning, and I sometimes had hangovers. Sometimes—often. That was what the Coca-Cola was for.

I am beginning to think the war has a lot to do with my not drinking anymore. Maybe if there were no war, I would still be having hangovers. But I doubt that, too.

There were some good things about that front room in Perry Street. The shiny new telephone. The grave and delicate writing desk. The sun pouring in the windows. The too-many street cries. Calling Wilma Reardon on the shiny phone. Lax called up and told me he had heard the election of Pope Pius XII announced on the radio, and that day, too, I had been crouching on the balcony in the sun. Another good thing was the record of "And the Angels Sing."

But just the same, I once in a while had hangovers. Also I had no real work to do but just thought some about writing a Ph.D. dissertation on Gerard Manley Hopkins.

The room was a great expensive luxury. No more of that in my whole life: I hope I can live always in monasteries or college cubicles or corners of libraries. The thought of having "one's own establishment"—one's own telephone, one's own six-month lease, a name in the phone book, "my apartment," a civil status—disturbs me tremendously. It is no sacrifice to renounce it now.

The back room was dark, but I spent a lot of time in it. It wasn't pleasant as a room; it was pretty dank. But starting at the end of August 1939, in a hell of heat and sweat and hangovers and wisdom teeth torn out of my hacked jaw with saws and hammers, I began to learn a lot of things in that room, and work there, too. But being in the country's better.

That summer when me and Lax and Rice were at the cottage up here was a good summer.

March 4, 1941

This has been a remarkable day to have looked in the face. I don't think of the contents of a day as "a day" ordinarily, but this one has to be seen that way. To begin with, it is a day I feared—it is the day I got all my notions together about war and said them briefly, all at once, on a few sheets of paper, on a prepared blank, and put them in the mail for the draft board.

I mean I made out my reasons for being a partial conscientious objector, for asking for noncombatant service, so as not to have to kill men made in the image of God when it is possible to obey the law (as I must) by serving the wounded and saving lives—or what may be a purely artificial situation: by the humiliation of digging latrines, which is a far greater honor to God than killing men.

The thing was that I wrote these pages out without trepidation and was amazed. Went quietly to Father Thomas and Father Gerald and got their approval. Went to Olean and had the thing notarized, mailed it. All through it I was tremendously happy in a strange quiet way. It was as if this were one of the good things for me to have done in my life—and all along I kept wondering at it. When the thing was in the box, I knew I was completely in God's hands. Everything goes according to His will. *I am free.* I have never felt such a cool sense of freedom as when I realized that I now belong to a decision by a board of strangers, which I will know is God's will, for He expresses His will through laws of states also. Whatever His will is, may it be done, through Christ our Lord.

Riding in to Olean in a small old car with one of the workmen from the monastery farm was as pleasant as any time in my whole life. Outside was good blue sky, and the hills were in shadow from the sun going down gradually, aslant of them somewhere. In Olean the wide streets were almost empty and people were coming home from work. Riding back to

Saint Bona's, I came with Bob O'Brien, the plumber from Olean House. Now the sun was below the hills, but the sky was the cleanest and clearest blue you ever saw and in it a couple of light, fiery, orange clouds, like in Bellini's pictures.

Bob O'Brien said, "Isn't it good to be here in the country now? Where else would it be better than in this good country?" We had been talking about how people go mad in the city. A simple topic. Everything Bob said about the country he meant completely: it had the greatest depth of conviction. He is a big happy guy and means what he says. I never meant anything so much either as when I agreed with him.

I walked up the road to the monastery and saw the cross on top of the low cupola over the rim of the roof and saw that bright, clean, fiery sky and heard the bell ringing, blowing down the hill from the open belfry up at Saint Elizabeth's for the Angelus, and once again I remembered clearly how I belong absolutely to God. This thing in the mail demonstrates that but does not make it so, for it always *was* so and will be, in a sense. But my consent is more open than ever, and I pray it be more and more and more so until I am all His.

March 18, 1941

The first insult of the day, after getting off the five-thirty train into the freezing storm, was when I found the letter from the *New Yorker* saying my poem containing a parody on "Beauty is truth etc. . . . " was a parody of Emily Dickinson and their readers would mostly be unfamiliar with that poem "of hers" so they couldn't use it.

I never read a line of Emily Dickinson.

Now I really think I shouldn't send anything more to them.

I was glad to get back here. The monastery at St. Bonaventure's is more of a home than anywhere I have had since my father died—or since Pop died in Douglaston, which emptied the house in a way. That house was my home, too, last year, before I went to Cuba—at exactly this time of the year. It would still be, except that—it isn't, and Uncle Harold is always thinking of moving out. The only thing that made it no home before was my own ingratitude. In a way, you have to be grateful for goodness before you know goodness.

March 23, 1941. Sunday (4th in Lent)

My father's death, in the Middlesex Hospital: for a long time he could not speak. On blue letter paper, with a fountain pen, he drew Byzantine saints. I told him one day I was going to learn Italian. That was a dreary hospital. This is another thing I can't understand: his death. His illness was something that was being "kept from me," that is, how bad it was. I knew all along father would die but didn't reflect upon it, because I couldn't: I mean I didn't know how. Anyway, I was too young and too selfish, and I had been away at school too much and at Aunt Maude's and other places too much on holidays. I didn't reflect about it, but on the other hand I have never ceased to dream about it. I never doubted the fact that father's soul, or mother's, was immortal—never. It was never possible even when I said I didn't believe anything.

Today in the Four Mile Valley, hearing the rush of waters down the ditches of the mountainside, I was reminded of Murat and Le Puy du Cantal. On the rock at Murat is a huge image to the Blessed Virgin: she was in my father's pictures, and I hope she prayed for him when nobody else did. All the saints to whom were dedicated the churches and cathedrals that my father loved, pray for him. The Saint of St. Antonin, where he was building a house, where we lived looking at the river and Rocher d'Angears, pray for him. I have never stopped thinking about that town or all the places around it. It is thirteen years since I was there.

Again today I thought of the time we were in Clermont-Ferrand. Or the time we were in Marseilles—the restaurant where everybody was afraid of the towels. The first day we were in Montauban. My exhilaration at the sweet-smelling barbershops in Montauban. I often think of the Marist College in Montauban, a place I wondered at: very mysterious. The brick tower of St. Jacques. The Musée Ingres. The guidebooks I devoured. Father working on the land he had bought on summer evenings, making flowers grow. The drawings of the house. The beginning of the house itself. His room, my room. Mine full of sun. His smelled of tobacco, a little. The kitchen, where we made cocoa out of goat's milk. I thought of the Medieval tanneries, the legend of the Saint, the rocks, the stunted oaks, the *causses*, the tough little chateaux, the Calvaire, where the rich people from Lille were trying to be country gentry. The Protestant cemetery, where there were nightingales in the cypresses. Eating at the Hôtel des Thermes: but above all: summer. And the rains of winter. And all father's pictures. The big screen he did for Bennett. The tunes he played on the piano in the movie house for the Buster Keaton movies: "I Want to Be Happy," "Chicago," "Tea for Two," "Toodle-oo."

Sometimes I think I don't know anything except the years 1926–27–28 in France, as if they were my whole life, as if father had made that whole world and given it to me instead of America, shared it with me.

I have not ceased to dream about all this, or won't, ever. Also, I want to write another novel.

April 7, 1941. Eastertime. Our Lady of Gethsemani, Kentucky

I should tear out all the other pages of this book and all the other pages of everything else I ever wrote, and begin here.

This is the center of America. I had wondered what was holding the country together, what has been keeping the universe from cracking in pieces and falling apart. It is this monastery if only this one. (There must be two or three others.)

Abraham prayed to the Lord to spare Sodom if there should be found in it one just man. The Blessed Mother of God, Mary Queen of Heaven and of Angels, shows Him daily His children here, and because of their prayers, the world is spared from minute to minute from the terrible doom.

This is the only real city in America—in a desert.

It is the axle around which the whole country blindly turns.

Washington is paint and plaster and noise-making machines and lunacy: this country hasn't got a capital or a heart or any focal point to it except Gethsemani. Gethsemani holds this country together the way the underlying substrate of faith, which goes with our own being and cannot be separated from it, keeps living in a man who is faithless.

This is a great and splendid palace. I have never in my life seen a court of a king or a queen. Now I am transported into one, and I can hardly breathe from minute to minute. I have been in the greatest capital cities of the world, but I have never seen anything that was not either a railway station or a movie house, instead of being the palace it tried to be. Here, suddenly, I am in the Court of the Queen of Heaven, where She sits enthroned and receives at once the proper praise of men and angels. I tell you I cannot breathe. (I tell who? When I am in the palace of the Queen of Heaven, who do I talk to? I only ask to kiss the earth this Holy Place is built on.)

April 8, 1941. Our Lady of Gethsemani

How does it happen that this abbey is an earthly paradise? It is as a result of a hierarchy of uses. For the good Trappists (and they are good, holy men) work is important—it is a mixture of penance and recreation. However hard it is, it is still a form of play. Even the strictest penance is play, too. The liturgy, too. The Trappist uses work to save his soul. To be as little as children, we must play like them, do things not because they are physically necessary, but *freely*, as if almost arbitrarily, for love. Behind the strictness of Trappist discipline is this complete metaphysical freedom from physical necessity that makes it, ontologically speaking, a kind of play. This use of work as play to save the monk's soul results, indirectly, in the abbey being an earthly paradise—because work necessarily produces results. The results, in this case, are a perfect community, a marvelous farm, beautiful gardens, a lovely chapel, woods, the cleanest guest house in the world, wonderful bread, cheese, butter— all things make this abbey the only really excellent community of any kind, political, religious, or anything, in the whole country.

April 9, 1941. Wednesday in Holy Week. Our Lady of Gethsemani, Ky.

The life in this abbey is not understandable unless you begin the day with the monks, with Matins at 2 A.M. If you get up for the low masses, at 4:30 (when each priest says his Mass), it still does not make the day completely comprehensible: because even then it is not clear that the high point of the day is High Mass at 8 o'clock. The hours from 2 to 8 (6 hours) are all devoted to prayer, pretty much filled up with prayer by the time Matins, Lauds, Prime, and all the little hours (at least in Lent) are said. The High Mass is the fullest, most sustained, and most splendid ceremony of the day and unquestionably the most significant, not excluding Compline and its hymn *Salve Regina*, which is also very moving and significant. But in the High Mass everything is deeper and more tremendous, naturally, since, after all, it is a High Mass, the highest kind of Liturgy. This is the heart of the whole day, its center, its foundation, its meaning: it *is* the day. But if you are up at 4 or 5 you don't immediately realize this—High Mass, then, seems to be only the day's beginning: then the work in the fields seems to be the important part of the day (9 to 11:30 and 1 to 5 perhaps), when of course the work is really not much more than recreation.

April 10, 1941. Holy Thursday. Abbey of Our Lady of Gethsemani

I have not written what a paradise this place is, on purpose. I think it is more beautiful than any place I ever went to for its beauty—anyway, it is the most beautiful place in America. I never saw anything like the country. A very wide valley—full of rolling and dipping land, woods, cedars, dark green fields—maybe young wheat. The monastery barns—vineyards. The knoll with the statue of St. Joseph in the middle of a great field where the road goes through a shallow cut toward the village and the railway station on the line from Louisville to Atlanta.

And in the window comes the good smell of full fields—*agri pleni.*

The sun today was as hot as Cuba. Tulips in the front court opened their chalices, widened and became blowsy. Bees were working, one in each flower's cup, although it is only April. Fruit trees are in blossom, and every day more and more buds come out on the trees of the great avenue leading to the gate house.

The Trappist brothers in their medieval peasant hoods and their swathed legs and big homemade boots tramp along in a line through the vineyards; bells ring in the steeple.

All the spring, which I had looked forward to finding here, from St. Bonaventure's, is here, and I haven't been looking at it—for fear of trying to claim I owned it, for fear of taking out title deeds to it and making it my real estate as I have everything else, for fear of devouring it like a feast, making it my party, and so losing it.

This morning after High Mass—a Pontifical High Mass celebrated by the Abbot at 8:30—I walked along the wall of the guest house garden under the branches of the fruit trees and in the hot sun, in the midst of more beauty than I can remember since I was in Rome. I remember Rome a lot here.

April 18, 1941. Friday. Douglaston, New York

Leaving Gethsemani was very sad.

After Benediction in the afternoon on Easter Day the monks had almost all left the church, and it was quiet and sun streamed in on the floor. I made the Stations of the Cross and wished I were going to stay there—which is impossible. I wished it was not impossible.

I left early in the morning Monday. Got to Louisville at 8—everybody was going to work—it would have been in the middle of the day at the abbey, not its beginning. I was very confused. There is a huge gap between the monastery and the world. Louisville is a nice enough town, but I wasn't happy to be thrown back into it. Then there were the papers with Germany about to enter Egypt in the war. There had been a big robbery on Fourth St., Louisville. I couldn't figure out half the time whether it was morning or afternoon.

It is terrible to want to belong entirely to God but see nothing around you but the world and not see Him. In the monastery you don't see Him either, but you have nothing to do but lament your separation from Him, pray to Him, and pray for the world. In the world itself your prayers are drowned by the noise of traffic: you have to watch out for cars, falling buildings, brimstone, thunder.

The world is beautiful with the sunlight, but the objects in the sunlight are not beautiful—they are strange. Candy in a drugstore window. Newspapers. Mannequins in store windows. Women's clothes have military insignia all over them now. Speech is violent and hard and blasphemous. You weep because already you see how terribly difficult it is to hold on to the cleanness and peace you had at the abbey!

I go everywhere talking about the abbey.

May 14, 1941. St. Bonaventure

That same old game of my happy childhood, entitled "Where was I this time last year, two years ago, etc. etc. . . . ."

May 14, 1940:

Either in Havana, Cuba, or just leaving Havana. Maybe I sailed on the 15th. If I was in Havana I was living in the Hotel Andino. There was an afternoon as hazy and indefinite as this one when I stayed with this

Manolo, the head waiter of one of those places at the Plaza—Oh! Club Pennsylvania was its name—and ate ice cream. But the day before I left I went to Rio Cristal and had a fabulous lunch that was much more than I wanted to eat.

Last year: flowers, birds, waterfalls, *arroz con pollo,* a special soup, *frijoles,* people playing guitars, a veranda. Back in Havana—the many plazas via the streets that opened into them. Mostly to the Churches of El Santo Cristo and San Francisco. The only really good thing about Havana was the mornings—going to church and Communion, then having breakfast with a huge glass of orange juice and reading, in the *Diario de la Marina,* about the English being chased out of Norway. The big fight in Belgium was just beginning. When I landed in New York after two days without news, things had suddenly become very terrible, Belgium folding up, British and French armies being cut to pieces, etc.

May 14, 1939:

35 Perry Street. I would sit on the unsafe balcony of that front room, while the loose boards rattled under me. I would wait for my telephone with the soft, subdued, and happy, expensive bell to ring. I would go to the World's Fair with Lax and Bob Gibney, to the Cuban village, to the French Building—or maybe that wasn't open yet. And I was reading *Finnegans Wake* and writing what? Those rather lousy poems. Except around the time I wrote "Dido," which is all right. I thought I was going to write a thesis on Gerard Manley Hopkins for my Ph.D. at Columbia.

May 1938:

We would sit in Dona Eaton's big room with no sunlight, in the heat, typing very fast to finish Lax's novel for Nobbe's novel-writing course about Mr. Hilquist and Mme. Choppy. Maybe drank Rhine wine. I had just been to Ithaca and would soon come to Olean with Lax. Just then we thought we would come to Olean on an oil barge up the Erie Canal in Buffalo, but we didn't, we took the train. It is three years since I first came here.

May 1937:

I guess I was sitting in Douglaston holding my head in confusion. I had just had most of my front teeth yanked out, and I guess I was waiting for nothing more important to happen than the appearance of the College Year Book, as I was Editor. I wanted to see all the pictures of myself I was having printed. Around this time was Russ Boyer's wedding, when we all—that is, a lot of people from Douglaston—drove out to Rothman's and I was relatively content to be full of champagne. It seemed like a good party.

May 1936:

This game gets more distressing as the years go back. I suppose we had all just had a jolly, jolly party in the old Alpha Delta house, and I was being interviewed about getting the job at Radio City. What an unhappy summer that was.

May 1935:

I sat in the garden at Douglaston and typed a stupid term paper for Irwin Edman on the function of art. Further than this I refuse to remember in 1935.

May 1934:

Cambridge. Stab me with swords and shower my head with garbage at the horror and embarrassment I feel upon remembering Cambridge in May 1934. I would rather be instantly dead than do one thing or say one sentence or think one thought that I was likely to have been happy about at that time.

May 1933:

I was in Douglaston. I had been in Rome, and I was just beginning to forget and stamp out of myself the grace that had been given me momentarily in Rome to try, in an obscure and proud and Protestant way, to love God by trying to pray in shame and secret, trying to read the Bible when nobody was looking, trying to do good, or be good, in some way. But I was also busy reading D. H. Lawrence and wondering more about how experienced I was and how shameful it was to know so little of "life" as I imagined I knew. I found out, I suppose.

May 1932:

I had been in the Sanitarium with blood poisoning up to now, only more than my blood was poisoned. I thought John Dos Passos was the world's greatest novelist and was busy writing an essay on modern novels.

May 1931:

I can bear remembering this year, when I believed in God and was still a kind of a child, anyway. But I was beginning to wonder when I would be a great man of the world—not so much, though. I was just going to sail on the *Minnetonka* for America. I was writing very silly and no good poems indeed. I thought Vergil's *Georgics* were swell (which they are), and I liked Tacitus. I was just going to be Editor of the School Magazine, and I had been reading Shelley.

Ten years is enough. This is not a satisfying game to play. It feels very much like hara-kiri.

June 26, 1941, St. Bonaventure

It is all the time hot and bright. In the mornings I sometimes write something in the *Journal of My Escape from the Nazis.* In the afternoons I read Dante and dull stuff about a course I have to give in Bibliography. Last summer we were all up at the cottage—or rather, I was here, thinking to be a Franciscan novice and reading a lot of Saint Thomas Aquinas.

I looked at the ten first pages of *Brighton Rock* and was not as happy about them as the very first time. The novel I wrote last fall, *The Man in the Sycamore Tree,* came back from Curtis Brown. I am not so sore at it as I was a few weeks ago. Last night I reread the Cuban part and liked it. Only, the beginning is terrible.

August 15, 1941. Saturday. 548 West 114th Street, New York City

Down in Harlem is the Baroness's place, Friendship House. Yesterday, full of Hail Marys, I went there. Today I sorted dresses in the clothing center and women's shoes until my hands were thick with the gray dirt of their whiting.

Walking across 135th Street between the clothing center and the Library where the Baroness has her desk, you see (looking West) City College on top of the hill, looking surprised. A big building saying Y.M.C.A.—white letters on black. A movie. Seven or eight pushcarts. The drabbest billiard parlor in the world, the subway at the corner of Lenox Avenue, and hundreds of little Negro kids, walking solemnly, holding kites.

A pair of army trucks go by full of colored soldiers leaning very far out and laughing excitedly at the strangers of their own race all along the street. Very fast, the trucks are gone.

I remember the kids in the play in Harlem—Merlin turns into a black and white cat. Wonderful costumes. The sad and earnest parents watching, ready to laugh and cry, so scared, so colored. The children on the tiny little stage in a converted store. It was very good. If I have done any work there, it has no proportion to the 2 meals and cups of black tea they have given me, Friday and today.

You don't get sentimental or exalted sorting dresses in an old store in a tenement. You work. It is safe; there is nothing aesthetic about it. And what happens? I don't know. I'll know better when I see the dresses given out Tuesday. But I already know something from the faces of the scared, earnest, devoted parents, last night, sitting outlandishly polite like bourgeois, listening to the Baroness before the play.

September 27, 1941, St. Bonaventure

It was a pretty day and a pretty evening with a clear half moon and the hills not misty yet. I keep seeing the pastures as they were last winter. But when I look toward Martiny's Rocks I am filled with awe, thinking of the earthly paradise I found under the tree last Sunday—a view over a road and farms and woods, the road leading back to a wild place, perhaps a wooded plateau with I don't know what miles of woods or with what uninhabited valley full of oil wells.

The grass like green silk under the tree: and the sun and the silence and the wind moving in the branches and the heat pouring on the landscape: and I sit under the tree full of all this, not able to say anything to myself about it because it was all incomprehensible as soon as I tried to describe it as a possessed experience. An individual material reality is unintelligible: what I was trying to describe was not an experience. It was nothing comprehensible, the matter of an experience, raw matter. *That* you can describe so as to *seem* to describe it, but you are really describing another thing, an experience—not this moment itself, but your experience in it.

The trick is to order your experience so that it doesn't get possessive but is lost in the object instead of trying to contain its object. That way it *does,* in fact, contain the object, but only by not trying.

It is the feast of Saints Cosmas and Damian, and I remember their church in Rome with the mosaic of Christ standing among the red clouds, small, firm clouds in a mackerel bank on a blue ground, receiving the two saints into heaven.

This was done when the Goths were at the gates of Rome and Saint Gregory the Great saw the avenging angel on the top of Hadrian's Tomb, putting the sword back into the scabbard.

I shall never cease to wonder at the love I suddenly got for these mosaics. It was certainly God's grace, and I cannot know in this life how much that love meant. It may have meant my whole life through the prayers of those Saints and others of the earliest times of the Church, who won by their prayers that I should love their churches, and by their prayers that I myself should also pray and read the Bible. After that, no matter where I went and what I came to for five years after, they still prayed until I came dragging back again, much more beaten and about ready to be dead!

They were physicians and they were martyrs and, I think, Arabs.

November 1, 1941. Feast of All Saints

I don't know how it started. Maybe the Baroness's letter saying I should write for the poor, for those who could scarcely read, for those who held a magazine clumsily. Anyway—big problem: how can I write for the poor? How can I tell them poverty was the condition of Christ and the Blessed Mother on earth and suffering was Christ's portion when, although I do not make any money ($45 a month and room and board), the life I lead here is as happy as the richest kind of life and as comfortable? How can I write about poverty when, although I am in a kind of way poor, I am in this happy country club? If I am to write for those who are poor and can hardly read, I cannot do it from this place. But that does not mean that if I live here and give away my salary—or live here and spend my salary—I am any less Christian than if I live among the poor.

Why do I ask myself questions all the time about what I ought to be doing? Why am I always unsatisfied and wanting to know what is my vocation if it *is* my vocation to stay here, reading and praying and writing and sometimes teaching a class? I came back to Saint Bonaventure's under a condition that occurred to me at the Trappists: wait and see about the other vocation. Meanwhile, go back to work and give away half your salary. All this merely postponed a lot of questions.

Did I know in advance that, when I had prayed to be poor, it would not satisfy me to give away $20 a month of my salary? Yes, I knew. Still, it didn't hurt to try it.

I have been happy here in a way, but never content, never completely at rest in the sense that this was where I belonged.

Whatever this vocation is, it involves a whole different attitude to the future. A sense of calm. A sense that I am going to do something hard, murderous to my pride and my senses. That it doesn't make sense to fear it or love it: I must refer everything to God. In the natural course of events I would never desire to do this unnatural thing (leave what is pleasant for what is unpleasant). I have no natural powers that will ever enable me, by themselves, to stand Harlem. If God has called me to that life of poverty, He will make it clear what I am to do and will also provide me with enough strength to do it. No sense in worrying or planning: only in continuing to pray that I may put my spirit entirely into His hands, which means doing, at the same time, what is better and harder, more holy and less rewarding, more merciful and less delightful. To do those things in which I am last and least. To submit my will to the Baroness's and to the priests.

All the arguments against going are jokes—transparently easy to see through, since they are all denied by the Gospels, the Beatitudes, the Baroness herself in asking me, and by me myself, who really desire no other thing than this which I have been praying for ceaselessly since August: that I may give myself entirely to God's service!

Before I had given the Baroness the first argument (about writing) I realized how foolish all the arguments would be.

That I am meant to stay here and write!

That I am meant to stay here and teach!

That I am meant to stay here and pray and meditate a lot!

If I am meant to write, I will write there also—and perhaps to more purpose. If I am meant to teach—the same thing. Pray and meditate—the same. There I will be living in poverty and doing the holy work of God's apostolate, *all* the corporal and spiritual works of mercy, instead of, here, only a couple of the spiritual!

November 4, 1941

Walking down from Martiny's Rocks on a day late in September, I think of the cowbells and the fields and the tree I have been sitting under, and I compare it all with Harlem. I do not quite convince myself that it is my calling to be "a contemplative" in the country.

One thing I cannot see myself trying to be now, even if I could be, is a Franciscan in this Province. But I still think of the Trappists. I still wonder if what was an obstacle to the Franciscans might not be one to the Trappists. I still keep thinking that maybe I could write to them and find out. But still I do not.

The choice between Saint Bonaventure and Harlem is definitely not a choice between two clear possible vocations. Harlem may be a vocation, but Saint Bonaventure isn't. Ever since I came here I have not regarded the place as anything permanent for myself: have always been wondering what else it was I was looking for. At first I thought another job. Then I feared I would be drafted into the army. Then I wondered if maybe I couldn't be a Trappist. Now this Harlem business. One thing is sure: I had better get settled on something. To me my life means two things: writing and voluntary poverty, both for the love of God. So far, here, there is no voluntary poverty—no sacrifice. Harlem will bring that, too. Beyond that, the Negro apostolate doesn't have to be the only thing I will ever turn to, but it begins to seem certain I should try the lay apostolate of poverty and writing and works of mercy and give my life to that.

November 17, 1941

It was a nice sunny day to be a pilgrim and an exile. I went into town and deposited my monthly paycheck in the bank, which did nothing whatever to make me happy. In spite of the sun, there is no real peace in this place, only inertia. Inertia is never the same as peace: peace is a kind of *active* order and harmony. It is vital, not inert.

There is often no real reason for preferring one place to another. Metaphysically it doesn't matter what town you happen to be in. You can work out your salvation in it and find peace there, if you want to, because for the peace we need we have to look inside ourselves.

Psychologically there are great differences between places, though. The limits they put upon your own spirituality are often very significant. I am beginning to think it was good, being quiet here for a year, but now perhaps I have used up the resources for recollection that the mere inertia of the place gave me. Maybe, if I stayed here, what I now seem to possess as peace would cease to deepen itself and turn into inertia (if such a thing is possible).

Perhaps there is in places a certain value: they make it possible for you to seek and find certain things in your own soul. When you have found them, you begin to know the place has served you: if the place is pleasant and pretty doesn't mean much anymore. It has only one further value: the value of a sacrifice. The only good thing that can be done with the place, the type of life, is to give it up. Renounce the temptation to keep what you have got as if it were a possession and to hold on to it in inertia.

November 24, 1941

I guess I am full of the kind of distress that means I ought to be writing a poem—or else what? Return to the chapel.

I got back from New York by the night train, having been wedged in various positions in the hard green seats of the day coach all night, but I am not physically tired, merely filled with a deep, undefined vague sense of spiritual distress as if I had a deep wound running inside me and it had to be stanched. I should go back to the chapel or try to say something in a poem. That wound is another aspect of the fact that we are exiles on earth.

The sense of exile bleeds inside me like a hemorrhage. It is always the same wound, whether it is a sense of sin or of loneliness or of one's own insufficiency or of spiritual dryness: they are all really the same in the way we experience them. In fact, spiritual dryness is one of the most acute experiences of longing we can have—therefore, of love.

I got back to this wonderful, quiet place. There is a little snow on the hills, a light, hard frozen powder. The roads are like iron. The air is cold and gray. The rooms are silent. Water runs in the pipes.

It is still and peaceful, but there is no peace for me here.

I am amazed at all this quietness, which does not belong to me. For a moment I get the illusion that the peace is real, but it isn't—not as soon as I hear the talk of the people. The peace here is not the peace of poverty and sacrifice, merely the "peace" of the absence of trouble, and that is not for me now nor can be anymore.

Before I was a Catholic I was half crazy with restlessness and boredom and sorrow. When I became a Catholic, I ceased to be bored or restless—in any natural sense. Most practicing Catholics are sure to lead a life full of more or less natural satisfactions, natural patience, even-temper, contentment, the level-temperedness of stoics. But that is not enough either—there is a lot of purely natural happiness around, among Catholics and people who are not. I have seen more of that everywhere in this last year than for 10 years before, in spite of the war. It probably comes of the fact that people are making money and are comfortable but not in so safe a way that their comfort palls on them.

When I was in the quicksand of my own exaggerated restlessness, I thought this firm ground was all that anyone needed for peace. There is plenty of this natural happiness, this evenness of life, at Saint Bonaventure.

But that evenness is illusory and dangerous. It is *based*, economically speaking, on violence and injustice, on the war and every injustice that led to the war. It is a purely natural contentment, and even if it were just, we cannot be content in merely natural satisfactions, our own selfish quiet and freedom from worry. We have to leave all and follow Christ, for only in Him is true peace. Christ is where men starve and are beaten.

We can either renounce all worldly quiet and ease and absence of trouble—living our lives out in the Liturgy before the tabernacle as pure contemplatives loving one another in our community—or else we must renounce all our own ease and minister to Christ in the poor as much as we can. If we renounce nothing except our cares, if our only idea is to live together without friction so that each of us may remain at peace, materially unruffled, we only get a false peace. It is a good enough peace in worldly terms, but it is not enough for Christians. Our peace is only in Christ and is only come by through mortification, sacrifice, and the Cross.

November 28, 1941

The one thing that appalls me is my own helplessness and stupidity: a helplessness and stupidity that come from a complete and total and uncompromising self-reliance that to the world appears to be a virtue in me and a great source of strength! What a lie and what a crazy deception that is—to be self-reliant is to be strong and smart; to be self-reliant will get you through all your problems without too much difficulty or anguish.

Ever since I was sixteen traveling all over Europe, some of it on foot by myself (always by preference alone), I have developed this terrific sense of geography, this habit of self-analysis, this knack of getting along with strangers and chance acquaintances—this complete independence and self-dependence, which turns out to be now not a strength but, in my big problem, a terrific weakness.

My instinct, when I have been faced by any such problem, has always been to go off and walk restlessly somewhere by myself until the problem turns itself over and over so many times that I get sick of it. Maybe a solution comes out later. Maybe the problem is not terribly tough—but this time it is a tough one.

At least I went first to the chapel—as I did when the Baroness asked me to come to Harlem. Last spring, I walked with the vocation problem in the woods. Two years ago—1939—I walked with the same problem, vocation to the priesthood, on the chicken dock in Greenwich Village.

In the chapel my heart was pounding so fast I couldn't even see straight, and I could hardly make the words of the prayers. All I could think was that it was very bad to be that disturbed. Eventually I calmed down and prayed. Then the idea it would be a good notion to see Father Philotheus gradually crystallized out.

I left the chapel. I went first not to his room but to mine. Then said a couple more prayers. Looked at a book about the Trappists, all the time knowing I was being a fool: I had no reason for standing around. (When my heart had pounded so fast in the chapel, I was saying to myself: "You are crazy: wait! wait! wait!")

When I got downstairs I went into the hall of the monastery and took two steps toward his door and rushed back out and walked up and down with ten conflicting ideas in my head—first, that I was being a fool—as disorganized as the French army was by the German fifth columns—second, that waiting was not relevant because it just protracted this confusion—third, that waiting was prudent—etc.

The next time I go in, I nearly get to his door, but then it is almost as if I were physically pushed away from it. The idea that pushed me away was "This is absurd! This huge big problem in this small, familiar room, thrown like a bomb in the middle of some routine piece of philosophical manuscript he is reading . . . disturb him . . . etc." I rushed out again.

Finally I walked across the campus and back. When I got back he was out of his room—I could see the light was out.

So then the first impulse was to say, "Now, see, let it all go for a few more days."

So I pray to Saint Theresa in the grove.

While I am praying to her, the question becomes clear: all I want to know is, do I have a chance to be a priest after all? I don't want him to argue for or against the Trappists. I *know* I want to be a Trappist. I remember the terrific sense of holiness and peace I got when I first stepped inside Gethsemani, something more certain and more terrific than had ever hit me anywhere else and that stayed with me until I got mixed up about the vocation at the end of the week in that terrible impasse: I want to be a priest—but I am told there is an impediment. Therefore the desire is just an emotional luxury: I am kidding myself.

While I am praying to Saint Theresa of the Child Jesus, it is like hearing the bells in the tower ringing for Matins in the middle of the night. I walk through the grove saying she will help me to be her Trappist—Theresa's Trappist—at Gethsemani.

I come back. No light in Father Philotheus's room. He is in the recreation room. I get him from there without any great fuss. I tell him my questions.

Instantly he says that in his opinion there is no canonical impediment in my case. He advises the thing that was so obvious I hadn't thought of it: go to Gethsemani as soon as the Christmas vacation begins and tell the whole story to the Abbot. (I thought of writing. He said that would be bad.)

He also advises me to be very careful about deciding to be a Trappist. What about my vocation to be a writer?

That has absolutely no meaning any more as soon as he has said what he has said.

So I run upstairs bursting with "*Te Deum laudamus—Te Dominum confitemur—Te aeternum Patrem omnis terra veneratur. . . .*" Then to the chapel and prayers and prayers and prayers.

I can't go to bed, and when I do I can't go to sleep.

I go through the grove again—my head full of a big double-talk mixture of *Te Deum* and good-bye to everything I don't want.

In bed: suddenly I am amazed—in four weeks, with God's grace, I may be sleeping on a board, and there will be no more future—not in the

world, not in geography, not in travel, not in change, not in variety,
conversations, new work, new problems in writing, new friends, none of
that: only a far better progress, all interior and quiet!!! If God only would
grant it! If it were only His will!

As to all this self-analysis on paper—it isn't important either. If the
twenty other things I have to say are important, I will find a chance to say
them. That I waited this long to ask Father Philotheus this question
about the vocation and to open the question again did no harm. All the
waiting I have done, and possibly must still do, is all quite important and
significant.

I earnestly pray to give myself entirely to God according to His will
and no longer get in the way with my own stupid will—only He can help
me out of my own clumsiness.

December 2, 1941
Now I know!

The whole business has burst into fire and flame like a terrific battle! I
can see some of the significance of the crisis the other night. This is a
battle, and a real one, maybe the most real one I have ever had to face in
my life—and the tremendousness of the forces engaged in it, for me and
against me, begin to be apparent. It appalls me.

I remember how an almost physical force tried to keep me from going
to Father Philotheus and finding out if there was, at least in his opinion,
every reason for me to take my vocation seriously! I was tempted to let
the whole thing wait several days.

Yesterday afternoon in the mail was a notice from the draft board—
completely unexpected. I thought my classification (1–B) last March was
final for a good long time: now I am to appear for a reexamination. They
have changed the rules about bad teeth. If I pass this time, it means I
might be in the army by January—in 1–A.

At least I had made up my mind and written the Trappists, saying I
wanted to come there December 18. I spent yesterday writing out
documents asking for time to find out whether or not the Trappists
would have me.

And I have been praying without ceasing.

PART II

BECOMING A MONK
AND WRITER

1941–1952

Once I can be in the place where I belong entirely to God and not to anyone less than Him, like some writer having my legal name, then I guess problems about writing and everything else will not be much problems any more. Harlem isn't it for me. Nor is any college. Nor is New York.

Maybe St. Lucy's Day I start out for Kentucky, full of prayer (next Saturday). There is absolutely no language to say the things that are to say about this except the language of love: there He will teach me to use that language like a child and a saint. Until which I cannot talk about Him, Who is all I want to talk about.

In Him, while I sing in the big church, will be also: Lax, Gibney, Seymour, Slate, Rice, Gerdy, Knight, Huttlinger, and Van Doren, and the Baroness, and Mary Jerdo, and my brother and my uncle and my aunt and my father and mother who died and Bramachari and the whole mystical body of Christ, everybody: Roger, Gil, all people, Jinny, Lilly. All people. The living and the dead. All days, all times, all ages, all worlds, all mysteries, all miracles. . .

Letter to Robert Lax, The Road to Joy

December 13, 1946. St. Lucy's Day. Abbey of Gethsemani

The years since I entered Gethsemani have gone by like five weeks. It was a bright day, not very cold, with little clouds very high up in the sky. Yesterday, although it is Advent and we are not supposed to receive any letters at all, Dom Frederic gave me a letter from Naomi Burton of Curtis Brown, Ltd. I had sent her the manuscript of *The Seven Storey Mountain.* Her letter about it was very good and she is quite sure it will find a publisher. Anyway, my idea—and hers also—is to turn it over to Robert Giroux at Harcourt, Brace.

At work—writing—I am doing a little better. I mean, I am less tied up in it, more peaceful and more detached. Taking one thing at a time and going over it slowly and patiently (if I can ever be said to do *anything* slowly and patiently) and forgetting about the other jobs that have to take their turn. For instance, Jay Laughlin wants two anthologies for New Directions Press. I wonder if I will ever be able to do them. If God wills. Meanwhile, for myself I have only one desire, and that is the desire for solitude—to disappear into God, to be submerged in His peace, to be lost in the secret of His Face.

April 20, 1947. Good Shepherd Sunday. Day of Recollection

If I were to make any resolutions, it would be the same old ones—no need to make them—they have been made. No need to reflect on them—it doesn't take much concentration to see how I keep them. I struggle along. It is useless to break your head over the same old details week after week and year after year, pruning the same ten twigs off the top of the tree. Get at the *root:* union with God. Drop everything and hide in yourself to find Him in the silence where He is hidden with you. Listen to what He has to say.

What a lot of things since last month's Day of Recollection, which seems like a year ago. I keep thinking of Solemn Profession, and every time it comes to my mind I am more profoundly happy. There is only one thing to live for: love. There is only one unhappiness: not to love God. That is what pains me on these Days of Recollection, to see my own soul so full of movement and shadows and vanities, of cross-currents of dry wind stirring up the dust and rubbish of desire. I don't expect to avoid this humiliation in my life, but when will it become cleaner, more simple, more loving? I can't give up writing, and everywhere I turn I find the stuff I write sticking to me like flypaper, the gramophone inside me playing the same old tune: "Admiration, admiration—You are my ideal—you are the one, original, cloistered genius, the tonsured wonder of the Western world."

It is not comforting to be such a confounded ape.

May 5, 1947

This was a day of grace.

After I had finished doing the Stations of the Cross, Father Anthony, my new confessor, called me into the confessional to tell me he thought I ought to be resolved never to willingly entertain any thought or desire of going and being a Carthusian or anything else. He reminded me that neither Reverend Father nor the Abbot General would ever give me permission to go. He said the best thing was to forget it all and leave the whole thing entirely in the hands of God.

Gethsemani—the place and the community, *locus et fratres,* the place and the brethren—is the spring where I am to drink the waters of life, and if I look somewhere else, it is to a broken cistern as far as I am concerned because, no matter how excellent it may be in itself, *it is not God's will for me.*

January 4, 1948. Day of Recollection

I just read some of the notes I wrote in the journal a year ago (the end of 1946), and I am wondering what I thought I was talking about. The first thing that impresses me is that practically all I wrote about myself and my trials was stupid because I was trying to express what I thought I *ought* to think, and not for any especially good reason, rather than what I actually did think. I couldn't very well know what I meant when I hardly meant it at all.

What was painfully artificial in that diary was that I was trying so much to write it like every other pious diary that was ever written: "I resolve this"—"I pray that." Well, I am very slow to learn what is useless in my life! I keep thinking that I have to conform to a lot of artificial standards, to things external and fragmentary that tend to keep my interior life on the surface, where it is easily scattered and blown away.

January 26, 1948. Feast of St. Alberic

Proofs of *The Seven Storey Mountain* came. There is a lot of it—still 8,000 words to cut, but that won't be hard. I'll cut more. Cutting is not merely something you have to do to save money for the publisher. It is part of the making of the book and just as much a part of it as writing the thing, especially with me. There is this whole mass of stuff, this big, frowzy, disheveled tree that has to be pruned into some kind of order and fruitfulness. St. Paul, help me out, sharpen my scissors! As usual with the fast writing, there was an awful lot of mediocrity and bad stuff. I am glad the thing waited long enough for my eyes to clear a little.

I bet it will snow tonight.

January 27, 1948

Zero weather today for St. Amadeus and yesterday for St. Paul and the days before: many days a lot of zero weather. The snow stays clean and dry, and somebody made a lot of false deer tracks in it under the trees of the garden.

The proofs of *The Seven Storey Mountain* are not as bad as they might be. In fact, as far as the printing goes, they are wonderful. I haven't found a misprint in 50 galleys, but some shark they have there has made all kinds of corrections of *my* faults, especially commas in the wrong places. On the whole I feel that is the way I really ought to write.

God defend me from the stuffy academic language and from the pious jargon I feel I got into in so many parts of *Exile Ends in Glory* on the theory that, since I was a monk, I *had* to write that way. NO! That is NOT the way to write! It does NO good.

On the other hand, it is chastening to see myself, I mean myself and not just my writing, in print. At times I sound nasty even to myself. My own bursts of indignation surprise me. They seem petulant and weak. I think many of my tirades are the fruit of something wrong with me and not with the world, and I don't know how to fix it. I need to stop shouting that way.

February 8, 1948. Quinquagesima. Forty Hours

Perhaps I am afraid of being absorbed in the public anonymity of the priest, of becoming one of those masks behind whom Christ hides and acts. I think of so many priests I know in their strange, sensitive isolation:

innocent, hearty men, decent and unoriginal, generally unperplexed, but all of them lost in a public privacy. They are Christ's property and everybody's property. Besides all that, they have their own characteristics, too, characteristics under which I don't recognize myself. I fear they will be disappointed if I don't act and think in all things the way they think that Cardinal Newman must have acted and thought, or Gerard Manley Hopkins for that matter.

February 22, 1948. Second Sunday of Lent

Today it is six years since I received the habit of novice, and not until today did I realize that I had received the habit on Washington's birthday. Father Hilary—he knows all these things—made me a sign that it was the "secular big day of the president who chopped wood."

Humble George is here again. He goes around praying with a medal in his mouth. The other day he was kneeling in church with a book, and he had a rosary around his neck and the cross of the rosary in his mouth. I think Humble George needs a little spiritual direction.

Maybe it will help me to do something about distractions if I restrain my famished appetite for the things that distract me—new books about the Order, my own work in print, etc. I don't expect to be without distractions: they are my cross. I suffer them with love in the sense that I am resigned to the drab business of remembering to sink below them when I can and keep with the God Who holds my will in His darkness. But I have given up expecting to overcome distractions by a method. I just have to love and love blindly and deepen the union that is there, in spite of everything, and not break it up by fighting the air.

Today it suddenly dawned on me: I am a *monk*, a Cistercian monk, under solemn vows, on the way to being a priest. It is almost unbelievable! I belong to this Order, this austere Order with a Rule that has such a terrific reputation with its long history and its twelfth century. I am part of all that. It is fantastic.

But that wasn't the way I felt last year.

March 19, 1948. St. Joseph

I spent the anniversary of my Solemn Profession in the infirmary, a piece of great kindness on the part of St. Joseph as I am beginning to realize. It has all the earmarks of a plot arranged for no other purpose than to give me a little consolation on this feast and make it a *very* happy one.

As soon as I get into a cell by myself I am a different person! Prayer becomes what it ought to be. Everything is very quiet. The door is closed, but I have the window open. It is warm—gray clouds fly—all night and all day the frogs sing. Reverend Father sold all the ducks (Father Peter kept proclaiming Brother Isidore and Brother Cyril because the ducks quacked all night). It is an improvement.

This is the way I happened to come to the infirmary.

Tuesday I got a cold. It was warm and damp, and when I walked into the church to pray in the afternoon interval before work, something got in my throat and I began coughing a lot. That night in the dormitory was no fun nor was the one after. The paint made me feel ill. I coughed a lot. Lungs full of green slime. Finally yesterday morning, Thursday, I came up to Father Gerard and found out I had a slight temperature, 99 or so. However, it got worse. Yesterday was full of penance. I tried to finish going over the ms. of *Waters of Siloe* but finally left it in good enough condition to be sent off though not completely gone over. Reverend Father sent me up to the infirmary again toward the end of the afternoon work, and since by that time the thermometer was up to 101, they put me to bed in the room marked St. Gertrude.

I was in the same room six years ago today with the same thing: "flu." It is the one Brother Hugh died in. It does not look, however, as though I am going to stay long.

Even with your eyes aching and your head spinning, how good it is to be alone, in silence. How close God is in this room! The presence of people around me is always something that divides my attention between the world and God: well, not always either. At meditation or after Communion in church I generally don't know that anyone else is there, but in the intervals people moving about are a distraction.

To have nothing to do but abandon yourself to God and love God! It is the greatest of luxuries. Silence and solitude are the supreme luxuries of life!

Anyway, I woke up about the time the bell was ringing for Lauds. I was soaked in sweat and that meant most of the fever was gone. I lay awake and listened to the frogs.

How this silence keeps claiming you for itself! As soon as you start anything, it says, "Come back for a moment! Pray! Be quiet! Rest in your God!"

Plenty of time! Plenty of time! No manuscripts, no typewriter, no rushing back and forth to church, no Scriptorium, no breaking your neck to get things done before the next thing happens!

I went down to Chapter because Reverend Father wants you to go to Chapter if your temperature is less than 100. Mine was. Father Amadeus preached vehemently on the sufferings of St. Joseph, his mental sufferings when he discovered that Mary was with child. I should not have made funny faces when he said Abraham was born 1,959 years after the creation of the world, nor can I figure out why he imagines that this event should be commemorated next year, 1949. But he says things like that; they come into his head and he says them.

Then I came back to the cell. On the table were bread and butter and a can of barley coffee, and before I said grace, Father Gerard came in with the bottle of Mass wine in which much was left because Father Odo could not say Mass. He said, "This is a *feast* day," and poured out half a tumbler of wine. He was not aware of any anniversary of mine, but it was then that I realized what was going on and that St. Joseph had arranged all this as a way of giving me some manifestation of God's love, that I might have joy.

So I drank the wine and it was good and it gave me back my appetite. Last night butter was hateful and I could not eat it.

Then I moved the table to the window and ate looking out of the window as the Carthusians do. The clouds flew and the huts of the ducks were empty and the frogs sang in the beautiful green pond.

It was a happy feast day.

Now it is evening. The frogs still sing. After the showers of rain around dinner time the sky cleared. All afternoon I sat on the bed rediscovering the meaning of contemplation, rediscovering God, rediscovering myself and the Office and Scripture and everything.

It has been one of the most wonderful days I have ever known in my life, yet I am not attached to that part of it either. My pleasure or the contentment I may have got out of silence and solitude and freedom from all care does not matter. But I know that is the way I ought to be *living:* with my mind and senses silent, contacts with the world of business and war and community troubles severed, not solicitous for anything high or low or far or near, not pushing myself around with my own fancies or desires or projects, and not letting myself get hurried off my feet by the excessive current of natural activity that flows through Gethsemani with full force.

Once again the question arises: is it possible to be quiet in an atmosphere like the one in this house? Should I move somewhere where I can find solitude and silence and peace to be alone with God in a pure tranquillity that is impossible for a Cistercian?

Father Anthony came up in the evening. He said that if I wanted to be a Carthusian, he would never oppose me. On the other hand, Europe is out of the question.

But there is no hurry. No need to be solicitous or anxious about that any more than anything else. God is hidden within me. I find Him by hiding in the silence in which He is concealed. All things that are not means to purify my heart and give it tranquillity in His will are useless. But if I follow Him, He will lead me to His peace.

Tomorrow I go back downstairs to the community and the dormitory full of paint. And I hope it will be with a mind to say "No" to all cares and anxieties and ambitions and ventures and images and things that have no profit for union with God in darkness above the level of change and desire and delight and sorrow and greatness and littleness and life and death and everything else that is not God alone.

I go to say Matins of Our Lady of Sorrows.

March 20, 1948. Our Lady of Sorrows

I feel as if I were in a hotel in Cuba. The landscape has something of the gray-green-yellow nondescript color that belongs to Cuba. The air is full of the sound of birds and water frogs and tree frogs and crows, too. As for those frogs, as I lay awake last night listening to them, I began to get a bit bored with their lyricism. They are inexhaustible and ring those same bicycle bells all day and all night. I began to think: "Don't they ever *do* anything, don't they ever stop to eat?" When I was just about to fall asleep, they all stopped for 30 seconds, and the silence was so astonishing that I woke up.

March 28, 1948. Easter Sunday

All the Easter *alleluia* antiphons come back to me with rich associations of the happiest days in my life—the seven Paschal seasons that I have had in the monastery—this being the seventh now beginning: the Sabbatical.

All the apple trees came out in blossom Good Friday. It rained and got colder, but today is very bright with a pure sky. The willow is full of green. Things are all in bud.

And in my heart, the deepest peace, Christ's clarity, lucid and quiet and ever-present as eternity. On these big feasts you come out on top of a plateau in the spiritual life to get a new view of everything. Especially Easter. Easter is like what it will be entering eternity when you suddenly, peacefully, clearly recognize all your mistakes as well as all that you did well: everything falls into place.

May 2, 1948. Day of Recollection

My interior activity must begin gradually to die down (but it tends to *increase!*).

All the useless twisting and turning of my nature, analyzing the faults of the community and the choir, figuring out what is wrong with everything and what *could* be right, comparing our life to the 12th century with what we have today, trying to figure some way to make a break and get into solitude: with all these things I have lost time and made myself suffer, and I have ruined the work of God in my soul.

Wind and sun. Catbirds bickering in a bush. Ringing bells and blowing whistles and birds squawking in a lamentable fashion. Trees are all clothed and benches are out: a new summer has begun.

May 30, 1948. Day of Recollection

I have a hard time trying to imagine what it is going to mean for me to become a priest. Sometimes I am terrified at the thought of being incorporated into a caste full of spiritual limitations and rigidity, but that is not what the priesthood really is, although some people make it look that way. Ultimately the only solution to that problem is obedience. I go ahead under obedience. If my superiors want me to be a priest, it is at least safe. God wants it, and He will do me good by it, although it might contain an unimaginable death.

Sometimes I want to run away and be a tramp and hang around on the roads without anything, like Humble George or Benedict Joseph Labre.

June 20, 1948. Fifth Sunday After Pentecost

I got a letter from Bob Giroux at Harcourt Brace saying Clare Boothe Luce had been reading page proofs of *The Seven Storey Mountain* and liked them and in fact that Henry Luce had swiped one set of proofs and her secretary had to call up Harcourt Brace for another.

The book has been accepted by the Catholic Book Club for August. The date assigned for publication is August 12th, Feast of St. Clare, the day on which with so many prayers I finished *The Journal of My Escape from the Nazis* seven years ago.

When I look at the way things have finally built up to this book, I cannot help getting a little understanding of what God has been doing all this time. It has been cooking for nine years, since I wrote *The Labyrinth* at Olean then couldn't sell it to Farrar and Rinehart or Macmillan or Harcourt Brace, nor could Naomi Burton sell it to Modern Age or Atlantic or Little Brown or the other people she tried.

Even so, the thing isn't finished. There are parts badly written, but on the whole it is the book in which I have tried to put something, although I scarcely began. The British edition is planned for next spring. It is beautifully printed. Bob has done a fine job. So on the whole I see now how God has taken the thing and how He had built up to it in His own time, how He prepared the Bob Giroux–Naomi Burton combination that has really *made* the book and how He brought F. X. Connolly into it. All this was completely beyond my control. I didn't even know what was going on, and now it is about to be launched.

Since I belong to God and my life belongs to Him and my book is His and He is managing them all for His glory, I only have to take what comes and do the small part that will be allotted to me: reading the letters of people who will hate me for having been converted and for having written about it, and the letters of people who will perhaps be pleased. It seems to me there can be great possibilities in all this and that

God has woven my crazy existence, even my mistakes and my sins, into His plan for a new society, "all things cooperating together for the good." So, if I get lynched, I'll offer that up for the glory of God and for the souls He will save by all this.

Now I see what it is all leading up to: to the happiness and the peace and the salvation of many people I have never known. There is no greater joy than to be drawn into union with God's great love for the souls of men, of Himself in them, and cooperate with Him in drawing them into His joy.

The best thing of all is that Bob Giroux or somebody did an index to *The Seven Storey Mountain:* the most peculiar collection of names you ever saw. Starts off with Abbot, Father, and goes on to Advent; Adler, Alfred; Ellington, Duke; and Fields, W. C.; Smith, Pete, is followed by Smith, Robert Paul, and there is Bob O'Brien, the plumber at the Olean House, and Pierrot the teamster at Saint Antonin, and the Privats at Murst, and Brother Fabian who went to Georgia, and Mary Jerdo and Helen Freedgood and Burton, Jinny, and Flagg, Nancy, and Wells, Peggy (Peggy wrote to me from Hollywood the other day. I can't figure out if she is acting or only writing or both at once).

I was fascinated. The index is beautiful. It is like the gathering of all the people I have known at a banquet to celebrate the publication of the Book. It is like a pledge that they will all belong to me somehow as trophies in heaven, or I will belong to some of *them* as a trophy.

Blake, William; Francis of Assisi, Saint; Bonaventure, Saint; Aquinas, St. Thomas; Bernard, Saint. I think this index is a partial, optimistic preview of the General Judgment with the four Marx Brothers among the sheep.

So God is very good. "Holy in all His ways." Though the natural pleasure of success sickens me a little and I get smoke in my eyes from thinking about how the book will look, still, I have to take all that on the chin and stay as tranquil and detached as God's grace will grant me to do.

July 11, 1948. Eighth Sunday After Pentecost

Last Wednesday the 7th—the anniversary of the departure of the Utah colony last year—I went to Dom Frederic just before the afternoon work to see if I couldn't go out into the fields. But he handed me the first copy of *The Seven Storey Mountain* and told me to look it over. It is a good job of printing, and I skipped through it with the general feeling that it is, with *Thirty Poems,* the only respectable book I have written. If I had never published anything but the *Mountain* and *Thirty Poems,* I would feel a whole lot cleaner. *Exile Ends in Glory* continues to be read in the refectory, and people in general seem to accept it all right. Nevertheless, there are parts of it that make my stomach turn somersaults. Where did I get all that pious rhetoric? That was the way I thought a monk was supposed to write, just after I had made Simple Profession.

About *The Seven Storey Mountain,* two Book Clubs and the Catholic Literary Foundation in Milwaukee have already guaranteed the sale of fourteen thousand copies. "Look out! Maybe this business is going to turn your whole life upside down for true!"

I caught myself thinking, "If they make it into a movie, will Gary Cooper be the hero?" Or maybe there is no Gary Cooper anymore. Anyway, that is the kind of folly I have to look out for now. I am reduced to that. I don't dare listen too closely for fear I might hear Dom Benedict roll over in his tomb. I pray to him to help me be very simple and tranquil and quiet in all this, which is God's will and is for Gethsemani. Here is the book I couldn't make a go of ten years ago. Now it is a success just when I am at Gethsemani and Gethsemani needs the money.

The business of being poisoned in spite of yourself by the pleasure you take in your own work! You say you don't want it, but it gets into your blood anyway. You don't taste the dish, but the smell of it goes to your head and corrupts you. You get drunk by sniffing the cork of the bottle.

August 4, 1948. Feast of St. Dominic. Wednesday

Reverend Father is dead.

This morning when we came down to choir he was not there. I had forgotten all about his leaving for Georgia. When he did not show up all through the Night Office, I began to worry and pray for him, and I was praying as much for him as for Dom Dominique, whose feast it was. At Prime there was a lot of confusion and running around. In Chapter Father Odilo told us that Dom Frederic had died on the train last night before they got to Knoxville, Tennessee.

Yesterday afternoon I had had a long talk with Reverend Father about work and books and so on. It was very pleasant and cheerful, and he was exhorting me to write something to make people love the spiritual life. He was glad about the Sheed and Ward job.

He has had a lot to suffer in the last two years. He has done a tremendous amount of work. The house is sad. He will come back from Knoxville embalmed and in an ambulance sometime tonight, and the funeral isn't supposed to be until Monday.

August 13, 1948

I have never been so busy in my life. But also very much at peace.

Yesterday I had to go to Louisville. It was the first time I was out of the monastery in seven years. I had to go in to act as interpreter for Dom Gabriel Sortais, who was called in to the Good Shepherd Convent because their Mother General from Anger was there and wanted him to talk to the community and hear her confession. The Sisters received us in a cool library with a lot of armchairs and carpets. The place was cool because all around the buildings were shade trees. On the whole, the convent is a pleasant one and very big. Big police dog, a laundry, and what not. So he told them in French to love their vocations, and I translated it into English, and I think they were happy. One Sister held the black hat I had been wearing in her hand while I drank a glass of ginger ale and ate a cookie.

August 14, 1948. Virgil of the Assumption

Going into Louisville the other day I wasn't struck by anything in particular. Although I felt completely alienated from everything in the world and all its activity, I did not necessarily feel out of sympathy with the people who were walking around. On the whole they seemed to me more real than they ever had before and more worthy of sympathizing with. Without any conscious effort being necessary, I went without remarking anyone, including women, except two. One wild-looking jane in a black dress with much lipstick—I thought of her all of a sudden when I was taking the discipline yesterday morning and hoped she didn't happen to be in the way of needing some vicarious penance.

The country was all color. Clouds. Corn in the bottomlands. Red rocks. A lot of rolling land and more hills between here and Bardstown than I realized. I had the impression of having remembered much more on my first journey, when I came to the monastery seven years ago. Now I realize I had forgotten practically everything.

It was nice saying the Office in the car and saying the *Gloria Patri* while looking at the woods and fields.

Louisville was boring. Anyway, the whole thing was obedience. It meant losing a day's work. We were back at seven, ate eggs in the guest house, and I was on time for the *Salve*.

August 25, 1948. Feast of St. Louis

The election lasted from 7:45 to 12:25: this included confirmation and installation of Dom James Fox, who, of course, was elected. It is easy to see from this end of the affair that he was the Holy Ghost's candidate—in more senses than one.

That afternoon, when he was in Louisville at the Archbishop's, I got a check for nine hundred dollars on *The Seven Storey Mountain*, so I gave it to him the next morning. He told me to go on writing.

September 6, 1948. Sixteenth Sunday After Pentecost

I have a terrific undefined longing to give everything to God and a constant feeling that I am not doing so here—or not now.

Really, though, I can't see what God wants of me. So far it seems to be this. But this writing business has become a chaos of correspondence, and that is certainly not our vocation.

However, I have to be content that I am more or less up against a blank wall interiorly. As soon as I ask too many questions about it, I suffer. But if I keep still, I have peace.

To make a Rule the whole meaning of my existence is not enough. To make an Order, a spiritual tradition, the center of my life is not enough. Contemplation is not enough: by itself it is not enough of an ideal. The complete gift of myself to Christ—transformation—total simplicity and poverty—these are some of the things I need. In other words, I need to get *rid* of everything. Here I am compelled to keep my hands full. And if I write, I am bound to live submerged in books.

October 10, 1948. Sunday

Sooner or later the world must burn and all things in it—all the books, the cloister together with the brothel, Fra Angelico together with the Lucky Strike ads, which I haven't seen for seven years because I don't remember seeing one in Louisville. Sooner or later it will all be consumed by fire and nobody will be left, for by that time the last man in the universe will have discovered the bomb capable of destroying the universe and will have been unable to resist the temptation to throw the thing and get it over with.

And here I sit writing a diary.

But Love laughs at the end of the world because Love is the door to eternity. He who loves is playing on the doorstep of eternity, and before anything can happen, Love will have drawn him over the sill and closed the door. He won't bother about the world burning because he will know nothing but Love.

March 6, 1949. First Sunday of Lent

Yesterday *Seeds of Contemplation* arrived, and it is very handsome. The best job of printing that has ever been done on any book by me. I can hardly keep my hands off it.

Every book that comes out under my name is a new problem. To begin with, every one brings with it an immense examination of conscience.

Every book I write is a mirror of my own character and conscience. I always open the final printed job with a faint hope of finding myself agreeable, and I never do.

So there is nothing to be proud of in this one either.

It is clever and difficult to follow, not so much because I am deep as because I don't know how to punctuate and my line of thought is clumsy and tortuous. It lacks warmth and human affection. I find in myself an underlying pride and contempt for other men that I had thought was all gone, but it is still there, as bad as ever. I don't see how the book will ever do any good. It will antagonize people or else make them go around acting superior and stepping on everybody.

Laughlin tells me a book club is taking it and advertising it as a "streamlined *Imitation of Christ*." God forgive me. It is more like Swift than Thomas à Kempis.

The Passion and Precious Blood of Christ are too little in the book—only hinted at here and there. Therefore the book is cold and cerebral. What is the good of trying to teach people to love God without preaching through those wounds? The reason I do not do so is because I am still selfish. I find myself thinking about what we ought to get for dinner in Lent and about how to distribute signed complimentary copies of the *deluxe* edition of this book. I should never have gone into such a thing as a boxed special edition. I must be nuts.

Ever since the death of Father Odo and the Forty Hours my mind has been overactive, and I didn't finally get back to resting in God in silence until this afternoon when I got into the vault for an hour and a half and once more became a rational being. All week I had been underwater with the whole world swimming between me and God like a fleet of large fish.

May Day, 1949. SS. Philip and James. Day of Recollection

Every day I get some idea of what is in myself when I have to swallow my own ideas about chant, the interior life, solitude, the Cistercian vocation, etc., etc. Every day I kill Isaac—my beautiful dream about a silent, solitary, well-ordered life of perfect contemplation and perfect monastic observance with no intrusion from the world, no publicity, no best-selling books, just God and that nice, archaic, little Carthusian cell!! I have to make that blind act of faith that God and Our Lady are drawing me—"through the Cross"—to something better, which I will probably never see this side of heaven.

May 15, 1949. 4th Sunday After Easter

God makes us ask ourselves questions most often when He tends to resolve them. He gives us needs that He alone can satisfy and awakens capacities that He means to fulfill. Any perplexity is liable to be a spiritual gestation leading to new birth and a mystical regeneration.

Here are a few points:

What is the Mass going to do to my interior life?

I am confronted with the fact of my past prayer. Acts, thoughts, desires, words became inadequate when I was a novice. Resting in God, sleeping, so to speak, in His silence, remaining in His darkness, have fed me and made me grow for seven years. Now that, too, is likely to become inadequate.

The Mass will hold the key to this inadequacy, I hope.

I cannot explain more at the moment except that Christ the High Priest is awakening in the depths of my soul in silence and majesty, like a giant Who means to run His course.

When practicing the ceremonies of Mass, when standing at the altar as Deacon, I have been more and more impressed by the fact that it would be utterly insufficient for me, as Priest, to stand at the altar and say prayers with great personal love and fervor to Christ in the Sacrament before me. I once thought that would be the consummation of all joy— to be united by a bond of love with Christ in the Sacrament of love—to be lost in His presence there as if nothing else matters.

But now there is much more. Instead of *myself* and *my* Christ and *my* love and *my* prayer, there is the might of a prayer stronger than thunder and milder than the flight of doves rising up from the Priest Who is the center of the soul of every priest, shaking the foundations of the universe and lifting up—me, Host, altar, sanctuary, people, church, abbey, forest, cities, continents, seas, and worlds to God and plunging everything into Him.

In the presence of this huge power, my own thoughts and words and affections cannot seem to mean anything! Not that they have no value whatever, but now they are lost and sublimated in a far greater and simpler prayer that is beyond my comprehension.

In the vault everything was clear. The page proofs of *Waters of Siloe* lay neglected on the table, and I expect them to lie that way more or less until after Ordination. I come out of myself and look at my books and at letters and am sad, but I return to God and know that my vocation is to be a priest and a contemplative—that my vocation is PRAYER—and that makes me happy.

May 29, 1949. Sunday Within the Octave of the Ascension
I could not begin to write about my Ordination, about saying Mass, about the *Agape* that lasted three days with all those who came down. Perhaps some day it will come out retrospectively in fragments.

A sense of the absolutely tremendous work that has been done in me and through me in the last three days, each day bringing its own growth. Ordination, anointing, Ordination Mass—then the first Low Mass and what followed, finally the Solemn Mass yesterday and talking in the afternoon out under the trees of the avenue. I am left with the feeling not only that I have been transformed, but that a new world has somehow been brought into being through the labor and happiness of these three most exhausting days full of sublimity and of things that none of us will understand for a year or two to come.

I wish I could explain something about the gradation that seems to have marked the three days of my festival. Each one seemed to represent some gigantic development that I am powerless to grasp or to explain. In the end I had the impression that all who came to see me were dispersing to the four corners of the universe with hymns and messages and prophecies, speaking with tongues and ready to raise the dead because the fact is for three days we have been full of the Holy Ghost and the Spirit of God seemed to be taking greater and greater possession of all our souls through the first three Masses of my life, my three greatest graces.

It is all unfamiliar to me. These graces belong to an apostolic order that are beyond my experience. Yet I cannot say, without ingratitude and stupidity, that they were outside my vocation since they were in a sense its crown: I mean the crown of this portion of my history—of the last seven years. I was brought here for this. For this I came into the world.

It seems like the triumphant conclusion of an epoch and the beginning of a new history whose implications are utterly beyond me.

Friday I said the Mass that I had promised to Our Lady of Cobre. It was the feast of St. Bede, but we don't celebrate that. I had been told that one got so mixed up in the rubrics that the first Mass was no fun. I did not find that to be true at all. On the contrary, I felt as if I had been saying Mass all my life, and the liturgical text of the Votive Mass of our dearest Lady in this season became immensely rich. It was at St. Anne's altar and the church was full of sun (after Chapter) and there was no one else saying Mass nearby so I could really speak it. Then there was a beautiful chalice Dan Walsh had brought down, and I had an amice and corporal and purificator and even a finger towel, which all came from colored boys and girls in Catholic High School in Mobile, Alabama, and I had a cincture given by a Sister in a hospital in St. Louis. If I had tried to say all the names of all the people I wanted to remember at the *Memento* I would have stood there until dinner time. I had kept forming intentions for them all the days beforehand, so they would all be included when the time came, but even then I took time to remember all those that God wanted me explicitly to remember over again at that moment.

Now I know that I had the whole Church in America praying for me and I am scared and consoled by so much mercy and the sense that I myself have contributed nothing to the whole business, that I have been worked on and worked in, carried upward on the tide of a huge love that has been released in people, somehow, in connection with a book printed over my name, and on this tide millions of us, a whole continent perhaps, are riding into heaven. It makes me truly the child of Our Lady ("Woman, behold your son!") to whom the greatest mercy was given. When she has produced in me something of her humility, there will be no end to what God will pour out upon me, not for myself alone, but for the whole world—even perhaps to make others very great while I remain in my nothingness. This would be, to me, a great joy.

In a way the experience of these last three days has been a reversal and contradiction of everything I was thinking about solitude on retreat. Or is it a fulfillment that I do not understand?

June 19, 1949. Sunday Within the Octave of Corpus Christi
The Mass each day purifies and baffles me at the same time. This beautiful mixture of happiness and lucidity and inarticulateness fills me with great health from day to day. I am forced to be simple at the altar.

For this I am eternally grateful to our Western Liturgy, which has a peculiar intensity of its own precisely because it is so straight-faced and noncommittal. There is never an exclamation. There is never an outcry.

But in the middle of this beautiful sobriety the indescribably pure light of God fills you with what can only be described as the innocence of childhood.

Day after day I am more and more aware how little I am my everyday self at the altar: this consciousness of innocence is really a sense of replacement. Another has taken over my identity, and this other is a tremendous infancy. I stand at the altar—excuse the language, these words should not be extraordinary—but I stand at the altar with my eyes all washed in the light that is eternity, as if I am one who is agelessly reborn. I am sorry for this language. There are no words I know of simple enough to describe such a thing, except that every day I am a day old, and at the altar I am the Child Who is God. Yet, when it is all over, I have to say, "The Light shines in the darkness and the darkness does not comprehend it." I have to fall back into my own poor self, which cannot receive Him altogether and even have to rejoice at being a shell. Well, I have contained some echo of His purity, and it has meant something tremendous for me and for the whole world, so that at my *Memento* of the living, which is very long, I swim in seas of joy that almost heave me off my moorings at the altar.

It is here, by the way, that I am deepest in solitude and at the same time mean something to the rest of the universe. It is really the *only* moment at which I can give anything to the rest of men. I am the only one who can give it to them, for unless I apply it to them, the special fruit of this Mass will never be theirs.

June 27, 1949. Feast of the Sacred Heart

Yesterday morning (Sunday) I went to Dom James and we were talking about solitude, and quite by surprise he gave me permission to go out of the enclosure into the woods by myself. So I took advantage of it in the afternoon, although there was a wall of black sky beyond the knobs to the west and you could hear thunder growling all the time in the distance. It was very hot and damp, but there was a good wind coming from the direction of the storm.

Anyway, I made Brother Hugh a sign to come and open the gates right after None, before the Brothers went to Catechism. (Before None, during the meridienne in the dormitory, I dreamed of going out, and in the dream I crossed the field where the platform still remains from the Centenary and walked up toward Aidan Nally's, but before I got to Nally's, in the dream, the wagon road developed sidewalks and I came not to solitude but to Jamaica High School, which we used to pass going up a hill on the way to the movies at Loew's Valencia in the days when I was generally drunk. But when I woke up and really went out, it was nothing at all like the dream.)

First I stopped under an oak tree on top of the hill behind Nally's and sat there looking out at the wide sweep of the valley and the miles of flat woods over toward the straight-line of the horizon where Rohan's Knob is.

As soon as I get away from people the Presence of God invades me. When I am not divided by being with strangers (in a sense anyone I live with will always remain a stranger), I am with Christ.

The wind ran over the bent, brown grasses and moved the shoulders of all the green trees, and I looked at the dark green mass of woods beyond the distillery on those hills down to the south of us and realized that it is when I am with people that I am lonely and when I am alone I am no longer lonely because I have God and converse with Him (without words) without distraction or interference.

I thought: "If it rains, I will have to go back to the monastery."

Gethsemani looked beautiful from the hill. It made much more sense in its surroundings. We do not realize our own setting and we ought to: it is important to know where you are put on the face of the earth. Physically, the monastery is in splendid solitude. There is nothing to complain about from the point of view of geography. One or two houses a mile and a half away and the woods and pastures and bottoms and cornfields and hills for miles and miles. And we huddle together in the midst of it and jostle one another like a subway crowd and deafen ourselves with our own typewriters and tractors.

I thought: "If we only knew how to *use* this space and this area of sky and these free woods."

Then the Spirit of God got hold of me and I started through the woods. I used to be afraid of lightning before I came to the monastery. Now there didn't seem to be any particular objection to walking right into the storm, although behind me was the big field where two boys were killed by lightning last summer or the one before.

I had a vague idea that there was a nice place beyond the field we call Hick's House, although there has been no house there for years. I went to the calf pasture beyond St. Malachy's field at the foot of the knob where the real woods begin. It is a sort of *cova* where Our Lady might appear. From there we started walking to get to the forest fire we went out to fight on All Saints Day two and a half years ago.

But this place was simply wonderful. It was quiet as the Garden of Eden. I sat on the high bank, under young pines, and looked out over this glen. Right under me was a dry creek with clean pools lying like glass between the shale pavement of the stream. The shale was as white and crumpled as sea biscuit. Down in the glen were the songs of marvelous birds. I saw the gold-orange flame of an oriole in a tree. Orioles are too shy to come near the monastery. There was a cardinal whistling somewhere, but the best song was that of two birds that sounded as wonderfully as nightingales and their song echoed through the wood. I could not tell what they were. I had never heard such birds before. The echo made the place sound more remote and self-contained, more perfectly enclosed, and more like Eden.

I thought, "Nobody ever comes here!" The marvelous quiet! The sweet scent of the woods—the clean stream, the peace, the inviolate solitude! And to think that no one pays any attention to it. It is there and we despise it, and we never taste anything like it with our fuss and our books and our sign language and our tractors and our broken-down choir.

One moment of that quiet washed clean the deep, dark inward mirror of my soul, and everything inside me was swamped in prayer that could not be quite pure because there was necessarily so much natural exultation. There was smoke in it, but I had to accept that; there wasn't much I could do about it because, anyway, I am full of grime.

To say I was happy is to say how far short the prayer was of perfection, but I was consciously and definitely and swimmingly happy, and I wonder how I ever stayed on the ground at all. The black clouds, meanwhile, piled up over the glen, and I went to where there was a shed down at the entrance to the wilderness, a shed for the calves to shelter in in cold weather in the fall.

Yet it did not rain.

I looked up at the pines and at the black smoke boiling in the sky, and nothing could make the glen less wonderful, less peaceful, less a house of joy.

When I finally decided it would soon be time for Vespers, I started back for the monastery the long-way round, keeping a screen of woods between me and the house so that I would not hit the road anywhere near where I might be seen from the back of the house where the monks were. I got in just after the first bell of Vespers, and only when we were in choir for first Vespers of the Feast of the Sacred Heart did it begin to rain. Even then it did not rain much. On my way home I turned to the storm and saw it was marching northeastward following the line of the knobs, over on the other side of them, following the line of the Green River turnpike that is far over there beyond our property in the woods going from New Haven to Bardstown.

I don't know what light this all throws on my vocation. I do not understand. Last night in my imperfection I came out of meditation with a wild scheme of starting a sort of Carmelite Desert out there. I know I'd never be allowed a one-man hermitage, but perhaps one might start a little house for special retreats where Priors and Guestmasters and what not could escape for a little recollection, where one could go for a month at a time or even more and get in some real and solid contemplation.

I can imagine no project less likely to meet with the favor of our General Chapter. Such a notion has almost nothing to do with our Order. For us a retreat means only one thing: a more complete immersion in the community.

That is where the graces are for a Cistercian: in choir with the rest, at the common work, in Chapter, reading with others.

And what about me? I wonder more and more about the whole business.

Most of the time my mind is in a jam. I make one movement to think about it and everything clogs and I remain helpless and thoughtless and open my hands and wait with my tongue-tied existence hanging on the inscrutable will of God.

One thing I must say: both in the woods and especially on my way back, crossing an open hillock, all that I had tasted in solitude seemed to have a luminously intelligible connection with the Mass. It seemed to be a function or an expression of that morning's offertory and of the next day's—the Feast's. It seemed to be, in my own very personal instance, the very heart of the Feast of Christ's Heart, its clear manifestation to me. It seemed to clarify and express in an ineffable way my identification with Christ in the Mass. My prayer in the wood was eminently the prayer of a priest, so that I wonder if my eyes have been momentarily opened and if what I have seen is really more than a poetic intuition—really something that could put in a claim to deeper and more directive significance. Could I end up as something of a hermit-priest, of a priest in the woods or the deserts or the hills, devoted to a Mass of pure adoration that would put all nature on my paten in the morning and praise God more explicitly with the birds?

Maybe that too is a dream and a sin.

July 10, 1949

Here I sit surrounded by bees and I write in this book. The bees are happy and therefore they are silent. They are working in the delicate flowers of the weeds among which I sit. I am on the east side of the house where I am not as cool as I thought I was going to be, and I sit on top of the bank that looks down over the beehives and the pond where the ducks used to be with Rohan's Knob in the distance. That big wobbly stepladder I nearly fell off, cleaning the church once, is abandoned out there at one of the cherry trees. The branches of a plum tree before me, right by the road, sag with plums.

In the Chapter Room they are finishing *Seeds of Contemplation,* reading a couple of pages each evening before Compline. It began when I was on retreat for Ordination. I do not know what the general feeling about it has been in the house—as far as I know, it is not unfavorable. Father Anthony told me, "Those who think they are intellectuals like it." Once or twice I felt as if everyone were a bit exasperated at passages that were at the same time excessively negative and subtle and obscure.

I am glad the book has been written and read. Surely I have said enough about the business of darkness and about the "experimental contact with God in obscurity" to be able to shut up about it and go on to something else for a change. Otherwise it will just get to be mechanical—grinding out the same old song over and over again. If it had not been read aloud at me, I might have forgotten how often I said all those things and gone on saying them again as if they were discoveries. For I am aware that this often happens in our life. Keeping a journal has taught me that there is not so much new in the interior life as one sometimes thinks. When you reread your journal you find out that your newest discovery is something you already found out five years ago. Still, it is true that one penetrates deeper and deeper into the same ideas and the same experiences.

As usual, after one of my own books has been read at me, I am left with the wish that I were simpler.

July 20, 1949

The community has never been so big as now. I do not know the official figure, but it must be around 185. Three postulants arrived one day last week and five more on Monday—all these for the choir. One of them stands in the lower stalls in front of me in a very distracting shirt, printed all over with huntsmen and foxhounds in green and brown. What disturbs me especially is that one of the huntsmen on a very fat horse is riding directly though the middle of the pack of hounds at right angles to the apparent direction of the chase. And I say to him, "Where do you think *you're* going?" when my mind ought to be on the psalms.

August 8, 1949

Merely to set down some of the communicable meanings that can be found in a passage of Scripture is not to exhaust the true meaning or value of that passage. Every word that comes from the mouth of God is nourishment that feeds the soul with eternal life. "Man does not live by bread alone but in every word that proceeds from the mouth of God." Whether Scripture tells of David hiding from Saul in the mountains and Saul's men surrounding his hiding place like a crown, or whether it tells about Jesus raising up the son of the widow of Nain or of the prescriptions for the evening sacrifice of incense, or sings the hymn of Deborah or tells us that Eli, the priest of Shilo, thought Hannah was drunk when she prayed to have a son, whether it tells us in the *Canticle* that the Spouse has gone down to see if the vineyards are in flower or shows us the new Jerusalem coming down from God adorned as a bride or rebukes the incestuous Corinthians or leads Paul to the river in Macedonia where the women gather and the Holy Spirit opened the heart of Lydia, the seller of dye, to hear the Gospel—everywhere there are doors and windows opened into the same eternity—and the most powerful communication of Scripture is the "implanted word," the secret and inexpressible seed of contemplation planted in the depths of our soul and awakening it with an immediate and inexpressible contact with the Living Word, that we may adore Him in Spirit and in Truth. By the reading of Scripture I am so renewed that all nature seems renewed round me and with me. The sky seems to be more pure, a cooler blue, the trees a deeper green, light is sharper on the outlines of the forest and the hills, and the whole world is charged with the glory of God and I feel fire and music in the earth under my feet.

The blessings of my Cistercian vocation are poured out on me in Scripture and I live again in the lineage of Bernard, and I see that, if I had been deeper in Scripture, all temptations to run to some other Order would have lost their meaning, for contemplation is found in faith, not in geography: you dig for it in Scripture but cannot find it by crossing the sea.

August 26, 1949

My pious Abbé Fillion suggests that, when we are stumped and cannot find out the meaning of a passage of Scripture, we ought to pray to the "sacred author," that is, to whomever it was that served as God's instrument in writing the work. The suggestion appeals to me, for I have a great though confused affection for the writers of the Bible. I feel closer to them than to almost any other writers I know of. Isaias, Job, Moses, David, Matthew, Mark, Luke, and John are all part of my life. They are always about me. They look over my shoulder, earnest men, belonging to the facade of a medieval cathedral. I feel that they are very concerned about me and that they want me to understand what God told them to write down, that they have always surrounded me with solicitous prayers, that they love and protect me.

They are more a part of my world than most of the people actually living in the world. I "see" them sometimes more really than I see the monks I live with. I know well the burnt faces of the Prophets and the Evangelists transformed by the white-hot dangerous presence of inspiration, for they looked at God as into a furnace and the Seraphim flew down and purified their lips with fire. I read their books with joy and with "holy fear," and their words become a part of me. They are solemn and dreadful and holy men humbled by the revelation they wrote down. They are my Fathers. They are the "burnt men" in the last line of *The Seven Storey Mountain*. I am more and more possessed by their vision of God's Kingdom, and I wonder at the futility of seeking anything else on earth but the truth revealed in them and in tradition—the Church's treasure to which she holds the keys.

I also have great reverence and love for the Patriarchs of the Old Testament—Abraham, Isaac, Jacob, and for the Prophets—Samuel, Elias, Eliseus. When I walk in the cemetery in the cool evening when the sun is going down—there is almost no sunlight left now in the interval after supper—I think of Isaac, meditating in the fields at evening, and of Rebecca coming to marry him from a far country, riding on a slick camel bigger than a ship.

September 1, 1949

This morning, under a cobalt blue sky, summer having abruptly ended, I am beginning the book of Job. It is not warm enough to sit for long in the shade of the cedars. The woods are crisply outlined in the sun, and the clamor of distant crows is sharp in the air that no longer sizzles with locusts.

Job moves me deeply. This year more than ever it has a special poignancy.

I now know that all my own poems about the world's suffering have been inadequate: they have not solved anything, they have only camouflaged the problem. It seems to me that the urge to write a real poem about suffering and sin is only another temptation because, after all, I do not really understand.

Sometimes I feel that I would like to stop writing precisely as a gesture of defiance. In any case, I hope to stop publishing for a time, for I believe it has now become impossible for me to stop writing altogether. Perhaps I shall continue writing on my deathbed and shall even take some asbestos paper with me in order to go on writing in purgatory. Except that I hope Our Lady will arrange some miraculous victory over my sins that will make purgatory unnecessary.

And yet it seems to me that writing, far from being an obstacle to spiritual perfection in my own life, has become one of the conditions on which my perfection will depend. If I am to be a saint—and there is nothing else that I can think of desiring to be—it seems that I must get there by writing books in a Trappist monastery. If I am to be a saint, I have not only to be a monk, which is what all monks must do to become saints, but I must also put down on paper what I have become. It may sound simple, but it is not an easy vocation.

To be as good a monk as I can and to remain myself and to write about it. To put myself down on paper, in such a situation, with the most complete simplicity and integrity, masking nothing, confusing no issue: this is very hard because I am all mixed up with illusions and attachments. These, too, will have to be put down. But without exaggeration, repetition, useless emphasis. No need for breast beating and lamentation before the eyes of anyone but You, O God, who see the depths of my fatuity. To be frank without being boring. It is a kind of crucifixion. Not a very dramatic or painful one. But it requires so much honesty that it is beyond my nature. It must come somehow from the Holy Ghost.

One of the results of all this could well be a complete and holy transparency: living, praying, and writing in the light of the Holy Spirit, losing myself entirely by becoming public property just as Jesus is public property in the Mass. Perhaps this is an important aspect of my priesthood—my living of my Mass: to become as plain as a Host in the hands of everybody. Perhaps it is this, after all, that is to be my way of solitude. One of the strangest ways so far devised, but it is the way of the Word of God.

Yet, after all, this only teaches me that nothing vital about myself can ever be public property!

November 16, 1949

Today on the eleventh anniversary of my Baptism, I began teaching theology, an introductory conference lasting an hour and a half, as a start for both my classes—Scripture and Mystical Theology. On Monday I began a series of orientation classes for the novices.

November 24, 1949. Feast of St. John of the Cross

The other day I read how Ezekiel saw the glory of God—those whales, those wings, those fires flashing, and those living creatures running to and fro—going back to Jerusalem from Babylon.

It was raining and there was a wind. I went out to the wagon shed. You could still see the hills in the distance, not too much rain for that—many black clouds, low and torn, like smoke from a disaster flying angrily over the wide open ruin of the old horse barn where I now love to walk alone. On sunny days it does not have this Castle of Otranto look about it. Today I was full of a melody that might have been related to something in Stravinsky's *Firebird,* which I have nevertheless forgotten. This was mostly my own and I sang it to God along with the angels. Then the melody went away and I sat on a stone and got into a deeper prayer than at any other time this day.

December 22, 1949

The Feast of St. Thomas yesterday was, I think, an important day. It was warm and overclouded and windy but tranquil. I had a kind of sense that the day was building up to some kind of deep decision. A wordless decision, a giving of the depths and substance of myself. There is a conversion of the deep will to God that cannot be effected in words— barely in a gesture or ceremony. There is a conversion of the deep will and a gift of my substance that is too mysterious for liturgy and too private. It is something to be done in a lucid secrecy that implies first of all the denial of communication to others except perhaps as a neutral thing.

I shall remember the time and place of this liberty and this neutrality, which cannot be written down. These clouds low on the horizon, the outcrops of hard yellow rock in the road, the open gate, the perspective of fence posts leading up the rise to the sky, and the big cedars tumbled and tousled by the wind. Standing on rock. Present. The reality of the present and of solitude divorced from past and future. To be collected and gathered up in clarity and silence and to belong to God and to be nobody's business. I wish I could recover the liberty of that interior decision, which was very simple and which seems to me to have been a kind of blank check and a promise.

To belong to God I have to belong to myself. I have to be alone—at least interiorly alone. This means the constant renewal of a decision. I cannot belong to people. None of me belongs to anybody but God. Absolute loneliness of the imagination, the memory, the will. My love for everybody is equal, neutral, and clean. No exclusiveness. Simple and free as the sky because I love everybody and am possessed by nobody, not held, not bound. In order to be not remembered or even wanted, I have to be a person that nobody knows. They can have Thomas Merton. He's dead. Father Louis, he's half dead too. For my part my name is that sky, those fence posts and those cedar trees. I shall not even reflect on who I am and I shall not say my identity is nobody's business because that implies a truculence I don't intend. It has no meaning.

Now my whole life is this—to keep unencumbered. The wind owns the fields where I walk, and I own nothing and am owned by nothing, and I shall never even be forgotten because no one will ever discover me. This is to me a source of immense confidence. My Mass this morning was transfigured by this independence.

They are pulling down the horse barn. The traxcavator was tethered to it in the rain after dinner. The barn was already half in ruins. "And house upon house shall fall." The roof was down in a hoisted heap, spreading its red old wings clumsily over the wreckage of the stables. The other half of the barn was tied to the monster and ready to fall. The stone pillars were already crooked and awry. When I was at work, I could hear the engine roar but did not hear the fall of the old building.

I seek no face. I treasure no experience, no memory. Anything I write down here is only for guidance because of my constant gravitation away from solitude. It will remind me how to go home. Not to be like the man who looked in the glass and straightaway forgot what manner of man he was. But, at the same time, not to be remembering myself lest I come to remember the person I am not.

December 27, 1949. Feast of St. John

On Christmas Day I walked in the woods and discovered many things I had never known before about the contour of our land—you can see the country from the knobs now because the trees are all bare.

Yesterday Father Cellarer lent me the Jeep. I did not ask for it, he just lent it to me out of the goodness of his heart so that I would be able to go over on the far side of the knobs. I had never driven a car before. *Once* or twice at St. Bonaventure's I took lessons. Father Roman tried to teach me to drive a little broken-down Chevy he had. Yesterday I took the Jeep and started off gaily all by myself in the woods. It had been raining heavily. All the roads were deep in mud. It took me some time to discover the front-wheel drive. I skidded into ditches and got out again, I went through creeks, I got stuck in the mud, I bumped into trees, and once, when I was on the main road, I stalled trying to get out of the front-wheel drive and ended up sideways in the middle of the road with a car coming down the hill straight at me. Thank heaven I am still alive. At the moment I didn't seem to care if I lived or died. I drove the Jeep madly into the forest in a happy, rosy fog of confusion and delight. We romped over trestles and I sang, "O Mary, I love you," went splashing through puddles a foot deep, rushed madly into the underbrush and backed out again.

Finally I got the thing back to the monastery covered with mud from stem to stern. I stood in choir at Vespers dizzy with the thought, "I have been driving a Jeep."

Father Cellarer just made me a sign that I must never, never under any circumstances, take the Jeep out again.

January 3, 1950

In the natural order, perhaps solitaries are made by severe mothers.

January 18, 1950. Feast of St. Peter's Chair in Rome

Last Saturday, the Feast of St. Hilary, I signed a long-term contract with Harcourt Brace for four books—St. Ailred, St. Bernard, *The Cloud and the Fire*, and a book on the Mass. I prayed hard over it for three days, especially at the Conventual Mass of the day itself, which was a Votive Mass of Our Lady. It is all her doing and her business.

I did not expect this legal act to have the effects it did. I put the thing in the mail, completely reconciled to my position and determined to waste no more time turning and turning around like a dog before lying down in the corner that has been prepared for me by Providence. That means the final renouncement forever of any dream of a Charterhouse or a hermitage. God will prepare for me His own hermitage for my last days. Meanwhile my work is my hermitage because it is *writing* that helps me most of all to be a solitary and a contemplative here at Gethsemani.

But the real reason why the signing of this contract left me in peace, with no more desire to rationalize my fate, was the fact that all my days are now completely ordered to God's work in prayer and teaching and writing. I have no time to be anything but a contemplative or a teacher of the contemplative life. And because I still know so little of my subject, I can no longer afford to waste time dramatizing my approach to it in mental movies or interior controversies. There is nothing left for me but to live fully and completely in the present, praying when I pray, and writing and praying when I write, and worrying about nothing but the wish and the glory of God, finding these as best I can in the sacrament of the moment.

January 27, 1950

Today, in a moment of trial, I rediscovered Jesus, or perhaps discovered Him for the first time. But then, in a monastery you are always discovering Jesus for the first time. Anyway, I came closer than ever to fully realizing how true it is that our relations with Jesus are something utterly beyond the level of imagination and emotion.

His eyes, which are the eyes of Truth, are fixed upon my heart. Where His glance falls, there is peace: for the light of His Face, which is the Truth, produces truth wherever it shines. His eyes are always on us in choir and everywhere and in all times. No grace comes to us from heaven except He looks upon our hearts.

The grace of this gaze of Christ upon my heart transfigured this day like a miracle. It seems to me that I have discovered a freedom that I never knew before in my life and with this freedom a recollection that is no impediment to moderate action. I have felt the Spirit of God upon me, and after dinner, walking along the road beyond the orchard by

myself under a cobalt blue sky (in which the moon was already visible), I
thought that, if I only turned my head a little, I would see a tremendous
host of angels in silver armor advancing behind me through the sky,
coming at last to sweep the whole world clean. I did not have to mortify
this fantasy as it did not arouse my emotions but carried me along on a
vivid ocean of peace. And the whole world and the whole sky were filled
with a wonderful music, as it has often been for me in these days. Sitting
alone in the attic of the garden house and looking at the stream shining
under the bare willows and at the distant hills, I think I have never been
so near to Adam's, my father's, Eden. Our Eden is the Heart of Christ.

January 31, 1950

Now I am thirty-five years old. Thirty-five is a nice number. It is the
middle of an average life. If I live the other thirty-five years, I hope they
will be as happy as this year—1950—has so far been.

February 10, 1950. St. Scholastica

I went to the garden house attic, as usual, after dinner. Climbed up the
ladder, observing all the hoes and shovels lying on the floor. I made my
way through the litter of old stovepipes and broken strawberry boxes to
the chair by the window. On the chair is a sack stained with either paint,
creosote, or the blood of something slaughtered. I opened the small
window (a pane fell out one day when I let it slam. I can still see the
fragments of glass on the red roof of the shed below).

Today it was wonderful. Clouds, sky overcast, but tall streamers of
sunlight coming down in a fan over the bare hills.

Suddenly I became aware of great excitement. The pasture was full of
birds—starlings. There was an eagle flying over the woods. The crows
were all frightened and were soaring very high, keeping out of the way.
Even more distant still were the buzzards, flying and circling, obscuring
everything from a distance. The starlings filled every hill tree and shone
in the light and sang. The eagle attacked a tree full of starlings, but before
he was near them, the whole cloud of them left the tree and avoided him
and he came nowhere near them. Then he went away and they all alighted
on the ground. They were there moving about and singing for about five
minutes. Then, like lightning, it happened. I saw a scare go into the cloud

of birds, and they opened their wings and began to rise off the ground, and in that split second, from behind the house and from over my roof, a hawk came down like a bullet and shot straight into the middle of the starlings just as they were getting off the ground. They rose into the air and there was a slight scuffle on the ground as the hawk got his talons into the one bird he had nailed.

It was a terrible and yet beautiful thing, that lightning flight, straight as an arrow, that killed the slowest starling.

Then every tree, every field, was cleared. I do not know where all the starlings went. Florida, maybe. The crows were still in sight but over their wood. Their guttural cursing had nothing more to do with this affair. The vultures, lovers of dead things, circled over the bottoms where perhaps there was something dead. The hawk, all alone in the pasture, possessed his prey. He did not fly away with it like a thief. He stayed in the field like a king with the killed bird, and nothing else came near him. He took his time.

I tried to pray afterward. But the hawk was eating the bird. And I thought of that flight, coming down like a bullet from the sky behind me and over my roof, the sure aim with which he hit this one bird as though he had picked it out a mile away. For a moment I envied the lords of the Middle Ages, who had their falcons, and I thought of the Arabs with their fast horses, hawking on the desert's edge, and I also understood the terrible fact that some men love war. In the end I think that hawk is to be studied by saints and contemplatives because he knows his business. I wish I knew my business as well as he does his.

I wonder if my admiration for you gives me an affinity for you, artist! I wonder if there will ever be something connatural between us, between your flight and my heart, stirred in hiding to serve Christ as you, soldier, serve your nature. And God's love a thousand times more terrible! I am going back to the attic and the shovels and the broken window and the trains in the valley and the prayer of Jesus.

March 3, 1951

March is St. Benedict's month. Clearing thorn trees from the rocky shoulder over the middle bottom where the new road is being made, I got to be good friends with his relic yesterday. How weary I am of being a writer. How necessary it is for monks to work in the fields, in the rain, in the sun, in the mud, in the clay, in the wind: these are our spiritual directors and our novice masters. They form our contemplation. They instill virtue into us. They make us as stable as the land we live in. You do not get that out of a typewriter.

The sanity of St. Benedict has something to do with the mystery of a monk becoming an American citizen. Yesterday I looked closely for the first time in ten years at the manuscript of the *Journal of My Escape from the Nazis,* which I wrote ten years ago at St. Bonaventure's at the beginning of the war.

There is some fair writing in the book. But it reflected great moral disintegration in my own life: more than I ever suspected! I revealed more of myself than I meant to in those pages that are by no means as cryptic as I thought, but I did not think of hiding anything. In being obscure I was only trying to discover something of myself. I could not see what was so plain.

It was a very inhibited book in spite of all the uninhibited explosives of an invented language, which I still like. The action can never progress forward. In fact, there is no action. A situation presents itself, and the stream of the book—which after all has a stream—stops and forms a lake. It is sometimes quite a bright lake. But I can do nothing with it.

Sitting in the garden house, I viewed the pale glare of sunlight on the roof of the distillery a mile away against the dark hills, and I thought about the whole business. Although my thinking was a little incoherent, circling the subject with a laziness appropriate to the hour—1:15 P.M.— I nevertheless came out of it more healthy than I went in and descended the ladders more in one piece than I had climbed them.

One of the problems of the book was my personal relation to the world and to the war. When I wrote it I thought I had a very supernatural solution. After nine years in a monastery I see that this was no solution at all. The false solution was this: the whole world, of which war is a characteristic expression, is evil. It has therefore to be first ridiculed, then spat upon, and at last formally cursed.

Actually, I have come to the monastery to find my place in the world, and if I fail to find this place, I will be wasting my time in the monastery.

It would be a grave sin for me to be on my knees in this monastery, flagellated, penanced, though not now as thin as I ought to be, and spend my time cursing the world without distinguishing what is good in it from what is bad.

Wars are evil, but the people involved in them are good, and I can do nothing whatever for my own salvation or for the glory of God if I merely withdraw from the mess people are in and make an exhibition of myself and write a book saying, "Look, I'm different!" To do this is to die, because any man who pretends to be either an angel or a statue must die the death. The immobility of that *Journal of My Escape* was a confession of my own nonentity, and this was the result of a psychological withdrawal.

On the other hand, if you let yourself be washed away with all the dirt on the surface of the stream, you pile up somewhere in another kind of immobility with the rest of the jetsam in the universe.

Coming to the monastery has been, for me, exactly the right kind of withdrawal. It has given me perspective. It has taught me how to live. Now I owe everyone else in the world a share in that life. My first duty is to start, for the first time, to live as a member of a human race, which is no more (and no less) ridiculous than I am myself. And my first human act is the recognition of how much I owe everybody else. There is a world that Christ would not pray for, but the world was made by God and is good, and, unless that world is our mother, we cannot be saints because we cannot be saints unless we are first of all human.

Thus God has brought me to Kentucky where the people are, for the most part, singularly without inhibitions. This is the precise place He has chosen for my sanctification. Here I must revise all my absurd plans and take myself as I am, Gethsemani as it is, and America as it is—atomic bomb and all. It is utterly peculiar but nonetheless true that, after all, one's nationality should come to have a meaning in the light of eternity. I have lived for thirty-six years without one. Nine years ago I was proud of the fact. I thought that, to be a citizen of heaven, all you had to do was throw away your earthly passport. But now I have discovered a mystery: that all the ladies in the Office of the Deputy Clerk of the Louisville District are perhaps in some accidental way empowered to see that I am definitely admitted to the Kingdom of Heaven forever.

For now I am beginning to believe that perhaps the only, or at least the quickest, way I shall become a saint is by virtue of the desires of many good people in America that I should become one. Last night I dreamt I was telling several other monks, "I shall be a saint," and they did not seem to question me. Furthermore, I believed it myself. If I do—I shall—it will be because of the prayers of other people who, though they are better than I am, still want me to pray for them.

March 4, 1951. Day of Recollection

Shall I reread the bits in St. John of the Cross's *The Ascent of Mount Carmel* about the memory? They seem to do me so much good—always. Year after year, returning to them. In what sense do they make a difference in my life?

This *Journal.* I mean this one I am writing right now. Apparently I have not yet written enough of it to become completely solitary and to be able to do without it. It is useless to drop the thing and say I am solitary just because I am not writing a *Journal,* when in fact the writing could help me find my way to where I am supposed to be traveling.

So I read about forgetting and write down all I remember. Somehow there is no contradiction here. It is simply a somewhat peculiar way of becoming a saint. I by no means insist that it is sanctity. All I say is that I must do what the situation seems to demand, and sanctity will appear when out of all this Christ in His own good time appears and manifests His glory.

June 13, 1951

It is sometime in June. At a rough guess, I think it is June 13, which may or may not be the feast of Saint Anthony of Padua. In any case, every day is the same for me because I have become very different from what I used to be. The man who made this Journal is dead, just as the man who finished *The Seven Storey Mountain,* when this Journal began, was also dead, and what is more, the man who was the central figure in *The Seven Storey Mountain* was dead over and over. Now that all these men are dead, it is sufficient for me to say so on paper, and I think I will have ended up by forgetting them. Writing down what *The Seven Storey Mountain* was about was sufficient to get it off my mind for good. Last week I corrected the proofs of the French translation of the book, and it seemed completely alien. I might as well have been a proofreader working for a publisher, going over the galleys of somebody else's book. Consequently, *The Seven Storey Mountain* is the work of a man I never even heard of. This Journal is getting to be the production of somebody to whom I have never had the dishonor of an introduction.

"Behold I make all things new!"

On Trinity Sunday I was named Master of the Scholastics. Dom Louis, Gethsemani's Father Immediate, had asked for the formation of a regular scholasticate. Some of our large monasteries have them. They are absolutely necessary when the young professed are too numerous to remain for a long time in the novitiate. They need a Spiritual Director as well as some sort of family life of their own. The problems of the young professed turn out to be perhaps the most crucial thing in their Cistercian formation.

The fact that I have suddenly ended up in this position clarifies all the foolish pages of the journal I have written about my own problems as a scholastic. For now I know that the reason why I had to resist the temptation to become a Carthusian was in order to learn how to help all the other ones who would be in one way or another tempted to leave the monastery. When I read such a lot of Duns Scotus, it was in order to learn, after all, the importance of keeping to the straight line of Thomism and of keeping scholastics out of difficulties that are too great for a Cistercian to solve. Our life is not designed for theological controversy, and Scotus is more than the Cistercian head can bear—at least until somebody distills his essence and gives it to us secondhand.

Finally, about the vault and the woods: I am appalled by the number of useless books that have piled up in the vault. As long as I was a writer I thought of them as possibly coming in handy for the compilation of a book. But now that I am a spiritual director I have to live beyond my own borders in the souls of those whom God has placed in my charge. It is immediately evident that very few of these books will ever help me to help them. On the contrary, most of the stuff on those shelves would only encourage me to disturb them. I am embarrassed at having walked with eyes wide open into such an obvious sin.

As for the woods, on Whitmonday (just before we cut down the last grove of cedars where one could still hide inside the enclosure) I explored a wooded bluff outside the east wall, which is sufficiently fenced in to be considered an extension of the enclosure. With the full approval of Dom Louis, Reverend Father has given me this wood as a refuge for my scholastics. It is a pleasant place, and one can more quickly find solitude there than in the forest, which is further away. So I find that now I spend more time praying and have less time for self-admiration. My prayer is more confusing and more obscure. I disappear and know nothing (except a confused awareness that I and the woods exist but that I have a center, which is outside the sphere of this existence). Two hours are the same as five minutes. The bell rings, and I am too often late for Vespers. Meanwhile, in the vault, I bless my children and talk to them one by one, and it is much more interesting than writing a book, besides being less fatiguing. Furthermore, since I am obliged to live the Rule in order to talk about it with any degree of authority, I go out to work as often as I can and now have blisters again the way I had them in the novitiate. I come home full of dirt and sweat and bathe and change and sit down under a tree behind the church where you can really pray.

Thus I sit on the threshold of a new existence. The one who is going to be most fully formed by the new scholasticate is the Master of the Scholastics. It is as if I were beginning all over again to be a Cistercian: but this time I am doing it without asking myself the abstract questions, which are the luxury and torment of one's monastic adolescence. For now I am a grown-up monk and have no time for anything but the essentials. The only essential is not an idea or an ideal: it is God Himself, Who cannot be found by weighing the present against the future or the past but only by sinking into the heart of the present as it is.

November 29, 1951

John the Baptist sends Andrew to Jesus, and Andrew gets Peter, and Peter tells Philip, and Philip speaks to Nathaniel, who does not think that anything good can come out of Nazareth. But Jesus says that Nathaniel's suspicions are without guile. He speaks to Nathaniel about the fig tree. All at once the Kingdom of God is formed in the world—"the kingdom of God is among you." The angels are ascending and descending upon the Church, the Mystical Body of the Son of Man. Before Advent gets a chance to start (at least this year's Advent), Christ appears among us—*Parousia*. He cometh. He is already formed before our eyes in His saints, even before the Church can begin to start from the beginning and draw Him forth from the types and mysteries of the Old Testament. Before the cycle has begun, it has already ended. The Vigil of St. Andrew is a prelude to Pentecost, it contains Pentecost. The Body that is to be vivified with the Breath of God is already being formed from the slime of the earth.

Elias was a man like unto us. Andrew, Peter, James, and John were men like unto us. Like them, we bring our infirmities to Christ in order that His strength may be glorified in the transformation of our weakness. Day after day the outward man crumbles and breaks down, and the inward man, the Man of Heaven, is born and grows in wisdom and knowledge before the eyes of men—who cannot recognize Him. Neither can we recognize ourselves in the image of Him which is formed in us because we do not yet have the eyes with which to see Him. Yet we suspect His presence in the mystery that is not revealed to the wise and prudent. We feel His eyes upon us as we sit under the fig tree, and our souls momentarily spring to life at the touch of His hidden finger. This flash of fire is our solitude, yet it binds us to our brethren. It is the fire that has quickened the Mystical Body since Pentecost so that every Christian is, at the same time, a hermit and the whole Church, and we are all members one of another. It remains for us to recognize the mystery that your heart is my hermitage and that the only way I can enter into the desert is by bearing your burden and leaving you my own.

It is now six months since I have been Master of the Scholastics and have looked into their hearts and taken up their burdens upon me. I have not always seen clearly, and I have not carried their burdens too well, and I have stumbled around a lot. On many days we have gone around in circles and fallen into ditches because the blind was leading the blind.

I do not know if they have discovered anything new or if they are able to love God more or if I have helped them in any way to find themselves, which is to say: to lose themselves. But I know what I have discovered: the kind of work I once feared because I thought it would interfere with "solitude" is, in fact, the only true path to solitude. One must be in some sense a hermit before the care of souls can serve to lead one further into the desert. But once God has called you to solitude, everything you touch leads you further into solitude. Everything that affects you builds you into a hermit as long as you do not insist on doing the work yourself and building your own kind of hermitage.

What is my new desert? The name of it is *compassion*. There is no wilderness so terrible, so beautiful, so arid, and so fruitful as the wilderness of compassion. It is the only desert that will truly flourish like the lily. It shall become a pool. It shall bud forth and blossom and rejoice with joy. It is in the desert of compassion that the thirsty land turns into springs of water, that the poor possess all things. There are no bounds to contain the inhabitants of this solitude in which I live alone, as isolated as the Host on the altar, the food of all men, belonging to all and belonging to none, for God is with me, and He sits in the ruins of my heart, preaching the Gospel to the poor.

Do you suppose I have a spiritual life? I have none, I am indigence, I am silence, I am poverty, I am solitude, for I have renounced spirituality to find God and He it is Who preaches loud in the depths of my indigence, saying: "I will pour out my spirit upon thy children and they shall spring up among the herbs as willows beside the running waters" (Isaias 44:3–4). "The children of thy barrenness shall say in thy ears: The place is too strait for me, make me room to dwell in" (Isaias 49:20). I die of love for you, Compassion; I take you for my Lady. As Francis married poverty, I marry you, the Queen of hermits and the Mother of the poor.

February 26, 1952. Shrove Tuesday
The blue elm tree near at hand and the light on the hills in the distance and the red bare clay where I am supposed to plant some shade trees: these are before me as I sit in the sun for a free half hour between direction and work. Tomorrow is Ash Wednesday, and today, as I sit in the sun, big blue and purple fish swim past me in the darkness of my empty mind, this sea that opens within me as soon as I close my eyes.

Delightful darkness, delightful sun, shining on a world that, for all I care, has already ended.

It does not occur to me to wonder whether we will ever transplant the young maples from the wood yonder to this bare leveled patch—the place where the old horse barn once stood. It does not occur to me to wonder how everything here came to be transformed. I sit on a cedar log half chewed by some novice's blunt axe and do not reflect on the plans I have made for this place of prayer because they do not matter. They will happen when they happen.

The hills are as pure as jade in the distance. God is in His transparent world, but He is too sacred to be mentioned, too holy to be observed. I sit in silence. The big deep fish are purple in my sea.

Different levels of depth.

First, there is the slightly troubled surface of the sea. Here there is action. I make plans. They toss in the wake of other men's traffic: passing liners. I speak to the scholastics. I make resolutions to speak less wildly, to say fewer of the things that surprise myself and them. Where do they spring from?

Second, there is the darkness that comes when I close my eyes. Here is where the big blue, purple, green, and gray fish swim by. Most beautiful and peaceful darkness: is it the cave of my own inner being? In this water-cavern I easily live, whenever I wish. Only dull rumors of the world reach me. Sometimes a drowned barrel floats into the room. Big gray-green fish with silver under their purple scales. Are these the things the blind men see all day? I close my eyes to the sun and live on the second level, a natural prayer, peace. When I am tired, it is almost slumber. There is no sound. Soon even the fish are gone. Night, night. Nothing is happening. If you make a theory about it, you end up in quietism. All I say about it is that it is comfortable. It is a rest. I half-open my eyes to the sun, praising the Lord of glory. Lo, thus I have returned from the blank abyss, reentering the shale cities of Genesis. Ferns and fish return. Lovely dark green things. In the depth of the waters, peace, peace, peace. Such is the second level of waters under the sun. We pray therein, slightly wavering among the fish.

Words, as I think, do not spring from this second level. They are only meant to drown there.

The question of socialization does not concern these waters. They are nobody's property. Animality. Game preserve. Paradise. No questions whatever perturb their holy botany. Neutral territory. No man's sea.

I think God intended me to write about this second level, however, rather than the first. I abandon all problems to their own unsatisfactory solutions, including the problem of "monastic spirituality." I will not even answer, as I answer the scholastics, that the Desert Fathers talked not about monastic spirituality but about purity of heart and obedience and solitude and about God. The wiser of them talked very little about anything. The divine life, which is the life of the soul, as the soul is the life of the body: this is a pure and concrete thing and not to be measured by your ascetic theory. God in you is not to be weighed in the scales of my doctrine. Indeed, He is not to be weighed at all.

Third level. Here there is positive life swimming in the rich darkness, which is no longer thick like water but pure like air. Starlight, and you do not know where it is coming from. Moonlight is in this prayer, stillness, waiting for the Redeemer. Walls watching horizons in the middle of the night. Everything is charged with intelligence, though all is night. There is no speculation here. There is vigilance: life itself has turned to purity in its own refined depths. Everything is spirit. Here God is adored. His coming is recognized. He is received as soon as He is expected, and because He is expected, He is received, but He has passed by sooner than He arrived. He has gone before He came. He has returned forever. He never yet passed by, and already He had disappeared for all eternity. He is and He is not. Everything and Nothing. Not light, not dark, not high, not low, not this side, not that side. Forever and forever. In the wind of His passing the angels cry, "Thy Holy One is gone." Therefore I lie dead in the air of their wings. Life and night, day and darkness, between life and death. This is the holy cellar of my mortal existence, which opens into the sky.

It is a strange awakening to find the sky inside you and beneath you and above you and all around you so that your spirit is one with the sky and all is positive night.

Here is where love burns with an innocent flame, the clean desire for death: death without sweetness, without sickness, without commentary, without reference, and without shame. Clean death by the sword of the spirit in which is intelligence. Everything in order. Emergence and deliverance. I think this also is the meaning of Ash Wednesday: mourn, man, because you are not yet dust. Receive your ashes and rejoice.

Receive, O monk, the holy truth concerning this thing called death. Know that there is in each man a deep will potentially committed to freedom or to captivity, ready to consent to life, born consenting to death, turned inside out, swallowed by its own self, prisoner of itself like Jonas in the whale.

This is the truth of death, printed in the heart of every man, which leads him to look for the sign of Jonas the prophet. But many have gone into hell crying out that they had expected the resurrection of the dead. Others, in turn, were baptized and delivered: but their powers remained asleep in the dark and in the bosom of the depths.

Many of the men baptized in Christ have risen from the depths without troubling to find out the difference between Jonas and the whale.

It is the whale we cherish. Jonas swims abandoned in the heart of the sea. But it is the whale that must die. Jonas is immortal. If we do not remember to distinguish between them, and if we prefer the whale and do not take Jonas out of the ocean, the inevitable will come to pass. The whale and the prophet will soon come around and meet again in their wanderings, and once again the whale will swallow the prophet. Life will be swallowed again in death, and its last state will be worse than the first.

We must get Jonas out of the whale and the whale must die at a time when Jonas is in the clear, busy with his orisons, clothed and in his right mind, free, holy, and walking on the shore. Such is the meaning of the desire for death that comes in the sane night, the peace that finds us for a moment in clarity, walking by the light of the stars, raised to God's connatural shore, dry-shod in the heavenly country, in a rare moment of intelligence.

July 4, 1952. The Fire Watch

"Watchman, what of the night!"

The night, O my Lord, is a time of freedom. You have seen the morning and the night, and the night was better. In the night all things began, and in the night the end of all things has come before me.

Baptized in the rivers of night, Gethsemani has recovered her innocence. Darkness brings a semblance of order before all things disappear. With the clock slung over my shoulder, in the silence of the Fourth of July, it is my time to be the night watchman, in the house that will one day perish.

Here is the way it is when I go on the fire watch:

Before eight o'clock the monks are packed in the belly of the great heat, singing to the Mother of God like exiles sailing to their slavery, hoping for glory. The night angelus unlocks the church and sets them free. The holy monster that is The Community divides itself into segments and disperses through the airless cloisters where yellow lamps do not attract the bugs.

The watchman's clock together with the watchman's sneakers are kept in a box, together with a flashlight and the keys to various places, at the foot of the infirmary stairs.

Rumors behind me and above me and around me signal the fathers going severally to bed in different dormitories. Where there is cold water some stay to drink from celluloid cups. Thus we fight the heat. I take the heavy clock and sling it on its strap over my shoulder. I walk to the nearest window on my silent feet. I recite the second nocturn of Saturday, sitting outside the window in the dark garden, and the house begins to be silent.

One late Father, with a change of dry clothes slung over his shoulder, stops to look out the window and pretends to be frightened when he sees me sitting around the corner in the dark, holding the breviary in the yellow light of the window, saying the Psalms of Saturday.

It is ten or fifteen minutes before there are no more feet echoing along the cloisters, shuffling up the stairs. (When you go late to the dormitories, you have to take off your shoes and make your way to bed in socks, as if the others were already asleep in such weather!)

At eight-fifteen I sit in darkness. I sit in human silence. Then I begin to hear the eloquent night, the night of wet trees, with moonlight sliding over the shoulder of the church in a haze of dampness and subsiding heat. The world of this night resounds from heaven to hell with animal eloquence, with the savage innocence of a million unknown creatures. While the earth eases and cools off like a huge wet living thing, the enormous vitality of their music pounds and rings and throbs and echoes until it gets into everything and swamps the whole world in its neutral madness, which never becomes an orgy because all things are innocent, all things are pure. Nor would I have mentioned the possibility of evil except that I remember how the heat and the wild music of living things drive people crazy, when they are not in monasteries, and make them do things that the world has forgotten how to lament.

That is why some people act as if the night and the forest and the heat and the animals had in them something of contagion, whereas the heat is holy and the animals are the children of God and the night was never made to hide sin but only to open infinite distances to charity and send our souls to play among the stars.

Eight-thirty. I begin my round in the cellar of the south wing. The place is full of naked wires, stinks of the hides of slaughtered calves. My feet are walking on a floor of earth, down a long catacomb, at the end of which there is a brand-new locked door into the guest wing, which was only finished the other day. So I punch the clock for the first time in the catacomb. I turn my back on the new wing. The fire watch is on.

Around one corner is a hole in the wall with a vat where they stew fruit. Under this vat Dom Frederic told me to burn all the letters that were in the pigeonholes of the room where he had been prior. Around another corner is an old furnace where I burned the rest of the papers from the same room. In this musty silence, which no longer smells of wine (because the winery is in another building now), the flashlight creates a little alert tennis ball upon the walls and floor. Concrete now begins under the watchman's cat feet, and moonlight reaches through the windows into a dark place with jars of prunes and applesauce on all the shelves.

Then suddenly, after the old brooding catacomb, you hit something dizzy and new: the kitchen, painted by the brother novices, each wall in a different color. Some of the monks complained of the different-colored walls, but a watchman has no opinions. There is tile under the shining vats and Scripture close to the ceiling: "Little children, love one another!"

There are blue benches in the scullery, and this one room is cool. Sometimes, when you go up the stairs making no noise, a brother comes in late from the barns through the kitchen door and runs into you by surprise in the darkness and is blinded by the flashlight and (if a novice) is probably scared to death.

For a few feet the way is most familiar. I am in the little cloister that is the monastery's main stem. It goes from the places where the monks live to the places where they pray. But now it is empty, and like everything else it is a lot nicer when there is nobody there. The steps down to the tailor shop have a different sound. They drum under my rubber soles. I run into the smell of duck and cotton mixed with the smell of bread. There is light in the bakery: someone is working late, around the corner, behind the oven. I punch the clock by the bakery door: it is the second station.

The third station is the hottest one: the furnace room. This time the stairs don't drum, they ring: they are iron. I fight my way through a jungle of wet clothes drying in the heat and go down by the flanks of the boiler to the third station, which is there up against the bricks, beneath an engraving of the Holy Face.

After that, I am in the choir novitiate. Here, too, it is hot. The place is swept and recently painted, and there are notice boards at every turn in the little crooked passageways where each blue door is named after a saint. Long lists of appointments for the novices' confessions and direction. Sentences from the liturgy. Fragments of severe and necessary information. The walls of the building have their own stuffy smell, and I am suddenly haunted by my first days in religion, the freezing tough winter when I first received the habit and always had a cold, the smell of frozen straw in the dormitory under the chapel, the deep unexpected ecstasy of Christmas—that first Christmas when you have nothing left in the world but God!

It is when you hit the novitiate that the fire watch begins in earnest. Alone, silent, wandering on your appointed rounds through the corridors of a huge, sleeping monastery, you come around the corner and find yourself face-to-face with your monastic past and with the mystery of your vocation.

The fire watch is an examination of conscience in which your task as watchman suddenly appears in its true light: a pretext devised by God to isolate you and to search your soul with lamps and questions in the heart of darkness.

God, my God, God Whom I meet in darkness, with You it is always the same thing! Always the same question that nobody knows how to answer!

I have prayed to You in the daytime with thoughts and reasons, and in the nighttime You have confronted me, scattering thought and reason. I have come to You in the morning with light and with desire, and you have descended upon me, with great gentleness, with most forbearing silence, in this inexplicable night, dispersing light, defeating all desire. I have explained to You a hundred times my motives for entering the monastery, and You have listened and said nothing and I have turned away and wept with shame.

Is it true that all my motives have meant nothing? Is it true that all my desires were an illusion?

While I am asking questions that You do not answer, You ask me a question which is so simple that I cannot answer. I do not even understand the question.

This night, and every night, it is the same question.

There is a special, living resonance in these steep hollow stairs to the novitiate chapel, where You are all alone, the windows closed tight upon You, shutting You up with the heat of the lost afternoon.

Here, when it was winter, I used to come after dinner, when I was a novice heavy with sleep and with potatoes, and kneel all the time because that was the only period in which we were allowed to do what we liked. Nothing ever happened, but that was what I liked.

Here, on Sunday mornings, a crowd of us would try to make the Way of the Cross, jostling one another among the benches. On Days of Recollection in summer we would kneel here all afternoon with the sweat running down our ribs, while candles burned all around the tabernacle and the veiled ciborium stood shyly in the doorway, peeping out at us between the curtains.

And here, now, by night, with this huge clock ticking on my right hip and the flashlight in my hand and sneakers on my feet, I feel as if everything had been unreal. It is as if the past had never existed. The things I thought were so important—because of the effort I put into them—have turned out to be of small value. And the things I never thought about, the things I was never able either to measure or to expect, were the things that mattered.

(There used to be a man who walked down the back road singing on summer mornings, right in the middle of the novices' thanksgiving after Communion, singing his own private song, every day the same. It was the sort of song you would expect to hear out in the country, in the knobs of Kentucky.)

But in this darkness I would not be able to say, for certain, what it was that mattered. That, perhaps, is part of Your unanswerable question! Only I remember the heat in the bean field the first June I was here, and I get the same sense of a mysterious, unsuspected value that struck me after Father Alberic's funeral.

After the novitiate, I come back into the little cloister. Soon I stand at the coolest station: down in the brothers' washroom, at the door of the ceramic studio. Cool winds come in from the forest through the big, wide open windows.

This is a different city, with a different set of associations. The ceramic studio is something relatively new. Behind the door (where they burnt out one kiln and bought a new one) little Frater John of God suddenly made a good crucifix, just a week ago. He is one of my scholastics. And I think of the clay Christ that came out of his heart. I think of the beauty and the simplicity and the pathos that were sleeping there, waiting to become an image. I think of this simple and mysterious child and of all my other scholastics. What is waiting to be born in all their hearts? Suffering? Deception? Heroism? Defeat? Peace? Betrayal? Sanctity? Death? Glory?

On all sides I am confronted by questions that I cannot answer because the time for answering them has not yet come. Between the silence of God and the silence of my own soul stands the silence of the souls entrusted to me. Immersed in these three silences, I realize that the questions I ask myself about them are perhaps no more than a surmise. Perhaps the most urgent and practical renunciation is the renunciation of all questions.

The most poignant thing about the fire watch is that you go through Gethsemani not only in length and height but also in depth. You hit strange caverns in the monastery's history, layers set down by the years, geological strata: you feel like an archaeologist suddenly unearthing ancient civilizations. But the terrible thing is that you yourself have lived through those ancient civilizations. The house has changed so much that ten years have as many different meanings as ten Egyptian dynasties. The meanings are hidden in the walls. They mumble in the floor under the watchman's rubber feet. The lowest layer is at once in the catacomb under the south wing and in the church tower. Every other level of history is found in between.

The church.

In spite of the stillness, the huge place seems alive. Shadows move everywhere around the small uncertain area of light that the sanctuary light casts on the Gospel side of the altar. There are faint sounds in the darkness; the empty choir stalls creak, and hidden boards mysteriously sigh.

The silence of the sacristy has its own sound. I shoot the beam of light down to Saint Malachy's altar and the relic cases. Vestments are laid out for my Mass tomorrow at Our Lady of Victories altar. Keys rattle again in the door, and the rattle echoes all over the church. When I was first on for the fire watch I thought the church was full of people praying in the dark. But no. The night is filled with unutterable murmurs, the walls with traveling noises, which seem to wake up and come back, hours after something has happened, to gibber at the places where it happened.

This nearness to You in the darkness is too simple and too close for excitement. It is commonplace for all things to live an unexpected life in the nighttime: but their life is illusory and unreal. The illusion of sound only intensifies the infinite substance of Your silence.

Here, in this place where I made my vows, where I have had my hands anointed for the Holy Sacrifice, where I have had Your priesthood seal the depth and intimate summit of my being, a word, a thought, would defile the quiet of Your inexplicable love.

Your Reality, O God, speaks to my life as to an intimate, in the midst of a crowd of fictions: I mean these walls, this roof, these arches, this (overhead) ridiculously large and unsubstantial tower. Lord, God, the whole world tonight seems to be made out of paper. The most substantial things are ready to crumble or tear apart and blow away.

How much more so this monastery, which everybody believes in and which has perhaps already ceased to exist?

O God, my God, the night has values that day has never dreamed of. All things stir by night, waking or sleeping, conscious of the nearness of their ruin. Only Man makes himself illuminations he conceives to be solid and eternal. But while we ask our questions and come to our decisions, God blows our decisions out, the roofs of our houses cave in upon us, the towers are undermined by ants, the walls crack and cave in, and the holiest buildings burn to ashes while the watchman is composing a theory of duration.

Now is the time to get up and go to the tower. Now is the time to meet You, God, where the night is wonderful, where the roof is almost without substance under my feet, where all the mysterious junk in the belfry considers the proximate coming of three new bells, where the forest opens out under the moon and the living things sing terribly that only the present is eternal and that all things having a past and a future are doomed to pass away.

This, then, is the way from the floor of the church to the platform on the tower.

First I must make a full round of the house on the second floor. Then I must go to the third-floor dormitories. After that, the tower.

Cloister. Soft feet, total darkness. The brothers have torn up the tent in the cloister garden, where the novices were sleeping two winters ago, and where some of them got pneumonia.

Just yesterday they put a new door on Father Abbot's room while he was away with Dom Gabriel, visiting the foundations.

I am in the corridor under the old guest house. In the middle of the hallway a long table is set with knives and forks and spoons and bowls for the breakfast of the postulants and family brothers. Three times a day they eat in the corridor. For two years there has been no other place to put them.

The high, light door into the old guest wing swings back, and I am on the stairs.

I had forgotten that the upper floors were empty. The silence astonishes me. The last time I was on the fire watch there was a retreat party of fifty lined up on the second floor, signing their names in the guest register in the middle of the night. They had just arrived in a bus from Notre Dame. Now the place is absolutely empty. All the notices are off the walls. The bookshelf has vanished from the hall. The population of holy statues has been diminished. All the windows are wide open. Moonlight falls on the cool linoleum floor. The doors of some of the rooms are open and I see that they are empty. I can feel the emptiness of all the rest.

I would like to stop and stand here for an hour, just to feel the difference. The house is like a sick person who has recovered. This is the Gethsemani that I entered and whose existence I had almost forgotten. It was this silence, this darkness, this emptiness, that I walked into with Brother Matthew eleven years ago this spring. This is the house that seemed to have been built to be remote from everything, to have forgotten all cities, to be absorbed in the eternal years. But this recovered innocence has nothing reassuring about it. The very silence is a reproach. The emptiness itself is my most terrible question.

If I have broken this silence and if I have been to blame for talking so much about this emptiness that it came to be filled with people, who am I to praise the silence anymore? Who am I to publicize this emptiness? Who am I to remark on the presence of so many visitors, so many retreatants, so many postulants, so many tourists? Or have the men of our age acquired a Midas touch of their own so that as soon as they succeed everything they touch becomes crowded with people?

In this age of crowds in which I have determined to be solitary, perhaps the greatest sin would be to lament the presence of people on the threshold of my solitude. Can I be so blind as to ignore that solitude itself is their greatest need? And yet, if they rush in upon the desert in thousands, how shall they be alone? What went they out into the desert to see? Whom did I myself come here to find but You, O Christ, Who have compassion on the multitudes?

Nevertheless, Your compassion singles out and separates the one on whom Your mercy falls and sets him apart from the multitudes even though You leave him in the midst of the multitudes.

With my feet on the floor I waxed when I was a postulant, I ask these useless questions. With my hand on the key by the door to the tribune, where I first heard the monks chanting the psalms, I do not wait for an answer, because I have begun to realize You never answer when I expect.

The third room of the library is called hell. It is divided up by wallboard partitions into four small sections full of condemned books. The partitions are hung with American flags and pictures of Dom Edmond Obrecht. I thread my way through this unbelievable maze to the second room of the library, where the retreatants used to sit and mop their brows and listen to sermons. I do not have to look at the corner where the books about the Carthusians once sang to me their siren song as I sail past with clock ticking and light swinging and keys on my hand to unlock the door into the first room of the library. Here the scholastics have their desks. This is the upper Scriptorium. The theology books are all around the walls. Yonder is the broken cuckoo clock, which Father Willibrod winds up each morning with a gesture of defiance, just before he flings upon the windows.

Perhaps the dormitory of the choir monks is the longest room in Kentucky. Long lines of cubicles with thin partitions a little over six feet high, shirts and robes and scapulars hang over the partitions, trying to dry in the night air. Extra cells have been jammed along the walls between the windows. In each one lies a monk on a straw mattress. One pale bulb burns in the middle of the room. The ends are shrouded in shadows. I make my way softly past cell after cell. I know which cells have snorers in them. But no one seems to be asleep in this extraordinary tenement. I walk as softly as I can down to the far west end, where Frater Caleb sleeps in the bell-ringer's corner. I find my station inside the door of the organ loft, punch the clock, and start off again on soft feet along the other side of the dormitory.

There is a door hidden between two cells. It leads into the infirmary annex, where the snoring is already in full swing. Beyond that, steep stairs to the third floor.

One more assignment before I can climb them. The infirmary, with its hot square little chapel, the room that contains the retreats I made before all the dates in my monastic life: clothing, professions, ordinations. I cannot pass it without something unutterable coming up out of the depths of my being. It is the silence that will lift me on to the tower.

Meanwhile I punch the clock at the next station, at the dentist's office, where next week I am to lose another molar.

Now the business is done. Now I shall ascend to the top of this religious city, leaving its modern history behind. These stairs climb back beyond the Civil War. I make no account of the long lay brothers' dormitory, where a blue light burns. I hasten to the corridor by the wardrobe. I look out the low windows and know that I am already higher than the trees. Down at the end is the doorway to the attic and the tower.

The padlock always makes a great noise. The door swings back on swearing hinges, and the night wind, hot and gusty, comes swirling down out of the loft with a smell of ancient rafters and old, hidden, dusty things. You have to watch the third step or your feet go through the boards. From here on the building has no substance left, but you have to mind your head and bow beneath the beams on which you can see the marks of axes with which our French Fathers hewed them out a hundred years ago.

And now the hollowness that rings under my feet measures some sixty feet to the floor of the church. I am over the transept crossing. If I climb around the corner of the dome, I can find a hole once opened by the photographers and peer down into the abyss and flash the light far down upon my stall in choir.

I climb the trembling, twisted stair into the belfry. The darkness stirs with a flurry of wings high above me in the gloomy engineering that holds the steeple together. Nearer at hand the old clock ticks in the tower. I flash the light into the mystery that keeps it going and gaze upon the ancient bells.

I have seen the fuse box. I have looked in the corners where I think there is some wiring. I am satisfied that there is no fire in this tower, which would flare like a great torch and take the whole abbey up with it in twenty minutes.

Now my whole being breathes the wind that blows through the belfry and my hand is on the door through which I see the heavens. The door swings out upon a vast sea of darkness and of prayer. Will it come like this, the moment of my death? Will You open a door upon the great forest and set my feet upon a ladder under the moon and take me out among the stars?

The roof glistens under my feet, this long metal roof facing the forest and the hills, where I stand higher than the treetops and walk upon shining air.

Mists of damp heat rise up out of the field around the sleeping abbey. The whole valley is flooded with moonlight, and I can count the southern hills beyond the water tank and almost number the trees of the forest to the north. Now the huge chorus of living beings rises up out of the world beneath my feet: life singing in the watercourses, throbbing in the creeks and the fields and the trees, choirs of millions and millions of jumping and flying and creeping things. And far above me the cool sky opens upon the frozen distance of the stars.

I lay the clock upon the belfry ledge and pray cross-legged with my back against the tower and face the same unanswered question.

Lord God of this great night: do You see the woods? Do You hear the rumor of their loneliness? Do You behold their secrecy? Do You remember their solitudes? Do You see that my soul is beginning to dissolve like wax within me?

"O my God, I cry out by day, but you do not answer; by night, but I find no rest."

Do you remember the place by the stream? Do You remember the top of the Vineyard Knob that time in autumn, when the train was in the valley? Do You remember McGinty's Hollow? Do You remember the thinly wooded hillside behind Hanekamp's place? Do You remember the time of the forest fire? Do You know what has become of the little poplars we planted in the spring? Do You observe the valley where I marked the trees?

There is no leaf that is not in Your care. There is no cry that was not heard by You before it was uttered. There is no water in the shales that was not hidden there by Your wisdom. There is no concealed spring that was not concealed by You. There is no glen for a lone house that was not planned by You for a lone house. There is no man for that acre of woods that was not made by You for that acre of woods.

There is greater comfort in the substance of silence than in the answer to a question. Eternity is in the present. Eternity is in the palm of the hand. Eternity is a seed of fire whose sudden roots break barriers that keep my heart from being an abyss.

The things of Time are in connivance with eternity. The shadows serve You. The beasts sing to You before they pass away. The solid hills will vanish like a worn-out garment. All things change and die and disappear. Questions arrive, assume their actuality, and also disappear. In this hour I shall cease to ask them, and silence shall be my answer. The world that Your love created and that the heat has distorted and that my mind is always misinterpreting will cease to interfere with our voices.

Minds that are separated pretend to blend in one another's language. The marriage of souls in concepts is mostly an illusion. Thoughts that travel outward bring back reports of You from outward things: but a dialogue with You, uttered through the world, always ends by being a dialogue with my own reflection in the stream of time. With You there is no dialogue unless You choose a mountain and circle it with cloud and print your words in fire upon the mind of Moses. What was delivered to Moses on tablets of stone, as the fruit of lightning and thunder, is now more thoroughly born in our souls as quietly as the breath of our own being.

You, Who sleep in my breast, are not met with words but in the emergence of life within life and of wisdom within wisdom. With You there is no longer any dialogue, any contest, any opposition. You are found in communion! Thou in me and I in Thee and Thou in them and they in me: dispossession within dispossession, dispassion within dispassion, emptiness within emptiness, freedom within freedom. I am alone. Thou art alone. The Father and I are One.

The hand lies open. The heart is dumb. The soul that held my substance together, like a hard gem in the hollow of my own power, will one day give in. Meanwhile I have beheld the light of the moon made prisoner in the heart of this gem, but I no longer believe the moon to be my own. Although I see the stars, I no longer pretend to know them. Although I have walked in these woods, how can I claim to love them? One by one I shall forget the names of individual things.

The Voice of God is heard in Paradise:

"What was vile has become precious. What is now precious was never vile. I have always known the vile as precious: what is vile I know not at all.

"What was cruel has become merciful. What is now merciful was never cruel. I have always overshadowed Jonas with My mercy, and cruelty I know not at all. Have you had sight of Me, Jonas, My child? Mercy within mercy within mercy. I have forgiven the universe without end, because I have never known sin.

"What was poor has become infinite. What is infinite was never poor. I have always known poverty as infinite: riches I love not at all. Prisons within prisons within prisons. Do not lay up for yourselves ecstasies upon earth, where time and space corrupt, where the minutes break in and steal. No more lay hold on time, Jonas, My son, lest the rivers bear you away.

"What was fragile has become powerful. I loved what was most frail. I looked upon what was nothing. I touched what was without substance, and within what was not, I am."

There are drops of dew that show like sapphires in the grass as soon as the morning sun appears and leaves stir behind the hushed flight of an escaping dove.

PART III

PURSUING THE MONK'S TRUE LIFE

1952–1959

Please pray for me to Our Lord that, instead of merely writing something, I may be something, and indeed that I may so fully be what I ought to be that there may be no further necessity for me to write, since the mere fact of being what I ought to be would be more eloquent than many books.

Letter to Etienne Gilson,
The School of Charity

The voice of silence speaks always to the monk reminding him
that he is a lost thing that is sought and found,
a perishing thing that is rescued and brought home to safety,
that there exists a world to be saved together with him.

Silence in Heaven

I have the immense joy of being *man*, a member of a race in which God Himself became incarnate. As if the sorrows and stupidities of the human condition could overwhelm me now that I realize what we all are. If only everybody could realize this! But it cannot be explained. There is no way of telling people they are all walking around shining like the sun.

Conjectures of a Guilty Bystander

September 3, 1952

I am now almost completely convinced that I am only really a monk when I am alone in the old tool shed Reverend Father gave me. (It is back in the woods beyond the horse pasture where Brother Aelred hauled it with the traxcavator the day before Trinity Sunday.) True, I have the will of a monk in the community. But I have the *prayer* of a monk in the silence of the woods and the tool shed. To begin with: the place is simple and really poor with the bare poverty I need worse than any other medicine and that I never seem to get. And silent. And inactive—materially. Therefore the Spirit is busy here. What is easier than to discuss mutually with You, O God, the three crows that flew by in the sun with light flashing on their rubber wings? Or the sunlight coming quietly through the cracks in the boards? Or the crickets in the grass? You are sanctified in them when, beyond the blue hills, my mind is lost in Your intentions for us all who live with hope under the servitude of corruption!

You have called me into this silence to be grateful for what silence I have and to use it by desiring more.

September 15, 1952

Out here in the woods I can think of nothing except God. It is not so much that I think of Him as I am as aware of Him as I am of the sun and the clouds and the blue sky and the thin cedar trees. When I first came out here, I was sleepy (because we are in the winter season and no longer have meridienne), but I read a few lines from the Desert Fathers and then, after that, my whole being was full of serenity and vigilance.

Who am I writing this for, anyway! It is a waste of time! Enough to say that as long as I am out here, I cannot think of Camaldoli: no question of being here and dreaming of somewhere else. Engulfed in the simple and lucid actuality that is the afternoon—I mean God's afternoon—this sacramental moment of time when the shadows will get longer and longer, and one small bird sings quietly in the cedars, one car goes by in the remote distance, and the oak leaves move in the wind.

High up in the late summer sky I watch the silent flight of a vulture, and the day goes by in prayer. This solitude confirms my call to solitude.

The more I am in it, the more I love it. One day it will possess me
entirely and no man will ever see me again.

September 26, 1952

I am writing this for myself because paper plays a definite part in the
spiritual formation of a writer, even in the formation that will make him
cease to be a writer and transform him into something else.

Because I believe this transformation is necessary.

For 37 years I have been writing my life instead of living it and the
effect is vicious, although by the grace of God it has not been as bad as it
might have been. But I cannot let myself become a hermit merely on the
grounds that the thing looks credible on paper.

October 22, 1952

Since my retreat I have been having another one of those nervous
breakdowns. The same old familiar business. I am getting used to it
now—since the old days in 1936, when I thought I was going to crack up
on the Long Island Railroad, and the more recent one since Ordination.
Now this.

I think it is good to write it down without asking too many questions
as to why it is good. The writing of it forms part of a documentation
that is demanded of me—still demanded, I think—by the Holy Ghost.

November 12, 1952

The truth is formed in silence and work and suffering, with which we
become true. But we interfere with God's work by talking too much about
ourselves—even telling Him what we ought to do—advising Him how
to make us perfect and listening for His voice to answer us with approval.
We soon grow impatient and turn aside from the silence that disturbs us
(the silence in which His work can best be done) and invent the answer
and the approval, which will never come.

Silence, then, is the adoration of His truth. Work is the expression of
our humility. Suffering is born of the love that seeks one thing alone: that
God's will be done.

November 29, 1952

The annual retreat is ending.

I was very deeply moved by Father Phelan's conference on the Sacred Heart. Great depth of theology in clear and simple terms. It showed me how there really is an abyss of light in the things the simplest faithful believe and love that sometimes seem trite to the intellectuals. Indeed, perhaps it is the simplest and most popular truths that are also the deepest after all.

For my own part, I think much has been done to me in the course of this retreat—in emptiness and helplessness and humiliation. Aware that I might crack up at any moment, I find, nevertheless, that when I pray, I pray better than ever. I mean that I no longer have any special degree of prayer. Simple vocal prayer, especially the Office and the psalms, seems to have acquired a depth and a simplicity I never knew in *any* prayer. I have nothing but faith in the love of God and confidence in the simple means He has given me for reaching Him. Suspended entirely from His mercy, I am content for anything to happen.

December 29, 1952. Feast of St. Thomas à Beckett

A week ago I was reading the Christmas sermon from T. S. Eliot's *Murder in the Cathedral* to the scholastics. I read them several of the choruses also. Today, after what has taken place in me since Christmas, I find I have lived through something of the same kind of decision as St. Thomas in the play.

You start by desiring something—an end, a vocation. You come to seek it with great imperfection, and there is a great danger of wanting the right thing for the wrong reason. And there is no decision possible. Suddenly occurs the "change of the right hand of the Most High." Now it is no longer we who question and plead and inquire and pray, but He who impels us. We feel the power of God suddenly upon us, and our desire is totally changed. It is objectively the same thing that we desire, but we see it in an entirely different light when we know that, by God's will, it is to be. For since in His intention it is already fulfilled, it is no longer a mere desire, no longer a wish we can *play* with. There is no playing with the will of God!

It is easy to understand why it is so easy and so pleasant to waste our lives playing with desires to which we unconsciously realize God is paying no attention. But what futility!

No—our joy is to be led by Him to the thing He desires, even though that thing be in some way terrible. As soon as He *desires* it, it ceases to be "our will." It becomes a sacrifice. It demands a gift of our whole being.

It was so with the priesthood. And now I think it will be so with solitude.

It is very serious. And very simple.

Yesterday, between two cedars, looking at the wagon tracks on the soft earth of the bottomlands and at the woods beyond, I knew that whatever God will have granted me—whatever solitude—will be truly for the salvation of my soul. I saw how much I need solitude for that reason.

Not solitude for the sake of something special, something exalted, but solitude as the climate in which I can simply be what I am meant to be: living in the presence of the living God. Solitude in order to be a simple Christian. Like climbing down from a mountain or a pillar and starting all over again to behave as a human being, I need solitude for the true fulfillment that I seek, that of being *ordinary.*

Life in the world was utterly abnormal.

Life in the monastery is not ordinary. It is a freakish sort of life. The freakishness is not St. Benedict's fault, but maybe it is necessary. In solitude I shall at last be just a person no longer corrupted by being known, no longer creating myself in the image of a slightly unbalanced society. Living in the likeness of the God who is my life: that is to say, living as unknown. For a Christian is one whom the world does not know.

February 9, 1953. Feast of St. Scholastica

Evening. St. Anne's. I got permission to stay out here until supper.

It is a tremendous thing no longer to have to debate in my mind about "being a hermit," even though I am not one. At least now solitude is something concrete—it is "St. Anne's"—the long view of hills, the empty cornfields in the bottoms, the crows in the trees, and the cedars bunched together on the hillside. When I am here there is always lots of sky and lots of peace and I don't have distractions and everything is serene—except for the rats in the wall. They are my distraction and they are sometimes obstreperous.

Here there seems to be less and less need of books. If I were only here always! Cold mornings, hot afternoons. Came out the other day (*Sexagesima* Sunday) when there was thick frost on the ground but the sun was already warm.

The Spirit is alone here with the silence of the world.

St. Anne's is like a rampart between two existences. On one side I know the community to which I must return. And I *can* return to it with love. But to return seems like a waste. It is a waste to offer to God. On the other side is the great wilderness of silence in which, perhaps, I might never speak again to anyone but God as long as I live.

(Back in the vault lies an existence that is already beginning to be remote and strange, a wayside station that I have passed in the desert, even though I still give direction there in the morning. The reviews of *The Sign of Jonas* lie under the typewriter table, stuffed into the first edition of the book, which still awaits some more correction. But all that has nothing to do with the silence of St. Anne's.)

February 14, 1953

Today we commemorate Blessed Conrad—one of the Cistercian hermits.

I might as well admit that in the novitiate I did not like the hermits of our Order: Blessed Conrad, St. Galgan, St. Firmian. Perhaps the stories of St. Albert of Sestri and Blessed John of Caramola were more congenial to me. The hermits, however, "never seemed to get anywhere." Their stories were inconclusive. They seemed to have died before finding out what they were supposed to achieve.

Now I know there is something important about the very incompleteness of Blessed Conrad: hermit in Palestine by St. Bernard's permission. Starts home for Clairvaux when he hears St. Bernard is dying. Gets to Italy and hears St. Bernard is dead. Settles in a wayside chapel outside Bari and dies there. What an untidily unplanned life! No order, no sense, no system, no climax. Like a book without punctuation that suddenly ends in the middle of a sentence.

Yet I know that those are the books I really like!

Blessed Conrad cannot possibly be solidified or ossified in history. He can perhaps be caught and held in a picture, but he is like a photograph of a bird in flight—too accurate to look the way a flying bird seems to appear to us. We never saw the wings in that position. Such is the solitary vocation. For of all men the solitary knows least where he is going and yet he is more sure, for there is one thing he cannot doubt: he travels where God is leading him. That is precisely why he doesn't know the way. That too is why, to most other men, the way is something of a scandal.

February 16, 1953

It seems to me that St. Anne's is what I have been waiting for and looking for all my life and now I have stumbled into it quite by accident. Now, for the first time, I am aware of what happens to a man who has really found his place in the scheme of things.

With tremendous relief I have discovered that I no longer need to *pretend.* Because when you have not found what you are looking for, you pretend in your eagerness to have found it. You act as if you had found it. You spend your time telling yourself what you have found and yet do not want.

I do not have to buy St. Anne's. I do not have to sell myself to myself here. Everything that was ever real in me has come back to life in this doorway wide open to the sky! I no longer have to trample myself down, cut myself in half, throw part of me out the window, and keep pushing the rest of myself away.

In the silence of St. Anne's everything has come together in unity, and the unity is not my unity but Yours, O Father of Peace.

I recognize in myself the child who walked all over Sussex. (I did not know I was looking for this shanty or that I would one day find it.) All the countries of the world are one under this sky: I no longer need to travel. Half a mile away is the monastery with the landscape of hills that haunted me for 11 years with uncertainty. I knew I had come to stay but never really believed it, and the hills seemed to speak, at all times, of some other country.

The quiet landscape of St. Anne's speaks of no other country.

If they will let me, I am here to stay—unless there is some invasion of tractors and construction. (There is a jeep now in the fields before me. First time since the corn harvest there has been anything there.) And if there be some other place to go to, it need only be a mile or two away!

This is a different situation. The silence of it is making me well.

February 17, 1953. Shrove Tuesday

Lent, which begins tomorrow, is a sunlit season.

Today—*carnivale*—farewell to the flesh. It is a poor joke to be merry about leaving the flesh, as if we were to return to it once again. What would be the good of Lent if it were only temporary?

Jesus nevertheless died *in order to return* to His flesh, in order to raise His own body glorious from the dead, and in order to raise our bodies with Him. "Unless the grain of wheat, falling into the ground, die, itself remains alone." So we cast off the flesh, not out of contempt, but in order to heal the flesh in the mercy of penance and restore it to the Spirit to which it belongs. And all creation waits in anguish for our victory and our bodies' glory.

God wills us to recover all the joys of His created world in the Spirit by denying ourselves what is really no joy—what only ends in the flesh. "The flesh profits nothing."

Looking at the crucifix on the white wall of St. Anne's—overwhelmed at the realization that I am a *priest*, that it has been given to me to know something of what the Cross means, that St. Anne's is a special part of my priestly vocation: the silence, the woods, the sunlight, the shadows, the picture of Jesus, Our Lady of Cobre, and the little angels in Fra Angelico's paradise. Here I am a priest with all the world as my parish. Or is it a temptation, the thought of this? Perhaps I do not need to remember the apostolic fruitfulness of this silence. I need only to be nothing and to wait for the revelation of Christ: to be at peace and poor and silent in the world where the mystery of iniquity is also at work and where there is also no other revelation. No, there is so much peace at St. Anne's that it is most certainly the heart of a great spiritual battle that is fought in silence. I who sit here and pray and think and live—I am nothing—and do not need to know what is going on. I need only to hope in Christ to hear the big deep bell that now begins to ring and sends its holy sound to me through the little cedars.

This is the continuation of my Mass. This is still my Eucharist, my day-long thanksgiving, work, worship, my hoping for the perfect revelation of Christ.

February 24, 1953. St. Matthias

Gone are the days when "mysticism" was for me a matter of eager and speculative interest. Now, because it is my life, it is torment to think about—like being in the pangs of childbirth and reading an essay on mother love written by a spinster.

In choir I am happier than I have ever been there, extremely poor and helpless, often strained, hardly able to hold myself in place. "Expecting every moment to be my last." Sometimes it is a great relief to be distracted. There is a "presence" of God that is like an iron curtain between the mind and God.

But here at St. Anne's I am always happy and at peace no matter what happens. For here there is no need for anyone but God—no need of "mysticism."

A fly buzzes on the window pane!

March 3, 1953

One thing is certain. Days of Recollection and afternoons at St. Anne's, Mass and the Office, and the terror of the dark, all are given to me for one thing: that I may find Christ and know Him, Who is "made to us power and wisdom from God." Not a question of examining myself, still less of planning work or how to be a spiritual director. Life is much more serious than that. Study has a serious place in it, too. Not as if Christ could offer us an alternative wisdom to other similar wisdoms—as if He had a doctrine that was one of many! We have not yet sufficiently "learned Christ," and we do not yet know sufficiently what it is to find Him.

Another thing: I have discovered the penitential psalms. You do not discover them until you know how much you need them. You do not know your need until you experience it. You do not experience your poverty when *you* tell yourself about it but when God tells you that you are poor. When God tells you of a sickness, it is because He means, at the same time, to provide a remedy. It is the Devil who tells us that we are ill and taunts us for it, reminds us of our helplessness by making us even more helpless.

In the penitential psalms Christ recognizes my poverty in His poverty. Merely to see myself in the psalm is a beginning of being healed. For I see myself through His grace. His grace is working; therefore I am on my way to being healed. O the need of that healing! I walk from region to region of my soul, and I discover that I am a bombed city.

While I meditated on Psalm 6, I caught sight of an unexpected patch of green meadow along the creek on our neighbor's land. The green grass under the leafless trees, the pools of water after the storm, lifted my heart to God. He is so easy to come to when even grass and water bear witness to His mercy! "I will water my couch with tears."

I have written about the frogs singing. Now they sing again. It is another spring. Although I am ruined, I am far better off than I have ever been in my life. My ruin is my fortune.

July 17, 1956

Either you look at the universe as a very poor creation out of which no one can make anything or you look at your own life and your own part in the universe as infinitely rich, full of inexhaustible interest opening out into the infinite further possibilities for study and contemplation and interest and praise. Beyond all and in all is God.

Perhaps the Book of Life, in the end, is the book of what one has lived and, if one has lived nothing, he is not in the Book of Life.

I have always wanted to write about everything. That does not mean to write a book that *covers* everything—which would be impossible. But a book in which everything can go. A book with a little of everything that creates itself out of nothing. That has its own life. A faithful book. I no longer look at it as a "book."

Prayer to Our Lady of Mount Carmel

What was it that I said to you, in the mirror, at Havana?

Were you not perhaps the last one I saw as the steamer left, you standing on your tower with your back to the sea, looking at the university?

I have never forgotten you. You are more to me now than then, when I walked through the streets reciting (which I had just learned) the *Memorare*. I have forgotten all the things I have prayed for to you. I think I have received them, but I do not remember. More important, I have received you.

Whom I know and yet do not know. Whom I love but not enough.

Prayer is what you bring—for prayer is your gift to us rather than what you ask of us.

If only I could pray—and yet I can and do pray.

Teach me to go to this country beyond words and beyond names.

Teach me not to pray on this side of the frontier, here where the woods are.

I need to be led by you. I need my heart to be moved by you. I need my soul to be made clean by your prayer. I need my will to be made strong by you. I need the world to be saved and changed by you. I need you for all those who suffer, who are in prison, in danger, in sorrow. I need you for all the crazy people. I need your healing hands to work always in my life. I need you to make me, as your Son, a healer, a comforter, a savior. I need you to name the dead. I need you to help the dying cross their particular river. I need you for myself whether I live or die. I need to be your monk and your son. It is necessary. Amen.

August 20, 1956

Our glory and our hope—We are the Body of Christ. Christ loves us and espouses us as His own flesh. Isn't that enough for us? But we do not really believe it. No! Be content, be content. We are the Body of Christ. We have found Him, He has found us. We are in Him, He is in us. There is nothing further to look for except for the deepening of this life we already possess. Be content.

August 29, 1956

The great thing and the only thing is to adore and praise God.

To seek Him is to adore Him and to say that He alone is God and there is no other.

We must lay down our life for His Truth. We must bear witness to what *is* and to what is the fidelity of God to His promises.

We must believe with our whole heart what God our Father has offered and promised us.

We must leave all things to answer His call to us and to reply to His grace.

When we have done this, we can talk of perfection but, when we have done this, we no longer need to talk of perfection.

August 31, 1956

A very small locust seedling, a few feet high, grows up triumphalistically out of the honeysuckle in the place where the wall is broken down. Beyond that, through a gap in the cedars, the old sheep barn with its plum-colored roof swelters in the noonday sun. A broken-down mowing machine is stranded among the stones of the road, and, beyond, the wind moves the massive, light and dark foliage of the oak trees.

A tractor, here under the woodshed, picks up a piece of machinery with which to worry the soil, and the latest postulant walks by, looking critically at the tractor.

I return to the small locust whose slow dance in the wind is like that of a Japanese dancer—she turns up her delicate branches in the wind and the undersides of the leaves smile at the sun.

September 12, 1956

Respect for mystery, sense of the mystery of God, veneration of the sacredness of mystery, awe and humility in approaching the ineffable holiness of Him who can be known in Himself only by His own revelation of Himself—these are essential virtues of a truly religious soul. To lose these characteristics is to lose our religious spirit. To grow in them is to grow in true interior life.

The gabby objectivity of a relationship in which familiarity has destroyed all sense of the reality of God's *Tremendum Mysterium* is almost as bad as agnosticism.

April 25, 1957

Macarius Bulgakov and Nicolas Berdyayev are writers of great attention. They are great men who will not admit the defeat of Christ who has conquered by His Resurrection. In their pages, for all the scandals one may fear to encounter, shines the light of the Resurrection, and theirs is a theology of triumph.

One wonders if our theological cautiousness is not after all the sign of a fatal coldness of heart, an awful sterility born of fear or of despair. These two men have dared to make mistakes and were to be condemned by every church in order to say something great and worthy of God in the midst of all their wrong statements.

They have dared to accept the challenge of the sapiential books, the challenge of the image of Proverbs where Wisdom is "playing in the world" before the face of the Creator. The Church herself says this. Sophia was somehow, mysteriously, to be revealed and "fulfilled" in the Mother of God and in the Church.

Most important of all—man's creative vocation to prepare, consciously, the ultimate triumph of Divine Wisdom. Man, the microcosm, the heart of the universe, is the one who is called to bring about the fusion of cosmic and historic process in the final invocation of God's wisdom and love. In the name of Christ and by His power man has a work to accomplish: to offer the cosmos to the Father, by the power of the Spirit, in the Glory of the Word. Our life is a powerful Pentecost in which the Holy Spirit, ever active in us, seeks to reach through our inspired hands and tongues into the very heart of the material world created to be spiritualized through the work of the Church, the Mystical Body of the Incarnate Word of God.

April 28, 1957

If I can unite *in myself,* in my own spiritual life, the thought of the East and the West, of the Greek and Latin Fathers, I will create in myself a reunion of the divided Church, and from that unity in myself can come the exterior and visible unity of the Church. For, if we want to bring together East and West, we cannot do it by imposing one upon the other. We must contain both in ourselves and transcend them both in Christ.

September 29, 1957

Mark and Dorothy Van Doren were here yesterday on their way to Illinois—long enough to walk to the cow barn and back—and for me to show Mark the novitiate.

I was happy to have him stand in these rooms, so wise a person, and lean against the bookshelf in the scriptorium and talk about some things that had come up when he was at the Hampton Institute the day before. The English professor there complained that his students had no preparation to read Shakespeare, and Mark said that everyone is prepared to read Shakespeare by the time they are 18. They have been born, they have had fathers, mothers; they have been loved, feared, hated, been jealous, etc.

At the cow barn we looked at brushfires being lit along the hillside of St. Bernard's field, and Mark talked about his love for fires and I talked of mine. We decided that everybody loves fires and those who admit it are not pyromaniacs but just love fires reasonably.

October 5, 1957

The warblers are coming through now. Very hard to identify them all, even with field glasses and a bird book. (Have seen at least one that is definitely not in the bird book.) Watching one, which I took to be a Tennessee warbler. A beautiful, neat, prim little thing—seeing this beautiful thing, which people do not usually see, looking into this world of birds, which is not concerned with us or with our problems. I felt very close to God or felt religious awe anyway. Watching those birds was as food for meditation or as mystical reading. Perhaps better.

Also the beautiful, unidentified red flower or fruit I found on a bud yesterday. I found a bird in the woods yesterday on the feast of St. Francis. Those things say so much more than words.

Mark was saying, "The birds don't know they have names."

Watching them, I thought: "Who cares what they are called?" But do I have the courage not to care? Why not be like Adam in a new world of my own and call them by my own names?

That would still mean that I thought the names were important.

No name and no word to identify the beauty and reality of those birds today is the gift of God to me in letting me see them.

(And that name—God—is no name! It is like a letter, X or Y. Yahweh is a better Name—it finally means "Nameless One.")

November 2, 1957

I must get to know something of modern physics. Even though I am a monk, that is no reason for living in a Newtonian universe or, worse still, an Aristotelian one. The fact that the cosmos is not quite what St. Thomas and Dante imagined it to be has, after all, some importance. It does not invalidate St. Thomas or Dante or Catholic theology, but it ought to be understood and taken into account by a theologian. It is futile to try and live in an expanding universe with atomic fission an ever-present possibility and try to think and act exclusively as if the cosmos were fixed in an immutable order centered upon man's earth. Modern physics has its repercussions in the monastery, and to be a monk one must take them into account, although that does nothing whatever to make one's spirituality either simple or neat.

One must get along without the security of neat and simple, ready-made solutions. There are things one has to think out, all over again, for oneself.

November 15, 1957. Feast of the Dedication of the Church

This always turns out to be a feast of anguish as well as one of joy.

Nothing could be more beautiful, nothing could make me happier than the hymn *Urbs Jerusalem*—to sing certain verses of that hymn in the evening looking at the sacramental flames of the candles upon the wall where the building was touched and blessed by Christ and made into a sacrament of Himself.

"They shall stand forever within the sacred walls."

I too "stand forever," placed in a permanent position. I am glad. I am truly happy, I am really grateful to God—for it means eternal salvation.

Yet it raises again the unanswerable question: "What on earth am I doing here?" I have answered it a million times. "I belong here." But that is no answer. In the end there is no answer like that. Any vocation is a mystery, and juggling with words does not make it any clearer.

It is a contradiction and must remain a contradiction.

I think the only hope for me is to pile contradiction upon contradiction and push myself into the middle of all contradictions.

Thus it will always remain morally impossible for me simply to "conform" and to settle down and accept the official rationalization of what is going on here. On the other hand, it in no way helps matters for me to replace the official statements with slightly better rationalizations of my own.

A great deal of the trouble comes from the fact that I look for a formula and expect to find a good one. If you want to find a satisfactory formula, you had better deal with things that can be fitted into a formula. The vocation to seek God is not one of them. Nor is existence. Nor is the spirit of man.

Obviously there is a certain amount of truth in the fact that my psychology is that of a bourgeois intellectual partly predetermined by economic influences. That is not the statement of a problem for which there is implied (in the very statement) a solution. It is merely a challenge: can I not prove by action that I can get free from this supposed determinism and rise above it?

This already throws a new light on my struggles here: it is a struggle against the determinism of what is socially "given"—what everybody else is in fact stuck with—the attitudes, the mores, the points of view, the sets of values that we all more or less have inherited from our class background and to which we cling to all the more peacefully because it all hides under a surface of religious formulas.

It is certain that I have no quarrel whatever with the formulas, though I generally think they can be stated more clearly and more specifically. My real struggle is with the psychology, the attitudes that are implied, that are so clearly printed between the lines. It is this psychology that really speaks, not the formulas.

Guilt and resentment at myself for having fled to America, to a country whose culture I secretly despise while loving it and needing it. The country of Pop's optimism—an optimism with no foundations, merely a facade for despair. All this Father laughed at, and I have identified myself with it out of cowardice perhaps. Yet at the same time I despise far more the more decadent and hollow values of the European bourgeoisie. Where then do I stand? Have I the courage to stand on my own feet, or do I have feet to stand on? What has it meant to stand on them?

All this has to boil up from time to time. This boiling is part of my life. Thank God for it.

There is no solution in withdrawal. No solution in conforming.

A Koan! What sound is made by one hand clapping against itself?

That is where I think Zen is smart: in its absolutely fundamental psychological honesty. This honesty is inseparable from the interior poverty and sincerity that Christ asked for when He said, "Can you believe? All things are possible to one who can believe."

December 29, 1957

In a world with a complicated economic structure like ours, it is no longer even a question of "my brother" being a citizen in the same country. From the moment the economy of another country is subservient to the business interests of my country, I am responsible to those of the other country who are "in need." In what does this responsibility consist? To what does it obligate me? Who can answer? Is Marx right in saying that the Capitalist world does not and *cannot* seek an honest answer? I am bound to agree with him.

Hence the problem of cooperation with those who exploit. A frightfully difficult problem. What have moral theologians done so far to open up new horizons? Nothing as far as I know.

Hence *my obligation to study questions of history, economics,* etc., in so far as I can.

This obligation is by no means in conflict with my "contemplative" vocation.

Until my "contemplation" is liberated from the sterilizing artificial limitations under which it has so far existed (and nearly been stifled out of existence), I cannot be a "man of God" because I cannot live in the Truth, which is the first essential for being a man of God.

It is absolutely true that here in this monastery we are enabled to systematically evade our real and ultimate social responsibilities. In any time, social responsibility is the keystone of the Christian life.

January 6, 1958. Epiphany

A beautiful sentence at the end of Paul Evdokimov's article on the Nativity ikon in *Bible et vie chrétienne.* (Concerning the angel in the ikon who comes up over the side of the mountain of God and leans toward men.) This is the angel whom we hear when we are silent, and when we get to heaven his voice will be the most familiar of voices to us and will be like our own voice. Too good for comment.

January 31, 1958

Dreamt the other night that I was in a general store somehow connected with the monastery. In the store were Soviet-manufactured articles, dreary and tawdry, which were being thrown away or destroyed—in particular, cheap desk lamps. I remember gathering up some of those things to appropriate them, thinking that, though they were useless, it was "against religious poverty" to let such things be thrown away, particularly since they symbolized the tragic suffering of millions of nameless people. The keeper of the store disdained my choice. These articles had been taken in in "the days when Father Placid was cellarer."

February 4, 1958

Beauty of the sunlight falling on a tall vase of red and white carnations and green leaves on the altar in the novitiate chapel. The light and shade of the red, especially the dark ones, the same color as blood but not "red as blood," utterly unlike blood. Red as a carnation. This flower, this light, this moment, this silence = *Dominus est,* eternity! Best because the flower is itself and the light is itself and the silence is itself and I am myself—all, perhaps, an illusion, but no matter, for illusion is nevertheless the shadow of reality and reality is the grace that underlies these lights, these colors, this silence.

The "simplicity" that would have kept those flowers off the altar is, to my mind, less simple than the simplicity that enjoys them there but does not need them to be there.

February 15, 1958. Saturday

This afternoon I suddenly saw the meaning of my *American* destiny—one of those moments when many unrelated pieces of one's life and thought fall into place in a great unity toward which one has been growing.

My destiny is indeed to be an American—not just an American of the United States. We are only on the fringe of the true America. I can never be satisfied with this only partial reality which is almost nothing at all, which is so little that it is like a few words written in chalk on a blackboard, easily rubbed out.

I have never so keenly felt the impermanence of what is now regarded as American because it is *North* American, or the elements of stability and permanence, which are in *South* America. Deeper roots, Indian roots. The Spanish, Portuguese, Negro roots also. The shallow English roots are not deep enough. The tree will fall.

To be an American of the Andes—containing in myself also Kentucky and New York. But New York is not, and never will be, really America. America is much bigger and deeper and more complex than that— America is still an undiscovered continent.

Waldo Frank has said many silly and callow things, but I agree with him on this deep and fundamental point: the *Great Vocation of America*, a hemisphere that is called and chosen.

America has her own vocation and no one else can help her to find it—least of all Russia (but Russia can perhaps place some bit of ferment in her that will start things working although no ferment is needed. It works mightily!)

The vocation of America is the vocation of men who are called and chosen from among the peoples. It depends on them. Men like Simón Bolívar who have seen and understood something of it.

My own vocation—it would have been dreadful to have returned to Europe, to Italy, to Camaldoli. It would have been fatal.

My vocation is American—*to see and to understand and to have in myself the life and the roots and the belief and the destiny and the orientation of the whole hemisphere*—as an expression of something of God, of Christ, that the world has not yet found out—something that is only now, after hundreds of years, coming to maturity!

The problems and the dangers (who cares about the dangers?).

To be able—possibly—to reach out and embrace all the extremes and have them in oneself without confusion—without eclecticism, without dilettantism, without false mysticism, without being torn apart.

No one fragment can begin to be enough—not Spanish colonial Catholicism, not 19th-century republicanism, not agrarian radicalism, not the Indianism of Mexico—but all of it, everything. To be oneself a whole hemisphere and to help the hemisphere to realize its own destiny.

February 28, 1958

Yesterday turned into a day of frustrations—minor ones, anyway.

But, after all these things, I had a dream. It may have had no connection with them whatever.

On the porch at Douglaston I am embraced with determined and virginal passion by a young Jewish girl. She clings to me and will not let go, and I get to like the idea. I see that she is a nice kid in a plain, sincere sort of way. I reflect, "She belongs to the same race as St. Anne." I ask her her name and she says her name is Proverb. I tell her that is a beautiful and significant name, but she does not appear to like it—perhaps the others have mocked her for it.

When I am awake, I rationalize it complacently. "I loved Wisdom and sought to make her my wife"—Sophia (it is the *sofa* on the back porch . . . etc., etc.). No need to explain. It was a charming dream.

March 4, 1958

Dear Proverb,

For several days I have intended to write you this letter, to tell you that I have not forgotten you. Perhaps now too much time has gone by and I no longer exactly know what I wanted to tell you—except that, though there is a great difference in our ages and many other differences between us, you know even better than I that these differences do not matter at all. Indeed, it is from you that I have learned, to my surprise, that it is as if they never existed.

How grateful I am to you for loving in me something that I had thought I had entirely lost and someone who, I thought, I had long ago ceased to be. In you, dear, though some might be tempted to say you do not even exist, there is a reality as real and as wonderful and as precious as life itself. I must be careful what I say, for words cannot explain my love for you. I do not wish by my words to harm that which in you is more real and more pure than in anyone else in the world—your lovely spontaneity, your simplicity, the generosity of your love.

I think what I most want to say is that I treasure in you the revelation of your virginal solitude. In your marvelous, innocent love you are utterly alone: yet you have given your love to me, why I cannot imagine. And with it you have given me yourself and all the innocent wonder of your solitude. Dear, should I ask myself seriously if I will ever be worthy of such a gift? No, I am not—not because I could never probably be worthy, but because of my own love for you. And so, I give you everything.

Dearest Proverb, I love your name, its mystery, its simplicity, and its secret, which even you yourself seem not to appreciate.

March 19, 1958. Feast of St. Joseph

In St. Anne's. It is so long since I have been here—I can hardly tell how long.

The peculiar peace and sweetness of St. Joseph's afternoon, the gentleness of the divine mercy, the silence of the air—eleven years since solemn profession, fourteen years since simple profession! How fantastic! A red-shouldered hawk wheels slowly over Newton's farm as if making his own special silence in the air—as if tracing out a circle of silence in the sky.

How many graces, here in St. Anne's, that I did not know about in those years when I was here all the time, when I had what I most wanted and never really knew it. Which only shows that solitude alone was not exactly what I wanted. How rich for me has been the silence of this little house, which is nothing more than a tool shed behind which on the hillside for two years they have tried without success to start a rock garden.

Yesterday, in Louisville, at the corner of 4th and Walnut, suddenly realized that I loved all the people and that none of them were or could be totally alien to me. As if waking from a dream—the dream of my separateness, of the "special" vocation to be different. My vocation does not really make me different from the rest of men or put me in a special category except artificially, juridically. I am still a member of the human race, and what more glorious destiny is there for man, since the Word was made flesh and became, too, a member of the Human Race!

Thank God! Thank God! I am only another member of the human race, like all the rest of them. I have the immense joy of being a man! As if the sorrows of our condition could really matter, once we begin to realize who and what we are—as if we could ever begin to realize it on earth.

It is not a question of proving to myself that I either dislike or like the women one sees in the street. The fact of having a vow of chastity does not oblige one to argue on this point—no special question arises. I am keenly conscious, not of their beauty (I hardly think I saw anyone really beautiful by special standards) but of their humanity, their womanness. But what incomprehensible beauty is there, what secret beauty that would perhaps be inaccessible to me if I were not dedicated to a different way of life. It is as though by chastity I had come to be unafraid of what is most pure in all the women of the world and to taste and sense the secret beauty of their girls' hearts as they walked in the sunlight—each one secret and good and lovely in the sight of God—never touched by anyone, nor by me, nor by anyone, as good as and even more beautiful than life itself. For the womanness that is in each of them is at once original and inexhaustibly fruitful, bringing the image of God into the world. In this each one is Wisdom and Sophia and Our Lady (my delights are to be with the children of men!).

Dear Proverb, I have kept one promise and I have refrained from speaking of you until seeing you again. I knew that when I saw you again it would be very different, in a different place, in a different form, in the most unexpected circumstances. I shall never forget our meeting yesterday. The touch of your hand makes me a different person. To be with you is rest and truth. Only with you are these things found, dear child sent to me by God!

Marvelous books for a few pennies—including *The Family of Man* for 50 cents. All those fabulous pictures. No refinements and no explanations are necessary! How scandalized some men would be if I said that the whole book is to me a picture of Christ, and yet that is the Truth. There, there is Christ in my own Kind, my own Kind—*Kind*, which means "likeness" and which means "love" and which means "child." Mankind. Like one another, the dear "Kind" of sinners united and embraced in only one heart, only one Kindness, which is the Heart and Kindness of Christ. I do not look for sin in you, Mankind. I do not see sin in you anymore today (though we are all sinners). There is something too real to allow sin any longer to seem important, to seem to exist, for it has been swallowed up, it has been destroyed, it is gone, and there is only the great secret between us that we are all one Kind. What matters is not what this or that one has committed in his heart, separate from the others, but the love that brings him back to all the others in one Christ. This love is not our love but the Divine Bridegroom's. It is the Divine Power and the Divine Joy. God is seen and reveals Himself as *man*, that is, in us, and there is no other hope of finding wisdom than in God-manhood: our own manhood transformed in God!

April 20, 1958

Day of Recollection resolutions:

1. My lot is cast with the future, which I do not yet know. The future of the whole of America, North and South.

2. My job is to shut up and avoid political mysticism and other forms of false mysticism and apply myself to learning and to open my eyes and see what is going on.

3. Learn to help the future to "go on" to where it is going. To keep myself from joining those who, one way or another, want everything stopped dead and kept that way—or everything to run the way they think it is supposed to be running.

4. But can I take a leaf out of the Marxist book by keeping my mouth shut and my eyes open and watching for what is to happen?

May 2, 1958. St. Athanasius

In the monastery, or at any rate in choir, I have been forgetting how to think, and only in the past few days have I woke up to the fact that this is very dangerous! I mean the constant, habitual passivity we get into. No matter how honest the surroundings and how clean the doctrine believed in them, no man can afford to be passive and to restrict his thinking to a new rehearsal, in his own mind, of what is being repeated all around him.

We are not as honest as we think, and our doctrine is not as pure as we hope it is. I, least of all, can afford to be passive in this place.

One must constantly be asking himself—"What do I mean by this? Am I saying what I mean? Have I understood what this implies? Have I some notion of the *consequences* of what I am saying?" I am particularly bad on the last question because usually I think on paper, that is, I often do not really know what I think until it is set out before me in black and white: then I can agree or disagree.

May 5, 1958

Thinking of the new and necessary struggle in my interior life.

I am finally coming out of a chrysalis. The years behind me seem strangely inert and negative, but I suppose that passivity was necessary.

Now the pain and struggle of fighting my way out into something new and much bigger. I must see and embrace God in the whole world.

(It is all very well to say I have been seeing God in Himself. But I have not. I have been seeing Him only in a very small monastic world. This is much too small.)

Said the Mass *Ad Tollendum Schisma*—For the End of Schisms—one of the most beautiful.

Cool again this morning. Many birds singing. The tops of the hills still hidden in mist. The lark still sings "Dr. Zhivago" (which I very much want to read).

June 22, 1958

The conviction that I have not yet even begun to write, to think, to pray, and to live and that only now am I getting down to waking up. By God's grace this comes from finally trying with great difficulty to be genuinely free and alone, as humbly as I can, in God's sight, without passively accepting all the standards and the formulas that have been adopted by others. I am at least now exercising a wider choice in my sources of inspiration.

July 25, 1958

A small monastery.

1. Without a "program."

2. Without a special job to do. Monks to *live*, not to be "monks" as distinct from every other kind of being, but to be *men*—sons of God.

3. Without a special future. No drive for postulants.

4. Without a special reputation or renown for anything.

5. A hidden monastery, not well known perhaps as a monastery. Perhaps not even wearing a special habit. Without observably distinctive buildings.

6.   Certainly isolated, cloistered and cut off.

7.   With hermit types—i.e., possibilities for personal solitude for a certain portion of the year. Special solitude in certain seasons. Advent, Lent.

8.   Made up of a nucleus of *mature* monks, each one able to decide for himself in fasting, etc.

9.   Taking an interest in art, music, literature, politics, etc., of our time.

10. Manual labor, of course. Maybe some teaching. *But care to keep the life from getting crowded with works and projects.*

One sensible thing: I can begin to live now, as far as possible, the life I would like to live in such a monastery and with the same spirit.

August 3, 1958

Always very fine ideas in Romano Guardini on Providence.

For instance, that the will of God is not a "fate" to which we submit but a creative act in our life producing something absolutely new (or failing to do so), something hitherto unforeseen by the laws and established patterns. Our cooperation (seeking first the Kingdom of God) consists not solely in conforming to laws but in opening our wills out to this creative act, which must be retrieved in and by us—by the will of God.

This is my big aim—to put everything else aside. I do not want to create merely for and by myself a new life and a new world, but I want God to create them in and through me. This is central and fundamental—with this one can never be a mere Marxian Communist.

I must lead a new life, and a new world must come into being. But not by *my* plans and *my* agitation.

August 14, 1958. Virgil of the Assumption

I must confess that I feel the lack of hard work. Enjoyed sweating and getting tired with a scythe in the weeds yesterday (fighting the jungle between the novitiate and the old mill). But it seems to me that I am obliged to study and put in as much time as I reasonably can in studying—in this I run the risk of being wrong, and I am at last simply running the risk for better or for worse. I am a writer. Though I don't intend to write so much any more, I feel I must know something about the world in which we live and in which we are supposed to fight for the Kingdom of God.

There are things I will not know about my faith and about my vocation if I fail to understand Communism. This I have to do for myself and for others as well. It is part of my solitude, which, as a matter of fact, is now very real.

August 25, 1958. Feast of St. Louis

The grip the *present* has on me. That is the one thing that has grown most noticeably in my spiritual life—nothing much else has. The rest dims as it should. I am getting older. The reality of *now*—the unreality of all the rest. The unreality of ideas and explanations and formulas. I am. The unreality of all the rest. The pigs shriek. Butterflies dance together—or danced together a moment ago—against the blue sky at the end of the woodshed. The buzz saw stands outside there, half covered with dirty and tattered canvas. The trees are fresh and green in the sun (more rain yesterday). Small clouds inexpressibly beautiful and silent and eloquent over the silent woodlands. What a celebration of light, quietness, and glory! This is my feast, sitting here in the straw!

September 27, 1958

It is a bright afternoon: what am I going to do? I am going to work with my mind and with my pen, while the sky is clear and while the soft white clouds are small and sharply defined in it. I am not going to bury myself in books and note taking. I am not going to lose myself in this jungle and come out drunk and bewildered, feeling that bewilderment is a sign that I have done something. I am not going to write as one driven by compulsions but freely, because I am a writer, because for me to write is to think and to live and also in some degree even to pray.

This time is given to me by God that I may live in it. It is not given to make something *out of it* but given me to be stored away in eternity as my own.

For this afternoon to be my own in eternity, it must be my own this afternoon, and I must possess myself in it, not be possessed by books, by ideas not my own, by a compulsion to produce what nobody needs. But simply to glorify God by accepting His gift and His work. To work for Him is to work that I myself may live.

How else shall I study Boris Pasternak, whose central idea is the sacredness of life?

October 2, 1958. Feast of the Guardian Angels

Brilliant and gorgeous day, bright sun, breeze making all the leaves and high brown grasses shine. Singing of the wind in the cedars. Exultant day in which even a puddle in the pig lot shines like precious silver.

Finally I am coming to the conclusion that my highest ambition is to be what I already am. That I will never fulfill my obligation to surpass myself unless I first accept myself, and if I accept myself fully in the right way, I will already have surpassed myself. For it is the unaccepted self that stands in my way and will continue to do so as long as it is not accepted. When it has been accepted—it is my own stepping stone to what is above me. Because this is the way man has been made by God. Original sin was the effort to surpass oneself by being "like God"—i.e., unlike oneself. But our Godlikeness begins at home. We must first become like ourselves and stop living "beside ourselves."

I no longer care about a foundation—the idea is done with—unless someone brings it upon me. If there is a "work" I think I should do, then let it be done here. The first thing is to get uncluttered so that I can be free to write if I have to. I have been living under an enormous heap of books from libraries—Louisville's and the University of Kentucky's— some useful, many useless. No matter—there were things I had to read up on. Now to take time and digest it all.

Everything adds up to these two points:

A. My instinct to regard as an evil and an oversimplification the thought of "losing oneself" in total identification with (submersion in) *any group* as such—this instinct is good. To be a

man of the church I have to be fully myself and fully responsible
and free before God—not a "unit" or a mere "number."

B.   My vocation and task in this world is to keep alive all that is
    usefully individual and personal to me, to be a "contemplative" in
    the full sense and to share it with others, to remain as a witness of
    the nobility of the private person and his primacy over the group.

October 12, 1958. Sunday

Thursday afternoon Reverend Father gave me a letter from Pasternak
inside an envelope from New Directions—air mail, registered, but
unopened. I explained with vehemence to Reverend Father that Boris
Pasternak was a great and basically religious writer. I could see he did not
believe me—or if he did, a little, it was against his will to do so. The
letter was brief but very cordial and confirmed my intuition of the deep
and fundamental understanding that exists between us. This is the thing I
have been growing to see is most important: *Everything* hangs on the
possibility of such understanding, which forms our interior bond, and is
the only basis of true peace and true community. External, juridical,
doctrinal, etc., bonds can never achieve this. This bond exists between me
and countless people like Pasternak everywhere in the world (genuine
people like Pasternak are never "countless"), and my vocation is
intimately bound up with this bond and this understanding for the sake
of which also I have to be a solitary and not waste my spirit in pretenses
that do not come anywhere near the reality or have anything to do with it.

October 18, 1958. Feast of St. Luke

Two letters have arrived from Pasternak—my letter and "Prometheus"
got through to him and apparently quite easily. He commented on
"Prometheus," saying that he liked especially sections IV and VII—and
that the last had some "fine individual Christosophic touches." I was very
pleased. Will write to him again. He keeps insisting that his early work is
"worthless." His heart is evidently in *Dr. Zhivago*—to which he does not
refer by the full name. Only as "Dr. Zh" or "the book published by
Pantheon."

Talking to Frater Lawrence about it, I remarked on the strange and marvelous fact of this apparently easy and natural communication between a monk in a strictly guarded Trappist monastery and a suspect poet behind the Iron Curtain. I am in closer contact with Pasternak than I am with people in Louisville or Bardstown or even in my own monastery. I have more in common with him.

All this while our two countries, deeply hostile to one another, have nothing to communicate between themselves, but spend millions trying to communicate with the moon!!

This simple and human dialogue with Pasternak and a few others like him is to me worth thousands of sermons and radio speeches. It is to me the true Kingdom of God, which is still so clearly and evidently "in the midst of us."

November 25, 1958. Day of Recollection
My Zen is in the slow swinging tops of sixteen pine trees.

One long thin pole of a tree fifty feet high swings in a wider arc than all the others and swings even when they are still.

Hundreds of little elms springing up out of the dry ground under the pines.

My watch among oak leaves. My T-shirt on the barbed wire fence. The wind sings in the bare wood.

The meaninglessness of any life that is not lived in the face of death. This has struck me forcibly, reading a passage from a Zen Samurai writer and warrior of the 17th century quoted by D. T. Suzuki.

Our great dignity is tested by death—I mean our freedom. There is no ordinary death, but there is all the difference in the world between flying from it interiorly and facing it with a man's freedom—with a man's acceptance. When the "parting of the ways" comes—to set one's foot gladly on the way that leads out of this world. This is a great gift of ourselves, not to death but to life. For he who knows how to die not only lives longer in this life (as if it matters) but lives eternally because of his freedom.

Never has man's helplessness in the face of death been more pitiable than in this age when he can do everything except escape death. If he were unable to escape so many other things, man would face death better.

But our power has only strengthened our illusion that we can cling to life without taking away our unconscious fear of death. We are always holding death at arm's length, unconsciously trying to think ourselves out of its presence. This generates an intolerable tension that makes us all the more quickly its victims. It is he who does not fear death who is more ready not to escape it, and when the time comes he faces it well.

So he who faces death can be happy in this life and in the next, and he who does not face it has no happiness in either. This is a central and fundamental reality of life, whether one is or is not a "believer"—for this "facing" of death implies already a faith and an uprightness of heart and the presence of Christ, whether one thinks of it or not. (I do not refer to the desperateness of the tough guy, but only to the sincerity of an honest and sober and sensitive person, assuming responsibility for his whole life in gladness and freedom.)

December 11, 1958

On the feast of the Immaculate Conception, tired and dry in the long Mass (Frater Linus made Solemn Profession), I bore up by asking myself, "What am I here for?" and discarding all the conventional answers. The only satisfying answer is "for nothing." I am here *gratis*, without a special purpose, without a special plan. I am here because I am here and not somewhere else. I am not here because of some elaborate monastic ideal or because this is "the best" (which it probably is not)—but simply this is where "God has put me." I live here. I work around here. The people who live in New Haven or down the road don't have to have some special answer to the question "What am I here for?" I know I have answered this differently in print, and what I have said about it in print still stands. For myself the only intelligible answer is an existential one—I am here *gratis*, for no special purpose, with no strings attached, freely. I have no serious reason for wanting to be elsewhere, though I might *like* to be elsewhere at times.

The fact remains that elsewhere is not where I am or where I am likely to be. The point is not that this is a sublimely wonderful and special place. Not at all. To try to convince myself of this after 17 years would be madness and insincerity. The point is that it does not much matter where you are as long as you can be at peace about it and live your life. The place certainly will not live my life for me, I have found that out. I have to live it for myself.

Yesterday—selecting poems for a paperback collection to be issued by New Directions.

Saw that my best ones were the early ones. I cannot go back to that.

The fervor of those days was special and young. It can inspire me to seek a new and different fervor, which is older and deeper. This I must find. But I cannot go back to the earlier fervor or to the asceticism that accompanied it. The new fervor will be rooted, not in asceticism, but in humanism. What has begun now must grow but must never seek to become spectacular or to attract attention to itself—which is what I unconsciously did in those days, proclaiming that I was a poet and a mystic. Both are probably true but not deep enough, because then it was too conscious. I have to write and speak, not as the individual who has cut himself off from the world and wants the world to know it, but as the person who has lost himself in the service of the vast wisdom of God's plan to reveal Himself in the world and in man. How much greater, deeper, nobler, truer, and more hidden. A mysticism that no longer appears transcendent but ordinary.

December 13, 1958. St. Lucy

Going into town yesterday was a kind of "retreat" for my seventeenth anniversary in the monastery. The things I wrote about the other day, about being here for nothing, are impossible to think about without immense qualifications. Really I am here for everything. Being out "in the world" would really be nothing and an awful waste. The "waste" of one's life in a monastery is the fruitful thing; at least it is for me.

The overwhelming welter of meaningless objects, goods, activities— the indiscriminate chaotic nest of "things" good, bad, and indifferent that pour over you at every moment—books, magazines, food, drink, women, cigarettes, clothes, toys, cars, drugs. Add to this the anonymous, characterless, "decoration" of the town for Christmas and the people running around buying things for no reason except that now is a time when everybody buys things.

Walking up and down Bardstown outside Kroger's in the cold, saluted by man, woman, and child. I thought that never, never could I make sense of life outside the monastery. I am a solitary and that is that. I love people okay, but I belong in solitude.

It was good to get back and smell the sweet air of the woods and listen to the silence.

December 28, 1958. Feast of the Holy Innocents
Feeling better because I slept and got a full 7 hours of sleep for a change.

Yesterday afternoon I spent a long time, as I had been promising myself, over in the lovely field where the Linton house used to stand. Tremendous view of four horizons, the vast sweep of strange hills, the great open sky with gray clouds overhead and tunnels of light into the west beyond the fire tower.

Really there is no problem but the act of accepting the solitude I have desired, solitude of the heart—in community. The whole trouble is I do not want it with my whole being. Half of me demands deference and consideration—expects everyone around me, at least in the novitiate, to see and do things my way. How necessary is this? Not as necessary as I seem to assume.

The house is boiling hot. I sit comfortably outside in summer clothes with only a winter cowl. In the house the heat is on full blast and is unbearable. I cannot stand ten minutes in choir without sweating. This is utterly ridiculous: a greenhouse for penitents—for monks or for geraniums?

With this and a thousand other things I cannot help thinking that life here has become to a great extent meaningless. Not that I am such a terrible ascetic—certainly I am not. But I wonder more and more to what extent a genuine and deep spiritual life is going to be at all possible in such a community. No question, of course, that the individual can maintain one on his own, but in order to do so he is going to have to cut his own way through the thicket and not just follow the community. At least that is my case.

More and more I am quietly going to have to do the difficult thing that no one else is free to do either for me or with me—really live my own interior life and seek God according to my own vocation—without fighting or condemning other people and without worrying at the differences between us in outlook, ideals, etc. Everybody knows me now, and I think they are quite willing, to a great extent, to mind their business and let me mind mine, except in the one place where they like to meddle, which is the novitiate. There I can't expect to have everything there to myself.

If I ever have a chance to lead a really solitary life, I must have the sense and the gumption to jump at it. I was not ready for it in 1955 when I agitated for it so wildly. I am not ready for it now. I am not ready to run a community either and have no longer any desire to start one. I hope that when the time comes I may really be ready to go off alone. May Christ grant me this great favor.

Dreamt last night that Father Tarcisius, my undermaster, insisted on the novices going to Communion, each one with a cookie suspended around his neck on a string.

January 2, 1959

This morning I went to the funeral of Herman Hanekamp in New Haven. Started out in the frost after dawn. The body laid out in the funeral parlor was that of a millionaire, a great executive. I never before saw Herman shaven, in a suit, least of all in a collar and tie. He looked like one of the great of the earth. I was a pallbearer along with Andy Boone, Hanekamp's old friend Glen Price (a great stout man with a lined face like the side of an old building but very humble and gentle). Brothers Clement and Colman were pallbearers and another man with a shoelace necktie.

Reverend Father sang the Mass, vexed with me because I begged off being deacon when he asked me at the last moment (because at the last moment it became a big affair, and if I had known that I would not have gone).

When we came out of the church into the sun, carrying the coffin, the bright air seemed full of great joy, and a huge freight train came barreling through the valley with a sound of power like an army. All the pride of the world of industry seemed, somehow, to be something that belonged to Herman. What a curious obsession with the conviction of him as a great, rich man, tremendously respected by the whole world! We drove back to bury him in the graveyard outside the monastery gate.

The bare woods stood wise and strong in the sun as if they were proud of some great success that had been achieved in secret with their connivance and consent.

As we carried the coffin through the sunlit yard, I listened with exaltation: it was hailed by the singing of skylarks on the second day of January.

What has triumphed here is not admired by anyone, despised even by the monks who also could not help thinking of Herman as a lazy man and an escapist. He had not taken seriously the world of business so important to us all. And now behold—a captain of industry!

March 15, 1959. Passion Sunday

Last night another night of high winds. Listened also to the winds outside while we sat in Chapter this morning. The cross is a sign of liberation. To this hope I cling blindly. There is no hope of freedom in myself alone or in simple conformity to what is said and done here. Freedom means battle and faith and darkness and a new creation out of darkness.

Darkness battling in the March wind.

The sky before Prime in the West: livid, "blasted," fast-running dark clouds, pale spur of the fire tower against the black west.

March 18, 1959

The old and the new.

For the "old man" everything is old—he has seen everything or thinks he has. He has lost hope in anything new. What pleases him is the "old" he clings to, fearing to lose it, but certainly not happy with it. So he keeps himself "old" and cannot change. He is not open to any newness. His life is stagnant and futile. Yet there may be much movement—but change that leads to no change. *"Plus ça change, plus c'est la même chose."*

For the "new man" everything is new. Even the old is transfigured in the Holy Spirit and is always new. There is nothing to cling to. There is nothing to be hoped for in what is already past—it is nothing.

The new man is he who can find reality where it cannot be seen by the eyes of the flesh—where it is not yet—where it comes into being the moment he sees it. And where it would not be (at least for him) if he did not see it.

The new man lives in a world that is always being created and renewed. He lives in this realm of renewal and creation. He lives in life.

The old man lives without life. He lives in Death and clings to what has died precisely because he clings to it. Yet he is crazy for change, as if struggling with the bonds of death. His struggle is miserable and cannot be a substitute for life.

Thought of these things after Communion today when I suddenly realized that I had—and for how long—deeply lost hope of "anything new." How foolish when in fact the newness is there all the time.

It is a year since I first found out about Pasternak in a chance reading of *Encounter*, which I picked up in Louisville: the Gerd Ruge interview. (The first thing Pasternak taunted him with was being "so young and yet so decrepit.")

May 3, 1959. Day of Recollection

"The secret power of the Message is found in the liberty to speak of everything, regardless of the manner of speaking, but always in the service of the Unique, the Other. One must go beyond the sociological, place oneself beyond it to proclaim justice in the service of Holy Truth." Paul Evdokimov, "Message aux Eglises," in *Dieu Vivant* XV.

Which I am now reading 10 years late. The whole answer is there. Am I wise enough to apply it?

Lax and Reinhardt were down last weekend, Bob Giroux yesterday. In between I went to Lebanon to get a rotten tooth pulled on a beautiful spring day (Thursday—April 30). Today—had to give the Conference Chapter—on the Will of God—Joseph, etc. It is like summer—or rather, it is summer though the trees are not fully out yet.

The thing is, when people come to see me, they are not really edified. I have to face this fact—it is disturbing. It is that I am not really a monk and a Christian. It is all very well to cast off invalid exterior forms. But is there anything on the inside? I think perhaps not.

Really need prayer in sorrow of heart.

And more humble thought of how to go about saying and doing what I say and do. I try to act as if I were wise, and I do not have the fear of God, without which there is no beginning of wisdom. I pray for mercy, but coldly. What will become of me? Mother of Mercy and of Wisdom, take pity on me, a sinner.

May 12, 1959

How far I have been from the Truth every day, wasting my time seeking something in vain. What I seek is simply being, and here it is. Here is the straw, here is the rain, here is the silence.

Oppressed with words, with the falsity and needlessness of most of the things I say to others. What do I expect to find in my words to them? What do I resent not finding? I have nothing to say. How happy I would be to admit it in practice. But I believe that all men, at all times, expect one to say something. What a fool I have made of myself by believing myself wise. And now I dare not be silent, though I have nothing to say.

May 28, 1959. Corpus Christi

A quiet morning reading in the woodshed (for the first time in seventeen years had nothing to do with the decorations). A clear, cool morning—got hot later. Reading Berdyayev's *Destiny of Man*, which is, I think, his best book.

In the clear sky two shiny kingfishers chased each other in a wide arc over the mill bottom.

What has become of my official request to leave Gethsemani and join Dom Gregorio at his monastery in Cuernavaca, Mexico?

Getting impatient to hear something from Dom Gregorio and the bishop. Tempted to think the letter has been stopped, though it is coming marked "conscience matter." And yet—indifferent about it.

How unprepared I am to start a new life. Yet that does not matter.

More prayer is necessary—uncomfortable prayer too, not just sitting under a tree.

How I hesitate to believe it can ever come about. Does that mean I am not really interested?

I am worried about the effects of my leaving.

It will be interpreted as simply giving up and "returning to the world." As a renunciation of my vocation. In a way it is a renunciation of the monastery because I am no longer satisfied with this kind of life. If that is the case, I must be willing to leave it so interpreted, though that is not my intention or my desire. However—am I really so dissatisfied? The question is almost impossible to answer. I am often convinced that I have "nothing in common" with Dom James and with the ideals of the Order at present. To what extent is this an evasion? There is certainly nothing wrong with these afternoons in the woods (but what have they to do with the ideals of the Order?).

The truth is that something inexplicable draws me away from here, something indefinable makes me uneasy here (I do not say unhappy)— always the old story of "something missing." What? Is it something essential?

Won't there always be "something missing"?

Yet always that urge to "go forth," to leave, to take off for a strange land and start another life. Perhaps this is inevitable, just a desire one is supposed to have without fulfilling it.

It was that kind of desire that brought me here.

Perhaps what I really want is to get away from ideals and a mental image of monasticism and simply live as best I can, just live.

June 14, 1959. IV Sunday After Pentecost
A beautiful, cool clear morning.

I am writing this after my Mass. It seems to me that during Mass and thanksgiving one of the big ambiguities has resolved itself out.

The fact is that I do not want purely and simply to "be a hermit" or to lead a life purely and ideally contemplative. At the same time, I want to break with all the fictions and pretenses, all the facade and latent hypocrisy of the monastic community in which I live.

Yet I truly seek a very solitary, simple, and primitive life with no special labels attached.

There must be love in it, however—not an abstract love—a real love for real people.

The conclusion, then, is that God is calling me to a kind of missionary solitude—an isolated life in some distant, primitive place among primitive and simple people to whose spiritual needs I would attend. *Not* a missionary life pure and simple, or a solitary life pure and simple, but a combination of both.

No nonsense about asking permission to live as a hermit here, raising all the futile questions and pretenses this would involve. It would get me into a whole network of lies for the sake of one grain of truth.

No nonsense about presenting the thing as a "desire for pure solitude" or for a more pure fiction than the fiction we already cherish in common. (I mean in this monastery. I am not condemning the monastic life, far from it. Perhaps I shall end up with a quasi-monastic community around me. But no set forms!)

June 16, 1959. Feast of St. Lutgarde

The great problem in this crisis of mine is to keep from going from one fiction to another: from the communal fiction, which we cherish as a group, to the private fiction, which I cherish as an individual. The more I let myself dwell with desire upon a "solution," the more I become involved in a new fiction of my own. I can tell immediately by the immense weariness that comes from entertaining falsity.

The truth is that almost everything I do to "solve" the problem becomes a kind of symbolic act that replaces something else, more real and more concrete, that I do not see how to do.

Hence the ritual of writing letters to bishops and Vicars Apostolic (such letters are already too many).

It is impossible to say what I ought to do. The situation is so vague and everything is uncertain. Is there any hope of obtaining an indult from Rome in the first place? It would be disastrous to stir up a great official fuss and then have nothing come of it.

More and more I realize that what I am really seeking is a spiritual and mystical action—which may need an exterior act, a geographic change, to make it really complete. But there is no hope that a legal act can solve a spiritual problem. It can only clear the way perhaps.

The more thought, the more silence, the more patience go into this, the better.

June 21, 1959

Summer solstice. This vocation business is making me miserable. Lay awake last night thinking about it. I try to keep off the futile and silly plane in which the advantages and disadvantages of each project go through my mind. In the end the whole thing becomes utterly absurd.

The one project to which I pay least attention is the original one proposed by Dom Gregorio—to go to Cuernavaca and "then see."

Perhaps what is upsetting me is the fear of uncertainty. If the whole business is really serious, that is, if my desire to leave here were serious, the uncertainty wouldn't matter. But the fact is—I must face it—I have no really strong and positive motives for launching out into something completely new. I am just not sufficiently interested in "starting something." More and more I see the futility, the absurdity, of simply becoming a "parish priest" in some isolated place. (That, of course, is not Dom Gregorio's idea, but the idea that struck me later.)

And I don't especially want to live in Mexico, as a hermit or otherwise.

Wherever I go as a "hermit," I will be at the mercy of everyone who writes, of course, and bothers me. Paradoxically, here I can arrange my time.

The question arises—would it be saner and truer simply to be "bothered" by people with real problems than to go through a lot of community routines that take up your whole day in a monastery?

If I am asked the question—what do I really want to do? It boils down to what I have done for the best afternoons of last week. The long hours of quiet in the woods, reading a little, meditating a lot, walking up and down in the pine needles in bare feet. If what I am looking for is more of that—why not just ask for "more of that"? It is the easiest solution, the request most likely to be granted and the one that involves no problem for me or my superiors or for the Order—no glory and no fuss either.

On the other hand, is that honest, and is it an interior life?

Or is it simply an escape from the routine of the community—the way a worker escapes from the factory on a weekend and goes swimming at Coney Island?

By accepting the escape am I conceding, surrendering to, the routine? It is a serious question. More serious still is the question whether I have by now been so destroyed by the routine that I can no longer do anything but accept it, although with suitable evasions?

June 28, 1959

Opened a new translation of Meister Eckhart and immediately hit upon this:

"Obedience has no cares, it lacks no blessings. Being obedient, if a man purifies himself, God will come to him in course. For where he has no will of his own, then God will command for him what God would command for Himself. When I do not choose for myself, God chooses for me."

I am sure that it has been a temptation all along to think that by staying here, where I like to pray in the woods, I would be cuddling in self-love. Yes, I like it. But the important thing = it is what God has chosen for me. Hence I cannot really start off to go anywhere else unless it is clear that God wants it for me. So far, no such thing is clear.

"A pure heart is one that is unencumbered, unworried, uncommitted, which does not want its own way about anything but which rather is submerged in the loving will of God, having denied self."

I cannot be loyal to that which is deepest and most genuine in my life if I am not first loyal to this principle.

August 18, 1959

What do I need?

Hard question to answer. This morning I need nothing. Perhaps what I have now is what I need at other times: leisure—time to think—time to look at the hills, at the horses in the distant pasture and at their beautiful brown color—to call it golden would be to insult it.

I need something beyond my capacity to know. If I call it solitude, I mistake it. Silence, a primitive life.

What I need—as far as I can interpret the desire in my heart—is to make a journey to a primitive place among primitive people and there die. It is at the same time a going out and a "return." A going to somewhere where I have never been or thought of going—a going in which I am led by God, a journey in which I go out of everything I now have. I feel that unless I do this my spiritual life is at an end.

September 22, 1959

The one thing necessary is a true interior and spiritual life, true growth, on my own, in depth, in a new direction. Whatever new direction God opens up for me. My job is to press forward, to grow interiorly, to pray, to break away from attachments and to defy fears, to grow in faith, which has its own solitude, to seek an entirely new perspective and new dimension in my life. To open up new horizons at *any* cost, to desire this and let the Holy Spirit take care of the rest. But really to desire this and *work* for it.

November 19, 1959

I have a koan to work on: "Who is this that wants to go to Mexico?"

I wonder what is going on in Rome?

Get clear about motives—or rather, write them down:

1. I really want to live alone in simplicity and devote myself to thought and prayer.

2. No *typewriter.*

3. Strictly selected books—about 100. Especially hope to work on *Philokalia.*

4. Renounce all *comfort,* the *reputation,* the *security,* the American friendships, which bind me here and make me part of the collective falsity and injustice of this society. Renounce this kind of cenobitism.

November 23, 1959

After dinner, looked out at the hills and woods and realized with a shock that perhaps within two weeks I will have seen them for the last time in my life.

This thing is like death, but it must be so.

It hardly seems possible—never seeing the woods again. Other woods will not be the same. The strangeness, the exile, the essential. I must be quite determined about that and not let myself be held prisoner emotionally by the soft embrace of this "mother"—this silent, gentle, circle of hills that has comforted me for eighteen years and whose secrets I have come to know perhaps better than anyone here (so many of the monks hardly know there is a forest around the abbey).

That is the one thing that will really hurt. Making up my mind, adjusting my mind to this, requires real determination, in the psalms especially. But it is a necessary "death," a detachment from one of the few things I really love deeply and purely.

Realized too how much I have in many ways failed here, failed in love. I have been weak in love and have broken with the community gradually because I did not have the strength to love it with all its faults and with all my faults—all my faults, which necessarily come out in this cramped and unnatural situation.

Yet I would prefer to die this way before dying in truth.

I would hate to die in this monastery. It would be a complete surrender to mediocrity. But of course it doesn't matter where you die, actually. Yet I do love the community, inarticulately, after all. It is better for them also that I leave here.

December 2, 1959

Though I am impatient at waiting, still I know that I need to wait. Every day that I wait is a better beginning of a preparation. Though there are many things that distract me from one thing that is important.

Yesterday was the anniversary of the death of Charles de Foucauld— my Mass partly for his canonization—partly for my Mexican intention—partly for the novices.

Today—visit with the Wassermans and their friends. Could hardly talk. Yet talking too is a preparation—I will have to meet new people, temporarily, before settling down in solitude.

The big reasons for solitude: the true perspectives—leaving the "world"—even the monastic world with its business, vanities, superficiality. More and more I see the necessity of leaving my own ridiculous "career" as a religious journalist. Stop writing for publication—except poems and creative meditations.

Solitude—witness to Christ—emptiness.

December 10, 1959

I have finally gotten around to reading Josef Pieper's fine little book *Leisure, the Basis of Culture.* It is very sound, and no amount of guilt should make us treat his view of contemplation as "pagan," as if that were to exclude "Christian." One thing is sure—we do not in this monastery have any faith in the basic value of *otium sanctum*—of "holy leisure." We believe only in the difficult and the unpleasant. That is why we, in practice, *hate* the contemplative life and destroy it with constant activity.

They have speeded up the machines in the cheese building. Everyone is agog with the orders. "I saw one going out to *Mrs. Irving Berlin!*" said one awestruck novice. We have finally justified our existence.

December 17, 1959

Yesterday, when I was least expecting it, a letter arrived from Rome.

It was a large envelope—had come by surface mail. Too large an envelope. I took it back to the novitiate and read it on my knees before the Blessed Sacrament. It said "No."

It was a long, personal, detailed letter, in fact a very fine letter, signed by the Cardinal Prefect and countersigned by Cardinal Larraona. Two cardinals. What could be more definite and more official—what could be more final?

They were very sorry. They wanted the right words to pour balm in certain wounds. But my departure would certainly upset too many people in the Order as well as outside it. They agreed with my superiors that I did not have an eremitical vocation. Therefore what they asked of me was to stay in the monastery where God had put me, and I would find interior solitude.

It was a serious letter, to be taken seriously.

I felt no anger or resistance. The letter was too obvious. It could only be accepted. My first reaction was one of relief that at last the problem had been settled.

Had to give a conference to the novices, which turned out to be a bit dizzy.

Afterward had to call Victor Hammer, who is coming over on Saturday, and he said he had heard in a roundabout way from Cuernavaca that the indult had been *granted.* But I knew this was impossible.

The letter from Rome was dated Dec. 7th.

The thing that strikes me is that the problem is settled. It is settled in some wider and deeper way than just by negation. It is not just that I must stay here.

Sat alone outside after dinner. Very quiet.

Actually it *is* a solution, and I don't yet know how much of a solution.

A kind of anesthesia. Certainly surprised myself by not getting at all upset and by not feeling the slightest disappointment. Rather felt only joy and emptiness and liberty. Funny.

Went out alone, in light rain, to get Christmas trees for the nuns.

Who cares about anything? Here or there.

The letter is obviously an indication of God's Will, and I accept it fully. So then what? Nothing. Trees, hills, rain. Prayer much lighter, much freer, more unconcerned. A mountain lifted off my shoulders—a Mexican mountain I myself had chosen.

Actually, what it comes down to is that I shall certainly have solitude but only by a miracle and not at all by my own contriving. Where? Here or there makes no difference. Somewhere, nowhere, beyond all "where." Solitude outside geography or in it. No matter.

Coming back, walked around a corner of the woods and the monastery swung in view. I was free from it. I remembered the anguish and resentment with which I saw that same view in March '47, before my Solemn Profession.

I will, of course, answer the letter and may take the opportunity to explain that my idea was not simply to "be a hermit." It will make no difference.

I woke up at 12, just when I was about to drink a milkshake in a dream. Could not get back to sleep, so went down at 1 for an hour of prayer in very silent darkness. Empty, silent, free, opening into nothing— a little point of nothing that alone is real. What do you ask? Nothing. What do you want? Nothing. Very quiet and dark. The Father. The Father.

Nothing. Nothing. Nothing. Nothing. The place where the tooth was pulled is only just beginning to hurt this morning.

December 20, 1959. IV Sunday Advent

Lax's Circus book is a tremendous poem, an Isaias-like prophecy that has a quality you just don't find in poetry today, a completely unique simplicity and purity of love that is not afraid to express itself. The circus as symbol and sacrament, cosmos and church—the mystery of the primitive world, of paradise in which men have wonderful and happy skills, which they exercise freely as at play. Also a sacrament of the *eschaton*, our heavenly Jerusalem. The importance of human love in the circus— for doing things well. It is one of the few poems that has anything whatever to say. I want to write an article about it.

Victor and Carolyn Hammer came over yesterday. We ate sandwiches in the jeep, in a sunny field near the shallow lake, drank coffee, ate apples and ginger. I lost a filling from a tooth. He came back to see the chapel—I have hopes that he will make a tabernacle for us and candlesticks. He looked at the chapel without inspiration and said, "This is an awful place." A prophetic utterance, quite unlike the words of Jacob used as Introit for the Feast of the Dedication. But he offered to lend us one of his painted crucifixes—one of those he did for Kolbsheim.

He gave me one of his little Japanese knives. I cleaned up the room in its honor.

Went out alone to get three large trees and a small one in the wasteland along by Andy Boone's. In the evening—two postulants to interview.

A sunny, happy day, yesterday.

December 26, 1959. St. Stephen's Day
I had been fearing that this Christmas would be a terrible one like the last one, but it has been quiet and neutral. Interiorly I have been aloof and resigned in all the community nonsense but also more united with the brethren on a simple human level *without* nonsense. In other words, the pretense kills me. When I can avoid the official myths and pretenses, everything is relatively sane.

On the 22nd—the only sunny day for a long time—I went to Lexington to get Victor's crucifix and came back with two of them.

Coming back, suddenly decided to go to Shakertown.

The approach from the west, through the big sycamores in the bottom, past a long stone fence to the old community house on "Pleasant Hill."

Only the guest house was open, and at first I found no one there. The marvelous double winding stair going up to the mysterious clarity of a dome on the roof. The empty third floor rooms with names scribbled all over the walls—the usual desecration—quiet sunlight filtering in—a big Lebanon cedar outside one of the windows. Mr. Renfrew came and we spoke—he lamented the lack of water. No one could come because there was no plumbing. "Who cares?" I said. "Everybody does," he said.

All the other houses are locked up.

There is Shaker furniture only in the center family house. I tried to get in it, and a gloomy old man living in the back told me curtly "it was locked up." He was putting water in a bucket from a pump in the yard. No plumbing, you see!

Mr. R. dug out an untidy, rolltop desk copy of the *Sacred Roll*, the Shaker bible, full of inspirations, which I borrowed and brought home but have only glanced at.

The empty fields, the big trees—how I would love to explore those houses and listen to that silence. In spite of the general decay and despair, there is joy and simplicity there still.

The Shakers fascinate me. Mother Ann Lee thought she was Sophia. The role of the sexes in their mysticism. The pure, entranced, immaculate dancing, shaking the sex out of their hands. The whirling. God, at least they had the sense to *dance!* I want to study them.

When I got home at night and went to bed, I thought I would have prophetic dreams. Dreamt only of a colored boy who had come from very far away to be my friend. Whatever else I dreamed I have forgotten.

December 29, 1959. Feast of the Holy Innocents
Read some of Peguy's "Mystery of the Holy Innocents" to the novices last evening. And, alone in the woodshed on St. Stephen's day, some Emily Dickinson, my own flesh and blood, my own kind of quiet rebel, fighting for truth against catchwords and formalities, fighting for independence of the spirit, maybe mistakenly, what the hell, maybe rightly too. Who else in Amherst in 1859 said anything worth being remembered? Said anything that remains living and natural now?

The very great thing Emily D. has done: she has hidden and refused herself completely to everyone who would not appreciate her and accept her on her own terms. Yet who "knew" and "saw" her. But she gave herself completely to people of other ages and places who never saw her but who could receive her gift anyway, regardless of space and time. It is like hugging an angel.

December 31, 1959

The last night of the year: a *Miserere*, a prayer for mercy, and a *Te Deum*, a prayer of thanksgiving.

I do not look back on the year. I do not look forward to the next one. I do not bother to step over an imaginary threshold.

Got permission today for a few sessions with Dr. James Wygal in Louisville, since I am sure Reverend Father's argument before the Congregation was based on a couple of wild remarks by Gregory Zilboorg that I was likely to take off with a woman and leave the Church, etc. It would do no harm to find out if I am just suffering from neurotic instability or what. I do not think I am.

January 31, 1960

I never thought to have had such a thing as a forty-fifth birthday. Yet here it is. Why was I always half convinced I would die young? Perhaps a kind of superstition—the fear of admitting a hope of life, which, if admitted, might have to be dashed. But now "I have lived" a fair span of life, and whether or not the fact be important, nothing can alter it. It is certain, infallible—even though that too is only a kind of dream. If I don't make it to sixty-five, it matters less. I can relax. Life is a gift I am glad of: I do not curse the day when I was born. On the contrary, if I had never been born I would never have had friends to love and be loved by, would never have made mistakes to learn from, would never have seen new countries. As for what I may have suffered, it is inconsequential and indeed part of the great good that life has been and will, I hope, continue to be. After all, as I suddenly realize, 45 is still young.

February 2, 1960. Feast of the Purification

At last we have a little sun warm enough to sit in the woods. Which I do.
It is not difficult to be content under this pine tree.

But I have not tried hard enough to be content in community. In fact, I have almost refused to let myself be content, as if there were danger in it—something to lose by it. As if by being content I would give in, lose my freedom, be trapped. But actually there is all the difference in the world between contentment and acquiescence. Contentment is an interior thing that goes with freedom. Freedom depends on it, and he who cannot be content in adversity cannot be free. Contentment has nothing to do either with defeat or compromise; it is the condition for victory. For when I am content I recognize that *I need no other conditions* and no other situation in order to be free and happy. This is, in one sense, to transcend the whole business!

Freedom, relaxation, and a sense of peace from active meditation—merely as an *exercise*—in the woods. We live without sufficient use of the intelligence or without right use of it. Forced, compulsive thought, which is not thought but verbalizing in the interests of conformity.

"I must be about My Father's business." The constant desire of interiority, meditation, the desire of liberation and purity, emptiness, is something I must always be following—not trying to see where it leads. If I follow, it will lead me where I cannot foresee the fulfillment that is waiting. Loyalty to this one call. All the rest is absurd.

February 3, 1960

One thing is sure: I have got to give up my secret justification of my own indolence and laziness, as if these could be a spirituality. My life is full of silly vanity. I hope I can begin to be honest about it and someday come to a certain degree of real intellectual and spiritual honesty, instead of a facile pose of honesty, which is useless, even for convincing myself.

First of all, forget myself, just not pay attention to my own feelings and desires all the time.

Then recognize the superficial thinking, the personal clichés, which enable me to indulge my vanity without having to admit it. One of these is the instinct—a pseudo-prophetic one—to condemn the whole world and preach the coming of the Last Judgment at every turn.

Eschatology is certainly a vitally important part of Christian revelation but is one that tends to be a pose and a vice if I am not very careful. On the contrary, what I need is the study, patience, effort, and self-effacement that will make me what I truly need to be, a genuine Christian humanist—and this is necessary for true contemplation as opposed to illuminism and quietism. I see it more and more.

I have to begin reading John Henry Newman, whom without cause I have neglected as though he were Chesterton. There is all the difference in the world. At the moment I am much more akin to the vanity and absurdity of Chesterton than I am to the solidity and brilliance of Newman. *Brilliance* is a bad word—for me to desire that is always fatal!

March 8, 1960

Yesterday I got a charming letter from a Shaker Eldress in New Hampshire in answer to an inquiry I wrote her. A touching little leaflet about how the Shakers now quietly face extinction, convinced they had not been a failure. I am convinced of it too. I think Shakerism is something of a sign—a mystery—a strange misguided attempt at utter honesty that wanted to be too pure—but ended up by being nevertheless pure and good, though in many ways absurd. This loyalty, absolute loyalty to a vision leading nowhere. But do such visions really lead nowhere? What they did they did, and it was impressive. It haunts me at times: the atmosphere and spirit, the image they created, the archetype.

March 18, 1960

Cold day with sun. The snow melts slowly.

A jet plane swooped low over the monastery with an interesting roar and then started climbing beautifully into the north, at great speed, with a flight I could not help but love and admire. In a few seconds it was high enough for the exhaust to come out white in a long trail.

Reading Al-Hallaj in Louis Massignon's translation—about which I wrote him a letter today. Hallaj is right: our piety is so safe as to be impious.

What a difference between the Greeks and this Moslem. I mean the classical Greeks. But in Aeschylus there's the same kind of fire none the less!

Perhaps I have been struggling with an illusory idea of freedom—as if I were not to a great extent bound up by my own history, the history of this community, of the country where I have become a citizen, etc. There are only certain very limited and special avenues of freedom open to me now, and it is useless to fight my way along where no issue is possible. This is true not only exteriorly but even interiorly and spiritually. To say that God can open up new ways is perhaps among other things to admit only that He has provided ways for me, of which I cannot yet be aware, since I am too intent upon imaginary and experimental ones.

March 25, 1960. Feast of the Annunciation

How little I really think. Since I write a lot I imagine I think a lot, but that is not true. Perhaps I do try to experience things rather than think them. Not enough.

Perhaps if I see less, I may learn to think and pray more.

One thing Christ has said: "He who sees me also sees the Father."

In emptying Himself to come into the world, God has not simply kept His reality in reserve, in a safe place, manifested only a kind of shadow or symbol of Himself. He has emptied Himself and is *all* in Christ. Christ is not simply the tip of the little finger of the Godhead, moving in the world, easily withdrawn, never threatened, never really risking anything. God has acted and given Himself totally, without division, in the Incarnation. He has become not only one of us but even our very selves.

May 8, 1960. III Sunday After Easter

Happy Sunday morning in the cell, which does all that tradition says it does! How eloquent are these four walls and the landscapes of hills and woods and crazy barns outside my window! I am high up as a stylite, the window goes down to the floor, my head almost touches the low ceiling. Birds fly past below me. I sit on the edge of the sky. The sunlight drenches my feet. I have a stool here, an old one, and a desk (my old scriptorium desk) by the bed, three icons and a small crucifix which Ernesto Cardenal made. Reading in here is a totally different experience from anywhere else, as if the silence and the four walls enriched everything with great significance. One is alone, not on guard, utterly relaxed and receptive; having four walls and silence all around enables you to listen, so to speak, with the pores of your skin and to absorb truth through every part of your being—I doubt if I would be any better off in Mexico!

Making plans for the retreat house up behind the sheep barn. Brother Clement is friendly to it and working to have it built, is even willing to pay good money to have it built rather than let the boys from Bellarmine College build it.

May 14, 1960. Saturday

After a week without sun, two brilliant May mornings. After Chapter I went out and sat on the trunk of one of the pines we felled in the last few days on the site for the Mount Olivet hermitage. Trying to think of the best kind of plan for it. A plan acceptable to Brother Clement and yet something more than a shack since it is for retreats. A kind of half cloister, facing the hills, catching the view and shade. And a chapel, an airy sanctuary. I think of a small tower as a kind of cage, so that there can be much air and yet shade and indirect light.

I hate to cut down the fifty- and sixty-foot pines, slim as grass, waving in the sky.

PART IV

The Pivotal Years

1960–1963

We do not see the way that lies ahead of us. It seems dark, but God is the Master of all destinies and His will is love. Let us then put aside everything else and trust ourselves completely to Him, giving ourselves to His love, asking Him to enlighten and guide us in the way of positive action, if any such action is feasible. For the rest, we must have great patience and sustained fidelity to His will and to our ideals.

Letter to Evora Arca de Sardinia,
Witness to Freedom

Father, I beg you to keep me in this silence so that I may learn from it the word of your peace, the word of your mercy, the word of your gentleness to the world, so that perhaps through me your word of peace may make itself heard where it has not been possible for anyone to hear it for a long time.

To study truth and learn to suffer for truth.

The Light itself and the contentment of the Spirit: these are enough. Amen.

Conjectures of a Guilty Bystander

June 5, 1960. Pentecost

With sore eyes, said Office privately in the novitiate, thus had about two hours for meditation. This is the first Pentecost here I have fully appreciated. The Office too was more illuminating. These quiet hours before and after dawn!

The other day (Thursday)—the *full meaning* of Lauds said against the background of waking birds and sunrise.

At 2:30—no sounds except sometimes a bullfrog. Some mornings, he says *Om*—some days he is silent. The sounds are not every day the same. The whippoorwill who begins his mysterious whoop about 3 o'clock is not always near. Sometimes, like today, he is very far away in Linton's woods or beyond. Sometimes he is close, on Mount Olivet. Yesterday there were two, but both in the distance.

The first chirps of the waking birds—"*le point vierge*" of the dawn, a moment of awe and inexpressible innocence, when the Father in silence opens their eyes and they speak to Him, wondering if it is time to "be"? He tells them, "Yes." Then they one by one wake and begin to sing. First the catbirds and cardinals and some others I do not recognize. Later, song sparrows, wrens, etc. Last of all doves, crows.

With my hair almost on end and the eyes of my soul wide open I am present, without knowing it at all, in this unspeakable Paradise and I behold this secret, this wide open secret which is there for everyone, free, and no one pays any attention ("One to his farm, another to his merchandise"). Not even monks shut up under fluorescent lights, face to face with the big books and the black notes and with one another, perhaps no longer seeing or hearing anything in the course of festive Lauds.

Oh, paradise of simplicity, self-awareness—and self-forgetfulness— liberty, peace. In this I have realized how silly and unreal are my rebellions, yet how unavoidable is the pressure and artificiality of certain situations that "have to be" because they are officially sacrosanct. Yet there is no need to rebel, only to ask *mercy*. To trust in mercy, which is what I have not done.

June 6, 1960. Whitsunday

To discover *all* the social implications of the Gospel, not by studying them, but by living them, and to unite myself explicitly with those who foresee and work for a social order—a transformation of the world—according to these principles: primacy of the *person* (hence justice, liberty, against slavery, peace, control of technology, etc.). Primacy of *wisdom and love* (hence against materialism, hedonism, pragmatism, etc.).

July 2, 1960. Feast of the Visitation. St. Anthony's Hospital

At 5:30, as I was dreaming in a very quiet hospital, the soft voice of the nurse awoke me gently from my dream—it was like awakening for the first time from all the dreams of my life—as if the Blessed Virgin herself, as if Wisdom had awakened me. We do not hear the soft voice, the gentle voice, the feminine voice, the voice of the Mother: yet she speaks everywhere and in everything. Wisdom cries out in the marketplace—"if anyone is little let him come to me." Who is more little than the helpless man, asleep in bed, having entrusted himself gladly to sleep and to night? Him the gentle voice will awaken, all that is sweet in woman will awaken him. Not for conquest and pleasure, but for the far deeper wisdom of love and joy and communion.

My heart is broken for all my sins and the sins of the whole world, for the rottenness of our spirit of gain that defiles wisdom in all beings—to rob and deflower wisdom as if there were only a little pleasure to be had, only a little joy, and it had to be stolen, violently taken and spoiled. When all the while the sweetness of the "Woman," her warmth, her exuberant silence, her acceptance, are infinite, infinite! Deep is the ocean, boundless sweetness, kindness, humility, silence of wisdom that is *not* abstract, disconnected, fleshless. Awakening us gently when we have exhausted ourselves to night and to sleep. O Dawn of wisdom!

July 4, 1960

Perhaps there is no good reason to disentangle the threads of thought that have been tied up together in these four or five days at St. Anthony's Hospital. What would have been very simple has been complicated by friends and my own reactions. The people who want to take you out—

when you shouldn't go and don't want to. I have been definitely at fault in yielding to them, and it has made me miserable. Of course, no one is to blame but myself. I suppose I have a way of implicitly encouraging that kind of invitation and not seeing it until I can no longer gracefully say "No"—or think I do not want to say "No."

What business have I to be sitting around in Jim Wygal's house in Anchorage, listening to records, trying to talk about something? I don't belong in that anymore, still less in the place where I went with Father John Loftus and his friend the other night to hear some jazz. At least I have found out by experience that this just does not go. I am dead to it. It is finished long ago. You don't drag a corpse down to 4th Street and set it up in a chair, at a table, in polite society.

This just made the reading of Chuang Tzu all the better and more meaningful. Here I am not dead because this is my life. I am awake and breathing and listening with all I have got and sinking to the root. There is no question that I am completely committed to interior solitude. Where makes no difference. Not a question of "where." Not "tampering with my heart" or with the hearts of others. This is imperative. "The mind is a menace to wisdom." To be one who "though walking on dry land is as though he were at the bottom of a pool."

The trouble is this being a "writer," and one of the most absurd things I have got into is this business of dialogues and retreats. This has to be faced. I can't completely back out now, but certainly no more pushing.

If the days here have taught me this, they are good enough.

August 16, 1960
Was in Louisville today and had dinner at the Little Sisters of the Poor.

The moral beauty of the place, the authentic beauty of Christianity, which has no equal. The beauty of the Church is the charity of her daughters.

The Good Mother, whom I shall never forget: her transparency, unearthliness, simplicity, of no age, a child, a mother, like the Blessed Virgin—as if no name could apply to her, that is, no name known to anyone but God. Yet more real than all the unreal people in the rest of the world.

The old people. The old man playing the piano and the old man dancing—or rather turning about stamping the floor with one foot, unaware that he was no longer able to move the muscles that would make for tap dancing. And the old man at the piano after all playing something far more alive than rock 'n' roll (though all askew).

The old Negro people: the sweet, dignified Negro lady who had worked for Father Greenwell; the old, beat, heavy Negro lady with wisps of white beard sunk in her dream, her blankness, slowly coming out of it when spoken to. The lady who had both legs cut off. The little girl lady who made the speech in the dining room; the old lady with the visor cap on. And the golden wedding couple.

The sisters, above all, and the little girls in blue and white uniforms, the "auxiliaries" and their song about playing the piano, the viola, and the triangle. The dark eyes of the girl going Thursday to be a postulant in Baltimore. Sweet, good people.

Now I have the prayers of the poor, the strong, merciful, invincible prayers of the poor behind me, and in me, changing my whole life and my whole outlook on life.

I have no regrets at this visit having been thought significant by them. No one can even say how significant for me.

September 8, 1960. *Nativity of Blessed Virgin*

Importance of being able to rethink thoughts that were fundamental to men of other ages, or *are* fundamental to men in other countries. For me, especially—contemporary Latin America—Greek Patristic period—Mt. Athos—Confucian China—T'ang dynasty—Pre-Socratic Greece. Despair of ever beginning truly to know and understand, to communicate with these pasts and these distances, yet sense of obligation to do so, to live them and combine them in myself, to absorb, to digest, to "remember." *Memoria.* Have not yet begun. How will I ever begin to appreciate their problems, reformulate the questions they tried to answer? Is it even necessary? Is it sane? For me it is an expression of love for man and for God. An expression without which my contemplative life would be senseless.

To share this with my own contemporaries.

September 17, 1960

Karl Barth had a dream about Mozart. (Mozart was a Catholic, and Barth is piqued by the fact that M. did not like Protestantism, for he said it was "all in the head" and that they didn't know the meaning of *Agnus Dei qui tollis peccata mundi*. Well, Barth dreamt he had to "examine" Mozart in Dogma. He wanted to make it as favorable as possible, and in his questions he alluded pointedly to Mozart's "Masses." But Mozart did not answer a word.

I am tempted to write Barth a letter about this moving dream, which of course concerns his own salvation. He says that for years he has played Mozart every morning before going to work on dogma himself. (Just think! Dogma is his daily work!!)

The Mozart in himself is perhaps in some way the better, hidden, sophianic fact that grasps the "center" of cosmic music and is saved by love (yes, Eros!). The other, the theologian, is seemingly more occupied with love, but it is a stern, actually more cerebral, agape. A love that is *not in us,* only in God.

I remember my own dream about "Protestants." (They are perhaps my *aggressive* side.)

Barth seeks perhaps to be saved by the Mozart in him.

September 25, 1960. Sunday

Reading Lorca again—what a marvelous poet, so alive, so much strength and vividness and sound. I can think of no modern poet that gives me more genuine poetic satisfaction. Wholeness. Primitive and modern. Beauty. Toughness. Music. Substance. Variety. Originality. Character. Color. Andalusian weather.

September 30, 1960

Is it a temptation for me to want to form judgments and enumerate them, judgments about the situation of man today? Sometimes I imagine that this is pride and megalomania—as if I were an authority. Who am I? The point is that I have acquired the power to be heard. There is every evidence that I should use it discreetly and modestly, when it seems that I have something to say. The humble and prudent solution is, then, to accept the responsibilities this entails, to mistrust my own observation and limitations but to study and think and, when opportune or fitting, to speak. There is no megalomania in this if I don't delude myself that I am a prophet or a doctor of the Church. This delusion, objectively speaking, should not be too hard to avoid, since it cannot have any visible or factual basis. Who am I? A priest and a writer, one who has the gift of speaking intelligently, I hope. Hence I must also think clearly and pray and meditate and, when circumstances require it, speak. Speak to as many as will listen to me about things concerning their happiness and their destiny—along with my own. In a word, about their salvation.

October 10, 1960

After the Night Office. The superb moral and positive beauty of the *Phaedo.* One does not have to *agree* with Plato, but one must hear him. Not to listen to such a voice is unpardonable, it is like not listening to conscience or to nature. I repent: I love this great poem, this "music." It is a purifying music of which I have great need.

And Gandhi—how I need to understand and practice nonviolence in every way. It is because my life is not firmly based on the truth that I am morally in confusion and in captivity under the half truths and prejudices that rule others and rule me through them.

October 16, 1960

The hermitage grows, but I find that anxiety grows with it because Reverend Father keeps intimating that it is something he does not want me to have or even use except in a very restricted way. I mean, he is very clear about my not *living* in it or sleeping in it or saying Mass there.

It is exceptionally frustrating to have such a beautiful place as this one is getting to be—tucked away among the pines—and to have to stay away from it. Along with this, the conviction that the abbot has no interest in how I might feel about this, is sure that my desires are absurd, and even fears them. But in that case why did he do something that would manifestly encourage them? I did not really ask for this, for rather I showed a great deal of hesitation and gave him five or six chances to reverse his decision and call the whole thing off. This by now he will have completely forgotten.

Meanwhile, I have a hard time appearing cheerful and sociable. I can't say I have tried too hard, either. Complete disgust with the stupid mentality we cultivate in our monasteries. Deliberate cult of frustration and nonsense. Professional absurdity.

Isn't life absurd enough already without our adding to it our own fantastic frustrations and stupidities?

Yet as soon as I set foot in the woods and climb to the place where the house is being built, I can forget all this. But as soon as I come back, I am in it worse than ever.

November 1, 1960. All Saints

This evening, after Office of the Dead, sat on the porch of the hermitage and watched the sunlight fade in the valley and saw the moon rise over the little maple saplings we planted on the east side yesterday.

Extraordinary peace and silence. If I have any desire left in the world it is to live there and die there.

December 1, 1960

Yesterday the workmen finished their job on St. Mary's hermitage. There only remains for them to remove their planks and scaffolding.

The building that was begun on the Feast of St. Thérèse is finished on the Feast of St. Andrew in the first week of Advent. Let's hope it will not be closed down or dynamited by the Abbot General in January.

December 10, 1960

Totally new perspectives on solitude. Afternoons at St. Mary of Carmel. It is true that places and situations are not supposed to matter. This one makes a tremendous difference. Real silence. Real solitude. Peace. Getting acclimated to the surroundings. The valley in front. The tall, separated pines to the west, the heavy, close-set, denser pine wood to the northeast, the sweep of pasture and the line of bare oaks to the east, various clumps of pine and poplar between east and south, bright sky through bare trunks of ash, elm, and oak to the southwest, where a shoulder of hill hides the abbey. A great dance of sky overhead. A fire murmuring in the fireplace. Room smells faintly of pine smoke. Silent.

After having thought for ten years of building a hermitage, and thought of the ten places where one might be built, now *having built* one in the best place, I cannot believe it.

It is nevertheless real—if anything is real. In it everything becomes unreal. Just silence, sky, trees.

Not to fear feelings of guilt, not to justify myself, not to wonder what this or that person might think. Nor what I myself might think. It is not thoughts that matter but hours of silence and the precious dimension of existence, which is otherwise completely unknown, certainly unknown when one thinks or mentally speaks or even writes. It must simply be seen, and it is not seen until one has been sitting still, alone in its own utter obviousness.

December 13, 1960. St. Lucy
White smoke rising up in the valley against the light, slowly taking animal forms, with a dark background of wooded hills behind. Menacing and peaceful, probably brush fires, maybe a house, probably not a house. Cold, quiet morning, watch ticks on the desk. Produce nothing.

Perhaps I am stronger than I think. Perhaps I am afraid of my strength and turn it against myself to make myself weak. Perhaps I am most afraid of the strength of God in me.

Work. To be a solitary and not an individualist. Not concerned with mere perfecting of my own life. This, as Marxists see, is an indecent luxury (because there is so much illusion in it). My solitude belongs to society and to God. Are these just words? Solitude for its special work, the deepening of thought and awareness. The struggle against alienation. The danger of a solitude that is the worst alienation. *Not* a matter of holding the community at arm's length. Important that I continue to be Novice Master for the time being (Dom James wants me to, anyway). But I think at night of St. Mary of Carmel. I go to sleep thinking of the quiet hermitage and wishing I were there in bed (there is no bed) in the silent woods where the owl cries. "Self-love," they would say.

It is simply time that I must pray intently for the needs of the whole world and not be concerned with other, seemingly "more effective," forms of action. For me prayer comes first, the other forms of action follow, if they have their place. They no doubt do to some extent. Prayer (yesterday's Mass) for Latin America, for all of America, for this hemisphere—sorrow for the dolts, for the idiot civilization that is going down to ruin and dragging everything with it.

December 26, 1960

After a feast day dinner, my hands smell sweetly of oranges.

St. Mary of Carmel (after Vespers) is tremendous: with the tall pines, the silence, the moon and stars above the pines as dark falls, the patterns of shadow, the vast valley and hills, everything speaks of a more mature and more complete solitude. The pines are tall and not low. There is frankly a house, demanding not attachment but responsibility. A silence for dedication and not for escape. Lit candles in the dusk. "Here is my resting place for ever and ever"—the sense of a journey ended, of wandering at an end. *The first time in my life* I ever really felt I had a home and that my waiting and looking were ended.

A burst of sun through the window. Wind in the pines. Fire in the grate. Silence over the whole valley.

January 19, 1961

To be freed from all involvement—on all sides. To work for the solitude that one has to keep preaching: not as a luxury but as a necessity. How my ideas have changed on that over the course of years. It is no longer a question of "sanctification" but of pure survival, survival in the integrity God gave me.

To know when, how, and to whom to say "No!" Considerable knots and difficulties. Not to want to hurt people, certainly, but not being too anxious to placate them.

People are constantly trying to use you to help them create an illusion by which they live. Especially various collective illusions. Through my own fault I have become a part of too many collective illusions—have wanted to.

A distinction in the order of love. I have been satisfied to be "thought of kindly" by many and to think of them kindly. A diluted benevolence that keeps us all secure.

I must sacrifice this diffuse aura of benevolence and pay attention only to the *genuine care* for individuals that are brought to me by God. This care *is* an involvement and a vital one. But it is good and right, since it is specific, personal. It is not a "movement." It is not diffuse, foggy, consuming, absurd.

The question of writing: definitely it has to be cut down or changed.

Someone accused me of being a "high priest" of creativity. Or at least of allowing people to regard me as one. This is perhaps true.

The sin of *wanting to be a pontiff*, of wanting to be heard, of wanting converts, disciples. Being in a cloister, I thought I did not want this. Of course I did, and everyone knows it.

St. William, says the Breviary this night, when death approached, took off his pontifical vestments (what he was doing with them on in bed I can't imagine) and by his own efforts got to the floor and died.

So I am like him, in bed with a miter on. What am I going to do about it?

One thing from which I must free myself is the popular Catholic image in this country. I am not at all that kind of a Catholic, and why should I be giving all these people the idea that I am an inspiration to them? I am not. The clergy that have opposed me will realize it. There is an abyss between us.

At the same time, the subtler temptation, the temptation of the French avant-garde Catholic, to want to be on good terms with the proletarian left. To want to be "part of the future." But that is another myth. In many ways a worse one. The temptation is pragmatic, because this myth is likely to be the more successful.

I have got to face the fact that there is in me a desire for survival as pontiff, prophet, and writer, and this has to be renounced before I can be myself at last.

January 21, 1961

You can make of your life what you want. There are various ways of being happy. Why do we drive ourselves on with illusory demands? Happy only when we conform to something that is *said* to be a legitimate happiness? An approved happiness?

God gives us the freedom to create our own lives, according to His will, that is to say in the circumstances in which He has placed us. We refuse to be content unless we realize in ourselves a "universal" standard, a happiness hypothetically prescribed and approved for all men of all time. Not just our own happiness. This, at least, is what I do. I am a happy person. God has given me happiness, but I am guilty about it—as if being happy were not quite allowed, as if everybody didn't have it within reach somehow or other—as if I had to justify God Himself by being zealous for something I do not and cannot have—because I am not happy in the same way as Pericles—or Khrushchev.

January 24, 1961

While I was getting my tonsure this morning I watched the novices milling around getting ready for work—standing in their patched coveralls and their funny hoods, some being very recollected, some very efficient, mostly quite happy. I was moved by the sight of them and the awareness of how much we all impede ourselves with useless spiritual baggage. How difficult it is to try to help them without adding to the baggage instead of relieving them of it.

I can at least love them and thus create, or keep alive, the climate in which the Holy Spirit does the work. I do love them, but what are they getting into? At least let me not give them illusions.

February 4, 1961

Tremendous discovery. The *Brihad-Aranyaka Upanishad!*

Kairos! Everything for a long time has been slowly leading up to this and—with this reading—a sudden convergence of roads, tendencies, lights, in unity! A new door. (Looked at it without comprehension 9 months ago.)

Yesterday's disgust with the trivial, shallow contemporary stuff I am tempted to read! No time for that. Scriptures. Greek patrology. Oriental thought. This is enough to fill every free corner of the day not given to prayer, meditation, duties.

February 14, 1961. Blessed Conrad

Today, feast of the Cistercian hermit whom no one in the Order loves— at least I think I am right in saying this. I myself obviously *do* love him very much and have more and more devotion to him, though when I was a novice and I wrote those absurd lives of saints of the Order, he bothered me. I don't think I even included him. He seemed like an oddball and a failure. His life seemed to end somewhere in midair, making no sense—he was a hermit on his way home, as the Breviary assures us, to his monastery? As if to give his life a semblance of security. As if at last he had repented of his folly, seen the light, hot-footed it back to the cenobium. And above all because he heard Our Father St. Bernard was "gravely ill." (St. B. was gravely ill ever since the foundation of Clairvaux thirty years before!!!) There is a note of anxiety: he did not make it back to France! Was he perhaps punished for his madness? He died in a "grotto dedicated to the Mother of God."

This morning, the splendor of my Mass! Sun pouring in on the altar and the glory of reflected lights from the hammered silver chalice splashed all over the corporal and all around the Host. Deep quiet. The Gospel— *Nolite timere,* "Do not fear, little flock." Where your treasure is, there your heart is also. May I learn the lessons of detachment, even from the little white house of St. Mary of Carmel. But no nonsense about not desiring solitude. On the contrary, to desire it in perfection and in truth. Interior and exterior.

February 20, 1961. 1st Sunday of Lent

This Sunday always moves me with joy. The liturgy is strong and appeals directly to monks. I wish my life were more genuinely ascetic. I am caught in confusions, which continue and continue to await clarification. Perhaps I am the one who resists their clarification. Yet in the bottom of my heart and in my conscience I know that the answer is *not* merely a question of conforming to approved and well-accepted standards or, at least, not merely a question of getting in line with the others (who in any case are by no means in line with one another).

It is true that a certain laziness and lack of generosity have always marked my life. My attempts to do anything about this are always too feeble and sporadic. "Behold, now is the acceptable time."

March 3, 1961

The rains of these days have waned. It was bright afterward, and now there will be more rain.

Dom Gabriel Sortais came to the hermitage Wednesday (it was George Washington's birthday and the 19th anniversary of my taking the habit). He sat in the chair by the redwood table and told me of a hermitess in the Dept. of Var and of her life. All to convince me not to leave to be a hermit alone, but that "this was a kind of solution," namely, having a hermitage to come to during the day. He seemed glad of it, eager for me to have it, not to live in it, "for you are the novice master." All his logic (and he is, after all, very logical) was that this was right for me. He was very kind.

The hermitage is right, even though to some it might be wrong. More right and less right. It is God's way of being right in my life in spite of everything—not for me or anyone to talk about or to discuss. He is greater than all possible blame.

A good loneliness, a good insecurity. Stone room, pines. His will, His mercy. An imperfection to say it and insist: lack of faith.

Do not explain.

March 7, 1961. Feast of St. Thomas Aquinas

Determined to write less, to gradually vanish. Do not know how and do not pretend it is easy. To vanish from popularity into insecurity and anguish by my own decision to be alone is perhaps dangerous and arbitrary. Yet this must be done. I must begin to do what I must do. Not insisting on it as a preference, which perhaps, after all, it really is not.

My motives are mired and confused, but the time has come to straighten them out if I can and "die" as an author or, at least, as a popular and celebrated one. Certainly if people read—really read—my most recent work, my popularity is done with.

The last thing I will give up writing will be this journal and notebooks and poems. No more books of piety.

March 11, 1961

I am still a 14th-century man: the century of Eckhart, Ruysbroeck, Tauler, the English recluses, the author of *The Cloud*, Langland, and Chaucer—more an independent and a hermit than a community man, by no means an ascetic, interested in psychology, a lover of the dark cloud in which God is found by love. This is what I am: I cannot consent to be it and not be ashamed that I am not something more fashionable.

March 16, 1961

The saints of the 15th century are among those who most move me. In the collapse of medieval society, corruption of the clergy, decadence of conventual life, there emerge men and women of the laity *supremely obedient to God,* especially Nicholas of Flue and Joan of Arc. Complete and simple signs of contradiction to worldliness and system and convention and prejudiced interest. *Not* rebels at all, but completely meek and submissive instruments of God. In them you see clearly and movingly revealed what it is *not* to be a mere rebel but to be obedient to God as a sign to men, a sign of mercy, a revelation of truth and of power. I am drawn to these "signs" of God with all the love of my heart, trusting above all in their love and their intercession, for they live in the glory of God. I would not love them if God had not made them "sacraments" to me. St. Catherine of Genoa also, whom Natasha Spender loves (she keeps wanting me to write about Catherine).

March 22, 1961. Feast of St. Joseph (transferred)

Continual rain.

Yesterday, the afternoon being partly clear (though I did not expect it to be), had a novitiate conference in St. Mary of Carmel. Very pleasant and peaceful. An altogether new atmosphere of light and peace (though there is plenty of both already in the novitiate). Sense of not being immersed in a fluid medium but out in the air.

Father John of the Cross said I would have less resentment in me if I were more concentrated on doing whatever it is God wills for me and not considering the defects of this institution.

One thing very clear after Mass: the "return to the Father."

The nonentity and insufficiency of all other concerns.

A going clear out of the midst of all that is transitory and inconclusive. The return to the Immense, the Primordial, the Unknown, to Him who loves, to the Silent, to the Holy, to the Merciful, to Him Who is All.

The misdirectedness, the folly, the inanity of all that seeks anything but this great return, the whole meaning and heart of all existence.

The absurdity of movements, of the goals that are not ultimate, the purposes that are "ends of the line" and therefore do not even begin.

To return is not to "go back" in time, but a going forward, a going beyond; to retrace one's steps is nothing on top of nothing, vanity of vanities, a renewal of the same absurdity twice over, in reverse.

To go beyond everything, to leave everything and press forward to the End and to the Beginning, to the ever new Beginning that is without End.

To obey Him on the way in order to reach Him in Whom I have begun, Who is the Way and the End—the Beginning.

March 24, 1961. Feast of Our Lady of Sorrows

There was a superb letter from Dr. John Wu in answer to one I had written to him about collaborating on some selections from Chuang Tzu. A letter of great humility and nobility from the depths of a great heart, of one who loves deeply his Chinese heritage and knows well the depths of that wisdom. I know once again we are touching something real that cries out for a hearing ("Wisdom cries out in the marketplace"). I can see no other way to be honest before God than to *hear* premonitions of His wisdom in one like Chuang Tzu. Dr. Wu had much to say about the Confucian and Taoist traditions that opened up exciting horizons. I think this will be a fine work, even though it may "accomplish nothing." (Why read Chuang Tzu and want to accomplish something? Wisdom takes care of herself. Tao knows what she is about. She has already "accomplished" it. I have had the first glimpse of a reservoir that is already full to the edges. It remains only for us to drink.)

March 28, 1961. Tuesday in Holy Week

Once again I dimly realize the enormous proportions of the ambiguities in myself. I cannot expect to resolve them. Nor should I be surprised at the ambiguities in others. The great ambiguity of the whole monastery on the question of "contemplation." We travel at all times in two opposite directions and do so quite serenely. As if it were enough to have some kind of ideal of contemplation in one's mind and then *do* anything one is impelled to do by latent activism to allay one's guilt feelings at being, perhaps, "unproductive." It is a peculiar problem of our time when we come from a world that is completely opposed to our ideal and do not really "come from" it but only bring it along with us.

At such a time the break should be more complete—more thorough. But being "drastic" is no answer. There is a kind of violence that does not take heaven by storm but serves only to justify our internal contradictions. This is an illusion.

April 2, 1961. Easter Sunday

A gay, bright, glorious day and a very fine Easter such as I do not remember for a long time. The Vigil was tremendous for me and the glory of Christ was in it. There has been splendor in everything (including the emptiness of Good Friday morning when rain came down in torrents and I stayed in the hermitage).

Yesterday—reading bits of Dame Julian of Norwich, and today I began Gregory of Nyssa's homilies on the Canticle.

Father Sylvanus was in town to the doctor and brought back a newspaper story about a man in the Kentucky mountains, a former coal miner who for 13 years has been living as a hermit, with a dog, in a pitiful little shack without even a chimney, with an old car seat for a bed. "Because of all these wars." A real desert father and probably not too sure why.

April 15, 1961

Thunderstorm. The first I have sat through in the hermitage. Here you really can *watch* a storm. White snakes of lightning suddenly stand in the sky and vanish. The valley is clouded with rain as white as milk. All the hills vanish. The thunder cracks and beats. Rain comes flooding down from the roof eaves, and the grass looks twice as green as before.

Not to be known, not to be seen.

LEFT: The young Thomas Merton in a passport photograph taken around 1939. (*Thomas Merton Center Archives, Bellarmine College, Louisville, KY*)

RIGHT: Merton as a young monk (about 1943–44) studies an illuminated manuscript in the Abbey of Gethsemani's rare books vault. (*Gethsemani Archives*)

RIGHT: Hair-cutting day at Gethsemani—Merton, center, receives his monthly trim in a photograph from the early 1960s. *(Gethsemani Archives)*

BELOW: During the 1960s, Merton teaches the novices and young professed monks in the novitiate at the Abbey of Gethsemani. *(Gethsemani Archives)*

ABOVE: Merton's
hermitage at Gethsemani.
He received permission to
live full-time here in
August 1965. *(Photo by
Brendan Egan; Gethsemani
Archives)*

RIGHT: Merton inside
his hermitage in 1967.
*(Photo by Ralph Eugene
Meatyard; Thomas Merton
Center Archives)*

LEFT: Thomas Merton, in the mid-1960s, poses in the Abbey of Gethsemani's monastic garden. The abbey church and enclosure wall appear behind him. *(Photograph by John Howard Griffin; Thomas Merton Center Archives)*

BELOW: Tommie O'Callaghan, Sr. Therese Lentfoehr, and Thomas Merton enjoy a picnic at Gethsemani in the mid-1960s. *(Thomas Merton Center Archives)*

ABOVE: Merton, while Novice Master at Gethsemani in the 1960s, relaxes in a woodshed where novices read and meditate on rainy days. *(Gethsemani Archives)*

RIGHT: Jacques Maritain, Fr. Stan Murphy, C.S.B., Dr. Daniel C. Walsh, and Thomas Merton picnic at the hermitage in the fall of 1967. *(Photograph by John Howard Griffin)*

RIGHT: Thomas Merton clowns for the camera in the mid-1960s. "This is the old Hillbilly who knows where the still is," he captioned this photograph. *(Photo by John Lyons; Thomas Merton Center Archives)*

BELOW: Patrick Hart, Thomas Merton, and Maurice Flood at Merton's hermitage on the morning before his departure for the Far East in 1968. *(Photo by Philip Stark; Gethsemani Archives)*

ABOVE: Merton with the Dalai Lama at Dharamsala, India, in November 1968. (*Gethsemani Archives*)

LEFT: Merton addressing attendees of the East/West Conference in Bangkok, Thailand, on December 10, 1968, just a couple of hours before his death. (*Gethsemani Archives*)

ABOVE: A portrait of Merton in his final year. *(Photo by John Howard Griffin; Thomas Merton Center Archives)*

LEFT: Thomas Merton's grave marker at the Abbey of Gethsemani. *(Gethsemani Archives)*

April 23, 1961. III Sunday After Easter

I love this mysterious and joyful Sunday. The responses about the
Heavenly Jerusalem and the Gospel about the joy that "no man shall take
from you." Remember twenty-one years ago in Havana: the Sunday of the
great joy in San Francisco Church. (That was April 29 that year.)

May 7, 1961. V Sunday After Easter

In the Night Office—St. Ambrose: all *must* rise from the dead.
Resurrection is our lot. Life is our destiny whether we want it or not.
But to be risen and not want it, to hate life, is the resurrection of
judgment. Man is not and cannot be a merely ephemeral thing. If he
wills to be evanescent, to remain in what he is *not*, he is a living
contradiction.

Thunder, lightning, and rain all night. Heaviest rain for a long time.
Floods in the bottoms. Water bubbling in under the basement wall into
the washroom. Novitiate garden flooded in the NW corner. (One day
the whole retaining wall will go if this keeps up.) Sound of water in the
valley.

   "My love is / The fragrance of the orchid / And the sound of
waters," says the Haiku of my lovely Zen calendar.

May 16, 1961

It is like an English summer day, cool and cloudy, with deep green grass
all around the hermitage and trees heavy with foliage. Occasional slow
bursts of gentle sunlight that imperceptibly pass by. Shafts of light and
great rooms of shadow in the tall tree-church beyond the cedar cross.
The path of creek gravel leads into the shadows and beyond them to the
monastery, out of sight down the hill, across fields and a road and a dirty
stream. All such things as roads and sewers are far from this place.

Reading Martin Luther King, Jr., and the simple, moving story of the
Montgomery bus boycott. Especially interested not only in the main
actions but in the story of his own spiritual development. Certainly here
is something Christian in the history of our time.

May 20, 1961

A Prayer to God My Father on the Vigil of Pentecost

Today, Father, this blue sky praises you. The delicate green and orange flowers of the tulip poplar praise you. The distant blue hills praise you, along with the sweet-smelling air, which is full of brilliant light. The bickering flycatchers praise you, with the lowing bulls and the quails that whistle over there, and I too, Father, praise you, with these creatures my brothers. You have made us all together, and you have placed me here this morning in the midst of them. Here I am.

For a long time I prayed, in the years that are past, and I was in darkness and sorrow and confusion. No doubt the confusion was my own fault. No doubt my own will was the root of my sorrow, and I regret it, O merciful Father. But whatever may have been my sin, the prayer of Your friends for me and my own prayers were answered: I am here in this hermitage before You. Here You see me. Here You love me. Here You ask the response of my own love and of my confidence. Here You ask me to be nothing else than Your friend.

To be Your friend is simply to accept Your friendship because it is Your Friendship. This Friendship is Your life, the Spirit of Your Son. You have called me here to be Your Son: to be born over again, repeatedly, in Your light, in knowledge, in consideration, in gratitude, in poverty, and in praise.

Here I will learn from the words of Your friends to be Your friend. Here I will be a friend to those in whom You send me Your Son.

If I have any choice to make, it is to live and even die here. But in any case, it is to speak Your name with confidence here in this place, to say it by being here and by having You in my heart as long as I can be here.

Father, I beg You to teach me to be a man of peace and to help bring peace to the world. To study here truth and nonviolence and patience and the courage to suffer for truth.

Send me Your Holy Spirit, unite me with Your divine Son, and make me one with You in Him, for Your great glory, Amen.

May 30, 1961. *Feast of St. Joan of Arc*

On Trinity Sunday, after the Night Office, I realized I had plenty of time to go to the hermitage and went as the sun rose. I wonder why I had not thought of it before—perhaps too obsessed with the reading I have been doing at that time and in which, to a great extent, I have been fruitlessly lost.

This morning I came up again, and I am doing my best to take as far as possible the whole day here, going down, of course, for exercises, which is possible as I have no conference or direction.

This morning at four. Great full moon over Nally's Hill, pale and clear. A faint mist hanging over the wet grass of the bottoms.

More and more I appreciate the beauty and solemnity of the "Way" up through the woods, past the bull barn, up the stony rise, into the grove of tall, straight oaks and hickories, and around through the pines on top of the hill, to the cottage.

Sunrise. Hidden by pines and cedars on the east side of the house. Saw the red flame of it glaring through the cedars, not like sunrise but like a forest fire. From the window of the front room, then he, the Sun (can hardly be conceived as other than "he"), shone silently with solemn power through the pine branches.

Now after High Mass the whole valley is glorious with morning light and with the song of birds.

It is essential to experience all the times and moods of this place. No one will know or be able to say *how* essential. Almost the first and most important element of a truly spiritual life, lost in the constant, formal routine of Divine Offices under the fluorescent lights in choir—practically no change between night and day.

May 31, 1961

The great work of sunrise again today.

The awful solemnity of it. The sacredness. Unbearable without prayer and worship. I mean unbearable if you really put everything aside and see what is happening! Many, no doubt, are vaguely aware that it is dawn, but they are protected from the solemnity of it by the neutralizing worship of their own society, their own world, in which the sun no longer rises and sets.

Sense of importance, the urgency of seeing, fully aware, experiencing what is *here:* not what is given by men, by society, but what is given by

God and hidden by (even monastic) society. Clear realization that I must be with these first elements. It is absurd to inquire after my function in the world, or whether I have one, as long as I am not first of all alive and awake. If that and no more is my job (it is certainly every man's job), then I am grateful for it. The vanity of all false mission, when no one is sent. All the universal outcry of people who have not been told to cry out, but who are driven to this noise by their fear, their lack of what is right in front of their noses.

June 6, 1961. In the Orthodox Calendar, Bessarion the Great, of Egypt
Dom Jean-Marie Leclercq came last Wednesday afternoon, before Corpus Christi, stayed three days, and gave some conferences. We had some talks together.

He told me I was a pessimist, too anxious and too negative.

Actually, I also had a feeling of an underlying disharmony between us, a kind of opposition and mistrust (*méfiance*) under the surface cordiality and agreement.

He is certainly one of those, one of the very many, who accept any writing I have done only with great reservations. That I can certainly understand. As a theologian I have always been a pure amateur, and the professionals resent an amateur making so much noise. Though he is friendly to a book like *Thoughts in Solitude,* I know he is not happy with something like *The Sign of Jonas,* which would obviously disturb most Europeans, most European monks. He protests he is not against journals as such. As for *Ascent to Truth*—all right, I know this was a foolish experiment, a false start and a mistake. I am ashamed of it. Perhaps it is not as bad as I feel it is in my guilt. So too some of the other fatuous didacticism I have gotten into.

The things I have said fairly well are things I needed to say: I stand by them. Most of *The Seven Storey Mountain,* and *Jonas,* and anything on solitude, esp. the notes in *Disputed Questions,* a lot of poems, *Seeds of Contemplation* and *New Seeds* (I think), a good part of *The Silent Life.* Perhaps a few pages of *No Man Is an Island,* a good bit of *Secular Journal,* and most of the recent work: *Behavior of Titans* especially. And the stuff on Herakleitos and Chinese thought? Maybe.

What hurts me most is to have been inexorably trapped by my own folly. Wanting to prove myself a Catholic—of course not perfectly succeeding.

They all admit and commend my good will, but, frankly, I am not one of the bunch, am I?

For my comfort a squirrel just ran across the porch.

June 16, 1961

Sweet afternoon! Cool breezes and a clear sky! This day will not come again. The bulls lie under the tree in the corner of their field. Quiet afternoon! The blue hills, the day lilies in the wind. This day will not come again.

June 20, 1961

Bruno Scott James sent a copy of a review of *Disputed Questions* he did for the *Tablet*. Partly very favorable and in part reproves me for being bitter and critical, trying to sound like a prophet in the lands of Sinai. I think he certainly exaggerates, and in any case he referred to the Pasternak article. There is no doubt that the problems of our time call for some strong protests and declarations. It is, however, sensitivity reaching to the element of harshness, to the impatience and the violence that are in me. My reprisals, my resentments. Really, he is right. I have got to stop making negative statements dictated by these sick drives, if I can. At least I must try more than I have. It has spoiled all my work from the beginning, a basic defect, deep in my character. Such a defect one must fight, especially in a monastery. I have tended not to but rather justified myself about it.

No need to overemphasize the importance of spiritual direction, but one thing I have certainly lacked is a director. Father John of the Cross is capable but says nothing.

June 27, 1961

Realization that I need to turn a corner, to slough off a skin.

Need for moral effort in the midst of dullness and boredom (*engourdissement*) and confusion. There is probably something sick about the mental numbness and anguish. It is hard to see exactly what is to be left and what is to be thrown overboard.

Once again, at the risk of getting involved in hopeless confusions, I try to face the incomprehensible problem (for me) of writing. Incomprehensible because I am too involved and committed. That is the bad thing. It is so true that I have to continue being a writer that I do not know where to begin to think about not being one. Where to make the divisions. I feel it is useless even to make them, though I know what they are in my own mind. Certainly I can write something and write, if possible, creatively. But not to *preach*, to dogmatize, not to be a pseudo-prophet, not to declare my opinions. Yet it is essential to take a moral stand on some points—like atomic war. Am I so far gone that I can't do this without putting a brazier on my head and running about like Solomon Eagle in the London fire?

June 29, 1961

It all cleared up after High Mass when I saw my only solution is to do what I have always wanted to do, always known I should do, always been called to do: follow the way of emptiness and nothingness, read more of the "nothing" books than those of the others, forget my preoccupations with ten thousand absurdities, to know without wanting to be an authority, or else I will forever be a lackey of pious journalists and editors: the right-thinking rabbit who gives birth to litters of editorials every morning before breakfast.

July 3, 1961

The "world" with its funny pants of which I do not know the name, its sandals and sunglasses, its fat arses, its bellies, its nerves (my nerves too, my belly too), its hair, its teeth. Its talk. I do not have words for the world. I do not understand my fear of it, which includes fascination and a sick feeling in the pit of the stomach, since I am also part of it. The smell of its lotions is already in our front wing and in our offices. The little printed pieces of paper we send out are responses to its sly intimations of complicity. I don't care what Bruno James says, I must write about this, not perhaps with the overtones of a preacher or of a prophet. Write about the sick feeling I get about the plague, the suntanned death. First I must collect all the words I do not know: the names of plastics, the drugs, the oils, the lubricants that make it smell so and move so. I do feel like a child who lives in a whorehouse (or right next door to one) who guesses what goes on, *feels* what goes on as if the whole place were impregnated with a sly fun for which you pay. Sex is, after all, what has gone wrong perhaps in everything, but that too is the temptation—that I too might indulge in my own way by raising a chorus of exacerbated protest.

July 9, 1961

Dawn at the hermitage.

I slept until 3 and came up here to say the Office—the long way round by the road. Very thin end of a moon in the morning sky. Crows bothering an owl.

Once again—the Office is entirely different in its proper (natural) setting, out from under the fluorescent lights. There Lauds is torpor and vacuum. Here it is in harmony with all the singing birds under the bright sky. Everything you have on your lips in praising God is there before you—hills, dew, light, birds, growing things. Nothing in the liturgy of light is lost.

I saw in the middle of the *Benedicite* the great presence of the sun, which had just risen behind the cedars (same time and place as Trinity Sunday). Now under the pines the sun has made a great golden basilica of fire and water.

Perspective: crows making a racket in the east, dogs making a racket in the south, and yet, over all, the majestic peace of Sunday. Is that, after all, the true picture of our world?

"God whose Providence never fails to accomplish its ends." This is the great truth. Christ has indeed conquered, and the world does indeed belong to Him alone. This cannot help but be reflected in society. Society cannot be left entirely to the forces of evil. But that does not mean, of course, that we must naively expect the triumph of the *civitas christiana*, of "Christian civilization" as we imagine and plan it, still less that we must believe in some kind of clerical fascism.

July 23, 1961. 9th Sunday After Pentecost

Jerusalem, and Christ's tears. The Holy City. "Thou hast not known the time of thy visitation."

I will stop making any kind of effort to justify myself to anybody. To prepare a place for myself anywhere, among any group. It is this that I have to face. This and the necessity to give up any activity that leaves the slightest (intended) impression upon the surface of the world. This and the necessity to renounce all surreptitious reaching for human immortality—for being remembered.

Peace is impossible until I fully, totally realize and embrace the realization that I am already forgotten. Not that I can help wanting to be remembered. But daily I am confronted with the price that would have to be paid!! I shrink from it yet want to pay it. This is what must not be done. Render unto God the things that are God's.

July 31, 1961

Very hot.

During Night Office and morning meditation, saw that my whole life is a struggle to seek the truth (at least I want it to be so), that the truth is found in the reality of my own life as it is given to me, that it is found by complete consent and acceptance. Not at all by defeat, by mere passive resignation, by mere inert acceptance of evil and falsity (which are nevertheless unavoidable) but by "creative" consent, in my deepest self, to the will of God, which is expressed in my own self and my own life. Indeed, there is a sense in which my own deepest self is in God and even expresses Him as "word." (Such is the deep meaning of our Sonship.)

Gradually I will come more and more to transcend the limitations of the world and of the society to which I belong—while fully accepting my own little moment in history such as it is.

To be detached from all systems without rancor toward them, with insight and compassion. To be truly "Catholic" is to be able to enter into everybody's problems and joys and be all things to all men.

August 6, 1961. Feast of Transfiguration and Day of Recollection

Thought much today of the tone and value of my own interior world. Culture, of a sort, has given it much of its tone. Christian and European culture, Christian spirituality, monastic life, occidental mysticism, plus a certain openness to other cultures and spiritualities, especially, I think, the Chinese. All this not only is relevant to my life and salvation but has crucial significance in my whole vocation.

That I have known the hill town of Cordes; that I have walked from Caylus to Puylagarde and know Caussade and Cahors and the church of Saint Jacques by the bridge in Montauban. That I have stood in the ruined castles of Penne and Najac and waited under the high bluff of Beziers among the wine barrels—or passed by the walls of Carcassonne.

That the quarterboys of Rye never cease to ring in my ears, that I know the silence of the broad marsh between Rye and Winchelsea and listen to it forever, the fens at Ely, the backs behind Clare and Kings and Trinity, the bell in the cloister tower of St. John's as heard by night on Bridge Street, Cambridge.

The tower of Oakham Church and the vale.

The Surrey Downs and the ruins of Waverly in the meadow on a September evening.

The high roofs of Strasbourg, Tauler's city, streets known to Meister Eckhart.

Today I read the wonderful sermon on the Divine Truth in which Eckhart says that as a person is about to be struck by a thunderbolt turns toward it, and as all the leaves of a tree about to be struck turn toward it, so one in whom the Divine Birth is to take place turns, without realizing, completely toward it.

The village church at West Horsley and the other one at Ripley. Newark Priory, where Christopher Pierce knew all about the drains.

I must not cease to read David Knowles but get the book back again and continue.

High Street, Guildford. St. Albans, as I passed by in the LMS. Limoges also. All this is important: it has all been in some way sacramental. Now I am in a world that is to a great extent without such *experiences* and *symbols*. Yet I have come to a place that has, or once had, something of that spiritual climate. I resent the lack of it, yet create it always for myself.

The point is that I need not be ashamed of this world because the communists want to build another. Let them build anything they can, for something has to be done. For my part, my vocation includes fidelity to all that is spiritual and noble and fine and deep. This I will keep alive in myself and hand on to anyone who is capable of receiving it.

August 7, 1961

Both Newman and Fénelon loved Clement of Alexandria, which is not at all surprising. To Newman he was "like music." This may look like a cliché, but it is profound. For there are people one meets—in books and in life—with whom a deep resonance is at once established.

For a long time I had no "resonance" with Newman ("heart speaks to heart"). I was suspicious of letting him enter my heart. Clement the same. Now I want all the music of Clement and am only with difficulty restrained from taking new books on Newman from the library where I have so many other things to read and finish.

Resonances: one of the "choirs." Maritain, Van der Meer de Walcheren, Bloy, Green, Chagall, Satie—or a string sextet!

Another earlier music: Blake, Eckhart, Tauler (Maritain got in here too), Coomaraswamy, etc.

Music: the marvelous opening of the *Protreptikos*—the "new song"—the splendid image of the cricket flying to replace by his song the broken string in the Lyre of Eunomos at Delphi. Though Clement repudiates the myth, he uses its splendidly. Humanity: a musical instrument for God.

August 8, 1961

Dream of being lost in a great city and walking "toward the center" without quite knowing where I was and suddenly coming to the road's end on a height overlooking a great bay, an arm of the harbor, and seeing a whole section of the city spread out before me on the hills, covered with light snow, realizing that, though I had far to go, I knew where I was because in this city there are two arms of the sea, which one always encounters and by which one can get one's orientation.

Then, in a library of this city, speaking with strangers, I suddenly realize there is a charterhouse here and that I have promised myself to visit and speak to the Prior about "my vocation." I ask someone, "Where is the charterhouse?" and he says, "I am just going to drive that way, I go right by it and I will take you." I accept this offer realizing that it is providential.

I think frequently that I may soon die, but I don't know what kind of conviction this thought carries with it. Rather that I *may* die and that, if it is God's will, I am glad. "Go out to meet Him." I realize the futility of my attachments, particularly the big one—my work as a writer. I do not feel inordinately guilty about this, but it is a nuisance and an obstacle. I feel hampered by it. Not fully free. But the love of God, I hope, will free me. The important thing is simply turning to Him daily and often, preferring His will and His mystery to anything that is tangibly "mine."

August 16, 1961

It is certainly true that man is most human and proves his humanity by the quality of his relationship with woman. (This, in Marx, surprised me.) How much more true than I realized in the past! Here in the monastery with our chastity we are ideally supposed to go still further in this dimension of humanism and love. This is one of the keys to our problems: how can one go further than that to which one has not yet attained?

Not that virginity cannot be deeply and purely human. But it has to be spiritual and positive. This spiritual character of chastity and virginity is *not* found in alienation. It is *not* found in sentimentality, in a "thought" of pure love for Jesus.

Inexorably life moves on toward crisis and mystery.

Everyone must struggle to adjust himself to this, to face the situation, for "now is the judgment of the world." In a way each one judges himself merely by what he does. Does, not says. Yet let us not completely dismiss words. They do have meaning. They are related to action. They spring from action and they prepare for it, they clarify it, they direct it. They are not, by themselves, enough. Yet, united with action, they constitute *testimony* and therefore decision, judgment.

August 19, 1961

Yet one must not be too quickly preoccupied with professing definitively what is true and what is false. Not that true and false do not matter. But if at every instant one wants to grasp the whole and perfect truth of a situation, particularly a concrete and limited situation in history or in politics, he only deceives and blinds himself. Such judgments are only rarely and fleetingly possible, and sometimes when we think we see what is most significant, it has very little meaning at all.

So it is possible that the moment of my death may turn out to be, from a human and "economic" point of view, the most meaningless of all.

Meanwhile, I do not have to stop the flow of events in order to understand them. On the contrary, I must move with them or else what I think I understand will be no more than an image in my own mind.

So, the flow of events: Terry Phillips with a wrecking bar smashing the plaster off the walls of the room in the old guest house where, twenty years ago, I first came on retreat, that moonlit night in Lent! He—our youngest postulant—was not even born then.

August 22, 1961

I finished Christopher Dawson's *Understanding Europe.* It is a fine book. He is completely right about the central importance of Christian culture, the danger of the theological dualism à la Karl Barth playing into the hands of secularism. Whether or not he came too late, who can say? In any case I have a clear obligation to participate, as long as I can and to the extent of my abilities, in every effort to help a spiritual and cultural renewal of our time. This is the task that has been given me, and hitherto I have not been clear about it in all its aspects and dimensions.

To emphasize and clarify the living content of spiritual traditions, especially the Christian but also the Oriental, by entering myself deeply into their disciplines and experience, not for myself only but for all my contemporaries who may be interested and inclined to listen. This for the restoration of man's sanity and balance, that he may return to the ways of freedom and of peace, if not in my time, at least someday soon.

September 12, 1961

A dream last night that was in many ways beautiful and moving—a hieratic dream.

I am invited to a party. I meet some of the women going to the party, but there is an estrangement. I am alone by the waterfront of a small town. A man says for five dollars I can get across on a yacht to where I want to go. I have five dollars and more than five dollars, hundreds of dollars and also francs. I am conscious of my clerical garb. The yacht is a small schooner, a workaday schooner and no yacht. It does not move from the shore—we make it move a little by pushing it from the inside. Then I am swimming ahead in the beautiful water, magic water from the depths of which comes a wonderful life to which I am not entitled, a life and strength that I fear. I know that by diving in this water I can find something marvelous but that it is not fitting or right for me to dive, as I am going to the further shore, with the strength that has come from the water, immortality.

Then in the summer house on the other side where I have arrived, first of all I play with the dog and the child brings me two pieces of buttered white bread, which I am to eat on arrival.

September 23, 1961

The last two or three days—great seriousness in prayer, sense of the meaning and value of vigils, of self-stripping and going in poverty "to the Father." Orientation out of this world, sense of its transiency and provisional character.

Silent afternoon at the hermitage—wind soughing in the hot pines, crickets in the yellow grass.

September 25, 1961

One of the people I most enjoy getting letters from is Doña Luisa Coomaraswamy. I am growing very fond of her and she has been most generous—writes long letters full of all sorts of interesting things and sends offprints of Ananda Coomaraswamy's articles. She is very much a recluse and remains generally suspicious of scholars and publishers, but I am happy that she accepts me completely. It is a friendship in which, it seems, we both recognize correlative needs and potentialities in each other and are grateful. This is good and consoling and is from God. Or at least I hope so. Why should it not be? One is happy for the mystery of mutual recognition in this great, confused, silent, and anonymous sea which is our world.

September 30, 1961

For my own part, I have one task left. To pray, to meditate, to enter into truth, to sit before the abyss, to be educated in the word of Christ, and thus to make my contribution to world peace. There is not much left to be said.

October 3, 1961

Yesterday, Feast of the Guardian Angels, a bright, cool afternoon, a fine half day of meditation at the hermitage. The Corbin book on Ibn al'Arabi is in ways tremendous. The plays and changes on the theme of the divine compassion, on the "sympathy" of the spirit and God, on God seeking to manifest Himself in the spirit that responds to a "Name," which it is meant to embody in its life. Compare the medieval Cistercians with their births of Christ in us. Need for compassion and tenderness toward the infinite fragility of the divine life in us, which is *real* and not an idea or an image (as is our conception of God as "object").

This could and should lead me more and more to a new turning, a new attitude, an inner change, a liberation from all futile concerns to let Him emerge in His mystery and compassion within me. Yielding to the inexplicable demand of His presence in weakness. To be very careful and timid now about those innumerable self-affirmations, which tend to destroy His weakness and littleness in me—fortunately indestructible. This mustard seed, His kingdom in me. The struggle of the very small to survive and change my self-affirmations.

October 21, 1961

Perhaps the last time we celebrate the Feast of St. Ursula in our calendar. Not that the same Mass texts will not be used over and over again in other Masses of Virgins. Special joy in listening to the Epistle and Gospel. To *become* attention from head to foot, to become all joy in hearing the Word of God. A deep pleasure of monks and, by rights, of all Christians.

Pleasure of fire in the grate at St. Mary of Carmel. The only talkative being, this child, this fire. The only one speaking in the quiet room outside—cold, damp, foggy day. Barely see the hills across the valley. You could not guess their presence unless you knew beforehand where to look.

Letter from Jim Forest at the *Catholic Worker*—that my article on the "War Madness" is published and that there will be controversy about it. That everyone has gone crazy, building fallout shelters and preparing to shoot their neighbors. Whole towns preparing to defend themselves against neighboring towns. What do the Russians need with bombs at all? Just get a false alarm going and we will all shoot each other up without giving them further trouble! A nice testimony to democracy and individualism!

October 23, 1961

I am perhaps at a turning point in my spiritual life: perhaps slowly coming to a point of maturation and the resolution of doubts and the forgetting of fears. Walking in to a known and definite battle. May God protect me from it. The *Catholic Worker* sent out a press release about my article, which may have many reactions or may have none. At any rate, it appears that I am one of the few Catholic priests in the country who has come out unequivocally for a completely intransigent fight for the abolition of war, for the use of nonviolent means to settle international conflicts. Hence by implication not only against the bomb, against nuclear testing, against Polaris submarines, but against all violence. This I will inevitably have to explain in due course. Nonviolent *action*, not mere passivity. How am I going to explain myself and defend a definite position in a timely manner, when it takes at least two months to get even a short article through the censors of the Order, is a question I cannot attempt to answer.

In a way I think the position of the Order is in fact unrealistic and absurd. That at a time like this *no one* in the Order should seem to be concerned with the realities of the world situation in a practical way— that monks in general, even those Benedictines who can speak out fully, are immersed in little scholarly questions about medieval writers and texts of minor importance even to scholars, this in the greatest moral crisis in the history of man: this seems to me incomprehensible. Especially when it is the definite policy of the Cistercian Order to impede and obstruct every expression of concern, every opinion in published written form, that has reference to the crisis. This seems to me extremely grave. The futility of taking the issue up and solving it is evident. I talked to Father Clément de Bourmont, the Abbot General's secretary, about it, and it was like talking to a wall. Total incomprehension and lack of sympathy. The General himself is more understanding, and Dom James too sees the point somewhat (they surprisingly released *Original Child Bomb* after the censors had definitively blocked it).

The Jesuit who condoned—even apparently encouraged—the business of sitting in your fallout shelter with a machine gun to keep others out! This is the best Catholic theology has had to offer in this country, so it appears.

At least I feel clean from having stated what is certainly the true Christian position. Not that self-defense is not legitimate but there are wider perspectives than that and we have to see them. It is not possible to solve our problems on the basis of "every man for himself" and saving your own skin by killing the first person who threatens it.

I am happy that I have turned a corner, perhaps the last corner of my life. The sense of abandon and home-going joy, love for the novices, whom I see as though dwelling in light and in God's blessing as we go home together. The thought is not negative nor destructive: it is a fulfillment. Whatever happens to the world, its infinitely varied dance of epiphanies continues, or is perhaps finally transfigured and perfected forever.

October 27, 1961

Tom McDonnell was here last week, working on the *Merton Reader*. It was a distraction. It brought me again into the realm of doubt and uncertainty. It seems to be necessary and right, and then at moments I glimpse all the possibilities of dishonesty and self-deception it brings with it. The creation of another image of myself—fixation on the idea that I am a "writer who has arrived," which I am, but what does it mean? Arrived where? Void. Has there been anything else in my life but the construction of this immense illusion? And the guilt that goes with it, what is this? A justification for it, a second illusion? Certainly I can have no peace in this kind of nonsense. My home is elsewhere.

October 30, 1961

The anchor in the window of the Old Zion church, before it burned in 1924 or 1925: this is the earliest symbol of which I remember being conscious. I was struck by it, aged perhaps seven or eight, but could not see why it was in a church window. Perhaps I did not know what it was. Yet I had seen the symbol somewhere in crossing the ocean (and I desired to be sailor). Anyway, there was an anchor in the window and I was aware of it. I have forgotten almost every other detail of the church except perhaps the Eagle on whose outspread wings the Bible rested, and even of this I am not sure. Was there really such an eagle? Whether or not, it is relevant that the anchor is a symbol of hope; hope is what I most need. And what the world needs most.

November 4, 1961

Aunt Kit is here on her way back to New Zealand, delighted at having hopped over New York in a helicopter. It rained yesterday. We sat in the gatehouse and made tea and talked about the family. She had already written to me about it, but I will try to put down the essentials as I remember them.

James Merton—from Stoke by Nayland in Suffolk. Bailiff of the Torlesse family. The Mertons were apparently the only ones in the village who could write. Was James's son Charles already schoolmaster there?

In 1856, with the Torlesses, James Merton, Charles his son, and their families went to New Zealand to settle (or did James stay in England?). Charles—musical precentor in St. John's Church (Christchurch? Rangiora?). Taught school. His wife—melancholy and silent. Alfred, my grandfather, his son, was born in New Zealand. Music master at Christ's College, Christchurch.

My grandmother—a Grierson—born in Wales of a Scotch father. Her mother's family Welsh, the Birds. Miniature of a Lieut. Bird in the navy was once over the mantle at Burston House. Don't remember. It is from the Bird family that our face comes—the one Father and I have and Kit has and Dick Trier has. The look, the grin, the brow.

Granny lived in Cardiff and as a child had infantile paralysis. They did not think she would live. She lived to be 101. When she came to Flushing with Kit in 1919, I was four. I remember her very well. The reason: her affection. Kit said Granny and my mother didn't get along. Mother said Granny was being too indulgent with me and that I ought to be made to obey. I remember Mother as strict, stoical, and determined. Granny believed children ought to be brought up by love.

Mother's integrity, directness, sincerity. She was "artistic but not an intellectual." She was practical. It was Granny who bought the house in Christchurch and kept everything together.

Granny in London would meet people "by the Elgin Marbles in the British Museum." Was greatly interested in architecture, history, etc. Kit was a history teacher. I told her to read Christopher Dawson.

November 5, 1961

My father was born in 1887 in Christchurch—left school about 16 to work in Bank of N.Z., but left for England about 1904, studied art—returned to N.Z., then back to England with money he had made in an exhibition in N.Z. Came steerage, his overcoat was stolen, reached England cold and penniless. Had an allowance from Aunt Maude. Studied in Paris, worked also for Tudor Hart in his studio. My mother, whom he met in Paris, was studying interior decorating. They married, hoping to sell pictures to tourists who came through south of France, but the war stopped that. They married about March 1914—came to U.S. about April 1916. My mother was strongly pacifist and opposed father going to war, saying it would be murder. She always was strong on poverty and did not want to have many possessions. Whatever asceticism I have in me seems to have to do with her, and my problems about asceticism are inseparable from my problems with her. Certainly I understand my vocation a bit better.

Sad to see Aunt Kit go. Forty-two years since I last saw her and will probably never see her again. The only blood relative I have seen for twenty years. Lots of lines in her face, but much animation. Thin and energetic, she reminds me of Aunt Maude.

November 27, 1961

Last night I was on the night watch. (Last Sunday after Pentecost.)

Wasted time, brooded. The cloud that hangs over everything is more than a mood now. It is difficult to realize that the source of that has always been just a kind of pretending that is now suddenly fitted out with objectivity. One may say, "Men have always expected a universal cataclysm and it has never come." Now that it is quite possible and within man's own power, one begins to think that man has always expected it because it was coming as the result of a self-fulfilling prophecy. But now, since he can destroy everything and *cannot* stand the tension of waiting, or face the labor of patient reconciliation. . . . Fortunately, one thinks such a thought without understanding it, as a child thinks of death.

On the night watch, hurrying by, I pushed opened the door of the novices' scriptorium and flashed the light over all the empty desks. It was as if the empty room were wholly full of their hearts and their love, as if their goodness had made the place wholly good and rich with love. The loveliness of humanity, which God has taken to Himself in love, and the wonder of each individual person among them. This is of final and eternal significance. To have been appointed by God to be their Father, to have received them from God as my children, to have loved them and been loved by them with such simplicity and sincerity, without nonsense or flattery or sentimentality: this is completely wonderful and is a revelation, a *parousia*, of the Lord of History. That that history may now end is not so relevant.

From this kind of love necessarily springs hope, hope even for political action, for here, paradoxically, hope is most necessary. Hope is always most necessary precisely where everything, spiritually, seems hopeless. This is precisely in the confusion of politics. Hope against hope that man can gradually disarm and cease preparing for destruction and learn at last that he *must* live at peace with his brother. Never have we been less disposed to do this. It must be learned, it must be done, and everything else is secondary to this supremely urgent need of man.

December 11, 1961

Yesterday, Day of Recollection, realized again above all my need for profound and total humility—especially in relation to any work I may do for peace. Humility is more important than zeal. Descent into nothingness and dependence on God. Otherwise I am just fighting the world with its own weapons, and there the world is unbeatable. Indeed, it does not even have to fight back: I will exhaust myself and that will be the end of my stupid efforts.

To seek strength in God, especially in the Passion of Christ.

December 27, 1961. St. John

It rained at first, but now the day has turned softly bright in the afternoon. There is a little, cutting wind and the sun is out, though it is pale. Most sit in the monastery writing their letters.

This morning I was praying much for a wise heart. I think the gift of this Christmas has been the real discovery of Julian of Norwich. I have long been around her and hovered at her door and known that she was one of my best friends, and just because I was so sure of her wise friendship, I did not make haste to seek what I now find.

She seems to me a true theologian with a greater clarity and organization and depth even than St. Teresa of Avila. I mean she really elaborates the content of revelation as deeply experienced. It is first experienced, then thought, and the thought deepens again into life, so that all her life the content of her vision was penetrating her through and through.

One of the central convictions is her eschatological orientation to the central, dynamic secret act "by which all shall be made well" at the last day, our *"great deed,"* "ordained by Our Lord from without beginning."

Especially the first paradox—she must "believe" and accept the doctrine that there are some damned, yet *also* the "word" of Christ shall be "saved in all things" and "all manner of thing shall be well." The heart of her theology is this apparent contradiction in which she must remain steadfastly. I believe that this "wise heart" I have prayed for is precisely in this—to stay in this hope and this contradiction, fixed on the certainty of the "great deed," which alone gives the Christian and spiritual life its true, full dimension.

January 25, 1962

In concluding this retreat:

1. There can be no doubt, no compromise, in my decision to be completely faithful to God's will and truth. Hence I must seek always and in everything to act for His will and in His truth and thus to seek, with His grace, to be "a saint."

2. There must be no doubt, no compromise, in my efforts to avoid falsifying this work of truth by considering too much what others approve of and regard as "holy." In a word, it may happen (or it may not) that what God demands of me may make me look less perfect to others, that it may rob me of their support, their affection, their respect. To become a saint therefore may mean the anguish of looking like and in a real sense "being" a sinner, an outcast. It may mean apparent conflict with certain standards, which may be wrongly understood by me or by others or by all of us.

3. The thing is to cling to God's will and truth in their purity and try to be sincere and to act in all things out of genuine love insofar as I can.

February 27, 1962

From a human and rational viewpoint there is every chance of a disastrous war in the next three to five years.

Although it is almost unbelievable to imagine this country being laid to waste, yet that is very probably what is going to happen.

Without serious reason, without people "wanting it," and without them being able to prevent it, because of their incapacity to use the power they have acquired, they must be used by it.

Hence the absolute necessity of taking this fact soberly into account and living in the perspectives which it establishes—an almost impossible task.

1. *Preeminence of meditation* and prayer, of self-emptying, cleaning out, getting rid of the self that blocks the view of truth. The self that says it will be here and then that it will not be here.

2. *Preeminence of compassion* for every living thing, for life, for the defenseless and simple beings, for the human race in its blindness. For Christ, crucified in His image. Eucharistic sacrifice, in humility and silence.

3. *Weariness of words,* except in friendship, in the simplest and most direct kind of communication, by word of mouth or letter.

4. *Preeminence of the silent and conclusive action*—if any presents itself—of meaningful suffering, accepted in complete silence, without justification.

June 12, 1962

The *Merton Reader* is finished and with the publisher. I am content with Tom McDonnell's final job and with him. He is a good editor, amiable too, simple, ingenuous, and sensible. The details of the war between the publishers are still not clear. Farrar, Straus & Cudahy wanted to trade me for Lowell and Eliot, which is exorbitant all right! Not flattering, just a little sickening.

Then Sister Thérèse Lentfoehr has come up with a remarkably interesting (to me) list of the items in her "collection."

But for me can all this have any serious meaning? I suppose I would earnestly like it to, and I secretly believe it does: as if the image were real. As if there were a genuine mosaic of achievement and as if all the little pieces added up to form the face of a real person. That is the illusion. Not that I must repudiate it all, but, still, it is not significant. The irony of total destruction hangs over it, to keep me wise.

July 21, 1962

A brilliant Saturday. Bright sky and clouds. Not too hot.

Everything I see and experience in Kentucky is to some extent colored and determined by the thoughts and emotions I had when I first came. It cannot be otherwise. So this day too is another day of that time, another link in the chain that began then, began long before then.

August 11, 1962

The thought of going somewhere, anywhere, especially of course to some fabulous mountain monastery to be a dreamer, a distraction avidly loved without too much guilt, almost a prayer.

But the thought of going anywhere is now all exhausted, a hopeless spasm of the heart, without life, without energy, without tone, without sense. There is no longer even any real conflict, it is beyond guilt, the nauseated turning away, the sufferance, the incomprehension that is beyond yes and no.

India, no. Himalayas (a faint flicker, but really no). Greece—a Greek island? Athos? No. Rome: if I were called to Rome by the Pope himself, I would want to refuse. *Anywhere* but Rome! Paris—no. A faint flicker for Devon and Cornwall, and almost a leap, still, for Ecuador (Quito, Cuenca). The Hebrides—yes, maybe the Hebrides. But one would have to go perhaps to Liverpool on the way. Rather die. Dublin? Rather die. Russia? Better dead. Better dead. The Grande Chartreuse? No, bud, leave me alone! No!

"People will do anything, no matter how absurd, to avoid facing their own psyches. They will practice Indian Yoga and all its exercises, observe a strict regimen of diet, learn theosophy by heart, or mechanically repeat mystic texts from the literature of the whole world—all because they cannot get on with themselves and *have not the slightest faith that anything useful could ever come out of the psyche.*" —C. G. Jung in *Spiritual Disciplines*, Papers from the *Eranos Yearbooks* 4. BS. XXX, p. 366.

September 7, 1962. Vigil of Our Lady's Nativity

A dream.

I am in a village "near Bardstown," out of the monastery, it is late, the monks are going to be asleep—will I get back by bedtime or be out after dark? It is dusk, still daylight.

With another man (Tony Walsh?), we meet two lovely young women dressed in white, in the almost deserted village. I say delightedly, "With you, we will easily get a ride!" We plan to hitchhike so as to get back to the monastery before it is too late.

They smile and do not object. I pair off with the less nunlike of the two (the other has a suggestion of a hood or veil), and with my arm around her waist, we walk off down the road. All through the dream I walk with my arm around her. She is fresh and firm and pure, a beautiful sweet person, a stranger yet freely intimate and loving. However, at one point she tells me seriously that I must never try to kiss her or to seduce her, and I assure her earnestly and sincerely I have absolutely no such intention. This does nothing to alter the intimacy of our relationship and friendship.

(Hereafter the other two vanish out of the dream. I am with A. Let us call her that, the question of knowing her *name* never really arises at all. It is totally irrelevant.)

Though the village has been dark and empty, now we are outside on the highway, at the crossroads. It is light. We decide that, if possible, we will take a bus to Bardstown and get from there to Gethsemani. Now there are half a dozen people waiting for the bus. They all know A. because she has preached in their village a new doctrine—sort of Shaker theology—and they twit her about it. One who kids her is an American Indian. Another says something with lewd implications, and I solemnly and hotly defend her—she lets me know it is hardly necessary.

The bus comes, I get in the front, there is nobody there. A. comes in through another door. We meet in the bus.

We are out of the bus, again in the midst of the country.

I see a chapel. It is the chapel of a novitiate of a foundation of Gethsemani, Genesee (*Je ne sais pas!*). We will go to the monastery and wake them up. They will understand. Someone will give us a ride.

Outside the monastery, a young secular and two or three girls. They are in bathing suits, have been swimming in a pond in the farmyard. We will not wake up the monks. This boy will drive us. But we must get to his car without awakening anyone.

Complication in the buildup. We do not find the car.

On the road. High columns of silver gray smoke go up from the direction of Bardstown. "Tactical atomic weapons." Beautiful, though. Some kind of test. It is here I think A. told me not to kiss her.

We turn back. Now all the monks led by their abbot, Dom Eusebius, are out on the road dressed as soldiers! He leads them with determination. Surely I will be caught. As we pass through the midst of them A. conceals my monastic crown with her hand. But is this going to be enough?

Are they after us?

I am in a barn (without A.). I set fire to straw—if the barn burns it will divert any pursuit. But can I myself get out? After seeming to be trapped, I am now completely out, on the "other side" in open country. I see a vast landscape, most moving, with a church in the middle, Dutch with a thin spire—sacred objects in the sky or country around, for instance, a cross.

I am going past the church in the open country when I wake up.

October 2, 1962

Though I am nearly 48 and it is doubtless time to feel a change of climate in my physical being, which begins to dispose itself for its end some one of these years, it is useless to interpret every little sign or suggestion of change as something of great significance. This is a temptation I yield to. I am still too young mentally to be in the least patient of any sign of age. My impatience is felt as an upheaval of resentment, disgust, depression. Yet I am joyful. I like life, I am happy with it, I have really nothing to complain of. But a little of the chill, a little of the darkness, the sense of void in the midst of myself, and I say to my body: "Okay, all right then, *die*, you idiot!" But it is not really trying to die, it just wants to slow down.

This war scare aggravates it, this sense of death and desperation running through my whole society with all its bombs and its money and its death wish. The colossal sense of failure in the midst of success that is characteristic of America (but that America cannot really face). I have a comfortable sense of success, which I know to be more or less meaningless, yet I want to make my will now—as a writer. Go on, fool! Forget it! You may write another twenty books, who knows? In any case, does it matter? Is this relevant? On the contrary, now is the time I must learn to stop taking satisfaction in what I have done, or being depressed because the night will come and my work will come to an end. Now is the time to give what I have to others and not reflect on it. I wish I had learned the knack of it, of giving without question or care. I have not, but perhaps I still have time to try.

December 9, 1962. II Sunday Advent

Hurt my hand falling on a sharp stone in the garden (in the dark) on the way to Prime. Moral: don't be looking at the stars on the way to Prime.

It is beautiful Advent weather, grayish and cold, with clouds of light snow howling across the valley, and I see it is really winter. I put some bread out for the birds.

Twenty-one years tomorrow since I landed here! I feel closer to my beginning than ever, yet perhaps I am near my end. The Advent hymns sound as they first did, as if they were the nearest things to me that ever were, as if they had been decisive in shaping my heart and my life, as if I had received their form, as if there could never be any other melodies so deeply connatural to me. They are myself, words and melody and everything. So also the *Rorate Coeli* that brought me here to pray for peace. I have not prayed for it well enough or been pure enough in heart or wise enough. Today before the Blessed Sacrament I was ashamed of the impertinences and the deep infidelities of my life, rooted in weakness and confusion.

December 11, 1962

Afternoon—the primary duty: to seek coherence, clarity, awareness, insofar as these are possible. Not only human coherence and clarity but those that are born of silence, emptiness, and grace. Which means always seeking the right balance between study, work, meditation, responsibility to others, and solitude.

Very cold. Some snow. Bright, silent afternoon.

I have been shocked at a notice of a new book by Rachel Carson on what is happening to birds as a result of the indiscriminate use of poisons (which do not manage to kill the insects they intend to kill).

Someone will say: you worry about birds. Why not worry about people? I worry about *both* birds and people. We are in the world and part of it, and we are destroying everything because we are destroying ourselves spiritually, morally, and in every way. It is all part of the same sickness, it all hangs together.

December 15, 1962

Charming letter from Eleanor Shipley Duckett, who, on returning to Smith College from England (Cambridge), found some notes I had sent and is making them her "Advent reading." I am very attracted to her. She is a sweet person. She wrote part of her letter in Latin. Though I have so far not had much contact with her (it began when the University of Michigan Press sent the proofs of her *Carolingian Portraits*), I feel we can be very good friends, that this friendship can be really precious to us both— with the autumn quality of detachment that comes from the sense that we are coming to the end of our lives (she must be quite older than I, in her sixties, I presume). This sense of being suspended over nothingness and yet in life, of being a fragile thing, a flame that may blow out and yet burns brightly, adds an inexpressible sweetness to the gift of life, for one sees it entirely and purely as a gift. One that one must treasure in great fidelity with a truly pure heart.

December 22, 1962

Joost Meerloo sent one of his offprints in French on the ritual of giving and receiving Christmas presents. It is really very amusing and interesting. In the middle of it I saw the connection with my own life, with my failure to really trust another person enough to give myself completely to her. My sexual adventures were always seductions—I wanted them to be conquests in which in reality I gave nothing, only "took." I believe my need and perhaps my latent capacity to give myself was once very deep. Now—well, I get depressed. I remember the frequency of Christmas depressions in the past few years and have come to expect them as a matter of course. Yet my first Christmas here, which was certainly an unreserved gift of myself to my vocation, was fantastically pure and happy. Nor has that happiness ever really left me, in the depths of my soul at least.

December 25, 1962. Christmas Day

Evening: rain, silence, joy.

I am certain that where the Lord sees the small point of poverty and extenuation and helplessness to which the monk is reduced, the solitary and the man of tears, then He *must* come down and be born there in this anguish and make it constantly a point of infinite joy, a seed of peace in the world. This is, and always has been, my mission. There is for me no truth and no sense in anything that conceals from me this precious poverty, this seed of tears and true joy. Hence the demonstrations and distractions that take me away from this are foolish and useless and can even constitute infidelities if they are evasions from it. I have a right to speak to others insofar as I speak to the same truth in them, assuage their doubts, and make them strong in this small spark of exhaustion in which the Lord becomes their wisdom and their life everlasting. What do the Psalms say but this?

"Stay vigilant, you will see the help of the Lord upon you!"

How deep is this truth, how tremendously important.

We do not *wait* for this *auxilium Domini,* this help from the Lord! Others announce it has arrived, but we feel that it has *not.* Stay vigilant: *Constantes estote.* It will arrive for me also at the proper time, in secret, in God's own freedom beyond all control of timetables, even ecclesiastical! This is a deeper and truer aspect of the Church's mystery: the freedom of her inner life, which may or may not correspond to the exterior indications of the ritual moment.

January 4, 1963

The New Year has begun well, though I have had a filthy cold.

The merger of the two novitiates is proceeding well, mainly because all the novices are so good. I am happy with the brother novices, one loves them immediately. They really have something, a special grace of simplicity and honesty and goodness. It is a great grace to have them there: choir and brothers seem happy with each other, and everyone seems agreed that the plan is working well. In fact, there seem to be all sorts of good things about it that one had not anticipated.

The unifying of the novitiate is certainly important and salutary. I think it will mean a great deal—and further I have to admit that though I am carrying it out, it is not originally my idea but the Abbot's. However, I did take a certain initiative and he was pleased to let me do so.

I think the grace the brothers have comes from their work, which keeps them perhaps (when properly done) from getting too obsessed with themselves and with their spirituality. It is wonderful how they will go into anything and get it done, not standing around scratching their heads with the dubiousness of the choir, not waiting to be told each next move.

January 15, 1963

The noise and concern about the novitiate, and all those who come to the classes, are having a deep effect on me. The work is hard, though I am doing more than I probably should in my concern to be well prepared. I also realize the limitations of anything short of prayer and abandonment as preparation, the limitations of my own capacity. Hence in everything I have come to feel more than ever my need for grace, my total dependence on God, my helplessness without His special intervention, which I may need at any moment. Never has this been so clear to me. Perhaps it was never before as true as now.

In consequence, my attitude toward the monastery changes. They have need of me and I have need of them. As if without this obedience and charity my life would not make sense. It is an existential situation which God has willed for me, and it is part of His Providence—it is not to be questioned, no matter how difficult it might be. I must simply obey God, and this reaches out into everything. Even at the hermitage it is less a question of seeking Him than of total submission and obedience to Him to whom I belong in love.

In this new condition my attitude toward the Abbot is changing. Of course it is obvious that my complaints and discontent have been absurd. Though I can perhaps back them up with plausible arguments, they have no real meaning, they don't make sense. He is what he is, he means well, and in fact does well. He is the superior destined for me in God's Providence, and it is absurd for me to complain. No harm will ever come to me through him—it *cannot*. How could I have thought otherwise?

January 17, 1963

The great trial of fidelity in Christian life—a trial that springs from the fact that we too closely identify *fidelity to God* and *fidelity to external organization* in the Catholic Church. Hence there is invariably a great trial when an apparent conflict is precipitated (and it is easily precipitated). There are times when it seems that fidelity to God is *not* compatible with mere obedience to an external norm, where fidelity to God requires something else: certainly not revolt nor disobedience but a presentation of alternative and deeper views.

A "fidelity" that *always* demands the sacrifice of the interior and the more perfect in order to conform to an external norm that is mediocre and requires of us only passivity and inertia is an infidelity to God and to His Church. Yet at the same time we must not make a fetish out of autonomy and be "faithful" only to our own will, for this is the other way to infidelity.

The answer is in the Church considered less as an organization than as a living body of interrelated freedoms. Fidelity belongs not so much to the realm of Law as to the realm of love. But it presupposes obedience and self-sacrifice.

January 21, 1963. St. Agnes

Very cold morning, about 8 above zero. Left for the hermitage before dawn, after retreat conference on sin. Pure dark sky with only moon and planets in it, stars already gone. The moon and Venus over the barns and Mars far over in the west over the road and the fire tower.

Sunrise—an event that calls forth solemn music in the very depths of one's being, as if one's whole being had to attune itself to the cosmos and praise God for a new day, praise Him in the name of all the beings that ever were or ever will be—as though *now* upon me falls the responsibility of seeing what all my ancestors have seen, acknowledging it and praising God so that, whether or not *they* praised God back then themselves, they now do so in me.

Sunrise demands this rightness, this order, this true disposition of one's whole being.

January 25, 1963

Still very cold and bright.

The best thing about the retreat has been working in the pig barn and then walking back alone, a mile and a half, through the snow.

I think I have come to see more clearly and more seriously the meaning, or lack of meaning, in my life. How much I am still the same self-willed and volatile person who made such a mess of Cambridge. That I have not changed yet, down in the depths, or perhaps, yes, I have changed radically somewhere, yet I have still kept some of the old, vain, inconstant, self-centered ways of looking at things. The situation I am in now has been given me to change me, if I will only surrender completely to reality as it is given me by God and no longer seek in any way to evade it, even by interior reservations.

Hitherto my interior reservation has been always "Of course there must be something better, and who knows if that is not for me?"

Well, there *is* something better: but it must come out of an inner transformation of my own self, in Christ. What is better is Christ, that is to say, for me to live completely in and by Him. I already do live in Him, of course, but there remains much to be surrendered that still remains "my own."

January 28, 1963

Here at the hermitage, in deep snow, everything is ordinary and silent.

Return to reality and to the ordinary, in silence. It is always there if you know enough to return to it.

What is *not* ordinary—the tension of meeting people, discussion, ideas. This too is good and real, but illusion gets into it. The unimportant becomes important, words and images become more important than life.

One travels all over vast areas, sitting still in a room, and one is soon tired of so much traveling.

William Miller of the Fellowship of Reconciliation and Paul Peachey of the Church Peace Mission were here. I was eventually strained and tense from all the talk. It was quieter this morning with Peachey alone. We discussed my peace book, which is not being published, and his translation of Dumoulin's *History of Zen*, which has just appeared. It was a fruitful morning.

Yet I need very much this silence and this snow. Here alone can I find my way, because here alone the way is right in front of my face and it is God's way for me—there is really no other.

February 27, 1963. Ash Wednesday

Our mentioning of the weather—our perfunctory observations on what kind of day it is—are perhaps not idle. Perhaps we have a deep and legitimate need to know in our entire being what the day is like, to *see* it and *feel* it, to know how the sky is gray, paler in the south, with patches of blue in the southwest, with snow on the ground, the thermometer at 18, and cold wind making your ears ache. I have a real need to know these things, because I myself am part of the weather and part of the climate and part of the place. A day in which I have not shared truly in all this is no day at all. It is certainly part of my life of prayer.

March 10, 1963. II Sunday of Lent

I thought today, at adoration of the Blessed Sacrament, what a blessing it was that I did not go in 1956 to be analyzed by Gregory Zilboorg! What a tragedy and mess that would have been—and I must give Z. the credit for having sensed it himself in his own way. It would have been utterly impossible and absurd. I think in great measure his judgment was that I could not be fitted into his kind of theater. There was no conceivable part for me to play in his life, on the contrary! And certainly it is true that the whole thing would have been unimaginably absurd. He had quite enough intelligence (more than enough, he was no fool at all!) to see that it would be a very poor production for him, for the Abbot (who was most willing), and for me. I am afraid that I was willing, at the time, to go, which shows what a fool I was.

In any case, all manner of better things were reserved for me. But I have not understood them.

In a Zen koan someone said that an enlightened man is not one who seeks Buddha or finds Buddha, but just an ordinary man who has *nothing left to do.* Yet mere stopping is not to arrive. To stop is to stay a million miles from it, to do nothing is to miss it by the whole width of the universe. Yet how close it is, how simple it would be to have nothing more to do—if I had only done it. Meanwhile, I am more content than I have ever been here with this unripeness. I know that one day it will ripen, and one will see there had been nothing there at all except an ordinary person with nothing to do in the first place.

The evening light. Purple coves and holes of shadow in the breasts of hills and the white gable of Newton's house smiling so peacefully amid the trees in the middle of the valley. This is the peace and luminosity William Blake loved. Today after dinner, a hawk, circling the novitiate and the church steeple, designed a free flight unutterably more pure than skating or music. How he flung himself down from on high and swooped up to touch lightly on the pinnacle of the steeple and sit there, then fell off to cut lovely curves all around the cedars, then off like an arrow into the south.

March 31, 1963

That notorious illuminist, the Holy Ghost.

Now the mauve hills are stained with green. As if I would write a novel about a southern place called Mauve Hill.

April 7, 1963. Palm Sunday

Quiet sunset. Cool, still day and another fire over toward Rohan's Knob.

Peace and silence at sunset behind the woodshed, with a wren playing quietly on a heap of logs, with a detached fragment of gutter hanging from the end of the roof, with bare branches of sycamores against the blue evening sky. Peace and solitude.

Daily I rot. My health is good, but little pieces and parts of me begin to work less and less well. I don't especially care. I am used and wearing.

April 24, 1963

The icon of St. Elias, which Jack Ford brought me from St. Meinrad's and which yesterday I put up on the east wall: fabulously beautiful and delicate and strong. A great red transparent globe of light, with angelic horses rearing in unison, and angels lifting all of it up to the blackness of the divine mystery—from below, the dark curve and shelves of the mountain from which Eliseus reaches into the globe to touch the mantle of the prophet, who stands in a little, finely drawn, very simple, Russian peasant's cart (in the globe of fire!).

Below, Elias sleeps: that was before, when he had sorrow. The angel leans over him and mentions the hearth-cake to the sleeping prophet.

What a thing to have by you! It changes everything! Transfigures everything!

Outside the door, a double bloom on one large violet iris, standing out of the green spears of the daylilies. On the tongue of the bloom walks a great black-gold bee, the largest honeybee I ever saw. To be part of all this is to be infinitely rich.

Father Alphonse died this morning. I was kneeling by his bed, and we said the wonderful prayers, calling upon all the prophets, patriarchs, martyrs. Such prayers! I discover that I was very fond of this crusty, simple, rude old man.

The relic of St. Bede over my heart, preparing me for May.

May 21, 1963

Marvelous vision of the hills at 7:45 A.M. The same hills as always, as in the afternoon, but now catching the light in a totally new way, at once very earthly and very ethereal, with delicate cups of shadow and dark ripples and crinkles where I had never seen them, the whole slightly veiled in mist so that it seemed to be a tropical shore, a newly discovered continent. A voice in me seemed to be crying, "Look! Look!" For these are the discoveries, and it is for this that I am high on the mast of my ship (have always been) and I know that we are on the right course, for all around is the sea of paradise.

May 26, 1963

Today is the fourteenth anniversary of my Ordination to the priesthood.

I wish I could say they had been fourteen years of ever-growing fulfillment and order and integration. That is unfortunately not so. They have been years of relative happiness and productivity on the surface, but now I realize more and more the depth of my frustration and the apparent finality of my defeat. I have certainly not fitted into the conventional—or even traditional—mold. Perhaps that is good. I am not a J. F. Powers character. Yet the frustration is the same. (I do not know if I am a George Bernanos character. I am not a Graham Greene character.) But this business of defeat is there, and I see it is perhaps in some way permanent. As if in a way my priestly life has been sad and fruitless—the defeat and failure of my monastic life. (Perhaps. For after all how do I know?)

I have a very real sense that it has all been some kind of a lie, a charade. With all my blundering attempts at sincerity, I have actually done nothing to change this.

I have certainly not been a model of priestly virtue. It does not seem that I have willfully sinned, i.e., with my eyes wide open, in a serious matter. But there have been repeated failures, failures without number, like holes appearing everywhere in a worn-out garment. Nothing has been effectively patched. The moths have eaten me while I was confusedly intent on what seemed to me to be good or important or necessary for survival.

There has been a kind of dazed desperation in my half-conscious attempts to preserve my identity, while being worn down by the ever-renewed futility of a half-productive existence.

I have not always been temperate. If I go to town and someone pours me a drink, I don't resist another or even a third. And I have sometimes gone beyond the *trivium perfectum*—the "perfect third." A monk?

Probably the chief weakness has been lack of real courage to bear up under the attention of monastic and priestly life. Anyway, I am worn down. I am easily discouraged. The depressions are deeper, more frequent. I am near fifty. People think I am happy.

My Mass every morning has certainly been a joy, and I have attended seriously to it. There has sometimes been great and simple meaning in it, and always the realization that it was far greater than I could understand. But there have also been moments of unspeakable anguish and tension.

I suppose that in the end what I have done is that I have resisted the superimposition of a complete priestly form, a complete monastic pattern. I have stubbornly saved myself from becoming *absorbed* in the priesthood, and I do not know if this was cowardice or integrity. There seems to be no real way for me to tell.

June 1, 1963. Vigil of Pentecost
It is hot. Pope John is dying and perhaps dead. Already yesterday at this time he was in a coma, in an oxygen tent, with the papal guards around

his apartments. Last night he was conscious for a moment, they say, and smiled and blessed those around him. I have been thinking of him all day and praying for him, especially at the High Mass after None. The world owes him a great debt, in his simplicity. It is hard to feel that we can do without someone like him. He has done so much in four years, four and a half, to remind people that Christian charity is not a pure fiction. Yet, in spite of it all, will people ever again have confidence in love? Will they not think that everyone who has spoken of love has finally betrayed them?

June 3, 1963. Whit Monday

Retreat at hermitage. Mass at 4, came up shortly after 5, through the mist and the wet grass. "Open the ground of hearing . . . " (Eckhart).

Time here seems quite a different kind of measure and, in fact, it is. For time is constituted by relationships, and here all the relationships are different. I am convinced that the tensions of our community life are delusions and obsessions because of the *unreality* of our activities—the basic unreality of our relationships. Unreal because much too artificial and contrived.

In any case, here one has a sense of being both fully relaxed and fully alive, of having nothing to do, or rather perhaps still wanting to read and think but not being able to because of the sweetness and fullness of time, which is too good to lose. The *immediacy* of the relationships is all too good to be lost. The sun, the summer tanager (I finally connected the song with the bird), the clear morning, the trees, the quiet, the barely born butterfly from the cocoon under the bench—etc.

Seriously, my projects and relationships, including correspondence and much of my work, are sheer waste. The only thing that can be said for them is that they seem at times to be more real than what goes on in the community and probably are.

Relationships with the novices, though, are meaningful and healthy, though I question the value of my conferences; maybe I am working in support of a delusion.

June 4, 1963

Solitude—when you get saturated with silence and landscape, then you need an interior work, psalms, scripture, meditation. But first the saturation. How much of this is simply a restoration of one's normal human balance?

Like waking up, like convalescence after an illness, my life here is most real because most simple. In the monastery it is also real and simple, at least in the novitiate. The more I reach out into "the world," the less simplicity, the more sickness. Our society is gravely ill. This is said so often and I have said it so often, but saying it does not seem to help. Knowing it does not seem to help. My concern has been probably sincere, but in great part futile. I don't want to turn off into desperation and negativism, but there has to be a far greater reserve and caution and *silence* in my looking at the world and my attempts to help us all survive.

Identity. I can see now where the work is to be done. I have been coming here into solitude to find myself, and now I must also lose myself: not simply rest in the calm, the peace, the identity that is made up of my experienced relationship with nature in solitude. This is healthier than my "identity" as a writer or a monk, but it is still a false identity, though it has a temporary meaning and validity. It is the cocoon that masks the transition stage between what crawls and what flies.

PART V

SEEKING PEACE IN
THE HERMITAGE
1963–1965

Everything the Fathers of the Church say about the solitary life is exactly true. The temptations and the joys, above all the tears and the ineffable peace and *happiness.* The happiness that is so pure because it is simply not of one's own making but sheer mercy and gift. Happiness in the sense of having arrived at last in the place destined for me by God, fulfilling the purpose for which I was brought here twenty-three years ago.

A Vow of Conversation

Who can free himself from achievement
And from fame, descend and be lost
Amid the masses of men?
He will flow like *Tao,* unseen,
He will go about like Life itself
With no name and no home.
Simple he is, without distinction.
To all appearances he is a fool
His steps leave no trace. He has no power.
He achieves nothing, has no reputation.
Since he judges no one
No one judges him.
Such is the perfect man:
His boat is empty.

The Way of Chuang Tzu

August 16, 1963

A lovely cool, dazzlingly bright afternoon yesterday. Blue sky, clouds, silence, and the immense sunlit sweep of St. Malachy's field. I found a mossy turf under pines in that little island of woods, along which the Lespedeza hedge we planted ten or fifteen years ago is still growing. Yesterday it was blooming with delicate, heather-like purple blossoms, and bees were busy in them.

An entirely beautiful, transfigured moment of love for God and the need for complete confidence in Him in everything, without reserve, even when almost nothing can be understood. A sense of the continuity of grace in my life and an equal sense of the stupidity and baseness of the infidelities that have threatened to break that continuity. How can I be so cheap and foolish as to trifle with anything so precious?

October 6, 1963

Dreamt last night of Italian cathedrals (not real ones, dream ones). First I am with others of the community in a crowded Cathedral at "Siena." Confusion. I am trying to pray, turned toward a stone-like tabernacle beyond the crowd. (Is it the tabernacle?) I think of going to the "Shrine of St. Catherine." Then I am in another spacious well-lighted Cathedral "nearer home" and I am trying to "remember" the name of the city which should be very familiar (Mantua?). I am struck and appeased by the airiness and spaciousness of the Cathedral, the high shadowy vaults with paintings. A Nazareth nun walks through the Cathedral. I am afraid she will recognize me. I pray. I cannot quite remember the name of the place where I am, a city perhaps beginning with *C?* Or "Mantua" perhaps? But no, Mantua is in the "North of Italy," and I am more in the center.

November 23, 1963

When I came in from the woods yesterday, Brother Aidan met me at the door of the novitiate and told me the president had been shot and died, in Texas, an hour and a half before.

The whole thing leaves one bewildered and slightly sick. Sick for the madness, ferocity, stupidity, aimless cruelty that is the mark of so great a part of this country. Essentially the same blind, idiot destructiveness and hate that killed Medgar Evers in Jackson, the Negro children in Birmingham. I do not know what was the motive of this absurd assassination—whether it was over the race question or not, or just fanaticism. The country is full of madness, and we are going to know this more and more.

December 1, 1963. First Sunday of Advent

Bright stars. I am still not going to the Night Office. Still need some traction to get the kinks out of my neck and shoulder when waking up. Take it again before going to sleep at night, so my timetable does not quite jive with that of the community. But I love this season, need the hymns. Loved the responseries again yesterday in the snow-flaked mist. Yet the old liturgy itself recedes in a "past" that is itself being rejected, as if one were no longer allowed to cling to it, as if it were no longer sure to be there tomorrow. It is my own past and the past of my civilization, and I must leave both, having them as though I had them not.

December 17, 1963

Cold stars. Steam coming up in the dark from the kitchens into the freezing night. Father Leonard with his routine in the grand parlor, in the dim light. Creak of the wooden steps leading down to the infirmary refectory. Flamingos on the Standard Oil calendar in the kitchen. Tea. Frost on the side of the coal pile. Dirty bread lying among the stones, frozen, for birds.

January 25, 1964

The need for constant self-revision, growth, leaving behind, renunciation of yesterday, yet in continuity with all yesterdays (to cling to the past is to lose one's continuity with it, for this means clinging to what was not there). My ideas are always changing, always moving around one center, always seeing the center from somewhere else. I will always be accused of inconsistencies. I will no longer be there to hear the accusation.

February 22, 1964

Today is the twenty-second anniversary of my reception of the habit. In all sobriety and honesty I must admit that the twenty-two years have not been well spent, at least as far as my part in them has been concerned, although from God there has been nothing but grace and mercy. Rather, twenty-two years of relative confusion, often coming close to doubt and infidelity, agonized aspirations for "something better," criticism of what I have, inexplicable inner suffering that is largely my own fault, insufficient efforts to overcome myself, inability to find my way, perhaps culpably straying off into things that do not concern me. Yet in the heart of it is a kind of standing aghast at the situation, the ambiguity in which I find myself. In the depths of my heart I do embrace the Cross of Christ, but I fear to verbalize about it and wonder if this failure is a failure of faith. "I do not know, Lord, have mercy on me!"

I do know this—that after the first half-year or so (beginner's consolations!) I ran into years of false fervor, asceticism, intransigence, intolerance: this lasted more or less until I was ordained. I am trying to get back now to a little of the asceticism (how awfully little!) without the intolerance and uncharity, yet I am still not broad and warm as a monk this long in a monastery ought to be. All this, I know, is useless talk. Better to find refuge in the psalms, in the chanted Office, the Liturgy. That is deep and real and one thing I have learned to trust— though I am suspicious of the nonsense and "projects" that always surround it.

March 3, 1964

I had been hoping to republish a few articles on nuclear war that had been permitted by Dom Gabriel—thinking that it was enough that he had permitted them once. Not so. The new General, Dom Ignace Gillet, dug into the files, held a meeting of Definitors, and declared that there was to be no republishing of these articles. Thus I am still not permitted to say what Pope John said in *Pacem in Terris*. Reason: "That is not the job of a monk, it is for the Bishops." Certainly it has a basis in monastic tradition. "The job of the monk is to weep, not to teach." But with our cheese business and all the other "weeping" functions we have undertaken, it seems strange that a monk should be forbidden to stand up for the truth, particularly when the truth (in this case) is disastrously neglected.

A grim insight into the stupor of the Church, in spite of all that has been attempted, all efforts to wake her up! It all falls into place. Pope

Pius XII and the Jews, the Church in South America, the treatment of Negroes in the United States, the Catholics on the French right in the Algerian affair, the German Catholics under Hitler. All this fits into one big picture, and our contemplative recollection is not very impressive when it is seen only as another little piece fitted into the puzzle. The whole thing is too sad and too serious for bitterness. I have the impression that my education is beginning—only just beginning—and that I have a lot more terrible things to learn before I can know the real meaning of hope.

There is no consolation, only futility, in the idea that one is a kind of martyr for a cause. I am not a martyr for anything, I am afraid. I wanted to act like a reasonable, civilized, responsible Christian of my time. I am not allowed to do this. I am told I have renounced this—fine. In favor of what? In favor of a silence that is deeply and completely in complicity with the forces that carry out oppression, injustice, aggression, exploitation, war. In other words, silent complicity is presented as a "greater good" than honest, conscientious protest—it is supposed to be part of my vowed life, for the "glory of God." Certainly I refuse complicity. My silence itself is a protest, and those who know me are aware of this fact. I have at least been able to write enough to make that clear. Also I cannot leave here in order to protest, since the meaning of any protest depends on my staying here. Anyway, I am definitely *silenced* on the subject of nuclear war.

The letter also seemed to indicate that the whole book (*Seeds of Destruction*) was stopped, but this must be a mistake, as *The Black Revolution* is appearing this month in France.

I have a splitting headache.

March 7, 1964
I am coming to see clearly the great importance of the concept of "realized eschatology"—the transformation of life and of human relations by Christ *now* (rather than an eschatology focused on future cosmic events—the Jewish poetic figures to emphasize the transcendence of the Son of God). Realized eschatology is the heart of genuine Christian humanism and hence its tremendous importance for the

Christian peace effort, for example. The presence of the Holy Spirit, the call to repentance, the call to see Christ in Man, the presence of the redeeming power of the Cross in the sacraments: these belong to the "last age," which we are in. But all these do not reveal their significance without a Christian Mission to peace, the preaching of the Gospel of unity, peace, and mercy, the reconciliation of man with man, and so with God. The duty, however, does not mean that there will not at the same time be great cosmic upheavals. The preaching of peace by a remnant in an age of war and violence is one of the eschatological characteristics of the life of the Church. By this activity of the Church the work of God is mysteriously accomplished in the world.

March 10, 1964

Heavy and steady rain with high winds for two days on end—and much rain before it. The Ohio Valley must be flooded. Here there is water everywhere, streams come from everywhere, and all night the air is full of the rushing of water and wind. Wonderful black skies over the woods, great strong expectancy of spring in all the wet, black trees. Yellow waterfall over the new dam at the waterworks.

Last night I dreamed that a distinguished Lady Latinist came to give a talk to the novices on St. Bernard. Instead of a lecture, she sang in Latin, with meters and flexes and *puncta*, what must have been a sermon of the saint—though I could not quite recognize it. The novices were restive and giggling: this made me sad. In the middle Dom Frederic entered. We stood. The singing was interrupted. I explained in an undertone that I had just now remembered the violation of enclosure and would remedy matters as soon as possible. Where did she come from? "Harvard," I said in a stage whisper she must have heard. Then the novices were in a big semi, loaded on the elevator (how?) to go down from the top of the building, and instead of the Latinist coming with us, I left the novices to escort her down safely by the stairs, but now her clothes were soiled and torn, she was confused and sad, she had no Latin and nothing much of anything to say. Is this my dream of the Liturgical revival and of Anglicanism, etc? Perhaps some Anglican *anima* of my own?

April 11, 1964

The time has probably come to go back on all that I have said about one's "real self," etc., etc., and show that there is after all no hidden mysterious "real self" *other than* or "hiding behind" the self that one is. The "real self" is not an object, but I have betrayed it by seeming to promise a possibility of knowing it somewhere, sometimes as a reward for astuteness, fidelity, and a quick-witted ability to stay one jump ahead of reality. However, the empirical self is not to be taken as fully "real" either. Here is where the illusion begins.

April 23, 1964

Real spring weather—these are the precise days when everything changes. All the trees are fast beginning to be in leaf, and the first green freshness of a new summer is all over the hills. Irreplaceable purity of these few days chosen by God as His sign!

Mixture of heavenliness and anguish. Seeing "heavenliness" suddenly, for instance, in the pure white of the mature dogwood blossoms against the dark evergreens in the cloudy garden. "Heavenliness" too of the song of the unknown bird that is perhaps here only for these days, passing through, a lovely, deep, simple song. Pure—no pathos, no statement, no desire, pure heavenly sound. Seized by this "heavenliness" as if I were a child—a child's mind I have never done anything to deserve to have and that is my own part in the heavenly spring. Not of this world, nor of my making. Born partly of physical anguish (which is really not there, though. It goes quickly). The sense that "heavenliness" is the real nature of things, not their nature, not "in themselves," but the fact that they are a gift of love, and of freedom.

April 28, 1964

The thought of traveling is perhaps soon going to be a real temptation, because soon it may happen that permission to travel may be given. (It could be given now, but Dom James is so afraid to let anyone out.) Hence I must decide and have decided against it, instead of idly wishing, for instance, that I could visit the Cistercian sites in Wales.

There seems to be trouble with another disk lower in my spine. Considerable pain early yesterday morning and most of the day, tapered off after I spent some time lying down flat on my back. I was afraid I might have to go back to the hospital.

Today I have the whole day in solitude with Dom James's permission.

One thing is certain—I am simply surfeited with words and typescript and print, surfeited to the point of utter nausea. Surfeited with letters, too. This is so bad that it amounts to a sickness, like the obsessive gluttony of the rich woman in Theodoret who was eating thirty chickens a day until some hermit cured her. The only hermit that can cure me is myself, and so I have to become that solitary in order to qualify as my own physician. I am so sick that the cure is going to take time. If by the end of the year it can be well begun, I can count myself fortunate. One plan to begin is perhaps in the area of letters—when I respond to *another* one asking for a blurb, I feel like a drunk and incontinent man falling into bed with another whore, in spite of himself. The awful thing is that I *can't* stop.

June 12, 1964

By surprise I got a letter Wednesday from Daisetz Teitaro Suzuki's secretary saying Suzuki was going to be in New York this month, could definitely not come here, but really wanted to meet me: so could I come there? I thought about it, and since it is probably the only chance I will ever have to speak to him, I thought it important enough to ask Dom James's permission. I certainly did not think he would give it, but, somewhat reluctantly, he did. A flight is booked for me next Monday the 15th. Since this decision has been reached, I am upset and distracted, certainly without much real joy at the thought of seeing Suzuki. I can think of nowhere I would less rather go than New York. I am to stay on the Columbia campus, or at any rate uptown, out of the midtown section where I would meet friends. That is all right.

The only way I can stomach the whole idea is that I think, in good faith, it was God's will for me to ask. For some reason I should go, not only for my own benefit. I am not supposed to understand but have to trust. There is more here than I know. I see how much I am attached to this place, these woods, this silence. That is as it should be. If I am to be shaken up a bit, shaken "loose," that is good also.

June 16, 1964

Extraordinary climb and lift of the jet (my first time on one) straight up into the clouds like a huge projectile, leaning over Louisville and the river, out of the dirty mist lying on the valley like a scum of water, fairly large wave of cumuli rising here and there out of the scum like something in a fair or dream.

After Columbus, Ohio (long stay during which I read a John Cheever story in the *New Yorker*), terrific climb to get over storms, and then the usual thing, as soon as you are 35,000 feet on top of piles of bright clouds in the absolutely pure sky, the girls start bringing you shrimps. Extraordinary—when the girl came to ask my destination and when New York came out as the most obvious and natural thing in the world, I suddenly realized after all that I was a New Yorker. When people had asked my destination in the past, it was New York to which I was coming back.

Actually I thought I was going to hate the trip. I loved it! As Sandy Hook came in sight I knew what it was, immediately. Then the long string of beaches on the Jersey shore, the twinkling water with boats in it, and dark brown hot Brooklyn and Manhattan over there. Idlewild, Kennedy Airport, enormous rumble of trucks and buildings, a vast congeries of airports, then in the American Airlines building, fantastic beings, lovely humans, assured yet resigned, some extraordinarily beautiful, all mature and sophisticated actual people with whom I was in a profound rapport with warmth and recognition—these are my people, for God's sake! I had forgotten—the tone of voice, the awareness, the weariness, the readiness to keep standing, an amazing existence, the realization of the fallible condition of man, the fantastic complexity of modern life.

I loved being here, seeing familiar houses and places and unfamiliar huge apartments yet knowing where I was (e.g., Forest Hills). Then sure enough the World's Fair, preposterous, just like the old one but tamer, no tower and ball, but the same place, same Jewish cemetery that I used to look at with river-dazed eyes. I tried to pick out Hillside Avenue (Elder Avenue) or whatever the street was where I lived forty years ago.

Morning of the 16th: bright clear sky and wind on Broadway, noble and vast with lots of new trees. Mass at Corpus Christi all by myself at

Our Lady's altar before that lovely Italian medieval triptych—no word for it.

My room in Butler Hall at Columbia looks out over Harlem. Out of Harlem—the noise of traffic and the uninterrupted cries of playing children, cries of life and joy coming out of purgatory, loud and strong, the voice of a great living organism. Shots too—and there is no rifle range! Frequent shots—at what? More frequent than the Kentucky woods behind the hermitage in hunting season. Drums, bongos, the chanting of songs, dogs barking, traffic, buses like jet planes. Above all the morning light, then the afternoon light, the flashing windows of the big new housing development.

The campus is better, the old south field track is gone, dorms there now (the sundial is gone), flashy new buildings and lots of foreign students.

About Suzuki later. How impressive and what a warm and charming visit today! The tea, the joy.

June 20, 1964

Two good long talks with Suzuki. He is now ninety-four, bent, slow, deaf, but lively and very responsive. Much support from Mihoko Okamura, his secretary, very charming and lively. They were both *extremely* friendly. Apparently he had read several of my books. It seems a lot of Zen people read *The Ascent to Truth.* That is somewhat consoling, though it is my wordiest and in some ways emptiest book. He was very pleased with the essay in *Continuum,* thought it one of the best things on Zen to have been written in the West. Mihoko made the green tea and whisked it up in the dark brown bowl, and I drank it in three and a half sips as prescribed: found it wonderful. (J. Laughlin had said it was awful.)

So I sat with Suzuki on the sofa and we talked of all kinds of things to do with Zen and with life. He read to me from a Chinese text—familiar stories. I translated to him from Octavio Paz's Spanish version of Fernando Pessoa. There were some things he liked immensely. (Especially "Praise be to God that I am not good!"—"That is so important," said Suzuki with great feeling.) He likes Eckhart, as I already knew from the book I got at the University of Kentucky several years ago. These talks were very pleasant, profoundly important to me—to see and experience the fact that there really is a deep understanding between myself and this extraordinary, simple man whom I have been reading for about ten years with great attention. A sense of being "situated" in this world. This is a legitimate consideration but must not be misunderstood.

I tried to explain things that perhaps did not need explaining. We both agreed on the need to steer clear of movements and to avoid promoting Zen or anything else. Mihoko seemed very eager about this too and obviously knows her Zen. I felt she and I were in close sympathy too, in fact I like her very much. For once in a long time I felt as if I had spent a moment in my own family. The only other person with whom I have felt so at home in recent years is Victor Hammer. And Carolyn. It was rather like one of their visits. (I hear Victor is to have an operation for cataracts.)

Perhaps Suzuki and Mihoko will come down to Gethsemani if they are in the United States next year. Suzuki said I must come to Japan— but I cannot. He said it with meaning, not in a polite formula. I know I should go there. God will provide that just as He provided this extraordinary meeting.

Said Mass two mornings entirely by myself without servers, deeply moved at the altar of Our Lady before which I made my profession of faith in Corpus Christi Church twenty-six years ago! No one recognized me or discovered who I was. At least I think not.

July 2, 1964. Gethsemani
Meadowlark sitting quietly on a fence post in the dawn sun, his gold vest—bright in the light of the east, his black bib tidy, turning his head this way, that way. This is a Zen quietness without comment. Yesterday a very small, chic, black and white butterfly on the whitewashed wall of the house.

July 10, 1964
Rafael Squirru's "New Man" pamphlet is very provocative. How much this is needed. The little that is published on Latin America is likely to be nonsense. There is no deep interest in the question—yet this is one of the deepest and most urgent questions. As for Antonio Cruz, a brilliant, violent book, but Cruz is still the Mexican stereotype, magnificently

redrawn. But is that the way Latin America is to be forever—as the United States wants it to be forever? There is much more to it, surely! I must read, read, and read. It is my vocation. The risk is not in seeking out and knowing these things but in claiming to intend more than I am able to intend. They are looking for a Savior and will take *anyone* as one. And I suppose I am looking for a Savior or an Earth Mother. I still believe in the idea of the dark Ecuadorian Virgin I got Jaime Andrade to carve in wood for the novitiate. She is there, I do not talk to her, nobody prays to her, but such a presence nonetheless! (Dom Gabriel did not like her.)

Some conclusions: literature, contemplation, solitude, Latin America—Asia, Zen, Islam, etc. All these things combine in my life. It would be madness to make a "monasticism" by simply excluding them. I would be less a monk. Others have their own way, I have mine. To write to Squirru. Follow Miguel Grinberg as he goes to San Francisco then to Argentina, with a letter when needed. To think with those new men. The opening to the South has not closed. One day to the monastic places in western Ireland!

July 14, 1964

This morning before High Mass Brother Simon (Patrick Hart) told me that a letter from the Definitor, Dom Laurence Bourget, had come and the long section on peace for *Seeds of Destruction* had been passed without change by the General! Thus the real heart of the forbidden book, *Peace in the Post-Christian Era*, is to be published after all. Now this would never have happened if Dom Gabriel had not been so stringent with the other three articles, which would have been used in *Seeds of Destruction* if he had not forbidden their reprinting. Thus in effect the very thing he wanted to prevent most has happened *because* of his own authoritarianism! This is something to remember when we think of religious obedience. The Church is *not* entirely run by officials! None of this was arrived at, in the end, by my own initiative! Again, Dom Ignace's part—demanding the reworking of the one article the publisher tried to insist on—led to this whole new approach! *How strange are the ways of God!*

August 12, 1964

Last night I dreamed that Dom James suddenly announced that we would have funeral and quasi-military "parades for the dead" along with every Office of the Dead from now on. Monks would march in spaced ranks slowly through the church for a long time. I saw this begin and saw that the sick were all forced to participate. Even the dead were in it, for Father Alphonsus was there, albeit stumbling. The Abbot was absolutely insistent on this preposterous new observance, as a firm manifestation of his will. I tried to reason with him, on the grounds of "simplicity," and even tried to find a copy of *The Spirit of Simplicity* for him to read but could find none anywhere.

October 13, 1964

One good result of the change in thinking on the part of Dom James is his desire for solitude. He gave me permission to sleep at the hermitage without any special restrictions, though not necessarily all the time. The understanding is that I can spend the night there once in a while, when I wish to. Last night I did this for the first time. (Brother Colman brought a bed up there Saturday evening.) It was most helpful. It finally helped me to get the noise and agitation of the Abbots' meeting out of my system.

Though it has been quite cold for several days, I got enough sun into the place in the afternoon to dry it out and warm it up. Got up there about nightfall. Wonderful silence, saying Compline gently and slowly with a candle burning before the icon of Our Lady. A deep sense of peace and truth. That this was the way things are supposed to be, that I was in my right mind for a change (around the community I am seldom in my right mind). Total absence of care and agitation. Slept wonderfully well, even though there was a great pandemonium of dogs in the woods when I got up about 12:20 and went out to urinate off the edge of the porch.

I thought I would hear the bell for Vigils at the monastery and didn't. However, I woke up soon after that and lit the fire and said Lauds quietly, slowly, thoughtfully, sitting on the floor. I felt very much alive, real, awake, surrounded by silence and penetrated by truth. Wonderful smell of predawn woods and fields in the cold night!

October 20, 1964

I am beginning to see that the question of solitude for me is finally getting to be no longer a question of *wish* but of *decision*. I still do not know what scope for decision may be given me, but I do know that I must prepare to face a serious decision, one about which I had more or less given up thinking. It seems to be a real "encounter with the Word" that I must not evade, and yet, as in all such things, I am not too sure just where the encounter is, except that my heart tells me that in this question of the solitary life there is for me a truth to be embraced that is not capable of a fully logical explanation, that is not rooted in my nature nor my biography but is something else. It may also cut clean through the whole network of my own recent work, ideas, writings, experiences, etc., even those that in some way concern the solitary life, monastic renewal, etc.

For the moment it seems to involve also cutting off a hundred contacts in the world and even legitimate and fruitful concerns with the events and needs of the time. I do not know or understand how far this needs to go, except that I am caught in all kinds of affairs that are no longer my business and that they may prove to be great distractions and evasions. Yet I do not yet see where to begin. It will also involve renouncing, definitively, some of the securities of the community.

Sleeping here has been a great grace. Last night, full moon. At midnight the whole valley was drenched in silence and dark clarity. Cold this morning. Going down to the monastery in the dark I could feel frost on the grass and the dry corn husks under my feet.

October 31, 1964

An impressive passage in Urs Von Balthasar's *Verbum Caro*—a deep and poignant essay. I will use part of it perhaps in conferences to novices and juniors on poetry and human experience. These nights I have been spontaneously been remembering the days when I first came to Gethsemani twenty-three years ago: the stars, the cold, the smell of night, the wonder, the *Verlassenheit* (which is something other than despondency), and above all the melody of the *Rorate Coeli*. That entire first Advent bore in it all the stamp of my vocation's peculiar character. The solitude inhabited and pervaded by the cold and mystery and woods and Latin liturgy. It is surprising how far we have got from the cold and the woods and the stars since those days.

My fiftieth year is ending. If I am not ripe now I never will be. It is the *Kairos*, say the stars, says Orion, says Aldebaran, says the sickle moon rising behind the dark tall cedar Cross. I remember the words I said to Father Philotheus, which may have been in part a cliché, but they were sincere and I know at the time that I really meant them. They were unpremeditated: that "I want to give God everything." Until now I really have not, I think. Or perhaps in a way I have tried to. Certainly not too hard! I cannot say my life in the monastery has been useless or a failure. Nor can I say where or how it has a meaning. Nor will I probably find where and how the hermitage has a meaning. It is enough that there is the same mixture of anguish and certitude, the same sense of walking on water, as when I first came to the monastery.

November 7, 1964

Reading Ezekiel 6. This is about our idolatry as well as Israel's. Idolatry is the basic sin. Therefore that which is deepest in us, most closely related to our final sin, most likely to deceive us under the appearance of true worship or integrity or honesty or loyalty or idealism. Even Christianity is often idolatrous without realizing it. The sin of craving a God who is "other" than He who cannot be made an idol—i.e., an object.

November 19, 1964

This Fellowship of Reconciliation retreat has been remarkably lively and fruitful. Sessions in the gatehouse mostly (because of rain), but we got to the hermitage yesterday afternoon. Ping Ferry has been very helpful (he and I talked a lot at first about Jacques Ellul), then John Howard Yoder spoke well this afternoon on protest from the Mennonite viewpoint, that is, biblical. Relation of technology to the "principalities and powers" of St. Paul (not at all akin to the mind of Ellul, whom in fact he quoted—a lecture of his). For personal intensity and sincerity I have also liked very much the remarks of Elbert Jean, a Methodist from the South—was a minister in Birmingham and was fired for his integrationist ideas ("Desegregation can be brought about by anyone, but integration only by the Holy Spirit"). A. J. Muste is impressive in real wisdom, modesty, gentleness.

Dan Berrigan said a way-out Mass in the novitiate chapel, yet it was beautiful too. We had two ministers (Nelson, Muste) read Gospel and Epistle. Dan's celebration of the sacrificial liturgy was simple and impressive. All in English and "uncanonical" even to the extreme point not only of Communion in both kinds but Communion to Protestants!! I suppose it will be the same again tomorrow—in the juniorate chapel, where the altar is better suited for standing around in a circle.

Last night—my dream of the Chinese "princess" has haunted me all day ("Proverb" again). This lovely and familiar archetypal person (no object! and how close and real, yet how elusive!) who comes in various mysterious ways into my dreams! She was with her "brothers," and I felt overwhelmingly the freshness, the youth, the wonder, the truth of her— her complete *reality*, more real than any other, yet unattainable. Yet the sense of understanding, of her "knowing" and loving me, yet not merely in my individuality and everyday self, as if this self were utterly irrelevant to her—not rejected, not accepted either.

Now—rainy night. I sit writing this in the green technological light of the Coleman lamp at the hermitage. They will leave tomorrow.

December 1, 1964

Will not easily forget the thin sickle of the old moon rising this morning just before dawn, when I went down to say Mass. Cold sky, hard brightness of stars through the pines, snow and frost, exaltation on the bright darkness of morning. In the cold of Advent I recapture the lostness and wonder of the first days when I came here twenty-three years ago, abandoned to God, with everything left behind. I have not felt this for a long time here. The monastery is too warm, too busy, too sociable for that! But breaking off and living (to a great extent) in the woods brings me back face-to-face with the loneliness and poverty of the cold hills and the Kentucky winter—incomparable, the reality of my own life!

December 3, 1964

Evening: "The heart is deceitful above all things, / The heart is deep and full of windings. / The old man is covered up in a thousand wrappings" (Lancelot Andrewes, *Pieces*).

True, sad words: I would not have felt the truth of them so much if I had not had so much solitude these days with rain coming down on the roof and hiding the valley. Rain in the night, the nuisance of water in the buckets. Cutting wood behind the house, a faint smell of hickory smoke from the chimney, while I taste and see that I am deceitful and that most of my troubles are rooted in my own bitterness. Is this what solitude is for? Then it is good, but I must pray for the strength to bear it! (The heart is deceitful and does not want this—but God is greater than my heart!)

December 4, 1964

It rained all night and is still raining.

How often in the last years I have thought of death. It has been present to me and I have "understood" it, known that I must die. Yet last night, only for a moment in passing and so to speak without grimness or drama, I momentarily experienced the fact that I, this self, will soon simply not exist. A flash of the "not thereness" of being dead. Without fear or grief, without anything. Just not there. This, I suppose, is one of the first tastes of the fruits of solitude. So the angel passed along thinking aloud to himself, doing his business, barely taking note of me, but taking note of me nonetheless. We recognized each other. Of course the other thing is that this "I" is not "I." I am not this body, this "self." I am not just my individual nature. Yet I might as well be, so firmly am I rooted in it and identified with it—with this which will cease utterly to exist in its natural individuality.

In the hermitage—I see how quickly one can fall apart. I talk to myself, I dance around the hermitage, I sing. This is all very well, but it is not serious, it is a manifestation of weakness, of dizziness. I feel within this individual self the nearness of disintegration. (Yet I also realize that this exterior self can fall apart and be reintegrated too. This is like losing dry skin that peels off while the new skin forms underneath.)

And I suddenly remember absurd things. The song Pop had on the record forty-five years ago! "The Whistler and His Dog." Crazy! I went out to the jakes in the rain with this idiot song rocking my whole being. Its utterly inane confidence! Its gaiety. It is in its own way joyful—the joy of people who had not seen World War II and Auschwitz and the Bomb. Silly as it was, it had life and juice in it. Confidence of people walking up and down Broadway in derbies in 1910! Kings of the earth! Sousa's whole mad band blasting out this idiot and confident song! The strong, shrill whistle of the whistler! ("O fabulous day, calao, calay!") and the bark at the end (that I liked best). Brave Whistler! Brave Dog! (As a child I had this Whistler confused with the one who painted his mother!)

December 5, 1964

In the hermitage one must pray or go to seed. The pretense of prayer will not suffice. Just sitting will not suffice. It has to be real—yet what can one do? Solitude puts you with your back to the wall (or your face to it!). This is good. One prays to pray. The reality of death. Donne's poems and Lancelot Andrewes.

The quality of one's nights depends on the sanity of the day. I bring there the sins of the day into the light and darkness of truth to be adored without disguise—then I want to fly back to the disguises. Who ever said that the solitary life is one of pretense and deception? As if pretense were *easy* in solitude!!! It is easy in the community, for one can have the support of a common illusion or a common agreement in forms that take the place of truth. One can pretend in the solitude of an afternoon walk, but the night destroys all pretenses. One is reduced to nothing and compelled to begin laboriously the long return to truth.

December 7, 1964

Guerric of Igny's beautiful Fourth Advent sermon on the consecration of the desert and the grace placed in it by Christ, "preparing a new place for the new life" and overcoming evil not for Himself "but for those who were to be future dwellers in the wilderness." Not just evil, the Evil One! The desert is given us to get the evil unnested from the crannies of our own hearts. Perhaps again my tendency to find this in solitude rather than in community is simply subjective. After twenty-three years all the nests are well established. But in solitude and open air they are revealed and the wind blows on them and I know they must go!

December 9, 1964

Last night after a prayer vigil in the novitiate chapel (didn't do a good job—was somewhat disorganized and distracted), went to bed late at the hermitage. All quiet. No lights at Boone's or Newton's. Cold. Lay in bed realizing that what I was, was *happy*. Said the strange word "happiness" and realized that it was there, not as an "it" or object. It simply was. And I was that. This morning, coming down, seeing the multitude of stars above the bare branches of the wood, I was suddenly hit as it were with the whole package of meaning of everything: that the immense mercy of God was upon me, that the Lord in infinite kindness had looked down on me and given me this vocation out of love, that he had always intended this, how foolish and trivial had been all my fears and twistings and desperation. No matter what anyone else might do or say about it, however they might judge or evaluate it, all is irrelevant in the reality of my vocation to solitude, even though I am not a typical hermit. Quite the contrary perhaps. It does not matter how I may or may not be classified. In the light of this simple fact of God's love and the form it has taken in the mystery of my life, classifications are ludicrous. I have no further need to occupy my mind with them (if I ever did)—at least in this connection.

The only response is to go out from yourself with all that one is, which is nothing, and pour out that nothingness in gratitude that God is who He is. All speech is impertinent; it destroys the simplicity of that nothingness before God by making it seem as if it had been "something."

December 16, 1964

Yesterday for the first time I was able to live a complete day's schedule as it "ought to be" (at least in this transition period) at the hermitage. Came down only for my own Mass and dinner. Cooked supper at the hermitage, etc. In fact, cooked too much rice, having miscalculated, and sat half an hour consuming it, with tea. But it was a splendid supper (looking out at the hills in the clear evening light). After that, washing dishes—the bowl, the pot, the cup, the knife (for oleo), the spoon— looked up and saw a jet like a small rapid jewel traveling north between the moon and the evening star—the moon being nearly full. Then I went for a little walk down to my gate (about 100 yards) and looked out over the valley. Incredibly beautiful and peaceful. Blue hills, blue sky, woods, empty fields, lights going on in the Abbey, to the right through the screen of trees, hidden from the hermitage. Out there, lights on three farms I can see. One at Newton's and two others out there in the hills behind Gethsemani Station.

Everything the Fathers say about the solitary life is exactly true. The temptations and the joys, above all the tears and the ineffable peace and happiness. The happiness that is so pure because it is simply not of one's own making but sheer mercy and gift! The sense of having arrived at last in the place destined for me by God and for which I was brought here twenty-three years ago!

December 22, 1964

Am finally reading Vladimir Lossky's fine book, *La Vision de Dieu*, which reminds me that the best thing that has come out of the Council is the Declaration on Ecumenism, particularly the part on oriental theology. If it were a matter of choosing between "contemplation" and "eschatology," there is no question that I am, and would always be, committed entirely to the latter. Here in the hermitage, returning necessarily to beginnings, I know where my beginning was: having the Name and Godhead of Christ preached in Corpus Christi Church. I heard and believed. I believe that He has called me freely, out of pure mercy, to His love and salvation and that at the end (to which all is directed by Him) I shall see Him after I have put off my body in death and have risen together with Him. That at the last day "all flesh shall truly see the salvation of God." What this means is that my faith is an eschatological faith, not merely a means of penetrating the mystery of the divine presence and resting in Him now. Yet because my faith is eschatological it is *also* contemplative, for I am even now in the Kingdom and I can even now "see" something of the glory of the Kingdom and praise Him who is King. I would be foolish then if I lived blindly, putting all "seeing" off until some imagined fulfillment (for my present seeing is the beginning of a real and unimaginable fulfillment!). Thus contemplation and eschatology are one in Christian faith and in surrender to Christ. They complete each other and intensify each other. It is by contemplation and love that I can best prepare myself for the eschatological vision—and best help the Church and all men to journey toward it.

The union of contemplation and eschatology is clear in the gift of the Holy Spirit. In Him we are awakened to know the Father, because in Him we are refashioned in the likeness of the Son. It is in this likeness that the Spirit will bring us at last to the clear vision of the invisible

Father in the Son's glory, which will also be our glory. Meanwhile, it is the Spirit who awakens in our heart the faith and hope in which we cry for the eschatological fulfillment and vision. In this hope there is already a beginning, a "promise" of fulfillment. This is our contemplation: the realization and "experience" of the life-giving Spirit in Whom the Father is present to us through the Son, our way, truth, and life. The realization that we are on our way, that because we are on our way we are in that Truth, which is the end and by which we are already fully and eternally alive. Contemplation is the loving sense of this life and this presence and this eternity.

In the afternoon (this is my whole day in the hermitage) the guns were pounding at Fort Knox while I was making my afternoon meditation. After all, I thought, this is no mere "distraction." I am here because they are there so that, indeed, I am supposed to hear them. They form part of an ever-renewed "decision" and commitment for peace. But what peace? I am once again faced with the deepest ambiguities of political and social action. One thing is clear is that there is a will and intention of God bearing upon me (to let it bear fully on me is to be free!). My life has no meaning except as a conscious and total self-dedication to the *fulfillment of His intention* (which in its details remains a complete mystery). As far as I know it, I must seek to be a man wholly given to prayer here in this place where I am, in which He has put me. But I am far from being "totally" a man of prayer. Obviously, even writing is not excluded.

My will, however, cannot simply lose itself in this or that, in meditation or writing or study or "tranquillity" or work, but simply must surrender in all this to the mysterious and dominant intention of the Lord, the Master whom I have come here to *serve.* I am not here to be this or that, but to obey Him in everything—*Gleichheit* (Eckhart). To learn slowly, patiently, the tempo of such obedience. If I had been a better cenobite I perhaps would be more familiar with it!

The REA men were here in the morning (cold and misty). The hermitage will tie in to a line that will eventually go to a sewage disposal plant to be built in the bottom, by the creek.

December 23, 1964

For Origen a man's "adversary" is his bad angel deputed to keep him firmly in subjection to the angelic prince of his nation or tribe, so that he will not free himself and belong only to God, in Christ (Who is above all nations and has vanquished all the powers).

January 30, 1965

There is a great need for discipline in meditation. Reading helps. The early morning hours are good, although in the morning meditation (one hour) I am easily distracted by the fire. An hour is not much, but I can be more meditative in the hour of reading that follows (and that goes by much too fast). The presence of Our Lady is important to me, elusive but, I think, a reality in this hermitage. Her influence is a demand of love, and no amount of talking will explain it. I need her and she is there. I should perhaps think of it more explicitly more often.

In the afternoon, work takes up so much time and there can be so much. Just keeping the place clean is already a big task. Then there is wood to be chopped, etc. The fire is voracious—but pleasant company. Sent off to *Holiday* a revised version of "Rain and the Rhinoceros."

Vigil of my fiftieth birthday. A bright, snowy afternoon, delicate blue clouds of snow blowing down off the frozen trees. Forcibly restrained myself from much work around the hermitage, made sure of my hour's meditation and will do more later. How badly I need it. I realize how great is the tempo and pressure of work I have been in down in the community—with many irons in the fire. True, I have there gained the knack of dropping everything and completely relaxing my attention and forgetting the work by going out and looking at the hills. Good that the novitiate work is not exceedingly absorbing. (Biggest trouble now is letter writing.)

More, then, of my vigil: Shall I look at the past as if it were something to analyze and think about? Rather I thank God for the present, not for myself in the present, but for the present, which is His and in Him. The past: I am inarticulate about it now. I remember irrelevant moments of embarrassment. My joys are seen to have been largely meaningless. Yet as I sit here in this wintry and lonely and quiet place, I suppose that I am the same person as the eighteen-year-old riding back alone into Bournemouth on a bus out of the New Forest, where I had camped a couple of days and nights. I suppose I regret most my lack of love, my selfishness and glibness (covering a deep shyness and need of love) with girls who, after all, did love me, I think, for a time. My great fault was my inability really to believe it and my efforts to get complete assurance and perfect fulfillment.

So one thing on my mind is sex, as something I did not use maturely and well, something I gave up without having come to terms with it. That is hardly worth thinking about now—twenty-five years nearly since my last adultery in the blinding, demoralizing summer heat of Virginia. That heat, that confusion and moral helplessness of those summer days, made me know what is in the weather of the South: what madness and what futility. I remember walking on the beach with her the next day and not wanting to talk to her, talking only with difficulty, not wanting to share *ideas* or things I really loved. Yet being attacked with something in my solar plexus.

I suppose I am the person that lived for a while at 71 Bridge Street, Cambridge, had Sabberton for my tailor (he made me that strange Alphonse Daudet coat and the tails I wore perhaps twice—once to the boat race ball, where I was very selfish and unkind to Joan). Clare was my College, and I was a damned fool, sitting on the steps of the boat house late at night with Sylvia, when the two fairies came down expecting to get in the boat house, saw us there, turned, and hurried away. All things like that. Adventures.

What I find most in my whole life is *illusion.* Wanting to be something of which I have formed a concept. I hope I will get free of that now because that is going to be a struggle. Yet I have to be something that I ought to be—I have to meet a certain demand for order and inner light and tranquillity. God's demand, that is, that I remove obstacles to His giving me these.

Snow, silence, the talking fire, the watch on the table. Sorrow. What would be the use of going into all this? I will get cleaned up (my hands are dirty). I will say the psalms of my birthday.

No matter what mistakes and illusions have marked my life, most of it, I think, has been happiness and, as far as I can tell, truth. There were whole seasons of insecurity, largely when I was under twenty-one and followed friends who were not my own kind. But after my senior year at Columbia things got straight. I can remember many happy and illumined days and whole blocks of time. There were a few nightmare times in childhood. But at Saint Antonin life was a revelation. Then again, at so many various times and places, in Sussex (at Rye and in the country), at Oakham, at Strasbourg, at Rome above all, in New York, especially upstate Olean and St. Bona's. I remember one wonderful winter morning arriving at Olean to spend Christmas with Lax. Arrivals and departures on the Erie were generally great. The cottage on the hill, too—then Cuba: wonderful days there. All this I have said before, and the whole world knows it.

Here? The profoundest and happiest times in my life have been in and around Gethsemani—and also some of the most terrible. But mostly the happy moments were in the woods and fields alone with the sky and the sun—and up here at the hermitage. And with the novices (afternoons at work). But good moments too with Protestants coming here, especially with the Hammers, of course (and one or two visits to Lexington), good visits with J. Laughlin, Ping Ferry—good days in Louisville with Jim Wygal—lunch at Cunningham's, etc. But the deepest happiness has always been when I was alone, either here in the hermitage (best of all) or in the Novice Master's room (that wonderful summer of the gardenias and Plato!) or simply out in the fields. Of course there was the old vault, too, and I must mention many happy moments with the students when I was their Father Master. Also a couple of good days in the hospital when I was well enough to go out and walk about near the grotto.

I could fill another page just with names of people I have loved to be with and love to hear from—Lax above all, Mark Van Doren, all the old friends, Ad Reinhardt, and so on. Naomi and Bob Giroux, all my Latin American friends, like Ernesto Cardenal and Pablo Antonio Cuadra. So many students and novices, especially for some reason the group that came in 1960–61. (Brothers Cuthbert, Denis, Basil, etc.) So many that have left—Father John of the Cross! Why go on? *Deo gratias* for all of them.

January 31, 1965

"When I enter my house, I shall find rest with her, for nothing is bitter in her company; when life is shared with her there is no pain, nothing but pleasure and joy" (Wisdom 8:16).

On this day I could set these words to very sweet music if I really knew how! I can imagine no greater cause for gratitude on my fiftieth birthday than that on it I wake up in a hermitage!

Fierce cold all night, certainly down to zero (I have no outdoor thermometer), and inside the house almost to freezing though embers still glowed under the ashes in the fireplace. The cold woke me up at one point, but I adjusted the blankets and went back to sleep.

But what more do I seek than this silence, this simplicity, this "living together with Wisdom"? For me there is nothing else. It is the pinnacle: *C'est le comble!* To think I have had the grace to taste a little of what all men really seek without realizing it. All the more obligation to have compassion and love and pray for them. Last night, before going to bed, realized what solitude really means: when the ropes are cast off and the skiff is no longer tied to land but heads out to sea without ties, without restraints! Not the sea of passion, on the contrary, the sea of purity and love that is without care. That loves God alone immediately and directly in Himself as the All (and the seeming Nothing that is all). The unutterable confusion of those who think that God is a mental object and that to love "God Alone" is to exclude all other objects to concentrate on this one! Fatal. Yet that is why so many misunderstand the meaning of contemplation and solitude and condemn it. But I no longer have the slightest need to argue with them. I have nothing to justify and nothing to defend. I need only defend this vast simple emptiness from my own self, and the rest is clear. (Through the cold and darkness I hear the *Angelus* ringing at the monastery.) The beautiful jeweled shining of honey in the lamplight. Festival!

February 2, 1965

Again very cold. On the 31st it was about four below, this morning it is almost down to zero. Yesterday it was warmer (about twenty-eight) and there was more snow. A great deal of wood I have for the fire is wet or not sufficiently seasoned to burn well—though finally this morning I got a pretty good fire going with a big cedar log on top of it. This is some of the coldest weather we have had in the twenty-three years I have been here. But sleeping was okay. No worse than anywhere else. In fact, very snug, with a lot of blankets.

It is hard but good to live according to nature with a primitive technology of wood chopping and fires rather than according to the mature technology that has supplanted nature, creating its own weather, etc., etc. Yet there are advantages, too, in a warmed house and a self-stoking furnace. No need to pledge allegiance to either one. Get warm any way you can, love God, and pray.

I see more and more that now I must desire nothing else than to be "poured out as a libation," to give and surrender my being without concern. The cold woods make this more real. And the loneliness, coming up last night at the time of a very cold sunset, with two little birds still picking up crumbs I had thrown for them on the frozen porch. Everywhere else, snow. In the morning, coming down: all tracks covered by snow blown over the path by the wind except tracks of the cat that hunts around the cold sheep barn. Solitude = being aware that you are one man in this snow where there has been no one but one cat.

February 4, 1965

Last night I had a curious and moving dream about a "Black Mother." I was in a place (where? somewhere I had been as a child, but there also seemed to be some connection with the valley over at Edelin's). I realized that I had come there for a reunion with a Negro foster mother whom I had loved in my childhood. Indeed, I owed, it seemed, my life to her love so that it was she really, and not my natural mother, who had given me life. As if from her hand had come a new *life* and there she was. Her face was ugly and severe, yet a great warmth came from her to me, and we embraced with great love (and I with much gratitude). What I recognized was not her face but the warmth of her embrace and of her heart, so to speak. We danced a little together, I and my Black Mother, and then I had to continue the journey I was on. I cannot remember more about this journey and many incidents connected with it. Comings and goings, and turning back, etc.

February 16, 1965

Yesterday in the morning, when I went out for a breath of air before my novice conference, I saw men working on the hillside beyond the sheep barn. At last the electric line is coming! All day they were working the holes, digging and blasting the rock with small charges, young men in yellow helmets, good, eager, hardworking guys with machines. I was glad of them and of American technology pitching in to bring me light as they would for any farmer in the district. It was good to feel part of this, which is not to be despised, but admirable. (Which does not mean that I hold any brief for the excess of useless developments in technology.)

Evening. About 2:45 the red-faced foreman (a very good simple man) came and set up the meter, and I put on the switch and had light. I was in the middle of translating some Pessoa poems for Suzuki in return for his calligraphy. The light is a great blessing.

I celebrated the great event with a good supper of potato soup, cooked on the old beat-up electric stove, which nevertheless works well. So it is an evening of *alleluia*.

February 24, 1965

Everything about this hermitage simply fills me with joy. There are lots of things that could have been far more perfect one way or the other—aesthetically or "domestically." But it is the place God has given me after so much prayer and longing—but without my deserving it. It is a delight. I can imagine no other joy on earth than to have such a place and to be at peace in it, to live in silence, to think and write, to listen to the wind and to all the voices of the wood, to live in the shadow of the big cedar cross, to prepare for my death and my exodus to the heavenly country, to love my brothers and all people, to pray for the whole world and for peace and good sense among men. So it is "my place" in the scheme of things. That is sufficient!

February 26, 1965

I see more and more that solitude is not something to play with. It is deadly serious. Much as I have wanted it, I have not been serious enough. It is not enough to "like solitude" or love it even. Even if you "like" it, it can wreck you, I believe, if you desire it only for your own sake. So I go forward (I don't believe I would go back. Even interiorly I have reached at least relatively a point of no return), but I go in fear and trembling, often with a sense of lostness, and trying to be careful what I do because I am beginning to see that every false step is paid for dearly. Hence I fall back on prayer, or try to. Yet there is great beauty and peace in this life of silence and emptiness, but to fool around with it brings awful desolation. When one is trifling, even the beauty of the life suddenly becomes implacable. Solitude is a stern mother who brooks no nonsense. The question arises: am I so full of nonsense that she will cast me out? I pray not and think it is going to take much prayer.

March 2, 1965. Shrove Tuesday

One thing the hermitage is making me see—that the universe is my home and I am nothing if not part of it. Destruction of the self that seems to stand outside the universe only as part of its fabric and dynamism. Can I find true being in God who has willed me to exist in the world? This I discover here not mentally only but in depth. Especially, for example, in the ability to sleep. Frogs kept me awake at the monastery, not here— they are comfort, an extension of my own being—and now also the hum of the electric meter near my bed is nothing (though at the monastery it would have been intolerable). Acceptance of nature and even technology as my true habitat.

April 4, 1965. Passion Sunday

Light rain all night. The need to keep working at meditation—going to the root. Mere passivity won't do at this point. Activism won't do either. A time of wordless deepening, to grasp the inner reality of my nothingness in Him who is. Talking about it in these terms is absurd. Nothing to do with the concrete reality that is to be grasped. My prayer is peace and struggle in silence, to be aware and true, beyond myself. To go outside the door of myself, not because I will it, but because I am called and must respond.

April 15, 1965. Holy Thursday

There is no question for me that my one job as a monk is to love the hermit life in simple direct contact with nature, primitively, quietly, doing some writing, maintaining such contacts as are willed by God, and bearing witness to the value and goodness of simple things and ways, and loving God in it all. I am more convinced of this than of anything contingent on my life, and I am sure it is what He asks of me. Yet I do not always respond with simplicity.

April 17, 1965. Holy Saturday

The great sin, the source of all other sins, is idolatry. Never has it been greater, more prevalent than now. It is almost completely unrecognized—precisely because it is so overwhelmingly total. It takes in everything. There is nothing else left. Fetishism of power, machines, possessions, medicine, sports, clothes, etc., all kept going by greed for money and power. The Bomb is only one accidental aspect of the cult. Indeed, the Bomb is not the worst. We should be thankful for it as a sign, a revelation of what all the rest of our civilization points to: the self-immolation of man to his own greed and his own despair. Behind it all are the principalities and powers whom man serves in his idolatry. Christians are as deeply involved in this as everyone else.

April 18, 1965. Easter Sunday

Peace and beauty of Easter morning: sunrise, deep green grass, soft winds, the woods turning green on the hills across the valley (and here too). I got up and said the old office of Lauds, and there was a wood thrush singing fourth-tone mysteries in the deep ringing pine wood (the "unconscious" wood) behind the hermitage. (The "unconscious" wood has a long moment of perfect clarity at dawn, and, from being dark and confused, now lit from the east it is all clarity, all distinct, seen to be a place of silence and peace with its own order in disorder—the fallen trees don't matter, they are all part of it!)

I wonder if I have not said ill-considered things about Christian tradition—things that will only add to the present confusion—motivated by some obscure desire to protect my heart against wounds by inflicting them myself—i.e., the wounds of loss and separation: as if I were saying, since the Middle Ages are no longer relevant to us, I might as well be the first to admit it and get it over with. But *are* the Middle Ages irrelevant? Of course not, and I have not begun to believe it! It is part of my vocation to make observations that preserve a living continuity with the past and with what is good in the past!

April 19, 1965. Easter Monday

Study of medieval exegesis is a way of entering into the Christian experience of that age, an experience most relevant to us, for if we neglect it, we neglect part of our own totality (in Henri De Lubac, Hans Urs Von Balthasar, etc.). But it must not be studied from the outside. Same idea in Kitaro Nishida on Japanese culture and the Japanese view of life. I have a real sense this Easter that my own vocation demands a deepened and experiential study, *from within* (by connaturality) of the Medieval tradition as well as of, to some extent, Asian tradition and experiences, particularly Japanese, particularly Zen: i.e., an awareness of a common need and aspiration with these past generations.

May 23, 1965. Fifth Sunday After Easter

One lovely dawn after another. Such peace! Meditation with fireflies, mist in the valley, last quarter of the moon, distant owls—gradual inner awakening and centering in peace and harmony of love and gratitude. Yesterday I wrote to the man at McGill University who thought all contemplation was a manifestation of narcissistic regression! That is just what it is not. A complete awakening of identity and of rapport! It implies an awareness and acceptance of one's place in the whole, first the whole of creation, then the whole plan of Redemption—to find oneself in the great mystery of fulfillment, which is the Mystery of Christ. *Consonantia* and not *confusio:* Harmony and not confusion.

Sometime in May 1965. Day of a Stranger

The hills are blue and hot. There is a brown, dusty field in the bottom of the valley. I hear a machine, a bird, a clock. The clouds are high and enormous. Through them the inevitable jet plane passes: this time probably full of passengers from Miami to Chicago. What passengers? This I have no need to decide. They are out of my world, up there, busy sitting in their small, isolated, arbitrary lounge that does not even seem to be moving—the lounge that somehow unaccountably picked them up off the earth in Florida to suspend them for a while with timeless cocktails and then let them down in Illinois. The suspension of modern life in contemplation that *gets you somewhere!*

There are also other worlds above me. Others jets will pass over, with other contemplations and other modalities of intentness.

I have seen the SAC plane, with the bomb in it, fly low over me, and I have looked up out of the woods directly at the closed bay of the metal bird with a scientific egg in its breast! A womb easily and mechanically opened! I do not consider this technological mother to be the friend of anything I believe in. However, like everyone else, I live in the shadow of the apocalyptic cherub. I am surveyed by it, impersonally. Its number recognizes my number. Are these numbers preparing at some moment to coincide in the benevolent mind of a computer? This does not concern me, for I live in the woods as a reminder that I am free not to be a number.

There is, in fact, a choice.

In an age where there is much talk about "being yourself" I reserve to myself the right to forget about being myself, since in any case there is very little chance of my being anybody else. Rather it seems to me that, when one is too intent on "being himself," he runs the risk of impersonating a shadow.

Yet I cannot pride myself on special freedom simply because I am living in the woods. I am accused of living in the woods like Thoreau instead of living in the desert like St. John the Baptist. All I can answer is that I am not living "like anybody." Or "unlike anybody." We all live somehow or other, and that's that. It is a compelling necessity for me to be free to embrace the necessity of my own nature.

I exist under trees. I walk in the woods out of necessity. I am both a prisoner and an escaped prisoner. I cannot tell you why, born in France, my journey ended here in Kentucky. I have considered going further, but it is not practical. It makes no difference. Do I have a "day"? Do I spend my "day" in a "place"? I know there are trees here. I know there are birds here. I know the birds in fact very well, for there are precise pairs of birds (two each of fifteen or twenty species) living in the immediate area of my cabin. I share this particular place with them: we form an ecological balance. This harmony gives the idea of "place" a new configuration.

As to the crows, they form part of a different pattern. They are vociferous and self-justifying, like humans. They are not two, they are many. They fight each other and the other birds, in a constant state of war.

There is a mental ecology, too, a living balance of spirits in this corner of the woods. There is room here for many other songs besides those of birds. Of Vallejo, for instance. Or Rilke, or René Char, Montale, Zukofsky, Ungaretti, Edwin Muir, Quasimodo, or some Greeks. Or the dry, disconcerting voice of Nicanor Parra, the poet of the sneeze. Here also is Chuang Tzu, whose climate is perhaps most the climate of this silent corner of woods. A climate in which there is no need for explanation. Here is the reassuring companionship of many silent Tzu's and Fu's; Kung Tzu, Lao Tzu, Meng Tzu, Tu Fu. And Hui Neng. And Chao-Chu. And the drawings of Sengai. And a big graceful scroll from Suzuki. Here also is a Syrian hermit called Philoxenus. An Algerian cenobite called Camus. Here is heard the clanging prose of Tertullian, with the dry catarrh of Sartre. Here the voluble dissonances of Auden, with the golden sounds of John of Salisbury. Here is the deep vegetation of that more ancient forest in which the angry birds, Isaias and Jeremias, sing. Here should be, and are, feminine voices from Angela of Foligno to Flannery O'Connor, Teresa of Avila, Juliana of Norwich, and, more personally and warmly still, Raïssa Maritain. It is good to choose the voices that will be heard in these woods, but they also choose themselves and send themselves here to be present in this silence. In any case, there is no lack of voices.

The hermit life is cool. It is a life of low definition in which there is little to decide, in which there are few transactions or none, in which there are no packages to be delivered. In which I do not bundle up packages and deliver them to myself. It is not intense. There is no give and take of questions and answers, problems and solutions. Problems begin down the hill. Over there under the water tower are solutions. Here there are woods, foxes. Here there is no need for dark glasses. "Here" does not even warm itself up with references to "there." It is just a "here" for which there is no "there." The hermit life is that cool.

The monastic life as a whole is a hot medium. Hot with words like *must, ought,* and *should.* Communities are devoted to high-definition projects: "making it all clear!" The clearer it gets the clearer it has to be made. It branches out. You have to keep clearing the branches. The more branches you cut back, the more branches grow. For one you cut, you get three more. On the end of each branch is a big question mark. People are running all around with packages of meaning. Each is very anxious to know whether all the others have received the latest messages. Has someone else received a message that he has not received? Will they be willing to pass it on to him? Will he understand it when it is passed on? Will he have to argue about it? Will he be expected to clear his throat and stand up and say, "Well, the way I look at it St. Benedict said . . . "? Saint Benedict saw that the best thing to do with the monastic life was to cool it, but today everybody is heating it up. Maybe to cool it you have to be a hermit. But then they will keep thinking that *you* have got a special message. When they find out you haven't . . . Well, that's their worry, not mine.

This is not a hermitage—it is a house. ("Who was that hermitage I seen you with last night?") What I wear is pants. What I do is live. How I pray is breathe. Who said Zen? Wash out your mouth if you said Zen. If you see a meditation going by, shoot it. Who said "Love"? Love is in the movies. The spiritual life is something that people worry about when they are so busy with something else they think they ought to be spiritual. Spiritual life is guilt. Up here in the woods is seen the New Testament: that is to say, the wind comes through the trees and you breathe it. Is it supposed to be clear? I am not inviting anybody to try it. Or suggesting that one day the message will come saying NOW. That is none of my business.

I am out of bed at two-fifteen in the morning, when the night is darkest and most silent. Perhaps this is due to some ailment or other. I find myself in the primordial lostness of night, solitude, forest, peace, a mind awake in the dark, looking for a light, not totally reconciled to being out of bed. A light appears, and in the light, an icon. There is now in the large darkness a small room of radiance with psalms in it. The psalms grow up silently by themselves without effort like plants in this light which is favorable to them. The plants hold themselves up on stems that have a single consistency, that of mercy or, rather, great mercy. *Magna misericordia.* In the formlessness of night and silence a word then pronounces itself: Mercy. It is surrounded by other words of lesser consequence: "destroy iniquity," "wash me," "purify," "I know my iniquity." *Peccavi:* I have sinned. Concepts without interest in the world of business, war, politics, culture, etc. Concepts also often without interest to ecclesiastics.

Other words: Blood, Guile. Anger. The way that is not good. The way of blood, guile, anger, war.

Out there the hills in the dark lie southward. The way over the hills is blood, guile, dark, anger, death: Selma, Birmingham, Mississippi. Nearer than these, the atomic city, from which each day a freight car of fissionable material is brought to be laid carefully beside the gold in the underground vault that is at the heart of this nation.

"Their mouth is the opening of the grave; their tongues are set in motion by lies; their heart is void."

Blood, lies, fire, hate, the opening of the grave, void. Mercy, great mercy.

The birds begin to wake. It will soon be dawn. In an hour or two the towns will wake, and men will enjoy everywhere the great luminous smiles of production and business.

—Why live in the woods?

—Well, you have to live somewhere.

—Do you get lonely?

—Yes, sometimes.

—Are you mad at people?

—No.

—Are you mad at the monastery?

—No.

—What do you think about the future of monasticism?

—Nothing. I don't think about it.

—Is it true that your bad back is due to Yoga?

—No.

—Is it true that you are practicing Zen in secret?

—Pardon me, I don't speak English.

All monks, as is well known, are unmarried, and hermits more unmarried than the rest of them. Not that I have anything against women. I see no reason why a man can't love God and a woman at the same time. If God was going to regard women with a jealous eye, why did he go and make them in the first place? There is a lot of talk about a married clergy. Interesting. So far there has not been a great deal said about married hermits. Well, anyway, I have the place full of icons of the Holy Virgin.

One might say I had decided to marry the silence of the forest. The sweet dark warmth of the whole world will have to be my wife. Out of the heart of that dark warmth comes the secret that is heard only in silence, but it is the root of all the secrets that are whispered by all the lovers in their beds all over the world. So perhaps I have an obligation to preserve the stillness, the silence, the poverty, the virginal point of pure nothingness that is at the center of all other loves. I attempt to cultivate this plant without comment in the middle of the night and water it with psalms and prophecies in silence. It becomes the most rare of all the trees in the garden, at once the primordial paradise tree, the *axis mundi*, the cosmic axle, and the Cross. "No forest produced such a tree." There is only one such tree. It cannot be multiplied. It is not interesting.

It is necessary for me to see the first point of light which begins to be dawn. It is necessary to be present alone at the resurrection of Day, in the blank silence when the sun appears. In this completely neutral instant I receive from the eastern woods, the tall oaks, the one word DAY, which is never the same. It is never spoken in any known language.

Sermon to the birds: "Esteemed friends, birds of noble lineage, I have no message to you except this: be what you are: be *birds*. Thus you will be your own sermon to yourselves!"

Reply: "Even this is one sermon too many!"

Rituals. Washing out the coffeepot in the rain bucket. Approaching the outhouse with circumspection on account of the king snake who likes to curl up on one of the beams inside. Addressing the possible king snake in the outhouse and informing him that he should not be there. Asking the formal ritual question that is asked at this time every morning: "Are you in there, you bastard?"

More rituals. Spray bedroom (cockroaches and mosquitoes). Close all windows on the south side (heat). Leave windows open on north and east sides (cool). Leave windows open on west side until maybe June, when it gets very hot on all sides. Pull down the shades. Get water bottle. Rosary. Watch. Library book to be returned.

It is time to visit the human race.

I start out under the pines. The valley is already hot. Machines out there in the bottoms, perhaps planting corn. Fragrance of the woods. Cool west wind under the oaks. Here is the place on the path where I killed a copperhead. There is the place I saw the fox run daintily and carefully for cover with a rabbit in his mouth. And there is the cement cross that, for no reason, the novices rescued from the corner of a destroyed wall and put up in the woods: people imagine someone is buried there. It is just a cross. Why should there not be a cement cross by itself in the middle of the woods?

A squirrel is kidding around somewhere overhead in midair. Tree to tree. The coquetry of flight.

I come out into the open over the hot hollow and the old sheep barn. Over there is the monastery, bugging with windows, humming with action.

The long yellow side of the monastery faces the sun on a sharp rise with fruit trees and beehives. This is without question one of the least interesting buildings on the face of the earth. However, in spite of the most earnest efforts to deprive it of all character and keep it ugly, it is surpassed in this respect by the vast majority of other monasteries. It is so completely plain that it ends, in spite of itself, by being at least simple. A lamentable failure of religious architecture—to come so close to nonentity and yet not fully succeed! I climb sweating into the novitiate and put down my water bottle on the cement floor. The bell is ringing. I have duties, obligations, since here I am a monk. When I have accomplished these, I return to the woods, where I am nobody. In the choir are the young monks, patient, serene, with very clear eyes, then reflective, gentle, confused. Today perhaps I tell them of Eliot's "Little Gidding," analyzing the first movement of the poem ("Midwinter spring is its own season"). They will listen with attention, thinking that some other person is talking to them about some other poem.

Chanting the *alleluia* in the second mode: strength and solidity of the Latin, seriousness of the second mode, built on the *Re* as though on a sacrament, a presence. One keeps returning to the *Re* as to an inevitable center. *Sol-Re, Fa-Re, Sol-Re, Do-Re.* Many other notes in between, but suddenly one hears only the one note. *Consonantia:* all notes, in their perfect distinctness, are yet blended in one. (Through a curious oversight Gregorian chant has continued to be sung in this monastery. But not for long.)

In the refectory is read a message of the Pope denouncing war, denouncing the bombing of civilians, reprisals on civilians, killing of hostages, torturing of prisoners (all in Vietnam). Do the people of this country realize who the Pope is talking about? They have by now become so solidly convinced that the Pope never denounces anybody but Communists that they have long ceased to listen. The monks seem to know. The voice of the reader trembles.

In the heat of noon I return with the water bottle, freshly filled, through the cornfield, past the barn under the oaks, up the hill, under the pine, to the hot cabin. Larks rise out of the long grass singing. A bumblebee hums under the wide shady eaves.

I sit in the cool back room, where words cease to resound, where all meanings are absorbed in the *consonantia* of heat, fragrant pine, quiet wind, bird song, and one central tonic note that is unheard and unuttered. This is no longer a time of obligations. In the silence of the afternoon all is present and all is inscrutable in one central tonic note to which every other sound ascends or descends, to which every other meaning aspires, in order to find its true fulfillment. To ask when the note will sound is to lose the afternoon: it has already sounded, and all things now hum with the resonance of its sounding.

I sweep. I spread a blanket out in the sun. I cut grass behind the cabin. I write in the heat of the afternoon. Soon I will bring the blanket in again and make the bed. The sun is overclouded. The day declines. Perhaps there will be rain. A bell rings in the monastery. A devout Cistercian tractor growls in the valley. Soon I will cut bread, eat supper, say psalms, sit in the back room as the sun sets, as the birds sing outside the window, as night descends on the valley. I become surrounded once again by all the silent Tzu's and Fu's (men without office and without obligation). The birds draw closer to their nests. I sit on the cool straw mat on the floor, considering the bed in which I will presently sleep alone under the icon of the Nativity.

Meanwhile, the mental cherub of the apocalypse passes over me in the clouds, treasuring its egg and its message.

June 8, 1965. Whit Tuesday

The great joy of the solitary life is not found simply in quiet, in the beauty and peace of nature, song of birds, etc., nor in the peace of one's own heart, but in the awakening and attuning of the heart to the voice of God—to the inexplicable, quiet, definite inner certitude of one's call to obey Him, to hear Him, to worship Him here, now, today, in silence and alone, and that this is the whole reason for one's existence, this makes one's existence fruitful and gives fruitfulness to all one's other (good) acts and is the ransom and purification of one's heart, which has been dead in sin.

It is not simply a question of "existing" alone but of doing, with joy and understanding, "the work of the cell," which is done in silence and not according to one's own choice or the pressure of necessity but in obedience to God. But the voice of God is not "heard" at every moment, so part of the "work of the cell" is attention so that one may not miss any sound of that Voice. When we see how little we listen, and how stubborn and gross our hearts are, we realize how important the work is and how badly prepared we are to do it.

June 12, 1965. Ember Saturday

Early mist. Trees of St. Anne's wood barely visible across the valley. A flycatcher, on a fencepost, appears in momentary flight, describes a sudden, indecipherable ideogram against the void of mist, and vanishes. On both sides of the house, the gossip of tanagers. The two lizards that operate on the porch scuttle away when I arrive on the porch, however quietly, from outside. But when I come from inside the house, even though I may move brusquely, they are not afraid and stay where they are. To be conscious of both extremes in my solitary life. Consolation and desolation; understanding and obscurity; obedience and protest; freedom and imprisonment.

June 26, 1965

Yesterday, Feast of the Sacred Heart, was very cool and clear—in the early morning (as also today) it was more like September than June. Father Lawrence, my undermaster when I was in the novitiate twenty-three years ago, returned from the monastery in Georgia for a while. I could not recognize him—he is much fatter (was very gaunt then). The Feast of the Sacred Heart was for me a day of grace and seriousness. Twenty years ago I was uncomfortable with this concept. Now I see the real meaning of it (quite apart from the externals). It is the *center*, the "heart" of the whole Christian mystery.

There is one thing more—I may be interested in Oriental religions, etc., but there can be no obscuring the essential difference—this personal communion with Christ at the center and heart of all reality as a source of grace and life. "God is love" may perhaps be clarified if one says that "God is void" and if in the void one finds absolute indetermination and hence absolute freedom. (With freedom, the void becomes fullness and 0 = ∞.) All that is "interesting," but none of it touches on the mystery of personality in God, His personal love for me. Again, I am void too—and I have freedom, or *am* a kind of freedom, meaningless unless oriented to Him.

The other day (the feast of St. John the Baptist perhaps) after my Mass, I suddenly thought of Ann Winser, Andrew's little sister. She was about twelve or thirteen when I used to visit him on the Isle of Wight, in that quiet rectory at Brooke. She was the quietest thing in it, a dark and secret child. One does not fall in love with a child of thirteen, and I hardly remember even thinking of her. Yet the other day I realized that I had never forgotten her, with a sort of Burnt Norton feeling about the part of the garden I never went to, and that if I had taken another turn in the road, I might have ended up married to Ann. Actually, I think she is a symbol of the true (quiet) woman I never really came to terms with in the world, and because of this there remains an incompleteness that cannot be remedied. The years in which I chased whores or made whores out of my girlfriends too (no, that is too strong and also silly, besides, there were plenty that I was too shy to sleep with) did nothing to make sense of my life. On the contrary. When I came to the monastery, Jinny Burton was the symbol of the girl I ought to have fallen in love with but didn't (and she remains the image of one I really did love with a love of companionship, not of passion).

July 5, 1965

Does my solitude meet the standard set by my approaching death? No, I am afraid it does not. That possibility which is most intimate, isolated, my own, cannot be shared or described. I cannot look forward to it as an experience I can analyze and share. It is not something to be understood and enjoyed. (To "understand" and "contemplate" it beforehand is a kind of imposture.) But the solitary life should partake of the seriousness and incommunicability of death. Or should it? Is that too rigid and absolute an ideal? The two go together. Solitude is not death, it is life. It aims not at living death but at a certain fullness of life. But a fullness that comes from honestly and authentically facing death and accepting it without care, i.e., with faith and trust in God. *Not* with any social justification: not with the reliance on an achievement that is approved or at least understood by others. Unfortunately, even in solitude, though I try not to (and sometimes claim not to), I still depend too much, emotionally, on being accepted and approved.

Now it is true that in my life the witness of solitude may perhaps be significant. But there is a great danger here. It is one of the points where I see my defensiveness, my weakness, my capacity to pretend and to be untrue. To face my untruth in solitude in preparation for the awful experience of facing it irrevocably in death with no more hope in anything earthly, only in God (totally unseen!). To do this without appealing to others for reassurance that I am not so untrue after all. How do they know, one way or the other? Certainly enough is evident merely in this Journal to destroy me forever after I am dead. But that is the point: not to live as one who can be so "destroyed." This means not ingeniously discovering infallible ways of being "true" in the eyes of others and of posterity (if any!), but of accepting my untruth in the untransferable anguish that is characteristic of death and leaving all "justification" to God. Everything else is only wrath, flame, torment, and judgment.

The greatest "comfort" (and a legitimate one, not an evasion) is to be sought precisely in the Psalms, which face death as it is, under the eyes of God, and teach us how we might face it, and they bring us at the same time into contact, rather communion, with all those who have so seen death and accepted it. Most of all the Lord Himself, who prayed from Psalm 21 on the Cross.

July 19, 1965

When I went to Father Abbot after Chapter, he ended by saying that on August 20, Feast of St. Bernard, he would make the change in the novitiate and I would be free to be in the hermitage all the time, with no further responsibility except to give *one* conference a week in the novitiate (Sunday). Father Baldwin is to be the new Novice Master. Father Timothy will go to Rome soon after that. This was a very pleasant surprise. I was jubilant about it and very moved and grateful. Things like this make me ashamed of my fears and worries and my derision. This, after all, is really remarkable and shows that he is not merely a politician. It is a most unusual step in the Order and one he could not possibly have taken two years ago. Hence he is certainly not guided merely by his own likes and dislikes, his own preferences and fears. He really does pay attention, more than many others, to objective indications of what God wants for His Church. Easy to say this when he gives me something I want. But it has been the same with the new liturgy, etc. Here he has given up strong repugnancies that he might have had to solitude in the Cistercian life (to which he is personally attracted). Concelebration after that was a moving, humbling, and consoling experience. I think I will have no more of my foolish feelings about it. Thank God for enough light to see my childishness.

Afternoon in the very quiet hollow behind the hermitage. A few sayings (*apothegmata*) of the Desert Fathers. Thinking seriously about the change that is to come. It is so momentous for me. One of the greatest mercies of God in my whole life! The answer to so many prayers, yet one sees here that everything has really been leading directly to this even when it appeared to be hopeless. How happy I am that I stayed on the path where I was all along and did not succeed in getting off it. (Though by God's grace my efforts to get off the path were just what kept me most truly on it, and, if I had not tried to go elsewhere, I would certainly not be in this hermitage now! I do not propose this as a working formula for everyone!)

In the evening I began a perpetual Psalter—a necessity—not to say a given quantity any period of time, but just to keep the Psalter going from now on until I die (or can no longer take it). Need for the continuity the Psalter offers—continuity with my own past and with the past of eremiticism. The Latin psalter is for me! It is a deep communion with the Lord and His saints of my Latin Church. To be in communion with the Saints of *my* tradition is by that fact to be more authentically in communion with those of the Greek, Syriac, etc., traditions, who reach me through my own Fathers.

July 28, 1965

How men fear freedom! How I have learned to fear it myself! I know that in fact, without faith, this would be a different matter, this living alone. But with faith it becomes an eschatological gift. I have never before really seen what it means to live in the new creation and in the Kingdom. Impossible to explain it. If I tried I would be unfaithful to the grace of it—for I would be setting limits to it. It is *limitless*, without determination, without definition. It is what you make of it each day, in response to the Holy Spirit!

The same freedom is everywhere. It is not limited to places. Yet solitude, these pines, this mist, are the chosen "places" of freedom in my own life.

August 10, 1965. St. Lawrence

The solitary life, now that I really confront it, is awesome, wonderful, and I see I have no strength of my own for it. Deep sense of my own poverty and, above all, awareness of the wrongs I have allowed in myself together with this good desire. This is all good. I am glad to be shocked by grace and to wake up in time to see the great seriousness of it. I have been merely playing at this, and the solitary life does not admit of mere play. Contrary to all that is said about it, I do not see how the really solitary life can tolerate illusion and self-deception. It seems to me that solitude rips off all the masks and all the disguises. It does not tolerate lies. Everything but straight and direct affirmation is marked and judged by the silence of the forest. "Let your speech be Yea! Yea!"

(I am frightened by the awful clarity of Anselm's argument in *De Casu Diaboli*. A view of liberty that is essentially monastic, i.e., framed in the perspective of an entirely personal vocation and grace.) The need to *pray*—the need for solid theological food, for the Bible, for monastic tradition. Not experimentation or philosophical dilettantism. The need to be entirely defined by a relationship with and orientation to God my Father, i.e., a life of sonship in which all that distracts from this relationship is seen as fatuous and absurd. How *real* this is! A reality I must constantly measure up to, it cannot be simply taken for granted. It cannot be lost in distraction. Distractedness here is fatal—it brings one inexorably to the abyss. But no concentration is required, only *being present*. And also working seriously at all that is to be done—the care of the garden of paradise! By reading, meditation, study, psalmody, manual work, including also some fasting, etc. Above all the work of *hope*, not the stupid, relaxed, self-pity of boredom, of *acedia*.

August 13, 1965

The joy that I am *man!* This fact, that I am a man, is a theological truth and mystery. God became man in Christ. In becoming what I am, He united me to Himself and made me His epiphany, so that now I am meant to reveal Him. My very existence as true man depends on this: that by my freedom I obey His light, thus enabling Him to reveal Himself in me. And the first to see this revelation is my own self. I am His mission to myself and, through myself, to all men. How can I see Him or receive

Him if I despise or fear what I am—man? How can I love what I am—
man—if I hate man in others?

The mere fact of my manness should be an everlasting joy and delight.
To take joy in that which I am made to be by my Creator is to open my
heart to restoration by my Redeemer. It is to taste the firstfruits of
redemption and restoration. So pure is the joy of being man that those
whose Christian understanding is weak may even take this to be the joy
of being something other than man—an angel or something. But God
did not become an angel. He became *man*.

August 17, 1965

Yesterday, finally, I finished cleaning out, sorting, throwing away, sending
to the library, etc., etc. I wonder how many wastepaper baskets I have
filled in the last week? With this absurd ritual of wastepaper has gone a
rending of the intestines, diarrhea at night, angst, etc. The revelation of
futility and interminable self-contradiction. What a poor being I am. If I
try to conceive myself as, on top of all this, "being a hermit," absurdity
reaches its culmination. Yet I am convinced that I am on the right way.
To turn back is infidelity and sin (there simply is no turning back) and
that in all this is hidden joy. Nor is it always hidden because I experience
it powerfully, not only in the silence of the early morning but also in the
hot, muggy afternoon, which in these days is tropical.

"Knowledge of the Spirit as Comforter adorns only the supreme
points of affliction," says Norossky. My supreme affliction is to see my
unbelief, my distrust of the Lord, my refusal to "let myself go" in hope.
But to see this at last is also a joy. I can begin to hope He will cure and
transform me. I got a very fine letter from Naomi in answer to one of
mine admitting my own confusion and self-contradiction. Full of mature,
realistic understanding and feminine comfort—the warmth that cannot
come from a man and that is so essential. Psychologically, my doubt is
based on this giant, stupid rift in my life, the *refusal* of woman, which is a
fault in my chastity (and in the chastity of so many religious!). But I am
learning to accept this love (of Naomi, for instance) even if it means
admitting a certain loss. (Chastity is in fact my most radical poverty. My
un-poverty—accumulating "things"—is a desperate and useless
expedient to cover this irreparable loss which I have not fully accepted. I

can learn to accept it in the Spirit and in love and it will no longer be "irreparable." The Cross repairs it and transforms it.)

The tragic chastity, which suddenly realizes itself to be mere loss and fears that death has won—that one is sterile, useless, hateful. I do not say this is my lot, but in my vow I can see this as an ever-present possibility. To make a vow is to be exposed to this possibility. It is the risk one must run in seeking the other possibility, the revelation of the Paraclete to the pure heart!

August 25, 1965. Feast of St. Louis

The five days I have had in real solitude have been a revelation. Whatever questions I may have had about it are answered. Over and over again I see that this life is what I have always hoped it would be and always sought. A life of peace, silence, purpose, meaning. It is not always easy but calls for a blessed and salutary effort. Everything about it is rewarding.

My stomach trouble has cleared up (except that it may flare up again when I go down to the monastery for Mass and dinner, e.g., yesterday). Everything is falling nicely into place. One can live at a good, quiet, productive tempo—manual labor in the morning, writing in the afternoon. There is time for reading and meditation, and I notice that the reading schedule simplifies itself and I want to spend more time on one thing. The dispersion and agitation of "those days" are settling of their own accord. Already the novitiate is becoming incredible (these last months there have not been reasonable, and the change is welcome). (I remember the novitiate of two—five—eight years ago as more "real"— the first year was a strain, as if I were playing some role I did not really want to play.)

Last week (the 20th, my first day here for keeps) I threw out some squirrel hunters. Thought there were probably no squirrels left anyway. This morning a beautiful, bushy-tailed, red squirrel appeared on the porch and darted about before leaving. It was a delight to see him! How can they kill such beautiful live things!

The blessing of Prime under the tall pines, in the cool of the early morning, behind the hermitage. The blessing of sawing wood, cutting grass, cleaning house, washing dishes. The blessing of a quiet, alert, concentrated, fully "present" meditation. The blessing of God's presence and guidance. I am very aware of the meaning of faith and fidelity. This place is marked with the blessed sign of my covenant with Him who has redeemed me. May I never fail this goodness, this mercy!

August 28, 1965. St. Augustine

The days go by and I am beginning to experience the meaning of *real* solitude. It is certainly real enough now. I go down at 10:45, to say Mass, do necessary errands, have dinner, and come back. Most days speak to no one, see very few members of the community and of course no one else. So I am beginning to feel the lightness, the strangeness, the desertedness of being really alone. It was far different when the ties had not been cut and when the hermitage was only *part* of my life. Now that everything is here, the work of loneliness really begins, and I feel it. I glory in it (giving thanks to God), and I fear it. This is not something lightly to be chosen. Unless I were convinced God had chosen it for me, I would not stay in it. There is an inner psychic strength and "fatness," a good comfortable complacency of being, that comes with the presence and support of other people. Without it, one becomes innerly wasted. It is this "wasting" that I feel beginning, ever so little, and it is what I have to bear.

Yet I feel closely united to my brothers in this above all. It is as if I had taken *their* loneliness upon me, for some mysterious purpose. I think I have assurance that many understand this and feel themselves concerned in it. Father Prior told me in confession yesterday that many were praying for me. Well, I must go ahead sensibly and quietly, without nonsense!

A hard day, two days ago—clearing brush I ran into a hornet's nest and was badly stung. Very painful, very "wasting"—ran to the house with hornets all over me. Fortunately, I pulled my blue denim work shirt up over my head or it would have been worse. The acrid smell of attacking hornets! One or two continued to hang around the house all day. It was very sobering! Reflected that this was due to the delusive impetuosity with which I work. This has to be changed! I must *really* be meek and nonviolent, but I see the roots of this are deep.

Yesterday, when I went down to say Mass, all the community, or a large group rather, were out gathering in the potato harvest under a blue, late summer sky. I remembered the communal beauty of work in this season—the sense of brotherhood and joy when I used to go over with the students to cut tobacco twelve years ago! Or cutting corn in the novitiate, or the general corn husking that went on all through October when I was a student (and late into November even). Now that is all done by machine and there is little really common work outdoors. Anyway, I felt lonely, seeing them out there.

September 6, 1965

Magenta mist outside the windows. A cock crows over at Boone's. Last evening, when the moon was rising, saw the warm burning soft red of a doe in the field. It was still light enough, so I got the field glasses and watched her. Presently a stag came out, then I saw a second doe and, briefly, another stag. They were not afraid. Looked at me from time to time. I watched their beautiful running, grazing. Everything, every movement was completely lovely, but there is a kind of gaucheness about them sometimes that makes them even lovelier. The thing that struck me most: one sees, looking at them directly in movement, just what the cave painters saw—something that I have never seen in a photograph. It is an awe-inspiring thing—the *Mantu* or "spirit" shown in the running of the deer, the "deerness" that sums up everything and is saved and marvelous. A contemplative intuition! Yet perfectly ordinary, everyday seeing. The deer reveals to me something essential in myself! Something beyond the trivialities of my everyday being and my individuality. The stag is much darker, a mouse gray or rather a warm gray-brown, like a flying squirrel. I could sense the softness of their coat and longed to touch them.

September 11, 1965

In a sense, a very true and solitary sense, coming to the hermitage has been a "return to the world," not a return to the cities, but a return to direct and humble contact with God's world, His creation, the world of poor men who work. Andy Boone is physically more my neighbor than the monastery. It is his sawmill I hear, not the monastery machines. His rooster crows in my morning, his cows low in the evening, and I just heard him give a guttural yell at some animal (again, another one, while the first bell for Prime rings at the monastery and a flycatcher squeals happily in the poplar tree).

I do not have the official "space"—sanctified, juridically defined, hedged in with elaborate customs—of the monastery as my milieu. To be out of that is a great blessing. It is a space rich with delusions and with the tyranny of willful fabrication. My space is the world created and redeemed by God. God is in this true world, not "only" and restrictively a prisoner in the monastery. It is most important to see this, and I think that what those who are leaving often see is this. It is crucially important for the monastery to abandon the myth of itself as a purely sacred space—it is a disaster for its real "sacredness." Curiously, the move is getting out in rumors. Though the situation is partly understood and partly not, it is interpreted with shock as my "leaving the monastery." This is true. The general reproach is then that I am not clinging, in spite of reason, grace, and everything else, to something God no longer wills for me: clinging to it just because society expects me to do so! My life is a salutary scandal, and that is another proof of the reality of my vocation, I believe. Here I see my task is to get rid of the last vestiges of a pharisaical division between the sacred and secular, to see that the *whole* world is reconciled to God in Christ, not just the monastery, not only the convents, the churches, and the good Catholic schools.

Late afternoon—a good rainstorm began before supper, and it is going on now as darkness falls. A moment ago there was a hawk up there flying against the wind in the dark and in the rain, with big black clouds flying and the pines bending. A beautiful storm: it has filled my buckets with water for washing and the house with cool winds. It is good and comforting to sit in a storm with all the winds in the woods outside and rain on the roof and sit in a little circle of light and read and hear the clock tick on the table. Tomorrow's Gospel is the one about not serving two Masters, and letting the Lord provide. That is what I must do.

September 20, 1965

I have been working on *Conjectures* in the afternoon—at moments it gets to be like Cantares Hopscotch—crisscross itinerary of the various pieces taken out of time sequence and fitted into what? An indefinite half-conscious pattern of associations that is never consistent, often purely fortuitous, often not there (and not sought in any case). A lot of rewriting. For instance, rewrote an experience of March 18, 1958 (entry of March 19) in light of a very good meditation of Saturday afternoon, developed and changed. A lot of telescoping, etc. In a word, transforming a journal into "meditations" or "*Pensées.*"

October 6, 1965

I see more and more the fruitfulness of this life here with its struggles, its long hours of silence, the sun, the woods, the presence of invisible grace and help. It has to be a creative and humiliating life, a life of search and obedience, simple, direct, requiring strength (I don't have it but it is "given"). There are moments of frightening disruption, then recovery. I am only just beginning to know what life really is—away from all the veils, cushions, and evasions of common life. Yet I see my great need of common life. Seriously, last night at supper, a deep awareness that I need the saints and angels with me in my loneliness.

I am called here to grow. "Death" is a critical point of growth, a transition to a new mode of being, to a *maturity* and fruitfulness that I do not know (they are in Christ and His Kingdom). The child in the womb does not know what will come after birth. He must be born in order to live. I am here to learn to face death as my birth.

This solitude—a refuge under His wings, a place to hide myself in His Name, therefore a sanctuary, where the grace of Baptism remains a conscious, living, active reality, valid not only for me but for the whole Church. Here, planted as a seed in the cosmos, I will be a Christ seed and bring fruit for other men. Death and rising in Christ.

Need to be "confirmed" in vocation by the Spirit (speaking through the Church, i.e., the abbot and community = the abbot's council at least). This ordains me to be the person I am and to have the particular place and function I have, to be myself in the sense of choosing to tend toward what God wants me to be, to orient my whole life to being the person He loves. Too often I have been simply the person, or the individual, who is indifferent to His love and who therefore in practice ignores it as the great option and possibility for each man. (We are all "loved in general," but we have to personally accept a *special* love of God for ourselves.)

Now is the time to see what great strength comes out of silence—and not without struggle.

Obedience to God means first of all *waiting*, having to wait, "wait for the Lord." The first thing then is to accept the fact that one will have to *wait*. Otherwise obedience is undermined by an implicit condition, which destroys it.

One thing is certain: if I merely look upon solitude and "eremiticism" as a culminating monastic ideal, I will find only the delusions that are so frustrating everywhere else. The last thing in the world I want is to "be a hermit." The image of the bearded man half-blind with tears, living in a cave, is not enough. (The grace of compunction that this figure is supposed to have is something else again!) I come into solitude to hear the word of God, to wait in expectation of a Christian fulfillment, to understand myself in relation to a community that doubts and questions itself, and of which I am very much a part. I come into solitude not to "attain the heights of contemplation," but to discover painfully for myself and for my brothers the true eschatological dimension of our calling. No easy solution is permissible. This is a hard way and a way of faith, in which I must struggle to come into the right relation of obedience to the words of God constantly present in my heart, and rest in God who moves in the ground of my being, to make me grow in Him.

November 5, 1965

Old-fashioned idea: that the solitary life and indeed the Christian life is a struggle with invisible powers. All this is dismissed even by monks. Yet is the Bible so far wrong? I think I experience it more and more. As to what these powers are, who can clearly say, but one experiences their persuasion, their use of our weakness to prompt us to choices that, if followed out logically, would wreck us totally. So much more than mere "prudence" is needed—and infinitely more than simple "personal responsibility—autonomy— authenticity," etc. A superficial existentialism can be a disaster. I see it in my writings, once they are printed. Just my arrogant tone, and then extreme statements that could do harm, faults of perspective perhaps. How can I complain if I am criticized? Yet I am often criticized for not being radical *enough*. Obviously I am a complex, alienated person myself, and this can upset everybody. I must meanwhile go on seriously working out my own problems, but without seeking the transient satisfaction of laying down the law.

November 7, 1965

I went out on the porch before dawn to think of these things, and of the words of Ezekiel (22:30): "And I sought among them for a man that might set up a hedge and stand in the gap before me in favor of the land that I might not destroy it, and I found none." While I was standing there quails began to whistle all over the field and in the wood. I had not heard any for weeks and thought sure they were all dead, for there have been hunters everywhere. No, there they are! Signs of life, of gentleness, of helplessness, of providence, of love. They just keep on existing and loving and making more quails and whistling in the bushes.

November 11, 1965. St. Martin

A sad day. Learned this morning by special delivery letter from Jim Douglass (a day late) that a kid from the *Catholic Worker* burned himself alive in front of the United Nations Building. This is fantastic and horrible. He was an ex-seminarian evidently. I cannot understand the shape of things in the Peace Movement or the shape of things at all in this country. What is happening? Is everybody nuts? This took place last Monday.

I am so disturbed by the events, and especially the suicide at the U.N., that I sent a telegram to Dorothy Day and this telegram to Jim Forest of the Catholic Peace Fellowship:

> Just heard about suicide of Roger Laporte. While I do not hold Catholic Peace Fellowship responsible for this tragedy, current developments in Peace Movement make it impossible for me to continue as sponsor for Fellowship. Please remove my name from list of sponsors, letter follows.

This thought came when I was asking Father Abbot permission to send the telegrams, and naturally he was much in favor, but afterward I wondered if I had been too hard on Jim and the Catholic Peace Fellowship. But with things as crazy as they are, I cannot let my name be used by an outfit as unpredictable as that is, with kids likely to do anything at any moment. The CPF is right in the middle of the draft card burning and now this. Five from *Catholic Worker* burned their cards. One burnt himself. Totally awful, the suicide at least.

Yesterday Dan Walsh said a newspaper man in Louisville was trying to get in contact with me—perhaps it had something to do with this affair. Sometimes I wish it were possible simply to be the kind of hermit who is so cut off that he knows *nothing* that goes on, but that is not right, either.

November 13, 1965

This morning, when I was saying Prime under the pine trees in front of the hermitage, I saw a wounded deer limping along in the field, one leg incapacitated. I was terribly sad at this and began weeping bitterly. Then something quite extraordinary happened. I will never forget standing there weeping and looking at the deer standing still looking at me questioningly for a long time, a minute or so. The deer bounded off without any sign of trouble.

November 20, 1965

Letters came from Dan Berrigan, Jim Forest, Dorothy Day. Good letters. I can see that in the trial they have been through (death of Roger Laporte) there has been much purity of love. Dan is now being shipped out by superiors. A statement on draft card burning by Tom Cornell is lucid. However, I have to clarify my own position since people are identifying me with the card burners. While I respect their conscience, I don't think this is the most valid or helpful kind of statement at the moment, and I will have to give some idea where I stand. This in turn shows that there is a certain incompatibility between my solitary life and active involvement in a movement.

November 27, 1965

At midnight I woke up, and there was a great noise of wind and storm. Rain, heavy as a freight train, was rolling over the roof of the hermitage. The porch was covered with water, and there was a lot of lightning. Now at dawn the sky is clear and all is cold again (yesterday warm). Yesterday I read some articles on psychedelics. There is a regular fury of drug-mysticism in this country. I am in a way appalled. Mysticism has finally arrived in a characteristic American mode. One feels that this is certainly it. The definitive turn in the road taken by American religion. The turn I myself will not take (don't need to!). This leaves my own road a lot quieter and more untroubled, I hope. Certainly the great thing, as I see it now, is to get out of all the traffic: peace movement traffic, political traffic, Church traffic, "consciousness-altering" traffic, Zen traffic, monastic reform traffic. All of it!

November 29, 1965

This morning I really opened the door of Rilke's *Duino Elegies* and walked in (previously I have only peeked in through the windows and read fragments here and there). For one thing I got the *sound* of the German really going, and got the feel of the First Elegy as a whole. (Did this before to a lesser extent with the Eighth.) I think I need this hill, this silence, this frost, to really understand this great poem, to live in it—as I have also lived in *Four Quartets.* These are the two modern poems, long poems, that really have a great deal of meaning for me. Like García Lorca (whom I have not read in years). Others I simply like and agree with: W. H. Auden, Stephen Spender to some extent, Dylan Thomas in an entirely different way. But the *Duino Elegies* and *Four Quartets* talk about my life itself, my own self, my own destiny, my Christianity, my vocation, my relation to the world of my time, my place in it, etc. Perhaps Pablo Neruda's *Residence on Earth* and of course Vallejo will eventually do this, but with *Residence* I have, once again, only looked through the windows.

December 7, 1965

What is primary? God's revelation of Himself to me *in Christ* and my response in faith. In the concrete, this means, for me, my present life in solitude, acceptance of its true perspectives and demands, and the work of slow reorientation that goes on. Each day I realize a little that my old life is breaking loose and will eventually fall off in pieces gradually. What then? My solitude is not like Rilke's, ordered to a poetic explosion. Nor is it a mere deepening of religious consciousness. What is it then? What has been so far only a theological conception, or an image, has to be sought and loved. "Union with God!" So mysterious that in the end man would perhaps do anything to evade it, once he realizes it means the *end* of his own Ego-self-realization, once and for all. Am I ready? Of course not. Yet the course of my life is set in this direction.

December 21, 1965. St. Thomas

While I was saying Mass, at my Communion I heard the bells ring for an agony and guessed they were for Brother Gerard (they rang for *thee!*), and he died about an hour later. Father Roger made me a sign, coming late to his dinner. Another of the old brothers, the past dying. Brother Gerard was from Europe, was long a gardener, tailor, etc., and was said to have visions.

A distant relative sent an old snapshot taken when he and his wife visited Douglaston thirty years ago. It shows them with Bonnemaman and myself—the back porch of the house, the birch tree. There is Bonnemaman as I remember her—within two years of dying. And there am I: it shakes me! I am the young rugby player, the lad from Cambridge, vigorous, light, vain, alive, obviously making a joke of some sort. The thing that shakes me: I can see that that was a different body from the one I have now—one entirely young and healthy, that did not know sickness, weakness, anguish, tension, fatigue—a body totally assured of itself and without care, perfectly relaxed, ready for enjoyment. What a change since that day! If I were wiser, I would not mind, but I am not so sure I am wiser. I have been through more. I have endured a lot of things, perhaps fruitlessly. I do not think that—but it is possible. What shakes me is that I wish I were that rugby player, vain, vigorous, etc., and could start all over again!! Yet how absurd. What would I ever do? The other thing is that those were, no matter how you look at it, better times! There were things we had not heard of—Auschwitz, the Bomb, etc. (Yet it was all beginning nevertheless.)

And now what kind of a body! An arthritic hip; a case of chronic dermatitis on my hands for a year and a half (so that I have to wear gloves); sinusitis, chronic ever since I came to Kentucky; lungs always showing up some funny shadow or other on X-rays (though not lately); perpetual diarrhea and a bleeding anus; most of my teeth gone; most of my hair gone; a chewed-up vertebra in my neck, which causes my hands to go numb and my shoulder to ache and for which I sometimes need traction. When you write it down it looks like something: there is no moment anymore when I am not *aware* that I have something wrong with me and have to be careful! What an existence! But I have grown used to it—something that thirty years ago would have been simply incredible.

Dreams—Night of Saturday-Sunday (Fourth Sunday of Advent). I have a little water or "coffee"—in a bowl. By stirring it, perhaps it will be drinkable coffee. I stir it, but it is like lukewarm, muddy water to look at and there are insects in it, which I can pick and throw out. But I see really I must find fresh water and make new coffee.

My own personal task is not simply that of poet and writer (still less commentator, pseudo-prophet); it is basically to *praise* God out of an inner center of silence, gratitude, and "awareness." This can be realized in a life that apparently accomplishes nothing. Without centering on accomplishment or nonaccomplishment, my task is simply the breathing of this gratitude from day to day, in simplicity, and for the rest turning my hand to whatever comes, work being part of praise, whether splitting logs or writing poems, or best of all simple notes. And there will remain occasional necessary letters.

If everything centers on my obligation to respond to God's call to solitude, this does not mean simply putting everything out of my mind and living as if only God and I existed. This is impossible anyway. It means rather *learning* from what contacts and conflicts I still have how deep a solitude is required of me. This means *now* the difficult realization that I have relied too much on the support and approval of others—and yet I do need others. I must now painfully rectify this. That is to say— there is a sense in which *some* of God's answers must come to me from others, even from those with whom I disagree, even from those who do not understand my way of life. Yet it would be disastrous to seek merely to placate these people—the mere willingness to do so would make me deaf to whatever real message they might have. To do this job rightly is beyond my power. Prayer is all I have left—and patient, humble (if possible) obedience to God's will. One thing is certain—I do not possess my answers ready at hand in myself. (It almost seems an axiom that a solitary should be one who has his own answers. . . .) But I cannot simply seek them from others either. The problem is in learning to go for some time, perhaps for long periods—*with no answer!!*

December 30, 1965

End of a year. Should one have something to say about a "year"? I have no need to be obsessed with time here, though I don't pretend to be lost in eternity either. Days go by. The moon of Ramadan, which was new on Christmas Eve, is growing fat, and I will save the fasting till after New Year—a token fast with the Moslems. Must write to Abdul Aziz.

The business with Jim Forest and Catholic Peace Fellowship is settled charitably. Dorothy Day wrote a splendid card. These are authentic Christians and I feel very indebted to them. I see too, how much I thrash around mentally and morally in the face of emptiness. It is interesting and curious how one's being reacts to solitude and nothingness. Automatic and compulsive routines that are simply silly—and I don't take them seriously. All the singing, the "speaking in tongues," etc. Funny. I see how easily I could go nuts and don't especially care. I see the huge flaws in myself and don't know what to do about them. Die of them eventually, I suppose, what else can I do? I live a flawed and inconsequential life, believing in God's love. But faith can no longer be naive and sentimental. I cannot explain things away with it. Need for deeper meditation. I certainly see more clearly where I need to go and how. (Surprising how my prayer in community had really reached a dead end for *years* and stayed there. Fortunately I could get out to the woods and my spirit could breathe.) Still, Gethsemani too has to be fully accepted. My long refusal to fully identify myself with the place is futile (and identifying myself in some forlorn and lonesome way would be worse). It is simply where I am. The monks are who they are: not monks but people. The younger ones are more truly people than the old ones, who are also good in their own way, signs of a different kind of excellence that is no longer desirable in its accidentals. The essence is the same.

Renounce accusations and excuses.

I continue with Rilke, seeing his greatness and his limitations. His poetic solitude is not what I am here for, but it says something too. So he is no mystic. But he *is* a poet. Is that a small thing?

PART VI

EXPLORING SOLITUDE
AND FREEDOM
1966–1967

When in the soul of the serene disciple,
With no more fathers to imitate,
Poverty is a success,
It is a small thing to say the roof is gone:
He has not even a house.

Stars, as well as friends,
Are angry with the noble ruin.
Saints depart in several directions.

Be still:
There is no longer any need of comment.
It was a lucky wind
That blew away his halo with his cares,
A lucky sea that drowned his reputation.

The Strange Islands

I am thrown into contradiction:
to realize it is mercy,
to accept it is love,
to help others do the same is compassion.

Notebook 17

February 17, 1966

Today was *the* prophetic day, the first of the real shining spring—not that there was not warm weather last week, or that there will not be cold weather again, but this was the day of the year when spring became truly *credible*. Freezing night but cold, bright morning and a brave, bright shining of the sun that is new and an awakening in all the land, as if the earth were aware of its capacities!

I saw the woodchuck had opened up his den and had come out, after three months or so of sleep, and at that early hour it was still freezing: I thought he had gone crazy. The day proved him right and me wrong.

The morning got more and more brilliant, and I could feel the brilliancy of it getting into my own blood. Living so close to the cold, you feel the spring. This is man's mission! The earth cannot *feel* all this. *We* must. Living away from the earth and the trees, we fail them. We are absent from the wedding feast.

There are moments of great loneliness and lostness in solitude, but often there come other deeper moments of hope and understanding, and I realize that these would *not be possible* in their purity, their simple secret directions, anywhere but in solitude. I hope to be worthy of them!

After dinner, when I came back to the hermitage, the whole hillside was so bright and new I wanted to cry out. I got tears in my eyes from it!

With the new comes also memory, as if that which was once so fresh in the past (days of discovery when I was 19 or 20) were very close again, as if one were beginning to live again from the beginning: one must experience spring like that. A whole new chance! A complete renewal!

March 2, 1966

A flash of sanity: the momentary realization that there is *no need* to come to certain conclusions about persons, events, conflicts, trends, even trends toward evil and disaster, as if from day to day and even from moment to moment I had to know and *declare* (at least to myself) that this is so and so, this is good, this is bad. We are heading for a "new era" or we are heading for destruction. What do such judgments mean? Little or nothing. Things are as they are in an immense whole of which I am a part and which I cannot pretend to grasp. To say I grasp it is immediately to put myself in a false position, as if I were "outside" it. Whereas to be *in* it is to seek truth in my own life and action, moving where movement is possible and keeping still when movement is unnecessary, realizing that things will continue to define themselves and that the judgments and mercies of God will clarify themselves and will be more clear to me if I am silent and attentive, obedient to His will, rather than constantly formulating statements in this age which is *smothered* in language, in meaningless and inconclusive debate in which, in the last analysis, nobody listens to anything except what agrees with his own prejudices.

March 6, 1966. Second Sunday of Lent

Cold again. I took a good long walk in the woods, watching the patterns of water in my quiet, favorite creek. Then walked up and down in the sheltered place where we used to go for Christmas trees, thinking about life and death. How impossible it is to grasp the idea that one must die and what to do to be ready for it! When it comes to setting my house in order, I seem to have no ideas at all.

In the evening, stood for about 15 minutes on the porch watching deer, etc., through field glasses. The deer—five of them—were out by the brush piles beyond my fence, barely a hundred yards—less perhaps—from the hermitage. Hence I could see them very clearly and could watch all their beautiful movements—from time to time they tried to figure me out and would spread out their ears at me and stand still, looking, and there I would be gazing right into those big brown eyes and those black noses. One, the most suspicious, would lift a foot and set it down again quietly, as if to stomp, but in doubt about whether there was a good reason. This one also had a stylish, high-stepping trot routine, which the others did not seem to have. But what form! I was entranced by their perfection!

Beauty and *necessity* (for me) of a solitary life—apparent in the sparks of truth, small, recurring flashes of a reality that is *beyond doubt*, momentarily appearing, leading me further on my way. Things that need no explanation and perhaps have none but that say: "Here! This way!" And with final authority!

It is for them that I will be held responsible. Nothing but immense gratitude! They cancel out all my mistakes, weaknesses, evasions, falsifications.

They lead me further and further in that direction that has been shown me and to which I am called.

March 8, 1966

The solitary life reduces itself to a simple need—to make the choices that constantly imply preference for solitude fully understood (better "properly" understood in relation to one's capacity at the moment). I find myself confronted with these choices repeatedly. They present themselves in their own ways, and what they add up to these days is the question of emotional dependence on other people, simply, collectively—the community, friends, readers, other poets, etc. Over and over again I have to make small decisions here and there in regard to one or another. Distractions and obsessions are resolved in this way. What the resolution amounts to, in the end, is letting go of the imaginary and the absent and returning to the present, the real, what is in front of my nose. Each time I do this I am more present, more alone, more detached, more clear, better able to pray. Failure to do it means confusions, weaknesses, hesitation, fear, and all the way through to anguish and nightmares. It is not purely up to me to "succeed" each time. I cannot calculate the force of unidentified emotion that will well out of my unconscious. There are days of obscurity, frustrations, and crises when *nothing* is straight. However, I know my aim and I try at least to meditate. Discovering how hostile I have been, how desperate, how mean and unjust. (For instance, today again it comes back to me that I had been unjust, suspicious, and ungrateful to Doherty, the Headmaster at Oakham, who had really been kind to me and concerned with my best interests. I could not believe him.)

So, when it comes to "preparing for death," in my case it means simply this reiterated decision for solitude as the reality called for me by God as my penance and cleansing, as my paying off debts, as my return to my right mind, and as my place of worship and prayer.

March 10, 1966

I was going to finish cutting brush this morning, but it looks like rain. I'll see. My back hurts anyway. I am to go into the hospital on the 23rd, and apparently the operation is the next day. In a way I have *not* adjusted to the idea and cannot fully do so. I distrust the mania for surgery in this country, although Dr. Mitchell is certainly a reasonable and prudent man and no fanatic. I can see that the condition of my back is such that, if he does not operate now, I will hardly be able to work with my arms and hands in a little while. (My hand, holding a pen and writing a few lines, gets numb fast.)

Having to undergo surgery is a kind of defeat, an admission that I have not lived right, that I have in fact been too much a prisoner of a very unreasonable culture. Honestly, I think it is too late for me to escape the consequences altogether. But I hope I can salvage something. My life in the hermitage is much saner and better balanced than it was in the monastery, my health is much better, I sleep well, have a good appetite, no colds, stomach a bit better. I suppose my eating is wrong.

When the operation is over, perhaps I can start afresh and really try to get everything in order. I hope so! But meanwhile I do not expect much help from doctors and their damned pills.

March 23, 1966

The bell tolls slowly in the dark for the Preface of the Conventual Mass. I listen to it with the wind swaying the heavy pines in the night. The icebox is already turned off. I have a little oleo to return to the infirmary kitchen when I go down. Mass at 9:30, then to the eye doctor, then to the hospital for the back operation. One other thing: a small tumor in my stomach (can be felt on the surface) has been growing a little in these last weeks and had better be investigated. Father Eudes thinks offhandedly that it is not a malignancy.

Anyway, if I can be serious, I suppose I am so now. Yet not terribly alarmed or concerned. I know I have to die sometime, and may this not all be the beginning of it? I don't know, but if it is I accept it in full freedom and gladness. My life stands offered with that of Christ my brother. If I am to start now on this way, I start on it gladly. Curious that the operation will coincide with the big protest against the Vietnam war. It is my way of being involved.

Bell for Consecration at the monastery!

The one thing for which I am most grateful: this hermitage. The ability to spend at least half a day (the afternoon) here frequently, sometimes daily, since December 1960. Then sleeping here and having also the predawn hours since October 1964. Finally being here all day and all night (except for Mass and dinner) since August 1965. This last was the best, and I am just beginning to really get grounded in solitude (getting rid of the writer of many articles and books) so that, if my life were to be on the way to ending now, this would be my one regret: loss of the years of solitude that might still be possible. Nothing else. But there are greater gifts even than this, and God knows what is best for my good and for the good of the whole world. The best is what He wills.

April 10, 1966. Easter Sunday

Back in the hermitage sooner than I expected (sleeping in the infirmary). The operation was much more smooth and effective than I expected and apparently went beautifully. Had a hard time the first walk and am still troubled by the leg from which they took the bone graft, but on the whole have had less trouble than I anticipated. The worst was just the strain of the abnormal, mechanized, routinized life of the hospital, poked and pushed and stuck and cut and fed and stuffed with pills, juices, etc. Got home yesterday and came up to the hermitage as soon as I could, silly with exaltation. I suppose it is all a bit childish really.

One week after the operation, Friday in Passion Week, I was able to get up and go out to walk a while on the grass. This made an enormous difference, as did the fact that I got a very friendly and devoted student nurse working on my compresses, etc. This livened things up considerably. In fact, we were getting perhaps too friendly by the time M. went off on her Easter vacation, but her affection—undisguised and frank—was an *enormous* help in bringing me back to life fast. In fact, all the nurses were very interested and friendly and warm. Being surrounded with all this care and esteem was a great indulgence! A huge luxury! I realized that though I am pretty indifferent to the society of my fellow monks (can live without being lonely for the community *at all* and it is a work of the will to go down and participate in the essentials, not an emotional need), I do feel a deep emotional need for feminine companionship and love. Seeing that I must irrevocably live without it ended by tearing me up more than the operation itself.

The best thing of all was lying down reading Meister Eckhart or sitting up when I finally could, copying sentences from the sermons that I can use if I write on him. It was this that saved me. When I got back to the hermitage last evening to say the Easter offices, everything else drained off and Eckhart remained as real. The rest was like something I had imagined.

April 12, 1966. Easter Tuesday

The community has moved out of the church (yesterday) to a temporary chapel on the third floor. Already there is a lot of banging in the church, getting ready to tear everything out and remodel the interior.

Beginning to think a little of work again—I mean writing. But I do not feel I can type yet and do not intend to try. Have no really serious ideas either. Yet I can feel them coming back again. I am more myself.

April 14, 1966. Easter Thursday

Yesterday I wrote a longish poem about the hospital experience, and I think it is a good poem too. Better than the others I have done so far this year. Today I revised the notes on solitude written as a preface for the Japanese *Thoughts in Solitude,* and I think I deepened and improved it. One thing has suddenly hit me—that nothing counts except love and that a solitude that is not simply the wide-openness of love and freedom is nothing. Love and solitude are the one ground of true maturity and freedom. Solitude that is just solitude and nothing else (i.e., *excludes* everything else but solitude) is worthless. True solitude embraces everything, for it is the fullness of love that rejects nothing and no one, that is open to All in All.

The work of writing for me can be, or can be very close to, the simple job of *being:* by creative reflection and awareness to help life itself live in me, to give its *esse* an existant, or, rather, for me to find a place in *esse* by action, intelligence, and love. To write is to love: it is to inquire and to praise or to confess or to appeal. This testimony of love remains necessary. Not to reassure myself that I am ("I write therefore I am"), but simply to pay my debt to life, to the world, to other men. To speak out with an open heart and say what seems to me to have meaning. The bad writing I have done has all been authoritarian, the declaration of musts and the announcement of punishments. Bad because it implies a lack of love, good insofar as there may yet have been some love in it. The best stuff has been more straight confession and witness.

April 19, 1966

Warm wind swaying the very leafed out branches of the rose hedge. The grass was cut yesterday for the first time (and smelled sweetly). The dogwood blossoms are just beginning to open. Brother Benedict finished planting those pecan trees yesterday.

A letter came from M. I was glad to hear from her. Have to think— my way around the problem of this tenderness—but anyway I will do the only thing possible and risk loving with Christ's love when there is so obvious a need for it. And not fear!

April 20, 1966

I can hear the demolishers shouting from the top of the steeple. They are now stripping it. A momentous change: the steeple has been so much a sign of the place—the thing one looks for when one is getting close— the expression of the abbey's identity—the sign that it is *there!* I was disquieted by the steeple's going. The church is raided and ruined inside (Sunday I concelebrated on the third floor and it was already hot, but I like the simplicity of the long room and the beams).

April 21, 1966

Dark day, colder. Andy Boone's buzz saw is going, and it sounds like winter again. But the grass is very green, the red buds show well against the green pines and the brush bursting into leaf, small red wildflowers everywhere, and the May apples opening their shiny new umbrellas. St. Anselm's day. It has been a day of struggle and prayer for me—the need for inner freedom, the urgency of constant work, and the difficulty of getting back into solitude after the hospital. In fact, there is now a real doubt in my mind about the value of the whole hermit experiment as it is here. Certainly it means more to me than the artificialities of the community, but this is artificial and arbitrary in its own way. I would organize it otherwise if I could—more open, less rigid. But I have no way of doing so, and perhaps it is really best to have to take it, as I do, on someone else's terms, especially if that other is an Abbot with whose views I in no way agree. But there *is* the question of charity, of being open to others. Of course I am really bothered and worried. M. wants to see me and I want to see her. I tell myself it is because I want to help her. Yet the bother is that one has to *calculate* how it might possibly be done. And then the letters: will they be stopped, interfered with, etc.? Things should not have to be this way. In the hospital, where I could confront everything directly and frankly, there were no such Byzantine problems of tactics and justifications.

However, I must admit that I can do her little or no good as long as I am emotionally attached to her. I must try to be more free and more sure of what I mean by love in Christ—and not kid myself.

April 22, 1966

More shouting on the steeple. Slowly the plates of lead come off and the old brown lumber appears. Warm afternoon. For a while I sat in the sun surrounded by lovemaking bumblebees. The other day I saw the feathers of a cardinal that a hawk had killed and was sad, thinking a pair had been broken up. Today I saw this male sitting beautifully on a fence post singing joyfully—but at first no female. Then I saw her flying in and out of a big rosebush in the hedge, where the new nest is, and was happy.

April 24, 1966. II Sunday After Easter

One warm gray day after another, continued struggle in my own heart. I am losing weight (five more pounds in the last week). Repugnance for food. Perhaps this has something to do with the antibiotic that made me sick in the hospital. It will be better for me when I can work again. Yesterday, the whole day revolved around a long (illegal) phone conversation with M. I got into the cellarer's office when everyone was at dinner (with his approval—he went off and left me locked in), reached her in the hospital cafeteria (cry of joy when she found out who it was!). We had a good long talk. It was in many respects necessary, cleared up a lot of confusion in my own mind (from sheer lack of information and communication). Yet, on the other hand, one thing led to another, and this is another link in an uncomfortable kind of karmic chain. In my heart I know it would really have been better if I had followed my original intuition and been content with a couple of letters and nothing more. But we want to see each other, etc., etc. Still, we both know there is no future to it and there is no sense making much of it. Sooner or later it will all end anyway. It would be better to end it before it gets more complicated than it is. But now I fear that a chain of events has started that cannot be stopped—only slowed down, directed, guided (I hope!).

Today—back to meditation on the *Dhammapada*—something sound to support me when everything else is quicksand.

April 25, 1966. Feast of St. Mark

Yesterday I went down to begin my conferences again, having thought of reading my hospital poem ("With the World in My Blood Stream")— yet doubting and hesitating. I read it, and though at the end I am sure that most of them did not understand much of it, they all seemed very attentive and moved—some (whom I would not have expected to be so) quite visibly. I think, to begin with, that they were first of all happy that I should share a poem with them (of my own—which I never do. Perhaps read one twelve years ago in the scholasticate). Also, they were obviously glad to have the conferences start again. In a word, in spite of my anxieties and doubts about myself and my hesitations about the community, I am someone they (at least those who come to the conferences, and others too) appreciate, to whom they look for something that seems to them alive and valuable. Usually it disturbs me to admit this, since it starts a conflict between narcissism on the one hand and self-doubt on the other. My usual reaction is flight.

Now I see more and more that there is only one realistic answer: Love. I have got to dare to love, to bear the anxiety of self-questioning that love arouses in me, until "perfect love casts out fear."

Same with M. (but with no nonsense!). The basic fact is that she does love me. She does need from me a certain kind of love that will support her and help her believe in herself and get free from some destructive patterns and attachments that are likely to wreck her. Her love arouses in me at once an overwhelming gratitude and the impulse to fling my whole self into her arms, and also panic, doubt, fear of being deceived and hurt (as I lay awake half the night tormented by the thought of the guy she is probably sleeping with!).

After several days of this conflict and anxiety, last night I took a sleeping pill and Brother Camillus, the infirmarian, gave me some old bourbon that had been tucked away in a closet since Dom Edmund's days (marvelous too!). I slept nearly 9 hours (sweated up and changed 3 times) and awoke with the deep realization that my response of love to M. was *right*. It might have nothing to do with the rule books or with any other system, it might be open to all kinds of delusions and error, but in fact so far, by and large, I have been acting right. I have been in the Truth, not through any virtue of my own, nor through any superior intuition, but because I have let love take hold of me in spite of all my fear. I have obeyed love. I have honestly tried to see her truly as she is and love her exactly as she is, to value her uniquely and share with her this deep faith in her. I know that the result has been a deep, clear, strong, indubitable resonance between us. Our hearts really are in tune. Our depths really communicate. This is all. It is the real root and ground of everything, and of this sexual love can only at best be a sign. Certainly it would be marvelous if we could communicate the whole thing in this sign, but I see no way of doing this without falling away completely from truth. Hence I will never touch her and will make sure that this is perfectly clear—without being sanctimonious about it. She is very aware of the problem too!

Then, too, of course, I have to continue my work of eliminating all craving, all passionate attachment, all self-seeking from this. It is work. Evasion is no answer, and I am not sure I have a real answer or know just what to do. I have only in the end to trust God in this as in all my other complexities and He will bring me through it all right.

*

April 27, 1966

There is no question that I am in deep. Tuesday (yesterday) M. met me at the doctor's. Appeared in the hall, small, shy, almost defiant, with her long black hair, her gray eyes, her white trench coat. (She kept saying she was scared.) Jim Wygal (on whom I depended for transportation and lunch) was along. He kept peppering everything with a kind of earthy crudeness that annoyed me, but it was a good thing, I guess. His house just burned down and he was upset, drank too much, left me and M. alone for a half hour in the booth at Cunningham's. It was a wonderful lunch, so good to be with her. More than ever I saw how much and how instantly and how delicately we respond to each other on every level. I can see why she is scared. I am too. There is a sense of awful, awesome rather, sexual affinity. Of course there can be no hesitations about my position here. I have vows and I must be faithful to them. I told myself that I can and will be, but I have moments of being scared too. Apart from that, though, we had a very good talk, and once again it was clearer than ever that we are terribly in love, the kind of love that can virtually tear you apart. She literally trembled with it. It also exists on other levels, really so, and I tried to make this clear, the meaning of it, trying desperately. I do so much want to love her as we began, spiritually. I do believe such spiritual love is not only possible but does exist between us deeply, purely, strongly, and the rest can be controlled. Yet she is right to be scared. We can simply wreck each other. I am determined not to give in to this, not to yield to fear and despair, to keep it on the level where it belongs, but I can see I really don't know how to handle this if it ever breaks loose. I have been imprudent. Wygal added to it afterward with his warnings, prophecies of doom, and gloomy insinuations. The man has an appalling death wish, and sadomasochism gets more and more into his friendship, and that is really depressing. Yet there were some peaceful moments sitting at the airport in the rain, drinking brandy and soda and watching the planes. Yet it was unreal. I do hope that my fondness for M. will not turn into an ugly, bloody conflagration. It would be so good to be able to help her, to have real sweet, tender, good friendship. I am going to fight for it against all odds because I *do* believe in this kind of love (look at Jacques and Raïssa Maritain), and in fact I do have plenty of friends on this basis (Mother Angela, for instance). It is that M. is terribly inflammable, beautiful, is no nun, and is so tragically full of passion and so wide open. My response has been too total and too forthright. We have admitted too much, communicated all the fire to each other, and now we are caught. I am not as smart or as stable as I imagined.

But such good things—her response to the poems, her words about her love, her fears, her hopes.

April 28, 1966

How does this all fit the standards of "the cell"? How does "the cell" judge it? There seems to be no problem. Solitude has not become distasteful to me or changed its meaning. It is true! I am not ready to go back to sleeping up here—medicinally and perhaps psychologically. This is the only place where I feel at home and feel I can be myself. I think, if the truth be told, what I am looking for is not to "be a hermit" but just to be myself, the person God made me to be, and also, incidentally, the person loved by M.

(She was looking at the pictures in *Jubilee*—which embarrass me—and said she was just doing this "because it was you." The hospital librarian came along and said what a miserable life I must be leading, etc., etc.).

May 7, 1966

The brilliant weather has continued all week, and now it seems to be the most brilliant day of them all. M. should be leaving Louisville about now with Jack Ford and his wife. (M. is scared that they will be scandalized at us—which is quite possible. How are the two of us going to sit politely at a picnic lunch without giving away the obvious fact that we are in love?) M. and I will have trouble providing safe small talk that will not let all the cats out of all the bags, because Thursday, with J. Laughlin and Nicanor Parra, I ended up in Louisville taking her out to supper at the airport. First I was only going to call her from Bardstown. Then I thought we could go to Bernheim Forest and call from there. But there were no public phones there. So we went out to the big restaurant and motel on the turnpike beyond the toll gate, and by the time I got there I decided that, since we were practically in Louisville, we might as well go all the way. So I called M. to expect us in twenty minutes, and soon there we were outside Lourdes Hall. She came out looking more lovely than ever. I had on only my Trappist overalls, but anyhow we got into the Luau Room at the airport. Lots of rich people were arriving for the Derby (which is today), and the place was full of brass and money, and there I sat having a marvelous time, looking like a convict, unable to turn my head to see all the swanky jets landing behind me, satisfied to look at M. I could hardly eat anything—not unusual, as it has been that way since the operation.

After supper M. and I had a little while alone and went off by ourselves and found a quiet corner, sat on the grass out of sight, and loved each other to ecstasy. It was beautiful, awesomely so, to love so much and to be loved, to be able to say it all completely without fear and without observation (not that we sexually consummated it).

Came home dazed, long after dark (highly illegal!), and wrote a poem before going to bed. I think Nicanor Parra was highly edified. He was saying something about how one must "follow the ecstasy," by which he meant evidently right out of the monastery and over the hill. This, of course, I cannot do.

May 9, 1966

M. and the Fords and Father John Loftus came Saturday—arriving late (an hour of waiting and I made desperate acts of patience). The woods were beautiful. It was a brilliant cool day, something like my Ordination day, lovely May weather. A good picnic with a bottle of St. Emilion. Then M. and I went off for a couple of hours together (Gladys Ford gave us some funny looks when we came back and I think Father John was worried). M. and I sat on the moss by the little creek in one of my favorite places and talked and loved and opened our hearts to each other. It was the longest, greatest time we had had together, not as ecstatic as the evening at the airport, but sweet and deep. There are in us both deep capacities for love, especially in her. I have never seen so much simple, spontaneous, total love. I realize that the deepest capacities for human love in me have never even been tapped, that I too can love with an awful completeness. Responding to her has opened up the depths of my life in ways I can't begin to understand or analyze now. Of course there could be all kinds of "danger." But what danger? Where does danger really lie? I am struck by the fact that the social rules of thumb for handling such situations offer no real structure, no authentic answer, and one cannot begin to make sense of norms!

May 10, 1966

Frost this morning. Bright sun now. Birds singing loudly. Wrens hopping about on the wood on the porch.

Whatever else I do, reading and meditation remain important, to keep in perfect touch with reality, to avoid the divisions created by yearning and speculation. One thing is evident—no use building my life on mere possibilities, whether on an ideal self as a perfectly solitary hermit or on a fulfilled and human self living with M. somewhere on an island. I *am* myself. I do not *make* myself or bring myself into conformity with some nonsensical ideal. One of the good sane things about this love is seeing myself as loved by M. True, she idealizes me impossibly, yet at the same time I am unavoidably known to her *as I am*. Many of the things she loves in me are things I find humiliating and impossible, but she loves them because they are concretely mine. I love her the same way. This surely is a very good thing!!

May 17, 1966

This morning we were awake thinking of each other at 1:30 (she likes this and so do I) but after I went back to sleep, I woke again at 3:30 in a splendid and terrible crisis of love.

I had been dreaming of some beautiful day and a voice said, "of course it is beautiful, it is Derby Day and Derby Day is always beautiful" (that was the 7th—the day she came out with the Fords). Then I woke up with a sense of eternal reality and validity of our love and became flooded with really ecstatic love and tears in which I could see her heart, so to speak, in all its preciousness before God, all its beauty and lovableness, the enormously valuable gift of her love to me! I wept for half an hour, shaken with sobs, still not completely awake, absorbed in the deep reality of this vision and this hope.

May 20, 1966

So yesterday, Ascension Day, was beautiful. She came out driven by another nurse in a light blue Ford, who came back to pick her up in the late afternoon.

We walked off into the woods at the foot of Vineyard Knobs, carrying things for a picnic, she with a bag of food dripping from the ice that was cooling the sauterne. Because of the dripping ice we could not go far—not to the place I had thought of, but just went off into the bushes and probably it was just as well because we were completely hidden—there was no special beauty to it and no one was likely to come there! It was good that we were hidden and totally alone!

We ate herring and ham (not very much eating!) and drank our wine and read poems and talked of ourselves and mostly made love and love and love for five hours. Though we had over and over reassured ourselves and agreed that our love would have to continue always chaste and this sacrifice was essential, yet in the end we were getting rather sexy. Yet really, instead of being all wrong, it seemed eminently right. We now love with our whole bodies anyway, and I have the complete feel of her being (except her sex) as completely me. Yet it seemed right because we do really belong to each other in our love (bad argument—it could justify anything!). Of course the grave thing is—this solemn and beautiful thing that we are doing is what lovers perhaps rarely do today. We are moving slowly toward a complete physical ripening of love, a leisurely preparation of our whole being, like the maturing of apples in the sun. I suddenly realized I had never permitted this before, had always in my youth been in a hurry and thought about it too much and tried to precipitate everything before its time. No wonder I was unhappy.

Now yesterday was this slow, gradual, new stage of ripening, and the grip of this deep warm sexual love disturbing me and flooding through me, shaking my whole being from the heart (not just genital excitation)—and it was as yet only a little! But this is awfully serious, because in spite of all we were wanting and saying, nature placidly and inexorably said something more profound and perhaps irreversible.

Yet I refuse to be disturbed by it. I am flooded with peace (whereas last Sunday the mere idea that this might happen tore me with anguish and panic). I have surrendered again to a kind of inimical womanly wisdom in M. which instinctively seeks out the wound in me that most needs her sweetness and lavishes all her love upon me there. Instead of feeling impure, I feel purified (which is in fact what I myself wrote the other day in the "Seven Words" for Ned O'Gorman). I feel that somehow my sexuality has been made real and decent again after years of rather frantic suppression (for though I thought I had it all truly controlled, this was an illusion). I feel less sick. I feel human. I am grateful for her love, which is so totally mine. All the beauty of it comes from this: that we are *not* just playing, we belong totally to each other's love (except for the vow that prevents the last complete surrender).

Always in the end there is this enormous, unthinkable problem of my vow and my dedication, which really come first and make the whole thing absurdly impossible. Yet she insists that she is totally mine and will never love anyone else. I have stopped trying to argue her out of this. I know we will have to suffer terribly. But now I just don't think of it. I cannot. There is all the reality and peace and beauty of yesterday. I find that if my love for her is in a way *less* ideal, more incarnate, it is also more ideal. To have body and earth more in it is to have a better grip on what supports the true ideal (as in the poem "Proverbs Arise out of Dreams").

Anyway, I love her more deeply than ever and just can't think about the future. It will take care of itself. God will take care of it.

Afternoon. Nevertheless, as always, I end up impatient of sex, backing away from domination by it, suspicious of its tyranny, and this afternoon I am turning with all my being toward freedom. I love her but do not want to think of her. I want to get to work, to write my conference for Sunday, to read, to meditate, to get the heaviness of passion off my mind. Once again too I want to *eat.* I have an appetite for the first time in two months—though I don't expect it will get very far. Try some herring left over from yesterday perhaps, later!

June 2, 1966

Since Tuesday, when M. came back from Cincinnati, I have had some good phone calls, the best of which was today. We get deeper and deeper in love. She challenged me on a point about "detachment" (I suppose I must have said something about that as she was so terribly lonely on the phone Saturday). But of course to talk about detachment when you are in love is just nonsense. Yet it came as a mild shock. Of course I am not detached and neither is she. We are profoundly and firmly attached to each other. I am more aware of it all the time because my nature at times rebels against being "held" like this. So today on the phone I made a frank commitment on this point. I *am* attached and I know it and my life

is profoundly changed—in a most serious way—by the fact. It is no joke
at all. This love of ours—very joyous today, very sure of itself,
triumphantly articulate—is still an immense reservoir of anguish,
especially for me. But I don't care. Now I can accept the anguish, the risk,
the awful insecurity, even the guilt (though we are doing nothing radically
wrong, i.e., not sinning). I hope I am not lying to myself anywhere.
Certainly I am not just loving now for the joy of it. I am loving because
of our commitment to each other, our bond to each other, what we mean
to each other. We are far beyond the point where I used to get off the bus
in all my old love affairs. I am in much deeper than I ever was before. (In
the light of M.'s love I realize for the first time how deeply I was loved
back in those days by girls whose names I have even forgotten.)

Anyway, I am seeing M. Saturday again in Louisville.

June 9, 1966. Corpus Christi

Concelebration early. I stood there among all the others, soberly aware of
myself as a priest who has a woman. True, we have done nothing
drastically wrong—though in the eyes of many our lovemaking is still
wrong even though it stops short of complete sex. Before God I think we
have been conscientious and have kept our love good. Yet is it reasonable
for me to be writing her love poems—even a song?

June 12, 1966

Yesterday I had to go to Louisville for a bursitis shot in the elbow. M.
and I had arranged with Jim Wygal that we would borrow his office and
get together there, which we did with a bottle of champagne.

When I got home I called her and we were talking again foolishly of
possibilities, living together, my leaving here, "marrying" her, etc. But it is
all preposterous. Society has no place for us, and I haven't the gall it takes
to fight the whole world, particularly when I don't really want married
life anyway; I want the life I have vowed.

This morning I woke up (after a night of light and fitful sleep)
without self-hate or undue guilt but with the realization that something
has to be done. We can't go on like this. I can't leave her. I have to try to
live the life I have chosen. Yet I love her.

June 14, 1966

Yesterday the Abbot came home. Last night I went down to the Steel building to call M. Brother Clement was there and said that Brother G. in the gatehouse had listened in on one of my many calls to M. (Thursday night? Sunday morning?—the worst!!) and had reported the matter to Dom James. I don't know how much he knows, but I know he is mad and is waiting to give me the devil about it, which is only natural. I have to face the fact that I have been wrong and foolish in all this. Much as I love M., I should never have let myself be carried away to become so utterly imprudent. But I suppose that I knew my time was limited and she loved me so much that I wanted to respond all I could. Well, it is clearly over now. I called her once more (she was desolate and so was I). She said, "I had the most terrible feeling something was wrong when I was waiting for you to call". . . ."Will we ever see each other again?". . . ."What will I do without you?". . . ."How unfair it is, even inhuman." But we have both anticipated this. However, the results may be very bad if they reported some of our frankest conversations! God knows what the Abbot knows! I will soon find out, I imagine.

In any case, from what I have been through since Saturday, I certainly realize the real spiritual danger I have got into. Things have really got close to going wrong, and it is providential that everything has been blocked at the moment. Perhaps it is saving me from a real wreck. Jim Wygal on the phone Saturday was saying, "Be careful you don't destroy yourself!" He is perhaps more right than I thought at the time. Hope I can see him about it.

Decided the best thing was to own up and face Dom James (about the phone calls *only!*) before he summoned me in. So I did. He was kind and tried to be understanding to some extent. His only solution was of course "a complete break." Wanted to write M. himself but I refused—that would be disastrous, and he does not know who she is and I don't think he needs to know. He was hinting around about how lonely I have been in the hermitage, how I ought to come down and sleep in the infirmary, etc. But I refused. The only concrete solution we arrived at was that I should go back to ecumenical work in the retreat house—as a cure for loneliness!! I suppose some constructive contacts with others would be a good thing. Obviously, though, he thinks the hermitage has been too much for me and has made me too vulnerable. He did, however, welcome the idea of my talking to the ecumenical groups, Protestants, Buddhists, etc.

I am going to write maybe a new book now, in a new way, in a new language too. What have I to do with all that has died, all that belonged to a false life? What I remember most is me and M. hugging each other close for hours in long kisses and saying, "Thank God this at least is real!"

June 25, 1966

Dream—"another" girl. I am supposed to date her soon but now she is in the hospital. I am talking to her mother (a heavy mother—battle-axe type), not interested in any of them much. But then someone suggests we go and see this girl in the hospital, and I feel an inner awakening of interest and love and know that briefly seeing her will awaken in us both a deeper rapport. I then wake up thinking—but this is *another*, not M., and go back to thinking consciously of M. with a little guilt. Is it another? Imagery later—after difficulty in starting.

I see a tangle of dark briars and light roses. My attention singles out one beautiful pink rose, which becomes luminous, and I am much aware of the silky texture of the petals. My Mother's face appears behind the roses, which vanish!

Also in there somewhere a student nurse who came to see me briefly in hospital one day when I was preparing to go out for a walk. I was short and rude with her.

Today I go for X-rays. Exactly 3 months since the operation. Am not supposed to see M., but I think she may come and meet me at the doctor's office, in which case I will give her "Midsummer Diary" (practically a book, I wrote it for her this last week).

June 1966. Selections from A Midsummer Diary for M.

Or the account of how I once again became untouchable. It is impossible for me to be what I was before I met M. The old life is a habit that no longer exists—a habit of isolation, of worry, of intent preoccupation with I no longer remember precisely what. A kind of poetic religiosity and an intention to be interiorly honest. Above all, the insistence on being different from other people.

I no longer know what these things mean or what their opposites might mean. I am not passing from this to something that stands against it. I am not going anywhere. I exist because I have the habit of existing. Perhaps I will in due time put other habits on top of this one, but they had better be more fruitful than sitting around drinking Christian Brothers' brandy out of an old marmalade jar big enough to get ice cubes in and not as big as a whole glass.

All the love and all the death in me are at the moment wound up in Joan Baez's song "Silver Dagger." I can't get it out of my head, day or night. I am obsessed with it. My whole being is saturated with it.

(June 19, 1966. Saturday—Late)

I went to bed like a good little monk at eight o'clock but could not sleep. Arm hurting, back hurting, heart empty and desolate, I lay there thinking. And thinking some more. Obsessed with the idea that M. might conceivably find her way out here though she has never seen the place and could not possibly find it in the dark, etc. If only there were a soft knock on the door and I opened it and it was she standing on the porch. Finally, I couldn't stand it anymore, got up, put my clothes on, and started wandering around. For a moment I had a strong desire to start down to the monastery and sneak into the office again and make another phone call. But I don't even know where she is, in Louisville or where? Perhaps she has gone home for the weekend. I no longer have any idea what she is doing and have no way of finding out.

I went out on the porch. Nothing. Silence. Vast silence of the woods full of fireflies. The stars. Down in the south the huge sign of the Scorpion. The red eye of Regulus. Just stars. Not a light from any house or farm. Only fireflies and stars and silence. A car racing by the road, then more silence. Nothing. Nothing.

When a car goes by you can feel the alien frenzy of it. Someone madly going somewhere for no reason. I am a complete prisoner under these stars. With nothing. Or perhaps with everything.

I sit on the porch and deliberately refuse to rationalize anything, to explain anything or to comment on anything, only on what is there. I am there. Fireflies, stars, darkness, the massive shadows of the woods, the vague dark valley. And nothing, nothing, nothing.

Is she thinking of me? Loving me? Is her heart calling to mine in the dark? I don't know. I can't honestly say that I know. I can't honestly say I know anything except that it is late, that I can't sleep, that there are fireflies all over the place, and that there is not the remotest possibility of making any poetic statement on this. You don't write poems about nothing.

And yet somehow this nothing seems to be *everything*. I look at the south sky, and for some ungodly reason, for which there is no reason, everything is complete. I think of going back to bed in peace without knowing why, a peace that cannot be justified by anything, by any reason, any proof, any argument, by any supposition. There are no suppositions left. Only fireflies.

I kneel down by the bed and look up at the icon of the Nativity. The soft shaded light plays over the shelves of Buddhist books in the silent bedroom. I want to tell you something, but I don't know how to begin to say it. I am afraid that if I start talking and writing, I will confuse everything. Nothing needs to be said.

(June 20, 1966)

Finally got five hours of sleep or so. At the end I was dreaming that I was being hazed by Jesuits in a sort of initiation into a fraternity into which I had no desire to be initiated. I can't remember details of the dream, only that I seemed to be mixed up with a lot of people with whom I had nothing in common, that they resented me, and that they were trying to ridicule and discredit me. I was thinking, "How did I get mixed up in all this?"

Solitude as act: the reason no one really understands solitude, or bothers to try to understand it, is that it appears to be nothing but a condition, something one elects to undergo—like standing under a cold shower. Actually, solitude is a realization, an actualization, even a kind of creation, as well as a liberation of active forces within us, forces that are more than our own, yet more ours than what appears to be "ours." As a mere condition, solitude can be passive, inert, and basically unreal: a kind of permanent coma. One has to work at it to keep out of this condition. One has to work actively at solitude, not by putting fences around oneself, but by destroying all fences and throwing away all the disguises, getting down to the naked root of one's inmost desire, which is the desire of liberty-reality. To be free from the illusion that reality creates when one is out of right relation to it and to be real in the freedom which reality gives when one is rightly related to it.

Hence the need for discipline, for some kind of technique of integration that keeps body and soul together, harmonizes their powers, brings them into one deep resonance, orients the whole being toward the root of being. The need for a "way." Presence, invocation, *mantram*, concentration, emptiness: all these are aspects of a realized solitude. Mere *being alone* is nothing. Or, at least, it is only a potential. Sooner or later he who is merely alone either rots or escapes.

The "active life" can in fact be that which is most passive: one is simply driven, carried, batted around, moved. The most desperate illusion and the most common one is just to fling oneself into the mass that is in movement and be carried along with it: to be part of the stream of traffic going nowhere but with a great sense of phony purpose. It is against this that I revolt. Because I revolt, my life at first must take on an aspect of total meaninglessness: the revenge of the social superego. The perception of the absurd. Freedom begins with the full acceptance of the absurd: the willingness to *realize* and experience one's life as totally absurd in relation to the apparent meaning that has been thrown over life by society, by illusion. But the experience of this absurdity is again only a potential, only a starting point for a deeper realization: the realization of that root reality in myself and in all life, *which I do not know and cannot know*. This implies the capacity to see that *realizing* and *knowing* are not the same. In realization the reality one grasps, or by which one is grasped, is actualized in oneself and one becomes what one realizes, one is what one realizes. Knowing is just a matter of registering that something is objectively verifiable—whether one bothers to verify it or not. Realization is not verification but "isness." Solitude is necessary for this "isness," and solitude itself is the fullness of realization. In solitude I become *fully able to realize what I cannot know.*

What does the lonely and absurd man have to teach others? Simply that being alone and absurd are not things to be feared. But these are precisely the two things that everybody fears: they spend all their time reassuring themselves that they make sense, that they are not ridiculous, that they are acceptable, desirable, valuable and that they will never have to regard themselves as really alone. In other words, they plunge into the reassuring stream of illusions that is created by all the other people like themselves. A great common work, a liturgy in which everyone agrees publicly to say that in these terms everything is real and makes sense. The terms are not, however, satisfactory. Everybody remains secretly absurd and alone. Only no one dares face the fact. Yet facing this fact is the absolutely essential requirement for beginning to live freely.

My apostolate: to realize that my life is absurd and not to care, to teach others that they do not have to care. But this has not been clear, for in fact I have spent too much time and effort in convincing others and even myself that all this makes sense. My work is in fact invalid in so far as it seems to make sense and in so far as it seems to say that solitude is something to be desired. One of course has to make some kind of sense: I do not deny that I want to write coherently in accord with a basic realization. But merely to spell out a logical message or, worse still, a sales pitch for something spiritual, something religious, something "interior," or, worse still, "monastic"—what a total waste. More than half my life and work have been wasted in this kind of thing.

(June 22, 1966, Wednesday)

I dreamt in several different ways of trying to contact M. I cannot remember what the dreams were, only that the last one, before I woke up, was that I was sending a child to the hospital to tell her that I loved her. I realized this was most unsatisfactory but there was nothing else I could do. (I was aware that the child would just go in and say "He told me today he loves you" in an embarrassed sort of way and walk out again.)

I almost never dream of M. as she is but of someone who, I instinctively know, represents her. Yet this girl is "different" from M. How does one explain this? Still, just when I wake up, the archetypal M. and the reality merge together. The M. I love in the depths of my heart is not symbolic and not just the everyday M. either. She is the deep, mysterious, personal, unique potential that is in her: the M. that is trying to become free in my love and is clinging to me for love and help. Yet not that either because it is the insecure and unreal self in each of us that clings so hard to the other. Even that has to be qualified. It was basically right that she should want me to make love to her fully, and there is no question that I wanted to do this in my heart. Yet because for me somehow the situation was all wrong, psychologically and spiritually, it did not matter. Our love (at least as I see it) was and is so much the important thing that the details do not make any difference. But precisely at this point everything was cut short, bombed out, gutted. What should naturally have turned into a long, warm, slow-growing, sweet love, expressed in all its depths, has been amputated just when it was about to begin. I have no right to complain because I have committed myself to another kind of life. As for her, I at least told her over and over what was coming, but the result is cruel for us both. I am only just beginning to discover how cruel it really is.

I cannot regard this as "just an episode." It is a profound event in my life and one that will have entered deeply into my heart to alter and transform my whole climate of thought and experience. In her, I now realize, I had found something, someone, that I had been looking for all my life. I know too that she feels the same about me. No matter what happens I think we will both always feel that this was and is something too deep and too real to be essentially changed. What we have found in each other will not be lost: yet it will not be truly possessed either. Hence the awful loneliness, deprivation, desolation of being without each other, even though in our hearts we continue to love each other deeply. Yet we are going to have to face the fact that we now go separate ways, and that is what I think neither of us is quite willing to face. *Can we* really go separate ways? In a sense, no. We have to travel together in our hearts as long as we live. She says she can never love anyone else. That moves me deeply and breaks my heart, yet

I know that she must someday love another, because it would be inhuman to expect such a deprivation in anyone's life. As for me, I am supposed to be lonely and live alone and sleep alone, so I have no problem and no complaint. It is merely what I have chosen and the choice is ratified over and over each day. Even though I so vividly remember her body and long for her love.

Last evening when Joe and John G. were leaving, I said jokingly, "Why not take me into Louisville with you?" But I was not really joking. I would certainly have gone if they had taken it seriously. But the whole thing was so futile and so desperately silly. I know now that, though I am drawn to this, it isn't what I should do. I am no longer the unknown kid that can do things like that. I do have a responsibility. Vocation is more than just a matter of being in a certain place and wearing a certain kind of costume. There are too many people in the world who rely on the fact that I am serious about deepening an inner dimension of experience that they desire and is closed to them. It is not closed to me: this is a gift that has been given me not for myself but for everyone, even including M. I cannot let it be squandered and dissipated foolishly. It would be criminal to do so. In the end I would ruin her along with myself.

It is a cool brilliant morning. The birds sing. The valley is full of sunlit mist. The tall fiery daylilies are opening to the June sun. I know I am where I belong. The books and papers are on the table and work is waiting. I know the poets I must read (yesterday for the first time really got into Louis Zukofsky, who is certainly one of the great classic poets of our time. Great mastery and richness and structure).

I know I have to read and understand and think and grasp and experience. This is easy and delightful to me. I have a rich life, but built on the central cost of cruel deprivation. That cruelty burns into my heart at times like a brand. But I know that I am not in a position to choose another kind of richness: that of love and living with M. I can have her love in a deep and lasting, very fruitful form as long as it is part of my solitude. If I try to take it on other terms, the wall will crumble. She has desperately refused to believe this and has, in her own silent and womanly way, challenged me on it and tried to force the issue. The issue cannot be forced.

What do I fear most? Forgetting, ignorance of the inmost truth of my being, to forget who I am, to be lost in what I am not, to fail my own inner truth, to get carried away in what is not true to me, what is outside me, what imposes itself on me from the outside. But what is this? It can take manifold forms. I must fear and distrust them all. Yet I cannot help being to some extent influenced by what is outside me, and hence I must accept that influence to some extent. But always in such a way that it increases my awareness, my remembrance, my understanding, instead of diminishing these.

Fear of ignorance in the sense of *avidya*: the ignorance that is based on the acceptance of an illusion about myself. The ignorance that comes from the decision to regard my ego as my full, complete, real self and to *work to maintain* this illusion *against* the call of secret truth that rises up within me, that is evoked within me by others, by love, by vocation, by providence, by suffering, by God. The ignorance that hardens the shell, that makes the inner core of selfhood determined to resist the call of truth that would dissolve it. The ignorance that hardens in desire and willfulness or in conformity or in hate or in various refusals of other people, various determinations to be "right at any price" (the Vietnam war is a clear example of the American people's insistence on refusing to see human truth). Fear of ignorance that comes from clinging to a stupid ideal. Fear of ignorance that comes from submersion in the body, in surrender to the need for comfort and consolation. Yet, at the same time, one must not fear the possibility of relative lucidity in all these things, provided they are understood. There is a *little* lucidity in love, a *little* lucidity in alcohol, a *little* lucidity in religion, but there is also the danger of being engulfed more or less easily in all this. The great fear is the fear of surrendering to sham lucidity and to the "one source" theory of lucidity—clinging to one kind of affirmation and excluding everything else—and sinking back into ignorance and superstition.

One of the worst sources of delusion is, of course, an exclusive attachment to supposed "logic" and to reason. Worse still when the logic and reason are centered on what claims to be a religious truth. This can be as deep a source of blindness as any in the world, sex included. One always has to distinguish and go beyond: one has to question reason in order to get to the deeper awareness of reality that is built into life itself. What I fear is living in such a way that life becomes opaque and one-sided, centered on one thing only, the illusion of the self. Everything else has to be defined in relation to this kind of ignorance. Once this is understood you can understand what makes me run—not only run in the sense of escape but run in the sense of tick. What runs and what ticks is, however, no longer important. What is important is that life itself should be lucid in "me" (whoever I am). I am nothing but the lucidity that is "in me." To be opaque and dense with opinion, with passion, with need, with hate, with power, is to be not there, to be absent, to non-exist. The labor of convincing myself that this non-existing is a real presence: this is the source of all falsity and suffering. This is hell on earth and hell in hell. This is the hell I have to keep out of. The price of keeping out of it is that, the moment I give in to any of it, I feel the anguish of falsity. But to extinguish the feeling of anguish, in any way whatever short of straight lucidity, is to favor ignorance and non-existence. This is my central fear and it defines my task in life.

(June 23, 1966)

What will I be without her? What will she be without me?

First of all, we cannot really be without each other any more. There is something completely permanent and irrevocable in our lives: the love that we have known in each other, that has changed us, that will remain with us in a hidden and transfigured—transfiguring—presence. "Derby Day is always beautiful." The beautiful "day" of our love, love's creation in our lives, will remain as the day in which we most deeply live and walk together. I will never be without the mysterious, transcendent presence of her essential self, which began to speak to me so stirringly and so beautifully those early mornings in May between sleeping and waking. She will always be to me her soft voice speaking out of the depths of my own heart, saying that the central reality of all is found in our love that no one can touch and no one can alter.

I have needed this love, and being without it is something I cannot yet grasp—that is, being without the chance to see her at all. Frankly,

if things were not what they were, I can see that it would be terribly
right and important for me to change everything and live the rest of
my life with her. From a certain point of view, that is what *should have
been*. But that was impossible. Hence all the ambiguities that follow.
To be without her is to be deprived of a central meaning in my life. It
is to remain incomplete and to some extent maimed. But also I
probably could not have coped fully with the problems that would
have arisen from our social situation. Anyway, what is, is.

(June 24, 1966—Friday)

The night did not turn out to be as hot as I feared. I slept more or less
(began waking up around one). Dreamt a series of dreams that were
more or less about the community. For instance: I am at the hermitage
and down in the valley are some people (monks) who are trying to
signal to me by semaphore, wig-wagging and whatnot. I do not know
how to read the message. I make helpless gestures about not knowing
"the rules." I really don't care that much. I just want to show I would
like to be in communication with them if it were possible. Later I
dream of the Abbot and Father Flavian (my confessor), we are walking
around more or less friendly and open to each other, talking pleasantly
about the hermit life and its possibilities.

In the last analysis what I am looking for in solitude is not happiness
or fulfillment but salvation. Not "my own" salvation, but the salvation
of everybody. Here is where the game gets serious. I have used the
word *revolt* in connection with solitude. Revolt against what? Against a
notion of salvation that gets people lost. A notion of a salvation that
is entirely legal and extrinsic and can be achieved no matter how false,
no matter how shriveled and fruitless one's inner life really is. This is
the worst ambiguity: the impression that one can be grossly unfaithful
to life, to experience, to love, to other people, to one's own deepest
self, and yet be "saved" by an act of stubborn conformity, by the will
to be correct. In the end this seems to me to be fatally like the very act
by which one is lost: the determination to be "right" at all costs, by
dint of hardening one's core around an arbitrary choice of a fixed

position. To close in on one's central wrongness with the refusal to admit that it might be wrong. That is one of the reasons why solitude is a dangerous thing: one may use it for that purpose. I don't think I can. I am not that stubborn. I am here for one thing: to be open, to be not "closed in" on any one choice to the exclusion of all others: to be open to God's will and freedom, to His love, which comes to save me from all in myself that resists Him and says no to Him. This I must do not to justify myself, not to be right, not to be good, but because the whole world of lost people needs this opening by which salvation can get into it through me.

(Friday evening)

It is usually a joy to finish a book. I am not able to finish this one and am not going to. Anyway, who says this is the end of it? I don't. If I make a point of "finishing" this—which does not need to be finished—it will look too much like good-bye. I don't want it even to look like that. I do not even want to think of that. Let us just say that our friendship and our love have gone into a new phase.

I find myself back at the beginning. It is exactly three months since the operation. (Tomorrow is the 25th, and the operation was on the 25th of March.) I will never forget the morning of March 31st. I will never forget the Wednesday in Holy Week, that rainy night when you came in before going to Chicago, and we were too tongue-tied to say what we almost knew. And the night after that when I lay awake and realized that I loved you. And that Good Friday when I decided to leave a note for you to write me. (How glad I am that I did that.) And your first letter, with its "opening." And my letter, impulsive and "intense," which began everything. How glad I am that all these things took place. How glad I am that they led to such wonderful days together. Such beautiful letters from you. All the phone calls that finally got me in trouble, as I expected. What about the future? Who knows? But I cling to one hope: that future morning in heaven which the morning of March 31st "prefigured." That is the beautiful day I live for. The rest is nothing but time to pass until the real morning comes. I am not patient. I don't expect you will be either.

June 30, 1966

Gehorsamsopfer—To offer oneself to God as a sacrifice of obedience in
faith. This is the crucial point. Too much emphasis on one's *own* truth,
on one's own authentic freedom. One forgets the limitations and
restrictions of this "my own." Tendency to take "my own" truth and
freedom as unlimited, ultimate, "in my own case." This is a total loss.
Paradox that only God's truth is ultimately my truth (there is not one
truth for me, another for my neighbor, another for God) and only God's
will is my freedom. When they appear to be opposed, am I acting freely?

"Blessed are the pure in heart who leave everything to God now as they
did before they ever existed" (Eckhart). This is what I have to get back
to. It is coming to the surface again. As Eckhart was my life raft in the
hospital, so now also he seems the best link to restore continuity: my
obedience to God begetting His love in me (which has never stopped!).

September 5, 1966. Labor Day

Can I hope that I am now in a new area, traveling more securely, and that
my commitment to the hermit life will be something more than a comic
gesture? Is the whole thing just a fantastic private comedy? I question
myself and my whole life very seriously. The real absurdity of it all! The
unreality of so much of it. I mean especially the unreality of years I look
back on when, being Master of Students, for example, my job gave an
appearance of substance and consistency, but actually I was floating in a
kind of void! I think I enjoyed it to a great extent, but if I had been more
fully aware, I would probably have not been able to cope with it.

In a word what I see is this: that while I imagine I was functioning fairly
successfully, I was living a sort of patched-up, crazy existence, a series of
rather hopeless improvisations, a life of unreality in many ways. Always
underlain by a certain solid silence and presence, a faith, a clinging to the
Invisible God. This clinging (perhaps rather His holding on to me) has
been in the end the only thing that has made sense. The rest has been
absurdity. What is more, there is no essential change in sight. I will
probably go on like this for the rest of my life. Here "I" am—this

patchwork, this bundle of questions and doubts and obsessions, this gravitation to silence and to the woods and to love. This incoherence!!

There is no longer anything to pride myself in, least of all "being a monk" or being anything—a writer or anything.

September 10, 1966

Thursday, the 8th, I made my commitment—read the short formula I had written (simplest possible form). Dom James signed it with me, content that he now had me in the bank as an asset that would not go out and lose itself in some crap game (is he sure? The awful crap game of love!). A commitment "to live in solitude for the rest of my life in so far as health may permit." After that I was at peace and said Mass with great joy.

For M. I have a happy, friendly, and loving affection, deep and nonobsessed (I hope), and it will last. I love her but no longer crave her. At least that is how I feel at the moment. But to what extent do I know myself? I know enough to know I may be kidding.

Bob Dylan's song "I Want You" rang through my head all day yesterday in Louisville. Another bright day. Went to Dr. Mitchell for X-rays. Operation is perfect. Other bad disc above it not that bad yet. Avoid making it worse. Bursitis better.

Finally on the way home called M. from a phone booth near Bardstown station. (She was by that time home from work.) It was a happy call. She is much more buoyant since her letter got through and her hard work in the hospital is a help. "I am very tired."—"I think of you constantly!" "Especially when I wake up." She was a little worried about the commitment but I told her everything went well. "I was thinking about that all day—" (the 8th, seriously). She was a little piqued that I liked Dylan's song "Just Like a Woman." "Well, it's *pretty*." (Sort of distant tone.)

I forgot to ask the exact date of her birthday. (She was born just about two months before I came through Cincinnati on my way to Gethsemani! I had walked through Cincinnati station with the words of Proverbs 8 in my mind: "And my delights were to be with the children of men!"—I have never forgotten this, it struck me forcibly then! Strange connection in my deepest heart—between M. and the "Wisdom" figure—and Mary—and the Feminine in the Bible—Eve, etc.—Paradise—wisdom. Most mysterious, haunting, deep, lovely, moving, transforming!)

At the beginning of the call she changed to the other phone (bedroom, I guess), where she could talk more openly. We talked of our love being deep and the same—of our "radar." I said, "Yes, but there is no consolation," and she said, "*This* is consolation." It was a happy, cheerful, friendly, affectionate call without hooks, without anguish, and without smoke. She said I ought to write a poem about freight trains going by (she was delighted at the strange place I was calling from— always wants to know exactly where I am). I said I could guarantee nothing, but I wrote a poem this morning.

September 21, 1966

A dream. I know that M. is swimming alone in one of our lakes. I am near there but I have refrained from joining her for fear of the consequences. But now I approach the lake and see her wading in the water over there by the shore (it is no recognizable lake here—what is it like?). She looks so disconsolate and alone, as if she had wasted her afternoon there to no purpose, since I have not come. I go down toward the lake dressed in my habit and wave to her that I am coming. She still looks disconsolate, unbelieving. I wish to join her, I think, even if I have to swim naked. There appears to be no one around. But as I go to her along the bank I find one of the monks sitting there in my way. I cannot get to her. At this I wake up in great distress.

October 13, 1966

On the evening of the 6th—Jacques Maritain, John Howard Griffin, Penn Jones, and Babeth Manual arrived. A wonderful visit. On the morning of the 7th they came to the hermitage (bright, cool). I read some poems for them. In the afternoon we went out to the woods. Late Mass for them all in the temporary exterior chapel, which I liked. It was a beautiful Mass, which, as a matter of fact to please Jacques, I said all in Latin and all in the old way. He was delighted. Began then reading his book—the new one—which he gave me in page proofs, *Le Paysan de la Garonne*. It is perhaps a bit self-conscious: he is very aware of himself as

"*Le vieux Jacques*" and half apologetic but says, I think, some very telling things about the novelty hunters and the *superficial* advocates of change in a naively progressive way ("anything is good as long as it's something new"). The morning in the hermitage was good because they liked the bits of *Edifying Cables* I read to them. That was encouraging. Jack Ford and Dan Walsh were also there. They came in the afternoon.

October 14, 1966

A dark October morning with clouds. Extraordinary purple in the north over the pines. Ruins of gnats on the table under the lamp. Camus's preface to *L'Etranger*, his letter to an American editor, has things to say on truth and silence that have deep monastic implications. I must refuse all declarations and affirmations of what I do not fully and actually know, experience, believe *myself*. Not making statements that are expected of me, simply because they are expected, whether by the monastery (or monastic life) or by the peace movement or by various literary orthodoxies and antiorthodoxies or routine rebellions. If I renounce all that, there will be precious little left to say. But above all (as Maritain and I agreed) to steer clear of the futilities of "Post-Conciliar" theological wrangling and image making.

November 1, 1966

The wilderness theme in the Bible. Am reading a good book on it by Ulrich Mauser (in that Protestant series). Terribly fruitful at the moment! I can compare it with my own life. How evident it becomes now that this whole thing with M. was, in fact, an attempt to escape the demands of my vocation. Not consciously, certainly, but a substitution of human love (and erotic love after all) for a special covenant with loneliness and solitude, which is the very heart of my vocation. I did not stand the test at all but allowed the whole essence to be questioned and tried to change it. I could not see I was doing this. Fortunately God's grace protected me from the worst errors. My difficult return to my right way is a gift of His grace. I think I am gradually getting back. Each morning I wake up feeling a little freer (though I don't remember dreaming of it), just as last May each morning I awoke a little more captivated. I now see how much anguish I suffered, but I could not let go!

Now, thank God, I can. What will happen if she writes me another love letter? Somehow I don't think she will. I think it is clear to both of us that the affair is over and that it has been very silly.

November 13, 1966

Gelassenheit—letting go—not being encumbered by systems, words, projects. And yet being free *in* systems, projects. Not trying to get away from all action, all speech, but free, unencumbering *"Gelassen"* in this or that action. Error of self-conscious contemplatives: to get hung up in a certain kind of non-action which is an imprisonment, a stupor, the opposite of *Gelassenheit*. Actually quietism is incompatible with true inner freedom. The burden of this stupid and enforced "quiet"—the self sitting heavily on its own head.

December 10, 1966

Two days ago, Feast of the Immaculate Conception, Joan Baez was here—memorable day! Ping Ferry had called the Abbot and arranged it (Ira Sandperl had written before and had been refused. I had sent Joan a book and a note last July). Wire said they would come sometime in the morning. I waited around, and they drove up around 12:30. Were here all afternoon.

Out on the tobacco farm—gray skies, cold wind, Joan running down the wide field alone in black sailor pants with her long hair flying. Ira and I talking about everything and drinking beer. They want me to leave and come with them. "Someone has to talk to the students and you are the one," etc. I can't fully explain why I don't. I mean I can't explain to them. This solitude is God's will for me—it is not just that I "obey" the authorities and the laws of the Church. There is more to it than that. Here is where my roots are.

We came up to the hermitage and spent the rest of the time here. Played one side of her new record, "Noel." Lit a fire. Sat on the floor, talked. Gray rugs spread out. Sitting around, lying around. Father Chrysogonus was here, entranced. Then he left and went down. Joan sat on the rug eating goat-milk cheese and bread and honey and drinking tea in front of the fire. Lovely!

She is an indescribably sweet girl. I love her. I know she loves me too.

She said she had discovered prayer in reading my books. She and Ira seem to have read and liked most of my recent work, great openness, warmth, support.

She is a very pure and honest girl, stays away from dope, everything, is rightly regarded as a sort of saint in the peace movement. Her purity of heart is impressive. A precious, authentic, totally human person. The thing I sense most, for some reason, is a kind of mixture of frailty and indestructibility in her. Here is this sweet living child and she is on earth for now, for the time being, with a kind of visible evanescence in her reality, solidity, truth. A manifestation given us for a while. Yet right close, available, open, "given" in the realist sense. "Here I am." A sort of epiphany of what we most need.

She was talking about their nonviolent institute—the people who come to it, what they think and do—(they can't be convinced she isn't using pot, etc.). The meditation—the periods of silence worry the neighbors. She is a person who needs much silence, a kind of bride of silence, a listening person, who when she speaks comes out of silence with a lot of love and care for everything. Love for all kinds of creatures. In close union with the Mother, is the Mother.

We talked of my love for M. and I read some of the poems. Joan was ready to drive ninety miles an hour through the rain to Cincinnati so I could see M. when she got off at the hospital (11:30 P.M.). So we went to Bardstown and called M. But then they could not get their reservations changed to a convenient time. Just as well I did not go!! Would have been totally exhausted. Tired enough after driving with them to the airport and then coming home with Jack Ford after watching a bit of the *Glass Menagerie* at his house. Guilt next day for this wild impulsiveness, this night ride.

February 6, 1967

I did a "graph" of my work—the biggest ups and downs were in the beginning. The lowest plunge was to "awful" in 1950 with *What Are These Wounds?* In the fifties the writing was consistently indifferent but got better in the end and most of my best work has been since 1957.

I would say I would be much better off if I had published only these:

Thirty Poems, The Seven Storey Mountain, Seeds of Contemplation, The Tears of the Blind Lions, The Sign of Jonas, The Silent Life, The New Man, Thoughts in Solitude, The Wisdom of the Desert, (Disputed Questions?), New Seeds of Contemplation, Seeds of Destruction, Chuang Tzu, Emblems of a Season of Fury, Raids on the Unspeakable, Conjectures of a Guilty Bystander.

That's 15 or 16—plenty. Yet the others, too—some of them—had something in them that had to be gotten out of my system, I guess.

February 22, 1967

It is the twenty-fifth anniversary of my taking the novice habit. I have been wondering about going back over the years and writing up some of the things I remember. Certainly a great deal has changed. In many ways we have swung around 180 degrees from the attitude that prevailed when I entered. Good or bad? Both. Neither. The old ways had to be changed but I do not know if the new makes sense. I find that I certainly do not believe in the monastic life as I did when I entered here when I was more sure I knew what it was. Yet I am much more convinced I am doing more or less what I ought to do, though I don't know why and cannot fully justify it.

March 5, 1967. Laetare Sunday

The crocuses multiply and are still there after nearly a month, with some very cold weather. Bees in them yesterday. I walked in the woods. Woods ringing with distant voices. Father Matthew is putting up a tent on top of one of the knobs where he will build a small hermitage (not to live in but for the Days of Recollection). Another communal hermitage is to be built in the flat shady spot where M. and I and the Fords had our picnic last May. I have loved to walk there all summer—reading Eugenio Montale, reading René Char, or just praying and thinking. Now that too will be over. I'll find other places. My place on the edge of St. Malachy's field is gone—people will be there for the statues (monument to Jon Daniels). Brother Giles is working there now, putting in dogwoods and so on. Anyway, I know that all this foolishness of mine must finally end. Though our phone calls were warm and affectionate, and though M. almost came down Monday (but the hospital called and she had to work), I know that our love affair is really all over and there is no point trying to keep it alive. Certainly I miss her, but one has to face facts. I am humbled and confused by my weakness, my vulnerability, my passion. After all these years, so little sense and so little discipline. Yet I know there was good in it somewhere, nevertheless.

March 31, 1967. Friday—Easter Week

Today is the anniversary of the day I first saw M. in the hospital. March 31 last year was Wednesday in Passion Week. That day she was assigned, as student nurse, to take special care of me, change the dressings on my hip, etc. She came in and made a little speech about how I was "her patient" and I little realized how true that would turn out to be. I remember those days when we talked and laughed and got on so well that in a week we were in love. I can't find it in me to regret that part of it. Certainly I made mistakes and we could have made plenty of worse mistakes. But the fact remains that we love and understand each other and still in some sense need each other, though obviously it is all over.

April 8, 1967

Last night I dreamed of M. Today, again, I realize how confused I have been, not just because of her but in general because of my slackness, my imprudence, my inconsistency, my frivolity. I suppose also my laziness. It is certainly true that a great deal has gone wrong in my life. Yet I do not know precisely how or where. I can hardly pin it on any one symptom. My falling in love so badly was not a cause but an effect. I think really it all comes from roots that had simply lain dormant since I entered the monastery. So too in my writing, my persistent desire to be somebody, which is really so stupid. I know I don't really need it or want it, yet I keep going after it. Not that I should stop writing or publishing, but I should not let myself be flattered and cajoled into the business, letting myself be used, making statements and declarations, "being there," "appearing." Pictures appear (without any desire of mine, to tell the truth) and I am ashamed of myself.

At the root—an attraction nevertheless for this kind of publicity. Or rather, I would like to be known, loved, admired, yet *not* in this cheap and silly way. But is there any other way? In my case, if I were more serious about remaining unknown, I would not be so quick to accept what eventually shames me.

April 15, 1967

A lovely day. Everything is two or three weeks ahead this year. The trees are almost in leaf. The redbuds are gone, the dogwoods are going. Bright sun. Bright, pure, little clouds. Deep blue sky. I was going to do some work on the "Rite for Ejection of Lepers" but took off to the woods instead—same place—by the hidden pond. All the old desires, the deep ones, the ones that are truly mine, come back now. Desire of silence, peace, depth, light. I see I have been foolish to let myself be so influenced by the current trends, though they perhaps have their point. On the other hand, I know where my roots really are—in the mystical tradition, not in the active and anxious "secular city" business.

May 13, 1967. *Vigil of Pentecost*

A rather foul, murky, damp day. I am making a sort of 1/2 day retreat in preparation for tomorrow. Another booklet on the Marian apparition at Garabandal came in. A lot of it is perhaps somewhat questionable in detail, but the overall impression is moving, and once again I was stirred by it. Quite apart from the authenticity of the apparitions (and they seem for the most part genuine), I experience in myself a deep need of conversion and penance—a deep repentance, a real sense of having erred, gone wrong, got lost, needing to get back on the right path. Needing to pray for forgiveness. Sense of revolt at my own foolishness and triviality. Shame and amazement at the way I have trifled with life and grace—how could I be so utterly stupid! A real sense of being flawed and of needing immense help, pardon—to recover some capacity to love God. Sense of the nearness and mercy of Mary.

May 14, 1967. *Pentecost*

Lightning, thunder, and rain on and off all night, and now at dawn there is still more of it. The lovely gray-green valley, misty clouds sweeping low over the hills and forest out there in the south, iron dark clouds heavy above them. The rainy gloom full of pale yellow irises and the cloudy white blossoming green masses of the rose hedge. I went out a while ago and a hawk flew fast away—it had been waiting on the cross or in the big poplar tree.

The return to unity, to the ground, the paradisiacal inner sacred space where the archetypal man dwells in peace and in God. The journey to that space, through a realm of aridity, dualism, dryness, death. The need of courage and of desire. Above all faith, praise, obedience to the inner voice of the Spirit, refusal to give up or compromise.

What is "wrong" in my life is not so much a matter of "sin" (though it is sin too), but of *unawareness*, lostness, slackness, relaxation, dissipation of desire, lack of courage and of decision, so that I let myself be carried along and dictated to by an alien movement. The current of "the world," which I know is not mine. I am always getting diverted into a way that is not *my* way and is not going where I am called to go. Only if I go where I must go can I be of any use to "the world." I can serve the world best by keeping my distance and my freedom.

May 30, 1967

Last night—curious dreams.

One—I am in a place where there are Buddhist nuns, separated from me by a curious paper-thin sort of iconostasis or printed partition, behind which I hear their soft erotic laughter as they are aware of me there. Sense of being drawn to them.

The other dream. The monastery building (Gethsemani) is on fire. The fire burns slowly on the inside of the building, but threatens to become violent. Meanwhile there are still people in the building. I think "Why don't they get *out*?" I myself am there, moving through small patches of fire, but get to safety. The building is not destroyed but all that is inside is consumed, more or less.

July 14, 1967

The Abbot: his elaborate little game of pretending he wants to retire. Actually he can't and won't let go of his power. Goes around telling everyone it is his "duty" to stay and help watch over the changes. Precisely what we need, if we are to have any real renewal, is for him to retire. So he will stay in office in order to prevent *real* change, and that will be his excuse for not embracing a solitary life he really doesn't want. Blame it on God!

I can see how Dom James is cheating: but so what? What good does that do me? What good can I do *him?* The more important thing is that I too am cheating and perhaps more than the others. Perhaps monstrously. For instance—the collection at Bellarmine, the collection of Sister Thérèse Lentfoehr, all the business of filing and cataloguing every little slip of paper I ever wrote on! What a comedy! But I like it and cooperate wholeheartedly because I imagine it is for real. That I will last. That I will be a person studied and commented on. This is a problem, man.

August 2, 1967

Evening. I sit up late again listening to crickets and frogs because I can't go to bed yet. I had to translate in Chapter again tonight—which is not my business at all. I realize I may be stuck with this for the rest of the Visitation. Came back feeling stupid, as if I had done wrong. And in fact these sessions in Chapter are, in their own way, stupid. Dom Ignace Gillet was very nice and simple and gave a talk on his impressions of Japan. I did a good job of translating and made everyone happy. It was childish. I am ashamed of myself. I did the best I could and it was silly. So I pretend I belong here (as if I belonged somewhere). The woods, Okay. But I came back feeling sad. I realize it is this way almost everywhere and with everyone except very few people. Going to Chapter is just as reprehensible as going to Thompson Willett's and playing with little Alice in the pool. Got back, read a happy underground paper from Cleveland, and felt the same about *that.* It is silly. It is stupid shit. Then I read a little poetry magazine. The same. Do I now have to think there is something the matter? This does not follow. I will no doubt have to go to Chapter for a few days and do my silly bit. But I don't have to read happy newspapers and poetry magazines that still take themselves seriously. Or anything else of the kind. The *Surangana Sutra*—maybe. That's different, but there's a lot of classic shit in that, too. Fortunately I had some bourbon in the hermitage.

October 2, 1967. Feast of Guardian Angels

I love this feast. Hope my angel is not mad at me. Are you?

The Indian emphasis on encounter with one's "vision person" and obeying him thereafter. Beautiful and very real.

This morning I read Ruth Benedict's essay on the Pueblo Indians as an Apollonian culture surrounded by Dionysians. Extremely comical for the insight it gives into Ruth Benedict surrounded by imagined rapists. The trouble she gets into, her efforts to justify breakthroughs of the Dionysian even in her favored area, above all, the business of ritual shit-eating and piss-drinking. I am afraid she doesn't win. Oh, all the poor dear lady anthropologists—and Margaret Mead is another.

More seriously: Gaston Bachelard's intuitions in *The Poetics of Space* are most fruitful psychologically. In his study on houses, rooms, etc., *"demeures,"* he suddenly opened up a whole set of obvious questions for me.

The hermitage—Okay. But the *Merton Room*—to which I have a silver key and where I never go but where the public goes—where strangers are and will be. A bloody cuckoo's nest. This becomes a *typical* image of my own stupid lifelong homelessness, rootlessness.

The ambiguities at work here: the pretended "roots" at Gethsemani, where I am alien and where most everyone else is alien too. Yet paradoxically to many people I am completely identified with this strange place I can't firmly believe in. Where all these people with vows of stability are so obviously on the point of taking flight (and don't know it) or else simply staying by force of repression. Even the ones who are at home here remain alien though they don't realize it. Dom James. Brother Clement. Father Anastasius. Certainly their deep personal investment in the place is so complete that they are inseparable from it. And all the dead whom no one remembers.

I am here to a great extent because of the guilt and force exercised by Dom James. He knows it and I know it. Yet there is nowhere else I want to go. Also I have a kind of legal, factual separation from the common roof and board, here in the woods. The hermitage is a more personal reality of some sort—however ambiguous.

But the *Merton Room*.

A place where I store away endless papers, in which a paper-self builds its nest to be visited by strangers in a strange land of unreal intimacy.

The *Merton Room* is a kind of escape from Gethsemani, a protest against their messing up, destroying, losing, frittering away, dispersing, rotting, canning, feeding to mice everything I have put my heart into.

The anxiety I have felt lately is due probably to the surfacing awareness that all this is futile—a nonsurvival, more alien to me even than Gethsemani to some extent. A last despairing childish effort at love for some unknown people in some unknown future. But this is Rilkean. Hell, it is Peter Pan. It is no good. All right if they do like what I have written or don't, if they understand or don't, this is only a kind of noncommunication in the end. It is not what I am so desperate for (and what I am supposed to have forgotten).

Merton Room again—ambiguity of an open door that is closed. Of a cell where I don't really live. Where my papers live. Where my papers are more than I am. I myself am open and closed. When I reveal most I hide most. There is still something I have not said: but what it is I don't know, and maybe I have to say it by not saying. Word play won't do it. Or *will* do it—*Geography of Lograire*. Writing this is most fun for me now, because in it I have finally got away from self-consciousness and introversion. It may be my final liberation from all diaries. Maybe that is my one remaining task.

PART VII

THE END OF
THE JOURNEY
1967–1968

In one sense we are always traveling,
Traveling as if we did not know where we were going.
In another sense we have already arrived.
We cannot arrive at the perfect possession of God in this life:
That is why we are traveling and in darkness.
But we already possess God by grace.
Therefore, in that sense, we have arrived and
Are dwelling in the light.
But oh! How far have I to go to find You
In Whom I have already arrived!

The Seven Storey Mountain

In the end it comes down to the old story that we are sinners, but that
this is our hope because sinners are the ones who attract to themselves
the infinite compassion of God. To be a sinner, to want to be pure, to
remain in patient expectation of the divine mercy and above all to
forgive and love others, as best we can. This is what makes us
Christians. The great tragedy is that we feel so keenly that love has
been twisted out of shape in us and beaten down and crippled. But
Christ loves in us, and the compassion of Our Lady keeps her prayer
burning like a lamp in the depths of our being. That lamp does not
waver. It is the light of the Holy Spirit, invisible, kept alight by her
love for us.

Letter to Czeslaw Milosz,
The Courage for Truth

November 14, 1967

Today I went in to Louisville with Naomi Burton and at Tommie O'Callaghan's we signed the Trust Agreement. I am glad that is done. It had to be done and now it is a weight off my mind. Whether or not everything is perfectly taken care of, at least I have done what was necessary. I think the agreement is about as practical as anything could be. John Ford was very efficient and cooperative about it. Having put all my writings in the hands of this Trust, I am much less concerned about getting anything "done"—still less about getting it published, obviously! I feel much freer and readier to forget all that and make more out of solitude.

November 25, 1967

All day it has been deceptively like spring. Not only because of light and cool-warm air (warm with a slightly biting Marchlike wind), but because I fasted and it felt like Lent. Then in the evening (I had my meal about 4 instead of supper at 5) it was suddenly much lighter, as though it were March.

At noon, when I was not eating, I was out by St. Bernard's lake (which is surprisingly low), and the sky, hills, trees kept taking on an air of clarity and freshness that took me back to springs twenty years ago when Lents were hard and I was new in the monastery.

Strange feeling! Recapturing the freshness of those days when my whole monastic life was still ahead of me, when all was still open. Now it is all behind me and the years have closed in upon their silly, unsatisfactory history, one by one. But the air is like spring and fresh as ever, and I was amazed at it. Had to stop to gaze and wonder: loblolly pines we planted ten or fifteen years ago are twenty feet high. The fire tower shines in the sun like new—though it was put up ten years ago (with what hopes, on my part!). Flashing water on the lake. A blue jay flying down as bright as metal. I went over to the wood where the Jonathan Daniels sculptures are now and read some selections from Origen. Again stood amazed at the quiet, the bright sun, the springlike light. The sharp outline of the pasture, the knolls, the brightness of bare trees in the hopeful sun. Yet it is *not* spring. We are on the threshold of a hard winter.

November 28, 1967

I went out this afternoon, read some stuff on meditation in one of Winston King's books—on Burmese Buddhism. Good. Then came back and began a new Penguin containing Basho's travel notes. Completely shattered by them. One of the most beautiful books I have ever read in my life. It gives me a whole new (old) view of my own life. The whole thing is pitched right on my tone. Deeply moving in every kind of way. Seldom have I found a book to which I responded so totally.

December 7, 1967

The last four or five days have been quite fantastic: among the most unusual in my life. I hardly know how to write about them. There should be a whole new key—a kind of joy unusual in this journal—where I am usually diffident and sad.

I have to change the superficial ideas and judgments I have made about the contemplative religious life, the contemplative orders. They were silly and arbitrary and without faith.

The retreat, or meeting, or whatever you want to call it, with the fifteen contemplative nuns who were here from Sunday evening (December 3rd) on has been wonderful. Much more than I expected.

First of all—their obvious *quality*. All of them—or almost all—real contemplatives, and they were really human (all of them certainly that)—completely simple, honest, authentic people. I have never before had such a sense of community with any group, including when Sister Mary Luke Tobin and Sister Jane Marie Richardson came over from Loretto, and two of our own monks, Brother Maurice and Brother Wilfrid, were up here this morning for Mass. Mass at the hermitage today was unutterably good, something I simply can't articulate. People who *should* have been undisposed finding themselves completely united, for instance, as we ended up singing "We Shall Overcome" with a sense that our own revolution was well under way! Sounds silly enough, but it was very real.

Sitting together in silence after Communion with the rising sun shining into the cottage was indescribably beautiful. Everyone so obviously happy! I was tired only on the first day. After that it was all easy. I'd like to write about them all but perhaps shouldn't try. I do feel very close to all of them—with each in some special way. A sense of awe and privilege at being able to come together with such people.

At Mass today I opened with a prayer of Lancelot Andrewes instead of the *Confiteor*. Sister Elizabeth read the Epistle. We had a dialogue homily (first time for me!). Everyone joined in with petitions in the prayer of the people, *mementoes*, etc. Afterward, another prayer of Lancelot Andrewes and a prayer from the Old Syrian Liturgy for hermits. Then we sat and had coffee and had a wonderful time. The hermitage is blessed with the memory of it.

These four days have been very moving and I feel completely renewed by them: the best retreat I ever made in my life.

December 23, 1967

It is going to be a cold night. Bright stars, cold woods, silence. A card from M. today. Thought of her suddenly the other day, almost saw her it was so vivid. That was the day the card was mailed. Certainly I feel less real, somehow, without our constant communication, our sense of being in communion (so intense last year). The drab, futile silences of this artificial life with all its tensions and its pretenses, but I know it would be worse somewhere else. Marriage, for me, would be terrible! Anyway, that's all over. In a month I'll be 53, and no one in his right mind would get married for the first time at such an age.

Yet this afternoon I wondered if I'd really missed the point of life after all. A dreadful thought!

December 26, 1967

Christmas night was good. Dom James's last sermon—simple and quite moving. The Mass was uncomplicated and everyone seemed much more awake and alive than last year, apparently because they had had a Vigil in English they enjoyed. Then there was the new church. When I got back I had several hours of curious, light, dream-filled sleep. I could not remember any dreams.

Fathers Flavian and Hilarion came up after dinner for a General Chapter of hermits and the three of us drank up all my Mass wine. General subject of conversation: Flavian *must* be abbot and what to do about this place.

Later I went over to the Gannons' and then their dog followed me back and I couldn't get rid of it all night. Wouldn't let it in or feed it. Finally, when I got up, it was so cold that I let the dog in. By that time it was starved, ran in triumphantly, and jumped on my bed with enormous tail wagging and saying, "I love you—*feed* me!" I finally took the dog back about 8:30—everybody worried and Mom G. out looking for it all over the place.

More good poems came in today for *Monks Pond*. I had to write a few letters and finally got out for a short walk.

January 6, 1968. Epiphany

Damp, leaden darkness. Falling snow (small wet flakes). Accidents. Yesterday in the frozen brightness I fell and badly bruised my knee—for a moment the pain gripped my guts with nausea and I thought I would pass out or vomit. Reeled—nowhere to sit. I think I may have broken the camera—the Rollerflex—i.e., bashed it so that the back may be letting in light. Will see what happens to this film in Gregory Griffin's tank.

Also another accident: yesterday morning woke up at the sound of a frozen water jug bursting, the unfrozen water running out all over the floor. And this morning dropped an egg as I was getting it out of the icebox. My hands don't feel and grip properly (awful clumsiness trying to load the camera).

Last night curious dreams, perhaps about death. I am caught suddenly in a flood, which has risen and cut off my way of escape—not *all* escape, but my way to where I want to go. Can go back to some unfamiliar place over there—where? Fields, snow, upriver, a road, a possible bridge left over from some other dream.

(Sudden recollection and, as it were, a voice: "*It is not a bridge*"—i.e., no bridge necessary!)

January 15, 1968. St. Paul the Hermit

Two momentous days, heavy with snow and heavier with happenings. Father Flavian Burns was elected abbot by a large majority and surprisingly fast (third ballot).

January 21, 1968. III Sunday After Epiphany

Another gray day. Snow still fairly thick on the ground, now black with coal dust around the monastery.

When I was making supper someone came banging on the door. It was Brother Thomas from the monastery with a message that Sy Freedgood was dead. I went down to call his wife, Anne, and found out that his house in Bridgehampton had burned down last night and he was not able to get out. Suffering with bursitis, he had been taking a lot of pills, drinking too, he was probably too groggy to escape—a very tragic thing—yet somehow last spring everything about him pointed to death—a kind of dysfunction. (His accident on the way here was sign enough!) I could not talk to Anne, who was on the way from Bridgehampton to New York, but spoke to one of her friends in the New York apartment. Poor Sy! I wired Lax, who is now in Olean.

Before I heard the news I was playing some Mozart Quintets on the record player and enjoying them. I no longer feel like listening to anything.

Sy's grandiose plans in the spring for getting me out, "like Faulkner," once a year, etc., etc. We did have a pretty good day in Lexington!

It is already a hard year and I don't know what else is coming, but I have a feeling it is going to be hard all the way and for everybody.

January 23, 1968

Poor Sy! Mass for him yesterday (Library Chapel) and today (hermitage). I remember so many things: Sy and Rice at my Baptism; the time we rented the house in Woodstock for the summer and then didn't go—a good thing—(I sublet my apartment to him). Bramachari. Sy's place in Long Beach, the brothers and uncles. That crazy paper—*The Long Beach Free Press*—we started with Ken Hart.

Last year Sy was looking terrible in his fur hat and bandaged face and I knew he was finished. Yet he was full of ideas and plans. We made a voluble, profane tape. Talked of his analysis and his analyst, on whom he greatly depended, and of death, which he had very much on his mind.

February 13, 1968

Bright morning—freezing, but less cold than before with a hint of the smell of spring-earth in the cold air. A beautiful sunrise, the woods all peaceful and silent, the dried old fruits on the yellow poplar shining like precious artifacts. I have a new level in my (elementary) star-consciousness. I can now tell where constellations may be in the daytime when they are invisible. Not many, of course, but for example: the sun is rising in Aquarius and so I know that in the blue sky overhead the beautiful swan, invisible, spreads its wide wings over me. A lovely thought, for some reason.

Since Hayden Carruth's reprimand I have had more esteem for the crows around here, and I find, in fact, that we seem to get on much more peacefully. Two sat high in an oak beyond my gate as I walked on the brow of the hill at sunrise saying the Little Hours. They listened without protest to my singing of the antiphons. We are part of a ménage, a liturgy, a fellowship of sorts.

February 22, 1968

Zero again. Heavy frost. Very cold night. I had a dream that President Johnson was assassinated in Louisville. It seemed like a rather trite event and few paid much serious attention, though of course the police and military went about finding the assassin. He was found almost immediately. This fact was heralded by a long, bizarre, sadistic bugle call. I asked a passing soldier who it was (three soldiers, dark silhouettes on a sloping lawn) and he said, "Some British pastor in Israel." After that I lay awake and listened to the hard ice cracking and hardening again in the rain barrel outside.

March 14, 1968

My solitude is radically changing. I no longer take for granted that the afternoon is for writing just because that was the way it had to be in the community. Why not early morning? Then in the afternoon I am free to go out to the woods and it gets me away from the hermitage at a time when people might be tempted just to "drop in" (as Father Tim Hogan did with Malcolm Boyd).

Yesterday afternoon, again in bright sun and cold wind, I took off for the East Farm (Linton's) and discovered a pond I had never seen. It was in the hollow over on the SE corner of the farm where the low cedars are. I had not been there for well over 10 years, maybe even 12 years. Anyway, this was a warm, quiet, out-of-the-way corner, lots of rocks, a steep dip, a small artificial pond half full of bulrushes—probably the one Father John of the Cross used to go swimming in when it was more clear. I stayed quiet in the sun there for a long time. Small clouds high above the bare trees. Sun on the pale green water. Warmth. Peace. A most fruitful afternoon. I came back out into the cold wind on the high fields wondering why I wasted my afternoons writing letters. Of course, I have to. I have to write some now. There will continue to be letters of refusal. Every week now I refuse two or three invitations to meetings and conferences—important ones—but I do not think I can get mixed up in them or that there is any point in so doing. Father Flavian would probably let me go if I insisted, but I am not going to insist. Still a question about Bangkok. This I *should* go to—Dom Leclercq is a good judge of such things. Father Flavian is still not definite about it. But will Bangkok be a place one can get to this December? Or will the whole place be up in flames?

March 16, 1968

Warmer. Rain in the night. Frogs again. At first the waterhole (four feet long at most) had one frog or two. Now they are a small nation, loud in the night. The innocent nation, chanting blissfully in praise of the spring rain. Last evening I pruned a few little trees—including the beeches I had planted.

Today I have to go down to see Father Vernon Robertson, who evidently wants to get me involved in something. I will try not to. He has been pestering me to come to Louisville to give a talk at Bellarmine. This is confirming me in my resolution to keep *out* of all that. Almost every day I have to write a letter to someone refusing an invitation to attend a conference or a workshop or to give talks on the contemplative life or poetry, etc. I can see more and more clearly how for me this would be a sheer waste, a Pascalian diversion, participation in a common delusion.

(For others, no: they have the grace and mission to go around talking.) For me what matters is silence, meditation, and writing: but writing is tertiary. To willingly and deliberately abandon this to go out and talk would be stupidity—for me. For others, retirement into my kind of solitude would be equally stupid. They could not do it, and I could not do what they do.

April 6, 1968

Wednesday evening Donald Allchin arrived (late) with a seminarian from General Theological Seminary, N.Y. Thursday we had planned to drive to Shakertown and did in fact do so. But when I got up Thursday it was raining in torrents and the rain continued all day. Apparently it was the end of a tornado that had hit Arkansas and Tennessee. We started out nevertheless, got to Pleasant Hill, walked from building to building in pelting rain. The restaurant wasn't open and we went to the Imperial House in Lexington. Then, when the seminarian went off to the University of Kentucky to hunt up a long-lost cousin, Donald and I sat in Gene Meatyard's shop. After that we stopped briefly at Carolyn Hammer's and went to a place called Lum's for supper. By then it was evening.

Lum's was a curious sort of goldfish-bowl place out in a flat suburb near a railway viaduct. Serves all kinds of beer—we drank Carlson's (Danish). The TV was on for the news. Some tanks plowed around in Vietnam, then Martin Luther King appeared—talking the previous night in Memphis. I was impressed by his tenseness and strength. A sort of vague, visual, auditory impression. At almost that very moment he was being killed. We left, and right away on the car radio came the news that he had been shot and had been taken to the hospital in a "critical condition." Later, long before we were in Bardstown, it was announced he was dead.

So then we decided to go to Hawk's, and there we sat for two or three hours talking to Hawk in an empty section of the place (a party was going on in the other section). It was a moving and sad experience. Got home late again (about 11:30) and again slept little—barely two hours.

The murder of Martin Luther King lay on the top of the traveling car like an animal, a beast of the apocalypse. It finally confirmed all the apprehensions—the feeling that 1968 is a beast of a year, that things are finally and inexorably spelling themselves out.

April 18, 1968. Easter Thursday

The problem of real solitude: I don't have it here. I am not really living as a hermit. I see too many people, have too much active work to do, the place is too noisy, too accessible. People are always coming up here. I have been too slack about granting visits, interviews, etc., going to town too often, socializing, drinking, all that. All I have is a certain privacy, but real solitude is less and less possible here. Everyone now knows where the hermitage is, and in May I am going to the convent of the Redwoods in California. Once I start traveling around, what hope will there be?

April 25, 1968

A beautiful spring day—one of those than which no more beautiful is possible. Everything green and cool (a light frost in the early morning). Bright sun, clear sky, almost everything now fully in leaf except that some of the oaks are still silver rather than green.

But then I went down to the mailbox and got terrible news. A rolled-up newspaper from New Zealand (I don't know who sent it) tells of a shipwreck, a "giant ferry" sunk in the entrance to Wellington Harbor. All the pictures and headlines and then, on the last page, in the list of the dead: Agnes Gertrude Merton, 79, Christchurch.

Poor Aunt Kit! It happened April 10, two weeks ago, Wednesday in Holy Week, and no one had told me about it. I said Mass for her—the Mass of the Holy Cross.

Off and on, kept wondering if it were really true. Perhaps there was some mistake.

In the afternoon, the workmen were here. They are finishing painting, putting in doors. I did a minimum of necessary work and went out to mourn quietly, walking in the bottoms. The need to lament, to express and offer up sorrow and loss. Finally, after the workmen had gone, I sat down and read everything in the paper—a supplement of the Sunday *Dominion-Times* or whatever it is. It was awful. All kinds of double-talk, complete mystery and confusion. No one really knows what happened. This ship was caught in a storm, and though it had "the latest" in all equipment, nothing worked, much of the life-saving equipment was inadequate, the people were constantly reassured there was "no danger." Then suddenly they had to abandon ship, life rafts capsized or were dashed upon the rocks, etc. A frightful mess. And in the middle of it all, poor, sweet Aunt Kit, old and without strength to fight a cold, wild sea! I look at the sweater she knitted to protect me against "the cold" and the whole thing is unbearable.

What can be said about such things? Nothing will do. Absurdity won't. An awful sense that somehow it had to be this way because it was, and no one can say why, really. "What did she ever do to deserve it?" Such a question does not make sense and the God I believe in is not one who can be "blamed," for it is He who suffers this incomprehensibility in me more than I do myself. But there is a stark absence of all relatedness between the quiet, gentle, unselfish courage of Aunt Kit's life and this dreadful, violent death. What have these waves and currents to do with her?

In the end—one gets poetic and wonders if somehow they became "worthy" of her, but there is still no proportion—none whatever.

I suppose that is what death really is for everyone, but it is usually made so comfortable—so faked. When it is naked and terrible, we remember what death really is.

Perhaps that is it: no faked death for Aunt Kit—the real thing with face unveiled. Still it is not easy for love to bear it! Or even possible. May God grant her peace, light, and rest in Christ. My poor dear. Now winter comes to her little garden on Repton Street and that is the end of it. It does not have another spring. I had hoped, if I went to Bangkok, to visit her in December. I don't know if I'll go to visit the others—or even if I will go to Bangkok at all.

April 30, 1968. (Tuesday)

Another bright, sunny morning. My chapel was finished Friday (Feast of Our Lady of Good Counsel). Worked late cleaning out, putting up the icons, said Mass there Saturday morning and on Sunday (II after Easter—Good Shepherd Gospel). John Howard Griffin was here briefly on Friday, talking of the wicked situation in the cities. He has a theory of white extremists provoking violence. It is certainly true that the people killed in riots are mostly black. We went to take pictures of the distillery and then he left with a fever (he is not supposed to walk around much).

My chapel is plain, bright, white-walled, the bright warm red of icons, simplicity, light, peace.

May 4, 1968. (Derby Day)

I am supposed to leave Monday for California—the convent at Whitethorn—for a series of conferences and seminars or what have you—discussions, as the French say, "with broken batons." I am on the whole glad to be going and look forward to it. Even if they don't get anything out of it, I probably will. One thing to talk about will be the curious question of the "contemplative mystique" and its relation with the cloistered feminine mystique, the pure victim souls shut away from the world and praying for it. There is so much hokum in this idea! Yet we do have to be serious about solitude, discipline, prayer.

This afternoon I cleaned up a bit, burned a big pile of brush and trash behind the hermitage—the cartons that the bathroom fixtures came in and a lot of other junk with pine branches brought down in the blizzard at the end of Lent. Tomorrow is already the III Sunday after Easter. "A little while and you shall see me, yet a little while and you shall not see me—because I go to the Father" (John 16:17). Which reminds me that I got a lovely card from Thich Nhat Hanh the other day—he must leave the country June 15 when his visa expires. Meanwhile the war goes on and Johnson's peace gesture was obviously another phony one.

May 13, 1968. California. Our Lady of the Redwoods Monastery

I am on the Pacific Shore—perhaps fifty miles south of Cape Mendocino. Wide open, deserted hillside frequented only by sheep and swallows, sun and wind. No people for miles either way. Breakers on the black sand. Crying gulls fly down and land neatly on their own shadows.

I am halfway between Needle Rock, where there is an abandoned house, and Bear Harbor, where there is another abandoned house—three miles between them. No human habitation in sight on all the miles of shoreline either way, though there is a small sheep ranch hidden beyond Needle Rock.

North, toward Shelter Cove, a manufactory of clouds where the wind piles up smoky moisture along the steep flanks of the mountains. Their tops are completely hidden.

Back inland, in the Mattole Valley at the convent, it is probably raining.

South, bare twin pyramids. Down at the shore, a point of rock on which there is a silent immobile convocation of seabirds, perhaps pelicans.

Far out at sea, a long low coastal vessel seems to get nowhere. It hangs in an isolated patch of light like something in eternity.

Yet someone has been here before me with a small box of sun-kissed, seedless raisins, and I too have one of these. So this other may have been a nun from the Redwoods.

A huge shark lolls in the swells making his way southward, close in shore, showing his dorsal fin.

Faint cry of a lamb on the mountain side muffled by sea wind.

When I came four or five days ago to Needle Rock, I told the rancher I would be out on this mountainside for a few days. He had just finished shearing. All the sheep were still penned in at the ranch. Now they are all over the mountain again.

This morning I sheltered under a low thick pine while sheep stood bare and mute in the pelting shower.

Song sparrows everywhere in the twisted trees—"neither accept nor reject anything" (*Astavakra Gita*).

Low tide. Long rollers trail white sleeves of foam behind them, reaching for the sand, like hands for the keyboard of an instrument.

May 14, 1968

Sister Katryn danced barefoot in the choir Sunday after Mass. Beauty of those Flemish nuns and of the American nuns too. More beautiful in their simple blue and gray dresses without veils than in the affected and voluminous Cistercian habit—the cowl and choker. They wear light cowls in choir and can wear such veils as they please. Some, like the chantress, a dignified mantilla. Others, a headband, others, nothing.

Not to run from one thought to the next, says Theophane the Recluse, but to give each one time to settle in the heart.

Attention: Concentration of the spirit in the heart. *Vigilance:* Concentration of the will in the heart. *Sobriety:* Concentration of feeling in the heart.

Bear Harbor is in many ways better than Needle Rock—more isolated, more sheltered. A newer house in better repair, with a generator. You reach it finally after barns and the tall eucalyptus grove.

Flowers at Bear Harbor. Besides wild irises three or four feet high, there are calla lilies growing wild among the ferns and the strange bank, a profusion of roses and a lot of flowering shrubs that I cannot name.

Bear Harbor—rocky cove piled up with driftwood logs, some of which have been half burned. Much of it could serve for firewood.

About a mile from Bear Harbor, there is a hollow in which I am now sitting, where one could comfortably put a small trailer. A small, loud stream, many quail.

The calm ocean: very blue through the trees. Calla lilies growing wild. A very active flycatcher. The sun shines through his wings as through a Japanese fan. It is the feast of St. Pachomius. Many ferns. A large unfamiliar hawk-type bird flew over a little while ago, perhaps a young eagle.

I called Ping Ferry in Santa Barbara last evening. He spoke of birds, of the shore, of Robinson Jeffers, and told me the name of the big jay bird all dark blue with a black crest, which I saw yesterday. It is called Steller's jay. Does the jay know whose bird he is? I doubt it. A marvelous blue!

Eight crows wheel in the sky. An interesting evolution of shadows on the bare hillside beneath them. Sometimes the crows fly low, and their dance mingles with the dance of their own shadows on the almost perpendicular olive wall of the mountain pasture. Below, the sighs of the ocean.

"How many incarnations hast thou devoted to the actions of body, mind and speech? They have brought thee nothing but pain. Why not cease from them?" (*Astavakra Gita*). Reincarnation or not, I am as tired of talking and writing as if I had done it for centuries. Now it is time to listen at length to this Asian ocean. Over there, Asia.

May 16, 1968

I am flying over snowy mountains toward Las Vegas and Albuquerque. I read Han Yu's versatilities about mountains in the book of late T'ang poets I got yesterday at City Lights Bookstore in San Francisco.

Downtown in San Francisco, I walked about a bit while the sisters went to find Portia, their postulant with whom they were to stay. Portia was getting off work at Penney's.

I called Lawrence Ferlinghetti. I went first to City Lights but he was not there. I got the T'ang poets, Heilo, something in Zen, William Carlos Williams's "Kora in Hell." We had supper at an Italian restaurant, Polo's. Ferlinghetti came after we had finished the bottle of Chianti. I went off with him to find an espresso place on Grant Avenue, the Trieste, where a young musician told of some visions he had had. Good visions, not on drugs either.

I stayed overnight last night at City Lights's publications offices. A bedroom with a mattress on the floor, a guitar, and a tape recorder and a window opening on a fire escape—a block from Telegraph Hill. Noise of cars roaring up the steep streets all night. Finally it got quiet about 1:30. I think I slept from 2 to 5 and also an hour somewhere around midnight.

Morning. Lovely little Chinese girls going in all directions to school, one with a violin.

A wide meteorite crater in the Arizona desert, like a brown and red morning glory.

I am the utter poverty of God. I am His emptiness, littleness, nothingness, lostness. When this is understood, my life in His freedom, the self-emptying of God in me is the fullness of grace. A love for God that knows no reason because He is the fullness of grace. A love for God that knows no reason because He is God, a love without measure, a love for God as personal. Love for all, hatred of none, is the fruit and manifestation of love for God—peace and satisfaction. Forgetfulness of worldly pleasure, selfishness in the love for God, channeling all passion and emotion into the love for God.

May 17, 1968. New Mexico

I am at the Monastery of Christ in the Desert, Abiquiu, New Mexico. I was bombarded by impressions getting here yesterday. The vast sweep of the Rio Grande Valley.

Sangre de Cristo Mountains, blue and snowy.

After Santa Fe, marvelous long line of snowless, arid mountains, clean long shapes stretching for miles under pure light. Mesas, full rivers, cottonwoods, sagebrush, high red cliffs, piñon pines. Most impressed of all by the miles of emptiness.

This monastery is thirteen miles by dirt road from the nearest highway. In that distance, only one other house is passed—Skull Ranch. Around the monastery, nothing. Perfect silence. Bright stars at night dimly light the guest room. The only noise, the puttering of the pilot light in the gas heater. The adobe building is full of beautiful *Santos*, old ones and new ones, serious as painted desert birds.

May 18, 1968

This morning I began looking at the copy of René Daumal's *Mount Analogue*, which Ferlinghetti just published and which he gave me in San Francisco.

Up the canyon from where I now sit, a couple of miles below the monastery, there is the heavy, domed architecture of a fat mountain ringed with pillared red cliffs, ponderous as the great Babylonian movie palaces of the 1920s, but far bigger. Fresh wind, song of an ordinary robin in the low gnarled cedars.

May 19, 1968. *Fifth Sunday After Easter*

From *Mount Analogue*: "How it was proved that a hitherto unknown continent really existed with mountains much higher than the Himalayas . . . how it happened that no one detected it before . . . how we reached it, what creatures we met there—how another expedition pursuing quite different goals barely missed destruction."

Last night at dusk, the three tame white ducks went running very fast through the green alfalfa to the river, plunging into the swift waters, swimming to the other side, standing up in the shallows, flapping their white wings. Then the fourth discovered their absence and followed them through another corner of the alfalfa field.

The calls of the crows here in New Mexico, as in California, are more muted, more melodious, briefer, less insistent than in the east. The crows seem to be flying at a great psychic altitude, in a different realm. Yes, of course, a realm of high rocks and stunted piñon pine.

The curvature of space behind Mount Analogue makes it possible for people to live as though Mount Analogue did not exist. Hence, everyone comes from an unknown country and almost everyone from a too well known country.

May 20, 1968

Evening. Sun setting over Memphis Airport. I have come in a slow prop plane over flooded Arkansas country from Dallas. Between Albuquerque and Dallas, I finished *Mount Analogue*, a very fine book. It ends at a strange moment, a sign for the eschatological conscience—or it does not end, for the climb has only begun.

May 21, 1968. *Back at Gethsemani*

The country that is nowhere is the real home, only it seems that the Pacific Shore at Needle Rock is more nowhere than this and Bear Harbor is more nowhere still. (I was tempted to cross that out, but in these notes I am leaving everything, permitting everything.)

Are you there, my dears? Still under the big trees, going about your ways and your tasks, up the steep slope to the roomy wooden place where the chasubles are woven—Sister Gerarda on a bicycle to the guest quarters, Sister William to bake hosts, big warm Sister Veronica in the kitchen. Sister Katryn seems to be an obscure descendent of Meister Eckhart's Sister Katrei. Sister Katryn and Sister Christofora were the ones who seemed to respond the most knowingly whenever Eckhart was mentioned.

Sister Dominique, the impulsive, the blue-dressed, the full of melodies, who drove me in the car to the store to buy Levis. Big, gentle Sister Leslie from Vassar, blue-eyed Sister Diane from Arizona interested in Ashrams, Sister Shalom and Sister Cecilia, who came later to the party, and Mother Myriam, the Abbess, who was responsible for this wonderful place. Which ones I have forgotten besides the two postulants, small dark Carole with the Volkswagen and big Portia from San Francisco?

Near the monastery, the tall silent redwoods, the house of the Looks and another house, neighbors by the Mattole River. The county line:

here Mendocino, there Humboldt. My desolate shore is Mendocino. I must return.

Then I arrived back here in Kentucky in all this rain. The small hardwoods are full of green leaves, but are they real trees? The worshipful cold spring light on the sandbanks of the Eel River, the immense silent redwoods. Who can see such trees and bear to be away from them? I must go back. It is not right that I should die under lesser trees.

In our monasteries we have been content to find our way to a kind of peace, a simple, undisturbed, thoughtful life. This is certainly good, but is it enough?

I, for one, realize that now I need more. Not simply to be quiet, somewhat productive, to pray, to read, to cultivate leisure—*otium sanctum!* There is a need of effort, deepening, change and transformation. Not that I must undertake a special project of self-transformation or that I must "work on myself." In that regard, it would be better to forget it. Just to go for walks, live in peace, let change come quietly and invisibly on the inside.

But I do have a past to break with, an accumulation of inertia, waste, wrong, foolishness, rot, junk, a great need of clarification of mindfulness, or rather of "no mind"—a return to genuine practice, right effort, need to push on to the great doubt. Need for the Spirit.

Hang on to the clear light!

May 24, 1968

Lonely for the Pacific and the Redwoods. A sense that somehow when I was there I was unutterably happy. Maybe I was. Certainly, every minute I was there, especially by the sea, I felt I was at home, as if I had come a very long way to where I really belonged. Maybe it's absurd, I don't know, but that is the way it feels. I seem to be alienated and exiled here, as if there were really no reason whatever—except a few tenaciously fictitious ones—for being here. As if I were utterly cheating myself by staying here where I am only a stranger and will never be anything else. I know how easy it is to be deluded by such things. So I try not to pay attention. In the end, I think I came to the best decision when I was out there: to try to get permission to spend Lent at least at Bear Harbor but to maintain my "stability" here. This evening the whole thing seems futile, as if it were not really an honest solution at all, only a compromise and a very unreal one. As if I ought frankly to ditch the place and go where I will have real solitude and won't be caught in this artificial *pretense* that keeps me here. Perhaps even Nicaragua.

Of course the problem arises from the fact that I felt very related to these bright and open nuns, mostly Europeans (and two bright Americans), much more in rapport with them than with people at Gethsemani (with many of whom I am nevertheless on very good terms—after all, most of them were my students or novices at one time or other. Yet we have so little in common!).

I must not kid myself about this. But it would certainly be good to live alone in the cove at Bear Harbor and come in once a week to give the nuns a talk and pick up supplies. That is, at least for Lent. I think Father Flavian would allow it, but he has not committed himself.

June 6, 1968

More sorrow. I went down to the monastery with my laundry—saw the flag at half-mast and asked someone if Robert Kennedy were dead. Of course, he was! The news was very depressing: there seemed to have been so much hope he would survive. I sent a telegram to Ethel.

June 7, 1968

I had a good talk with Father Flavian. He seems open to the idea of my spending some time in solitude by the Pacific, even perhaps to my going to Asia to see some Buddhist centers.

Meanwhile, whether I ever get to Asia or not, I see the importance of real seriousness about meditative discipline and deepening—not just quiet and privacy (which I don't always have anyway). Have really reached the point in my life where one thing only is important: call it "liberation" or whatever you like. Though I may write or not, I no longer *need* to and will more and more refuse to write so many prefaces and articles. (The ones I do write I am interested in, but even in these I am losing interest.) I know I have been through this before, but now it does seem to be more decisive. Now I do think it is *final.*

June 14, 1968

Another fine day. I had a good talk with Father Flavian. He had received a letter from the Prior of our monastery in Indonesia. The latter, assuming I was going to the regional meeting of Asian Abbots at Bangkok, asked if I could preach a retreat at Rawa Seneng. Father Flavian said I could do this if I wanted to. I want to. It is an opportunity to get to Asia and to get some badly needed experience. However, it is a long way off. Five months at least.

It will mean my not taking any more writing jobs for next winter, as I hope to get to Japan, too, to see some Zen places, perhaps go from there to San Francisco and the northern coast.

June 29, 1968. Saturday. SS. Peter and Paul

I am spending the afternoon reading Santi Deva in the woods near the hermitage—the oak grove to the sw—a cool, breezy spot on a hot afternoon. Thinking deeply of Santi Deva and my own need of discipline. What a fool I have been, in the literal and biblical sense of the word: thoughtless, impulsive, lazy, self-interested, yet alien to myself, untrue to myself, following the most stupid fantasies, guided by the most idiotic emotions and needs. Yes, I know, it is partly unavoidable. But I know too that in spite of all contradictions there is a center and a strength to which I *always* can have access if I really desire it. The grace to desire it is surely there.

It would do no good to anyone if I just went around talking—no matter how articulately—in this condition. There is still so much to learn, so much deepening to be done, so much to surrender. My real business is something far different from simply giving out words and ideas and "doing things"—even to help others. The best thing I can give to others is to liberate myself from the common delusions and be, for myself and for them, free. Then grace can work in and through me for everyone.

What impresses me most—reading Santi Deva—is not only the emphasis on solitude but the idea of solitude as part of the clarification which includes living for others: dissolution of the self in "belonging to everyone" and regarding everyone's suffering as one's own. This is really incomprehensible unless one shares something of the deep, existential Buddhist concept of suffering as bound up with the arbitrary formation of an illusory ego-self. To be "homeless" is to abandon one's attachment to a particular ego—and yet to care for one's own life (in the highest sense) in the service of others. A deep and beautiful idea.

"Be thou jealous of thine own self when thou seest that it is at ease and thy fellow in distress, that it is in high estate and he is brought low, that it is at rest and he is at labor. Make thine own self lose its pleasures and bear the sorrow of its fellows . . . " etc.

Preference to be given to helping others to enlightenment, therefore helping those who are *closest* to it.

July 3, 1968

(Evening) In the morning I went out early and finished cutting down and trimming the young pines still bent over since last winter's big blizzards. The bush boundary of my yard, toward the woods, is now clear— relatively (some sumac coming up along the fence line, however!). This work made my back sore again—so I have to be careful. In the afternoon I went to the farthest end of the soybean field on Linton's and took off my shirt to get the sun on my neck and shoulders while I meditated (*Hatha* and *Yoga Vasishta*). A quiet and profitable afternoon and God knows I need much more of this! How much precious time and energy I have wasted in the last three years, doing things that have nothing whatever to do with my real purposes and that only frustrate and confuse me. It is a wonder I haven't lost my vocation to solitude by trifling and evasion.

One thing is very clear: all that passes for *aggiornamento* is not necessarily good or healthy. One has to remain pretty critical and independent about *all* ideas. Come to one's own conclusions on a basis of one's own frank experience. Both the conservatives and the progressives seem to me to be full of the same kind of intolerance, arrogance, empty-headedness, and to be dominated by different kinds of conformism: in either case the dread of being left out of their reference group. I have to go my own way in terms of needs that to me are fundamental: need to live a life of prayer, need to liberate myself from my own "cares" and "unique" need for an authentic monastic solitude (not mere privacy), and need for a real understanding and use of Asian insights in religion.

July 29, 1968

This evening—cool and bright—I walked out on the brow of the hill after supper. Looked down at the bottom where pipe is strung out for the new sewage plant. Crisp green line of the hills across the valley. Dark green of the oak tops—there has been lots of rain this summer. In eight weeks I am to leave here. Who knows, I may not come back. Not that I expect anything to go wrong—though it might—but I might conceivably settle in California to start the hermit thing Father Flavian spoke of: it depends. Someone may give him a good piece of property, for instance. In any case I don't expect to be back here for a few months.

Really I don't care one way or another if I never come back. On an evening like this the place is certainly beautiful, but you can seldom count on it really being quiet (though it is at the moment). Traffic on the road. Kids at the lake. Guns. Machines. Boone's dog yelling in the wood at night. People coming all the time. All this is to be expected and I don't complain of it. But if I can find somewhere to *disappear* to, I will. If I am to be in a relatively wandering life with no fixed abode, that's all right too.

I really expect little or nothing from the future. Certainly not great "experiences" or a lot of interesting new things. Maybe, but so what? What really intrigues me is the idea of starting out into something unknown, demanding and expecting nothing very special, hoping only to do what God asks of me, whatever it may be.

August 20, 1968. Feast of St. Bernard

I have been three years officially in this hermitage. I spent some of the morning cleaning out papers from the bedroom—where most of my work is stored or filed.

Files too full. Shelves too full. Boxes.

It is really clear that I have written too much useless trivial stuff, whether on politics or on monastic problems. I don't take account of earlier books, which perhaps had their place.

I regret less some of the recent poetry, especially *Cables* and *Lograire*. I wish I had done more creative work and less of this trivial, sanctimonious editorializing.

Today, among other things, I burned M.'s letters. Incredible stupidity in 1966! I did not even glance at any one of them. High hot flames of the pine branches in the sun!

I have prayed much more in these days. More and more a sense of being lost without it.

September 1, 1968. 13th Sunday After Pentecost

What (very slowly) sinks into my mind is that soon I will really leave this place, to live for a long time out of a suitcase—everything I "have" will be within the 44 lbs. a plane will take for you. Leaving my books, cottage, security, time to write, time to be alone, and going on where I don't know, with only a few plans ahead that can all be changed. This may not be easy at all—in fact it might be very difficult. Certainly difficult to do well. It leaves me confused, and the only way to make sense of it is prayer.

I now have a flight booked out of Louisville on September 11. Nine days to get everything in order. Am supposed first to go to New Mexico, Christ in the Desert. I had them on the end of my itinerary, assuming I would come back here in February or March. Now I don't know if I will come back at all. New Mexico is one of the places where I might eventually settle. Dom Aelred has invited me to his place any time I want to come. I can live there as a hermit if I want to. First I'll look elsewhere! But certainly the nights are silent there in that empty canyon.

September 9, 1968

Rainy and warm, a misty night of bells and insects. It is hard to believe this is my last night at Gethsemani for some time—at least for several months.

Lest I regret going, the shooters were out again this afternoon, blasting off in the rain and evidently in Boone's cornfield. I can't figure it out! Can't be *that* many doves. But whereas you saw doves fly over in fives and sixes two weeks ago, now you see—and rarely—one alone. It flies like mad away from you into the far distance!

I go with a completely open mind. I hope without special illusions. My hope is simply to enjoy the long journey, profit by it, learn, change, perhaps find something or someone who will help me advance in my own spiritual quest.

I am not starting out with a firm plan never to return or with an absolute determination to return at all costs. I do feel there is not much for me here at the moment and that I need to be open to lots of new possibilities. I hope I shall be! But I remain a monk of Gethsemani. Whether or not I will end my days here, I don't know. Perhaps it is not so important. The great thing is to respond perfectly to God's Will in this providential opportunity, whatever it may bring.

September 13, 1968. Christ in the Desert Monastery, New Mexico
A journey is a bad death if you ingeniously grasp or remove all that you were before you started, so that in the end you do not change in the least. The stimulation enables you to grasp more raffishly at the same, familiar, distorted illusions. You come home only confirmed in greater greed— with new skills (real or imaginary) for satisfying it.

I am not going "home." The purpose of this death is to become truly homeless.

Bardo of small, bad hermitage, empty, quiet, musty smell, a cobweb, some cardboard boxes.

Very quiet. Good river. Good cliffs. Blue clouds arising after noon. Silence!

The big red dog, wet ears full of burrs, his stomach roaring with some grass he had eaten while I was swimming.

Go on! Go on! There is no place left.

September 19, 1968. Alaska
Louisville—Christ of the Desert—Jicarilla Apache Reservation—Santa Fe—Chicago—Anchorage—Eagle River Convent.

I am now here on a bright cold morning, and the first thin dusty snow is on the lower hills. Mt. McKinley is visible in the distance from the Precious Blood Convent, next to which I live in a trailer (very comfortable).

The flight to Alaska was mostly over clouds. Quiet. A soldier on the outside seat; the middle seat of the three empty. We didn't talk except for a little bit just before landing. (He said Anchorage wasn't any colder in winter than Syracuse but that there was a lot of snow.)

The clouds opened over Mt. St. Elias, and after that I was overwhelmed by the vastness, the patterns of glaciers, the burnished copper sheen of the sun on the bright blue sea. The shoreline. The bare purple hills. The high mountains full of snow, the dark islands stark in the sun—burnish on the water.

We swung slowly down into Anchorage and got out into the cold, clear, autumn air. Everywhere the leaves have turned. Gold of the aspens and birches everywhere.

Without going actually into Anchorage, we (Msgr. Lunney met me) drove out on Route 1 to the convent, at Eagle River. It is a nice house among the birches, at the foot of low mountains, looking out through the trees toward Cook Inlet and Mount McKinley. The nuns may move in a few months, as the place is not quite suitable.

I have a sense of great warmth and generosity in the clergy here. The Archbishop is away at Juneau but will be back next week. All are very eager to help and I feel that they are eager to have me settle here. Meanwhile I'm busy on a workshop with the nuns. They are a good community, and like all, they have their troubles.

This afternoon—in the sun at the foot of a birch, in the bushes near the monastery at a point where you can see Mt. McKinley and Mt. Foraker—great, silent, and beautiful presences in the afternoon sun.

September 24, 1968. Valdez

Most impressive mountains I have seen in Alaska: Drum and Wrangell and the third great massive one whose name I forget, rising out of the vast birch plain of Copper Valley. They are sacred and majestic mountains, ominous, enormous, noble, stirring. You want to attend to them. I could not keep my eyes off them. Beauty and terror of the Chugach. Dangerous valleys. Points. Saws. Snowy nails.

September 30, 1968

Flew to Dillingham in a Piper Aztec (two engines), a fast plane that goes high. Bristol Bay area—like Siberia! Miles of tundra. Big winding rivers.

At times, lakes are crowded together and shine like bits of broken glass, or are untidy and complex like the pieces of a jigsaw puzzle.

Two volcanoes: Iliamna—graceful, mysterious, feminine, akin to the great Mexican volcanoes. A volcano to which one speaks with reverence, lovely in the distance, standing above the sea of clouds. Lovely, near at hand, with small attendant peaks. Redoubt (which surely has another name, a secret and true name)—handsome and noble in the distance but ugly, sinister as you get near it. A brute of a dirty busted mountain that has exploded too often. A bear of a mountain. A dog mountain with steam curling up out of the snow crater. As the plane drew near there was turbulence, and we felt the plane might at any moment be suddenly pulled out of its course and hurled against the mountain, as if it would not pull itself away, but finally it did. Redoubt. A volcano to which one says nothing. Pictures from the plane.

October 8, 1968

More than a week since I last wrote in this thing. I am now at the Redwoods monastery. Dawn. Cold, hard frost, and a quiet crow softly cawing outside. It is good to be here.

Last Monday—flew to Dillingham (Alaska) over the volcanoes. A fine wild spot—desolate as Siberia. I like the lakes that are to the north of it. Tuesday—a Day of Recollection for priests there. Many chaplains. I spoke most of prayer. The Bishop was pleased. Wednesday I flew south to San Francisco.

October 15, 1968

The Pacific is very blue. Many small white clouds are floating over it, several thousand feet below us. It is seven o'clock in Honolulu, toward which we are flying. The planeload of people on Pan American: the silent Hawaiian soldier, the talking secretaries, the Australians, the others who like myself had to pay for excess baggage. Lesson: not to travel with so many books. I bought more yesterday, unable to resist the bookstores in San Francisco.

Yesterday I got my Indonesian visa in the World Trade Center on the Embarcadero. Said Terce standing on a fire escape looking out over the bay, the Bay Bridge, the island, the ships. Then I realized I had apparently lost the letter with addresses of the people I was to meet. However, I did jot down an address in Djakarta.

There was a delay getting off the ground at San Francisco: the slow ballet of big tailfins in the sun. Now here. Now there. A quadrille of planes jockeying for place on the runway.

The moment of takeoff was ecstatic. The dewy wing was suddenly covered with rivers of cold sweat running backward. The window wept jagged shining courses of tears. Joy. We left the ground—I with Christian mantras and a great sense of destiny, of being at last on my true way after years of waiting and wondering and fooling around.

May I not come back without having settled the great affair. Without having found also the great compassion, *mahakaruna.* We tilted east over the shining city. There was no mist this morning. All the big buildings went by. The green parks. The big red bridge over the Golden Gate. Muir Woods, Bodega Bay, Point Reyes, then two tiny rock islands, then nothing, only blue sea.

I am going home, to the home where I have never been in this body, where I have never been in this washable suit (washed by Sister Gerarda the other day at the Redwoods), where I have never been with these suitcases (in Bangkok there must be a catharsis of the suitcases!), where I have never been with these particular books, Evans-Wentz's *Tibetan Yoga and Secret Doctrines* and others.

Last week I had a dream about planes. It was at Yakutat, one of the small airstrips to which I had been flown in Alaska. There is a low ceiling and we are waiting to take off in a small plane. But a large plane, a commercial prop plane, is about to land. It comes down, then I hear it leave again. The way is clear. Why don't we take off now? The other plane is never seen though it lands and takes off nearby.

October 17, 1968. Bangkok

I had breakfast on the hotel terrace by the river. A hot wind. Choppy water and a great activity of boats: motorboats waiting to take tourists on a tour of the canal markets, rowboats as ferries to and fro across the river—one sculled by a strong woman who fought the current bravely and effectively, though I thought she and her passengers would be carried away!

Then about 10 A.M. I took a taxi to Wat Bovoranives. We drove through Chinatown with its clutter of shops and wild, dirty streets. Crowds. Motorbikes. Taxis. Buses. Trucks fixed up to look like dragons, glittering with red and chrome. Dirt. Camp. Madness. Enormous nightmare movie ads. Lovely people. Beautiful, gentle people, except those who are learning too fast from Americans. A long ride to the *wat*, but we finally got there. I pass through a gate into a quiet maze of shady lanes and alleys, large houses, canals, temples, school buildings. I ask a *bhikkhu* for directions and arrive at the domicile of Phra Khantipalo. He is extremely thin, bones sticking out in all directions. He has the look of a "strict observer." But sensible. ("These people here are very tolerant and uncritical.") Khantipalo is the author of two books on Buddhism. He says he is going to a forest monastery in the northeast part of Siam in four or five days. He will have a quasi-hermit life there with a good meditation teacher, in the jungle. We talked of *satipatthana* meditation.

In the evening I met the Abbot, Venerable Chao Khun Sasana Sobhana, who was very impressive. He was tired—he had just returned from the cremation of some *bhikkhu*—but he got talking on the purpose of Theravada. He spoke of *sila, samadhi, panna (prajna), mukti,* and the awareness of *mukti* (freedom), with emphasis on following one step after another, ascending by degrees. I enjoyed the conversation—there were occasional translations of difficult parts by Khantipalo. I felt it was fruitful.

What is the "knowledge of freedom?" I asked. "When you are in Bangkok you know that you're there. Before that you only knew about Bangkok. And," he said, "one must ascend all the steps, but then, when there are no more steps, one must make the leap. Knowledge of freedom is the knowledge, the experience, of this leap."

October 18, 1968. Bangkok

Yesterday afternoon I was driven out into the country to see Phra Pathom Chedi, one of the oldest and largest *stupas.* Rice fields. Coronet palms. Blue, shiny buffaloes. Endless lines of buses and trucks traveling like mad. A small *wat* in the fields. Many of the Buddhas were flaked with small bits of gold leaf stuck on by the faithful. At another tiny country *wat*, a side Buddha had his face masked and buried in gold by some benefactor, as though he were being smothered by it. Behind the entrance and around the *stupa* was a cloister with desks, books, little *bhikkhus* studying Pali. A master was correcting a *bhikkhu* who had written something wrong on a blackboard. Khantipalo and I circumambulate the *stupa* with incense and flowers, he in bare feet and all bony, I sweating with my camera around my neck. The gold-roofed temples against the clouds made me think of a picture of Borobudnur. There were men high up on the side of the *stupa* replacing old tiles, a boy up there pulling out weeds that had grown in between the tiles. Then I wandered interminably around under the trees (mostly frangipani) looking at small, good and bad Buddhas, *stupas*, reproductions, imitations, a rundown meditation garden confided to the Chinese. Buddhas smothered with gold, one enormous, lying down, with chicken wire at his back, a protection against graffiti.

October 19, 1968. Calcutta

When we landed in Calcutta the customs gave two utterly lovely—and haughty—Indian girls in saris a rough time. I got through quite fast, though with no rupees yet, and Susan Hyde, a secretary of Peter Dunne, was there to meet me with a garland of flowers: "Welcome to India." V.I.P. treatment. I felt confused, trying to talk sense to Susan about religious affairs. The Indian darkness was full of people and cows. Rough roads on which cars sped toward each other head-on. It takes some time here to discover which side anyone is driving on—he may take either side, right or left. Then into the big, beat-up, hot, teeming, incredible city. People! People! People! Campfires in the streets and squares. Movie posters—those Asian movie posters with the strange, enormous faces of violent or demented Western gods, the enormous gunners surrounded by impossible writings. They are a crass, camp deification of the more obvious emotions: love, hate, desire, greed, revenge. Why not John Wayne with eight arms? Well, he has enough guns already. Or the Dance of Shiva—with Frank Sinatra?

The situation of the tourist becomes ludicrous and impossible in a place like Calcutta. How does one take pictures of these streets with the faces, the eyes of such people, and the cows roaming among them on the sidewalks, buzzards by the score circling over the main streets in the "best" section? Yet the people are beautiful. The routine of the beggars is heart-rending. The little girl who suddenly appeared at the window of my taxi, the utterly lovely smile with which she stretched out her hand, then the extinguishing of the light when she drew it back empty. I had no Indian money yet. She fell away from the taxi as if she were sinking in water and drowning. I wanted to die. I couldn't get her out of my mind. Yet when you give money to one, a dozen half-kill themselves running after your cab. This morning one little kid hung on to the door and ran whining beside the cab in the traffic while the driver turned around and made gestures as if to beat him away. Sure, this is a well-practiced routine, an art, a theater, but a starkly necessary art of dramatizing one's despair and awful emptiness. Then there was the woman who followed me three blocks sweetly murmuring something like "Daddy, Daddy, I am very poor" until I finally gave her a rupee. Okay, a contest, too. But she *is* very poor. And I have come from the West, a Rich Daddy.

Clearly seeing the "Body City" makes one a *lokavidu:* "one who knows the worlds," one who has investigated all the realms of existence. So, too, the antitourism of the external city—the true city, the city out of control, whether it be Los Angeles or Calcutta. Whether it be the trace of new cars on superhighways or of old cars on bad highways or of blood, mucus, fecal matter in the passages of the body. Calcutta, smiling, fecal, detached, tired, inexhaustible, young, old, full of young people who seem old, is the *unmasked* city. It is the subculture of poverty and overpopulation.

Calcutta is shocking because it is all of a sudden a totally different kind of madness, the reverse of that other madness, the mad rationality of affluence and overpopulation. America seems to make sense but is hung up in its madness, now really exploding. Calcutta has the lucidity of despair, of absolute confusion, of vitality helpless to cope with itself. Yet undefeatable, expanding without and beyond reason but with nowhere to go. An infinite crowd of men and women camping everywhere as if waiting for someone to lead them in an ultimate exodus into reasonableness, into a world that works, yet knowing already, beyond contradiction, that in the end *nothing* really works, that life is all *anicca, dukkha, anatta,* that each self is the denial of the desires of all the others yet somehow a sign to others of some inscrutable hope. The thing that haunts me: Gandhiji led all these people, exemplified the sense they might make out of their life, for a moment. Then, with him, the sense was extinguished again.

October 24, 1968

Yesterday I drove with Amiya Chakravarty and his friend, Naresh Guha, to the home of the painter Jamini Roy. Walking barefoot on the cool tiles through low quiet rooms filled with canvases of unutterable beauty: simple, formalized little icons with a marvelous sort of folk and Coptic quality, absolutely alive and full of charm, many Christian themes, the most lovely treatment of Christian subjects I have ever seen and also, of course, Hindu subjects from the *Ramayana* and the *Mahabharata.* Amiya bought a Christ, which he will take to the nuns at Redwoods. I wish I could afford to buy a dozen canvases; they are very cheap, $35 or $40. But money gets away from me like water on all sides and I have to watch it. Some things in the hotel are extremely expensive, others not.

Jamini Roy himself, a warm, saintly old man, saying: "Everyone who comes to my house brings God into it." The warmth and reality of his hand as you shake it or hold it. The luminous handsomeness of his bearded son, who is, I suppose, my age. Marvelous features. All the faces glowing with humanity and peace. Great religious artists. It was a great experience.

October 28, 1968. New Delhi

The flight this morning from Calcutta to New Delhi turned out beautiful. At first it was very stormy and cloudy. Then all of a sudden I looked out and there were the Himalayas, several hundred miles away, but an awesome, great white wall of the highest mountains I have ever seen. I recognized the ones, like Annpurna, that are behind Pokhara. I could pick out the highest ones in the group, though not individually. Everest and Kanchenjunga were in the distance. Later, a big, massive one stood out but I did not know what it was. And the river Ganges. Below, the enormous plain cut up with tiny patches of farms and villages, roads and canals. A lovely pattern. Then the dry plain around Delhi. Rock outcrops. Burnt villages. As soon as I got out of the plane, I decided that the air of Delhi was much better than that of Calcutta and that I was happy to be here. Harold Talbott was at the airport. We are to go by train to Dharamsala next Thursday.

Real India. I haven't seen much of New Delhi yet, except a long avenue leading to a squat, huge red dome. The hotel is cleaner, newer, less crumbling than the Oberoi in Calcutta.

The taxis of Calcutta lowing mournfully in the wild streets like walruses or sea cows. Now in New Delhi—more bicycles, motorcycles, trees. A Moslem leaning in the dust toward a tree. The great death house of Humayun. Smoke in the evening. The moon rising in the first quarter over gray domes. There are more guns in the movie posters here. More military bases. More soldiers.

"Therefore have no fears, have no terror of that deep blue light of dazzling, terrible and awful splendor, since it is the light of the Supreme Way" (*Tibetan Book of the Dead*).

November 1, 1968. Dharamsala

I came up by train from Delhi to Pathankot with Harold Talbott last night. Then by jeep with a Tibetan driver to Dharamsala. Slept well enough in a wide lower berth, my first overnight train trip since I went to Gethsemani to enter the monastery twenty-seven years ago. When light dawned, I looked out on fields, scattered trees, tall reeds, and bamboo, brick, and mud villages, a road swept by rain in the night and now by a cold wind from the mountains, men wrapped in blankets walking in the wind. Teams of oxen plowing. Pools by the track filled with purple flowering weeds. A white crane starts up out of the green rushes. Long before Pathankot I was seeing the high snow-covered peaks behind Dalhousie.

On our arrival at Pathankot there was a madhouse of noise, bearers balancing several suitcases and packages on their heads and all trying to get through one small exit at once with a hundred passengers. We were met by a jeep from the Dalai Lama's headquarters.

It was a beautiful drive to Dharamsala—mountains, small villages, canyons, shrines, ruined forts, good, well-cared-for forest preserves. Then the climb to Dharamsala itself and the vast view over the plains from the village. It rained when we arrived, and thunder talked to itself all over and around the cloud-hidden peaks. We came to the cottage Talbott lives in—everything very primitive.

In the afternoon I got my first real taste of the Himalayas. I climbed a road out of the village up into the mountains, winding through pines, past places where Tibetans live and work, including a small center for publication and a central office. Many Tibetans on the road, and some were at work on a house, singing their building song. Finally I was out alone in the pines, watching the clouds clear from the medium peaks— but not the high snowy ones—and the place was filled with a special majestic kind of mountain silence. At one point the sound of a goatherd's flute drifted up from a pasture below. An unforgettable valley with a river winding at the bottom, a couple of thousand feet below, and the rugged peaks above me and the pines twisted as in Chinese paintings. I got on a little path where I met at least five Tibetans silently praying with rosaries in their hands, building little piles of stones. An Indian goatherd knocked over one of the piles for no reason. Great silence on the mountain, except for two men with axes higher up in the pines. Gradually the clouds thinned before one of the higher peaks, but it never fully appeared.

On the way down I met a man on the road, a man in European clothes walking with a lama. He introduced himself as Sonam Kazi, the man who translated for Desjardins. He sent the lama on his way and we went to the Tourist Hotel to drink tea and talk.

November 3, 1968

Quiet after sunrise. In the silent, cool, misty air of morning a sound of someone chanting *puja* floats up from the village. The report of a gun far down in the valley echoes along the walls of the mountain. Now too they are shooting. Yesterday, near the army post at Palampur, there was machine-gun fire in the mountains while we stayed by the road in the tea plantation talking with Khamtul Rinpoche.

We had some trouble locating Khamtul Rinpoche. We went to the place where he is setting up a new monastery and lay colony, but he wasn't there. A monk served us some tea. We waited a while but Khamtul did not come. Later we met him on the road at a lovely place with many pines and a fine view of the mountains. He is an impressive, heavily built Tibetan with a brown woolen cap on his head. We sat on the ground amid young tea plants and pines and talked, with Sonam Kazi translating. Khamtul Rinpoche spoke about the need for a guru and direct experience rather than book knowledge, about the union of study and meditation. We discussed the "direct realization" method. We discussed the need for a guru. "And," he asked, "have you come to write a strange book about us? What are your motives?"

November 4, 1968. Afternoon

I had my audience with the Dalai Lama this morning in his new quarters. It was a bright, sunny day—blue sky, the mountains absolutely clear. Tenzin Geshe sent a jeep down. We went up the long way round through the army post and past the old deserted Anglican Church of St. John in the Wilderness. Everything at McLeod Ganj is admirably situated, high over the valley, with snow-covered mountains behind, all pine trees with apes in them, and a vast view over the plains to the south. Our passports were inspected by an Indian official at the gate of the Dalai Lama's place. There were several monks standing around—like monks standing around anywhere—perhaps waiting to go somewhere. A brief wait in a sitting room, all spanking new, a lively, bright Tibetan carpet, bookshelves full of Kangyur and Tangyur scriptures presented to the Dalai Lama by Suzuki.

The Dalai Lama is most impressive as a person. He is strong and alert, bigger than I expected (for some reason I thought he would be small). A very solid, energetic, generous, and warm person, very capably trying to handle enormous problems—none of which he mentioned directly. There was not a word of politics. The whole conversation was about religion and philosophy and especially ways of meditation. He said he was glad to see me, had heard a lot about me. I talked mostly of my own personal concerns, my interest in Tibetan mysticism. Some of what he replied was confidential and frank. In general he advised me to get a good base in Madhyamika philosophy (Nagarjuna and other authentic Indian sources) and to consult qualified Tibetan scholars, uniting study and practice. *Dzogchen* was good, he said, provided one had a sufficient grounding in metaphysics—or anyway Madhyamika, which is beyond metaphysics. One gets the impression that he is very sensitive about partial and distorted Western views of Tibetan mysticism and especially about popular myths. He himself offered to give me another audience the day after tomorrow and said he had some questions he wanted to ask me.

The Dalai Lama is also sensitive about the view of other Buddhists concerning Tibetan Buddhism, especially some Theravada Buddhists who accuse Tibetan Buddhism of corruption by non-Buddhist elements.

The Dalai Lama told me that Sonam Kazi knew all about *dzogchen* and could help me, which of course he already has. It is important, the Dalai Lama said, not to misunderstand the simplicity of *dzogchen* or to imagine it is "easy" or that one can evade the difficulties of the ascent by taking this "direct path."

In the afternoon I got a little reading done and then had quite a good meditation. Talking with various *rinpoches* has certainly been helpful, above all with the Dalai Lama himself. I have great confidence in him as a really charismatic person. The Tibetans are all quite impressive, and their solidity does a great deal to counteract the bizarre reports about some of their practices. It is all very good experience.

Thinking about my own life and future, it is still a very open question. I am beginning to appreciate the hermitage at Gethsemani more than I did last summer when things seemed so noisy and crowded. Even here in the mountains there are few places where one does not run into someone. Roads and paths and trails are all full of people. To have real solitude one would have to get very high up and far back!

For solitude, Alaska seems the very best place. Everyone I have talked to says I must also consider others and keep open to them to some extent. The *rinpoches* all advise against absolute solitude and stress "compassion." They seem to agree that being in solitude much of the year and coming "out" for a while would be a good solution.

The idea of being in Alaska and then going out to Japan or the U.S. strikes me as a rather good solution. And, in some small way, helping in Alaska itself. On the way back from this trip I think I will need to go to Europe to see Trungpa Rinpoche's place in Scotland and the Tibetan monastery in Switzerland. To see Marco Pallis and then John Driver in Wales. I must write to Donald Allchin about Wales.

The way in which I have been suddenly brought here constantly surprises me. The few days so far in Dharamsala have all been extremely fruitful in every way: the beauty and quiet of the mountains, my own reading and meditation, encounters with lamas, everything.

In a way it is wonderful to be without letters. No one now knows where to reach me.

Trying to get a better perspective on the earlier part of this year, there is a lot I cannot quite understand. Perhaps do not need to understand. The last months have been demanding and fruitful. I have needed the experience of this journey. Much as the hermitage has meant, I have been needing to get away from Gethsemani and it is long overdue.

This evening the lights in the cottage went dead for a while. I stood out in the moonlight, listening to drums down in the village and looking up at the stars. The same constellations as over the hermitage and the porch opening in about the same direction, southeast toward Aquila and the Dolphin. Aquarius out over the plain, the Swan up above. Cassiopeia over the mountains.

November 5, 1968

Last night I dreamed that I was, temporarily, back at Gethsemani. I was dressed in a Buddhist monk's habit, but with more black and red and gold, a "Zen habit," in color more Tibetan than Zen. I was going to tell Brother Donald, the cook in the diet kitchen, that I would be there for supper. I met some women in the corridor, visitors and students of Asian religion, to whom I was explaining I was a kind of a Zen monk and *Gelugpa* together, when I woke up. It was 6 A.M. Time to get up.

Other recent dreams, dimly remembered. Strange towns. Towns in the south of France. Working my way along the Riviera. How to get to the "next place"? I forget what the problem is, or if it is solved. Another: I'm in some town and have a small, silvery toy balloon, but it has a dangerous explosive gas in it. I throw it in the air and hope it will float completely away before anything happens. It rises too slowly, departs too slowly— but nothing happens. The dream changes.

November 6, 1968. Second Audience with the Dalai Lama

We drove up earlier, at 8:30, a bright, clear morning. More people and more trucks on the road: army trucks roaring toward the corners, ambling buffaloes, students on their way to school, and the Jubilee Bus Company's silver dragons. At the entry to the Dalai Lama's residence there were pilgrims, maybe *sadhakas*, with marigolds on their hats or in their hair.

Most of the audience was taken up with a discussion of epistemology, then of *samadhi*. In other words, "the mind." A lot of it, at first, was rather scholastic, starting with *sunyata* and the empirical existence of things known—the practical empirical existence of things grounded in *sunyata*—enhanced rather than lessened in a way. I tried to bring in something about *sila*, freedom, grace, gift, but Tenzin Geshe had some difficulty translating what I meant. Then we discussed various theories of knowledge, Tibetan and Western-Thomist. There is a controversy among Tibetans as to whether in order to know something one must know the *word for it* as well as apprehend the concept.

We got back to the question of meditation and *samadhi*. I said it was important for monks in the world to be living examples of the freedom and transformation of consciousness that meditation can give. The Dalai Lama then talked about *samadhi* in the sense of controlled concentration.

He demonstrated the sitting position for meditation that he said was essential. In the Tibetan meditation posture the right hand (discipline) is above the left (wisdom). In Zen it is the other way round. Then we got on to "concentrating on the mind." Other objects of concentration may be an object, an image, a name. But how does one concentrate on the mind itself? There is division: the I who concentrates . . . the mind as object of concentration . . . observing the concentration . . . all three one mind. He was very existential, I think, about the mind as "what is concentrated on."

It was a very lively conversation and I think we all enjoyed it. He certainly seemed to. I like the solidity of the Dalai Lama's ideas. He is a very consecutive thinker and moves from step to step. His ideas of the interior life are built on very solid foundations and on a real awareness of practical problems. He insists on detachment, on an "unworldly life," yet he sees it as a way to complete understanding of and participation in the problems of life and the world. But renunciation and detachment must come first. Evidently he misses the full monastic life and wished he himself had more time to meditate and study. At the end he invited us back again Friday to talk about Western monasticism. "And meanwhile think more about the mind," he said as we left him.

November 7, 1968

The contemplative life must provide an area, a space of liberty, of silence, in which possibilities are allowed to surface and new choices—beyond routine choice—become manifest. It should create a new experience of time, not as stopgap, stillness, but as *"temps vierge"*—not a blank to be filled or an untouched space to be conquered and violated, but a space that can enjoy its own potentialities and hopes—its own presence to itself. One's *own* time, but not dominated by one's own ego and its demands. Hence open to others—*compassionate* time, rooted in the sense of common illusion and in criticism of it.

I had a fine visit with Chobgye Thicchen Rinpoche, a lama, mystic, and poet of the Sakyapa school, one of the best so far. Sonam says Chobgye Thicchen is very advanced in Tantrism and a great mystic. He even knows how to impart the technique of severing one's soul from the body. He taught this to another lama who was later captured by the Communists. The lama, when he was being led off to prison camp, simply severed soul from body—pfft!—and that was the end of it. Liberation!

We talked about *samadhi,* beginning with concentration on an object, then going beyond that to meditation without object and without concept. I asked a lot of questions about *bodhicitta, maitreya,* and *karuna.* "*Bodhicitta,*" Thicchen said, "is the most fundamental of these three concepts, which all center on love and compassion." He spoke of three kinds of *bodhicitta:* (1) "kingly"—in which one seeks spiritual power to save oneself and then save others; (2) "that of boatman"—in which one ferries oneself together with others to salvation; (3) "that of shepherd"— in which one goes behind all the others and enters salvation last—and this is the most perfect.

Chobgye Thicchen quoted something from the founder of the Sakyapa school that went more or less like this:

If you are attached to worldly things, you are not a religious man.

If you are attached to appearances, you cannot meditate.

If you are attached to your own soul, you cannot have *bodhicitta.*

If you are attached to doctrines, you cannot reach highest attainment.

He asked me to give an outline of Christian meditation and mysticism, which I did. He seemed very pleased and wrote a poem for me. I wrote one for him. He also spoke of the need for good interpreters, Sonam Kazi being the best.

On the way down we met the Gadong oracle, an old lama and a former member of the Tibetan cabinet, an old man with a big brown beard who had also formed part of a delegation that went to look for and identify the present Dalai Lama as a child.

The Dalai Lama's proper name is Gejong Tenzin Gyatso.

November 8, 1968

My third interview with the Dalai Lama was in some ways the best. He asked a lot of questions about Western monastic life, particularly the vows, the rule of silence, the ascetic way, etc. But what concerned him most was:

1. Did the "vows" have any connection with a spiritual transmission or initiation?

2. Having made vows, did the monks continue to progress along a spiritual way, toward an eventual illumination, and what were the degrees of that progress? Supposing a monk died without having attained to perfect illumination? What ascetic methods were used to help purify the mind of passions? He is interested in the "mystical life" rather than in external observances.

Some incidental questions: What were the motives for the monks not eating meat? Did they drink alcoholic beverages? Did they have movies? And so on.

I asked him about the question of Marxism and monasticism, which is to be the topic of my Bangkok lecture. He said that from a certain point of view it was impossible for monks and Communists to get along but that perhaps it should not be entirely impossible *if* Marxism meant *only* the establishment of an equitable economic and social structure. There was perhaps some truth in Marx's critique of religion in view of the fact that religious leaders had so consistently been hand in glove with secular power. Still, on the other hand, militant atheism did in fact strive to suppress all forms of religion, good or bad.

Finally, we got into a rather technical discussion of mind, whether as consciousness, *prajna*, or *dhyana*, and the relation of *prajna* to *sunyata*. In the abstract, *prajna* and *sunyata* can be considered from a dialectic viewpoint, but not when *prajna* is seen as realization. The greatest error is to become attached to *sunyata* as if it were an object, an "absolute truth."

It was a very warm and cordial discussion, and at the end I felt we had become very good friends and were somehow quite close to each other. I feel a great respect and fondness for him as a person and believe, too, that there is a real spiritual bond between us. He remarked that I was a "Catholic *geshe*," which, Harold said, was the highest possible praise from a Gelugpa, like an honorary doctorate!

November 12, 1968. Darjeeling

This is a much finer place that I expected—a king of places, full of Tibetans, prayer flags, high in mists, wonderful mountains, all hidden as we came up the wretched road along which there have been some seventy very bad landslides. We were held up an hour in Kurseong waiting for the worst stretch to open up again.

From the plane, which we took from Calcutta to Bagdogra, all the high mountains were visible above the clouds: Kanchenjunga nearest, Everest several hundred miles away, tall with a black side, a stately mountain. And the lovely pointed one next to it. Directly below, it might have been Indiana as well as India. We went over the Ganges. The ride from Bagdogra was long, through thick woods, then higher and higher into the clouds. Finally we came to the Windamere Hotel, the most pleasant place I have been to in India. We arrived, up a long flight of steps, out of breath, in the dark. Had tea. It is cold.

November 16, 1968

We started out early on a cold morning, about 7:45, in our friend's jeep with Jimpa Rinpoche and a big picturesque Tibetan type as guide to find other *rinpoches.* Also, Father Sherburne and Harold Talbott. I was feeling the cold as we hurried up the road toward Ghoom. I've had a bad throat; it seems to be aggravated by the coal smoke that fills the air. We went looking first for Chatral Rinpoche at his hermitage above Ghoom. Two *chortens,* a small temple, some huts. In the temple there is a statue of Padma Sambhava, which is decorated with Deki Lhalungpa's jewels. But I did not see it. Chatral Rinpoche was not there. We were told he was at an *ani gompa,* a nunnery, down the road, supervising the painting of a fresco in the oratory. So off we went toward Bagdogra and with some difficulty found the tiny nunnery—two or three cottages just down behind the parapet off the road—and there was Chatral, the greatest *rinpoche* I have met so far and a very impressive person.

Chatral looked like a vigorous old peasant in a Bhutanese jacket tied at the neck with thongs and a red woolen cap on his head. He had a week's growth of beard, bright eyes, a strong voice, very articulate, much more communicative than I had expected. We had a fine talk, and all through it Jimpa, the interpreter, laughed and said several times, "These are hermit questions" and "This is another hermit question." We started talking about *dzogchen* and Nyingmapa meditation and "direct realization" and soon saw that we agreed very well. We must have talked for two hours or more, covering all sorts of ground, mostly around about the idea of *dzogchen,* but also taking in some points of Christian doctrine compared with Buddhist: *dharmakaya*—the Risen Christ, suffering, compassion for all creatures, motives for "helping others," all leading back to *dzogchen,* the ultimate emptiness, the unity of *sunyata* and *karuna,* going "beyond the *dharmakaya*" and "beyond God" to the ultimate perfect emptiness. He said he had meditated in solitude for thirty years or more and had not attained to perfect emptiness. I said I hadn't either.

The unspoken or half-spoken message of the talk was our complete understanding of each other as people who were somehow *on the edge* of great realization and knew it and were trying, somehow or other, to go out and get lost in it, that it was a grace for us to meet each other. I wish I could see more of Chatral. He burst out and called me a *rangjung Sangay* (which apparently means a "natural Buddha") and said he had been named a *Sangay dorje*. He wrote "*rangjung Sangay*" for me in Tibetan and said that when I entered the "great kingdom" and "the palace," then America and all that was in it would seem like nothing. He told me, seriously, that perhaps he and I would attain to complete Buddhahood in our next lives, perhaps even in this life. The parting note was a kind of compact that we would both do our best to make it in *this* life. I was profoundly moved: he is so obviously a great man, the true practitioner of *dzogchen*, the best of the Nyingmapa lamas, marked by complete sincerity and freedom. He was surprised at getting on so well with a Christian. He at one point laughed and said, "There must be something wrong here!" If I were going to settle down with a Tibetan guru, I think Chatral would be the one I'd choose. But I don't know yet if that is what I'll be able to do, or whether I need to.

November 17, 1968

Several times during the long silent ride in the Land Rover to the Mim Tea Estate today I wondered, "Why am I going there?" But I am glad to be here in this utterly quiet bungalow. The owners are out and won't be back until late. I have already refused dinner and asked for tea only, tea to be sent to the bungalow. A fire is lit in the bungalow grate. Hah! It is good. Fog hides the mountains. Fog gets in the sore throat. No matter. Fire and a variety of remedies and a big bed, with covers and fresh sheets turned back, awaits the tired *penseur.*

"Dear Father Merriton (sic)," said the note. "Please make yourself at home the moment you arrive and just ask the bearer for anything you may require." Without my having to ask, the generator went on, the lights began to work, tea was provided in the big comfortable drawing room. I escaped quickly to the bungalow, aside, apart, alone, silent. Fire lit. Books unpacked, including one on Japan by Ruth Benedict and also Anaïs Nin's *Under the Glass Bell,* which I hope to finish, along with the Buddhist books I have to return to Harold Talbott, who remains in the Windamere Hotel where he reads wrapped in a blanket.

I'm glad I came here. All morning alone on the mountainside, in the warm sun, now overclouded. Plenty of time to think. Reassessment of this whole Indian experience in more critical terms. Too much movement. Too much "looking for" something: an answer, a vision, "something other." This breeds illusion. Illusion that there *is* something else. Differentiation—the old splitting-up process that leads to mindlessness, instead of the mindfulness of seeing all-in-emptiness and not having to break it up against itself. Four legs good; two legs bad.

I am still not able to fully appreciate what this exposure to Asia has meant. There has been so much, yet also so little. I have only been here a month! It seems a long time since Bangkok, even since Delhi and Dharamsala. Meeting the Dalai Lama and the various Tibetans, lamas or "enlightened" laymen, has been the most significant thing of all, especially in the way we were able to communicate with one another and share an essentially spiritual experience of "Buddhism," which is also somehow in harmony with Christianity.

On the other hand, though the Jesuits at St. Joseph's have repeatedly dropped hints about the need for contemplative Catholic foundations in India, I do not get any impression of being called to come here and settle down. Certainly not in this "sensitive" border area where there would be constant problems with the government.

If I were to be a hermit in India it would have to mean something other than this comfortable bungalow! Something more like what Dom Le Saux (Swami Abhishiktananda) is doing.

Though I fully appreciate the many advantages of the hermitage at Gethsemani, I still have the feeling that the lack of quiet and the general turbulence there, external and internal last summer, are indications that I ought to move. So far the best indications seem to point to Alaska or to the area around the Redwoods.

Another question: would this move be *temporary* or *permanent?* I do not think I ought to separate myself completely from Gethsemani, even maintaining an official residence there, legally only. I suppose I ought eventually to end my days there. I do in many ways miss it. There is no problem of my wanting simply to "leave Gethsemani." It is my monastery, and being away has helped me see it in perspective and love it more.

Now suppose some loon comes up to me and says, "Have you found the *real* Asia?" I am at a loss to know what one means by "the real Asia." It is *all* real as far as I can see. Though certainly a lot of it has been corrupted by the West. Neither Victorian Darjeeling nor the Kennedy-era Oberoi Hotel can be called the *ideal* Asia. I remember Deki Lhalungpa laughing at the phony American minarets in the Taj dining room at the Oberoi. Still, that is Asia too.

Darjeeling is a quaintly fraudulent relic of something incredible. The Indians, or the Nepalese, Sikkimese, and others around here, are still trying to believe in it and maintain it. English hats, tweeds, walking sticks, old school ties (St. Joseph's)—for the rich ones at least. Shivering in the Windamere over Madhyamika dialectic—is that the "real Asia"? I have a definite feeling it is a waste of time—something I didn't need to do. However, if I have discovered I didn't need to do it, it has not been a waste of time.

This deep valley, the Mim Tea Estate, above Darjeeling: it is beautiful and quiet and it is right for Martin Hall, the manager, and his wife, who are in their own way hermits and who appreciated my need for a couple of days of silence. Yet it has nothing I could not, essentially, have found at Needle Rock or Bear Harbor—nothing I did not find there last May. Or did I find an illusion of Asia that needed to be dissolved by experience? *Here?*

What *does* this valley have? Landslides. Hundreds of them. The mountains are terribly gashed, except where the forest is thick. Whole sections of tea plantations were carried away six weeks ago. It is obviously going to be worse the next time there are really heavy rains. The place is a frightening example of *anicca*—"impermanence." A good place, therefore, to adjust one's perspectives. I find my mind rebelling against the landslides. I am distracted by reforestation projects and the other devices to *deny* them, *forbid* them. I want this all to be *permanent*. A permanent postcard for meditation, daydreams. The landslides are ironic and silent comments on the apparent permanence, the "eternal snows" of solid Kanchenjunga. And *political* instability. Over there, only a couple of hundred miles as the crow flies, is the Tibetan border where the Chinese armies are!

The sun is high, at the zenith. Clear soft sound of a temple bell far down in the valley. Voices of children near the cottages above me on the mountainside. The sun is warm. Everything falls into place. Nothing is to be decided; nor is "Asia" to be put in some category or other. There is nothing to be judged. But it must be cold for the lamas, at night, in their high, draughty little *gompas!*

November 19, 1968. Mim Tea Estate

Last night I had a curious dream about Kanchenjunga. I was looking at the mountain and it was pure white, absolutely pure, especially the peaks that lie to the west. I saw the pure beauty of their shape and outline, all in white. And I heard a voice saying—or got the clear idea of: "There is another side to the mountain." I realized that it was turned around and everything was lined up differently; I was seeing the Tibetan side. This morning my quarrel with the mountain is ended. Not that it is a big love affair—but why get mad at a mountain? It is beautiful, chastely white in the morning sun—and right in view of the bungalow window.

There is another side of Kachenjunga and of every mountain—the side that has never been photographed and turned into postcards. That is the only side worth seeing.

Later: I took three more photos of the mountain. An act of reconciliation? No, a camera cannot reconcile one with anything. Nor can it see a real mountain. The camera does not know what it takes: it captures materials with which you reconstruct, not so much what you saw, as what you thought you saw. Hence the best photography is aware—mindful—of illusion and uses illusion, permitting and encouraging it—especially unconscious and powerful illusions that are not normally admitted on the scene.

The three doors (they are one door).

1. The door of emptiness. Of no-where. Of no place for a self, which cannot be entered by a self. Therefore it is of no use to someone who is going somewhere. Is it a door at all? The door of no-door.

2. The door without sign, without indicator, without information. Not particularized. Hence no one can say of it "This is *it!* This is *the door.*" It is not recognizable as a door. It is not led up to by other things pointing to it: "We are not it, but that is it—the door." No

signs saying "Exit." No use looking for indications. Any door with a sign on it, any door that proclaims itself to be a door is not the door. But do not look for a sign saying "Not-door." Or even "No Exit."

3. The door without wish. The undesired. The unplanned door. The door never expected. Never wanted. Not desirable as a door. Not a joke, not a trap door. Not select. Not exclusive. Not for a few. Not for many. Not *for*. Door without aim. Door without end. Does not respond to a key—so do not imagine you have a key. Do not pin your hopes on possession of the key.

There is no use asking for it. Yet you must ask. Who? For what? When you have asked for a list of all the doors, this one is not on the list. When you have asked the numbers of all the doors, this one is without a number. Do not be deceived into thinking this door is merely hard to find and difficult to open. When sought it fades. Recedes. Diminishes. Is nothing. There is no threshold. No footing. It is not empty space. It is neither this world nor another. It is not based on anything. Because it has no foundation, it is the end of sorrow. Nothing remains to be done. Therefore there is no threshold, no step, no advance, no recessing, no entry, no non-entry. Such is the door that ends all doors; the unbuilt, the impossible, the undestroyed, through which all the fires go when they have "gone out."

Christ said, "I am the door." The nailed door. The cross: they nail the door shut with death. The resurrection: "You see, I am *not* a door." "Why do you look up to heaven?" "Lift up your heads, O gates!" For what? The King of Glory. *Ego sum ostium:* "I am the door." I am the opening, the "shewing," the revelation, the door of light, the Light itself. "I am the Light," and the light in the world from the beginning. (It seemed to be darkness.)

Kanchenjunga this afternoon. The clouds of the morning parted slightly, and the mountain, the massif of attendant peaks, put on a great, slow, silent *dorje* dance of snow and mist, light and shadow, surface and sinew, sudden cloud towers spiraling out of icy holes, blue expanses of

half-revealed rock, peaks appearing and disappearing with the top of
Kanchenjunga remaining the visible and constant presence over the whole
slow show. It went on for hours. Very stately and beautiful. Then toward
evening the clouds cleared some more, except for a long apron of mist
and shadow below the main peaks. There were a few discreet showings of
whorehouse pink, but most of it was shape and line and shadow and
form. O Tantric Mother Mountain! Yin-yang palace of opposites in
unity! Palace of *anicca*, impermanence and patience, solidity and
nonbeing, existence and wisdom. A great *consent* to be and not-be, a
compact to delude no one who does not first want to be deluded. The
full beauty of the mountain is not seen until you too consent to the
impossible paradox: it is and is not. When nothing more needs to be
said, the smoke of ideas clears, the mountain is SEEN.

Testament of Kanchenjunga. Testament of fatherless old Melchizedek.
Testament from before the time of oxen and sacrifice. Testament without
Law. NEW Testament. Full circle! The sun sets in the East!

November 24, 1968. The 24th Sunday After Pentecost
"What is a vocation? A call and a response. This definition does not say
everything. To conceive the call of God as an expressed order to carry out
a task certainly is not always false, but it is only true after a long interior
struggle in which it becomes obvious that no such constraint is apparent.
It also happens that the order comes to maturity along with the one who
must carry it out and that it becomes in some way this very being, who
has now arrived at full maturity. Finally, the process of maturing can be a
mysterious way of dying, provided that with death the task begins. There
has to be a dizzying choice, a definitive *déhiscence* (rupture) by which the
certitude he has gained of being called is torn asunder. That which—and
the word is rightly used here—*consecrates* a vocation, and raises it to the
height of the sacrifice that it becomes, is a breaking with the apparent
order of being, with its formal full development or its visible efficacy"
(Pierre Emmanuel, "*La Loi d'exode*").

November 28, 1968. Madras
A sense of silence and of space at Mahabalipuram, of unpredictable
views, the palms and nearby sea. I would have liked to wander a long time

among the rocks, but the kids selling postcards and trying to act as guides were a nuisance, so I moved on to the beach, which is also admirable. Bright blue of the Bay of Bengal. A cool wind coming in strong off the sea. The shore temple, smaller than I expected, very weather-beaten, but a real gem. It is especially interesting when seen in relation to the rest of the complex. And in relation to Sankara, a contemporary of this shrine, who lived at Kancheepuram, which I did not see.

A conversation last evening with Dr. Raghavan on *rasa* and Indian aesthetics. He spoke of the importance of suggestion to convey aesthetic implications, which transcend ordinary speech. Poetry is not ordinary speech, nor is poetic experience ordinary experience. It is closer to religious experience. *Rasa* is above all *santa:* contemplative peace. We discussed the difference between aesthetic experience and religious experience: the aesthetic lasts only as long as the object is present. Religious knowledge does not require the presence of "an object." Once one has known *brahman,* one's life is permanently transformed from within. I spoke of William Blake and his fourfold vision.

December 4, 1968. Colombo

Polonnaruwa with its vast area under trees. Fences. Few people. No beggars. A dirt road. Lost. Then we find Gal Vihara and the other monastic complex *stupas.* Cells. Distant mountains, like Yucatán.

The path dips down to Gil Vihara: a wide, quiet hollow, surrounded with trees. A low outcrop of rock, with a cave cut into it, and beside the cave a big seated Buddha on the left, a reclining Buddha on the right, and Ananda, I guess, standing by the head of the reclining Buddha. In the cave, another seated Buddha. I am able to approach the Buddhas barefoot and undisturbed, my feet in wet grass, wet sand. The silence of the extraordinary faces. The great smiles. Huge and yet subtle. Filled with every possibility, questioning nothing, knowing everything, rejecting nothing, the peace not of emotional resignation but of Madhyamika, of *sunyata,* which has seen through every question without trying to discredit anyone or anything—*without refutation*—without establishing some other argument. For the doctrinaire, the mind that needs well-established positions, such peace, such silence, can be frightening. I was knocked over with a rush of relief and thankfulness at the *obvious* clarity of the figures, the clarity and fluidity of shape and line, the design of the monumental bodies composed into the rock shape and landscape, figure, rock, and tree. And the sweep of bare rock sloping away on the other side of the hollow, where you can go back and see different aspects of the figures.

Looking at these figures, I was suddenly, almost forcibly, jerked clean out of the habitual, half-tired vision of things, and an inner clearness, clarity, as if exploding from the rocks themselves, became evident and obvious. The sheer *evidence* of the reclining figure, the smile, the sad smile of Ananda standing with arms folded (much more "imperative" than Da Vinci's Mona Lisa because completely simple and straightforward). The thing about all this is that there is no puzzle, no problem, no "mystery." All problems are resolved and everything is clear, simply because what matters is clear. The rock, all matter, all life, is charged with *dharmakaya*—everything is emptiness and everything is compassion. I don't know when in my life I have ever had such a sense of beauty and spiritual vitality running together in one aesthetic illumination. Surely, with Mahabalipuram and Polonnaruwa, my Asian pilgrimage has come clear and purified itself. I mean, I know and have seen what I was obscurely looking for. I don't know what else remains, but I have now seen and have pierced through the surface and have got beyond the shadow and the disguise. This is Asia in its purity, not covered with garbage, Asian or European or American. It is clear, pure, complete. It says everything. It needs nothing. Because it needs nothing it can afford to be silent, unnoticed, undiscovered. It does not need to be discovered. It is we, Asians included, who need to discover it.

December 6, 1968. Singapore

I am now preparing to leave Singapore, the city of transistors, tape recorders, cameras, perfumes, silk shirts, fine liquors—carrying away only a stock of 35 mm. Plus X film. I am glad I came here. It is an interesting, "worldly" town, very different from India, a new Asian city, the cosmopolitan kind, "worldly" too in a Chinese sense. Singapore has a Chinese kind of practicality and reality along with the big Western buildings, which, as it happens, are clean and well kept. The place is not run down, and hence Calcutta is not a *necessary* pattern for all Asia! These evidences are needed in order to give a complete picture of Asia. Out in the suburbs by the university, it is like Santa Barbara or Sacramento.

I saw the other side of Colombo going out to the Katunayake airport. There were many screwy Catholic statues exhibited in public but sometimes under glass, so that the Catholic saints come a little closer to Ganesha and Hindu "camp" after all. Suddenly there is a point where religion becomes laughable. Then you decide that you are nevertheless religious.

My next stop will be the Bangkok meeting, to which I do not especially look forward. Then Indonesia; a whole new journey begins there. I am still not sure where it will take me or what I can or should plan on. Certainly I am sick of hotels and planes. But the journey is only begun. Some of the places I really wanted to see from the beginning have not yet been touched.

"Most men will not swim before they are able to" (Novalis).

December 8, 1968. Bangkok

Today is the Feast of the Immaculate Conception. In a little while I leave the hotel. I'm going to say Mass at St. Louis Church, have lunch at the Apostolic Delegation, then on to the Red Cross place this afternoon.

INDEX